The Cultural Revolution on Trial

The trial of Cultural Revolution leaders, including Mao's widow and her Gang of Four, was the signal event in China's post-Mao transition. In its wake, Chinese socialism emerged from the rubble of the Cultural Revolution to create the China that we know today. This spectacular show trial was a curious example of transitional justice, marking a break from the trauma of the past, a shift to the present era of reform, and a blueprint for building the future. In this groundbreaking account of the most famous trial in Chinese history, Alex Cook shows how the event laid the cornerstone for a new model of socialist justice. At the same time, a juxtaposition of official political and legal sources against works of popular literature reveals the conflicted cultural dimensions of this justice. The result, Cook argues, saved socialism as China's ruling ideology, but at the cost of its revolutionary soul.

Alexander C. Cook is Assistant Professor of Modern Chinese History at the University of California, Berkeley.

Studies of the Weatherhead East Asian Institute,
Columbia University

The Studies of the Weatherhead East Asian Institute of Columbia University were inaugurated in 1962 to bring to a wider public the results of significant new research on modern and contemporary East Asia.

A list of titles in this series can be found at the back of the book.

The Cultural Revolution on Trial

Mao and the Gang of Four

Alexander C. Cook

University of California, Berkeley

CAMBRIDGE
UNIVERSITY PRESS

University Printing House, Cambridge CB2 8BS, United Kingdom

Cambridge University Press is part of the University of Cambridge.

It furthers the University's mission by disseminating knowledge in the pursuit of education, learning, and research at the highest international levels of excellence.

www.cambridge.org
Information on this title: www.cambridge.org/9780521135290

© Alexander C. Cook 2016

First published 2016

Printed in the United States of America by Sheridan Books, Inc.

A catalogue record for this publication is available from the British Library.

Library of Congress Cataloging-in-Publication Data
Names: Cook, Alexander C., author.
Title: The Cultural Revolution on trial: Mao and the Gang of Four /
Alexander C. Cook (University of California, Berkeley).
Description: Cambridge, United Kingdom; New York, NY:
Cambridge University Press, 2016. |
Series: Studies of the Weatherhead East Asian Institute, Columbia University |
Includes bibliographical references and index.
Identifiers: LCCN 2016024206| ISBN 9780521761116 (hardback) |
ISBN 9780521135290 (paperback)
Subjects: LCSH: Gang of Four Trial, Beijing, China, 1980–1981. |
Jiang, Qing, 1914–1991 – Trials, litigation, etc. | Trials (Political crimes and
offenses) – China – History – 20th century. | Zhongguo gong chan dang –
Purges. | Criminal justice, Administration of – China – History – 20th
century. | China – History – Cultural Revolution, 1966–1976 – Influence. |
Socialism – China – History – 20th century. | Social change – China –
History – 20th century. | China – Politics and government – 1976–2002. |
BISAC: HISTORY / Asia / General.
Classification: LCC KNQ42.G36 C66 2016 | DDC 345.51/0231–dc23
LC record available at https://lccn.loc.gov/2016024206

ISBN 978-0-521-76111-6 Hardback
ISBN 978-0-521-13529-0 Paperback

Contents

Figures

Acknowledgments

Many people and institutions contributed to the completion of this book. Research for this project began at Columbia University, where I benefited from the guidance of Madeleine Zelin, Eugenia Lean, David Wang, Sam Moyn, and Yang Guobin, among others. I also enjoyed the warm support of a community of collaborators, coaches, and friends at Columbia and later Stanford, including Tom Mullaney, Alan Melowsky, Ben Martin, Song Weijie, Jonathan Ocko, Hayes Moore, Lee Pennington, Lisa Ford, Tim Davis, Nicole Cohen, Dominique Reill, the staff and fellows at the Institute for Social and Economic Research and Policy, Alan Mikhail, the Stanford Humanities Fellows, Haiyan Lee, and Ban Wang.

Generous funding was provided by fellowships and grants from numerous sources, including Columbia University and its Weatherhead East Asian Institute, the Mr. and Mrs. Giles Whiting Foundation, the V. K. Wellington Koo Fellowship, a William J. Fulbright Grant, the Mellon Foundation, Stanford University and its Humanities Center, the University of California at Berkeley and its Center for Chinese Studies, and a UC Regents Fellowship. In China at various stages of the project I had institutional support from the Institute of International Education, the Chinese Academy of Social Sciences, the Shanghai Academy of Social Sciences, the Shanghai Municipal Library, and the Institute of Law. Special thanks to Wu Jianfan, Liu Hainian, and Ye Yonglie for taking the time to meet with me.

Along the way, portions of my research were presented at Allegheny College, Birkbeck College (London), Cambridge University, California State University at Long Beach, Columbia University, Georgia Southern University, the Institute for International Education in Beijing, the Massachusetts Institute of Technology, Ramapo College, Stanford University, the State University of New York at Albany, the University of California at Berkeley, the University of California at Santa Barbara, the University of Iowa, the University of Miami, the University of Richmond, University College (London), Wayne State University, the Association for Asian Studies Annual Meeting, the Triangle East Asian Colloquium at Duke University, and the Sherman Emerging Scholar Lecture at the University of North Carolina, Wilmington. I am grateful for the valuable feedback I received from the participants at each of these venues.

This book was completed at the University of California, Berkeley. Nearly every member of the History Department there read and commented on at least some portion of this book. Several colleagues performed extraordinary service: Wen-hsin Yeh, Michael Nylan, David Johnson, Nick Tackett, Mark Peterson, Beth Berry, Martin Jay, Rebecca MacLennan, Victoria Frede, Tom Lacquer, Andrew Jones, and the anonymous members of two review committees. Daniel Leese offered many excellent suggestions. Special thanks to my editors at Cambridge University Press, Marigold Acland and Lucy Rhymer.

Most of all, I am thankful for the enduring support of my extended family: my mother Janice and my father John, my brothers Gareth and Andy, my mother-in-law Nhi, my stepfather Clayton, and my faithful writing partner Tom. My mother, especially, helped pull me over the finish line. Finally, my wife Tram and my daughter Beatrix deserve special commendation for suffering with grace and humor the grouchiness and grind of dissertating, editing, writing, and rewriting. Yes, finally, it is done.

Abbreviations

BGC	Beijing Garrison Command
CASS	Chinese Academy of Social Sciences
CCP	Chinese Communist Party
CCRD	Chinese Cultural Revolution Database
CDI	Central Commission for Discipline Inspection
CSB	Central Security Bureau
FBIS	Foreign Broadcast Information Service, Far East (China)
GMRB	*Guangming ribao (Guangming Daily)*
HQ	*Hongqi (Red Flag)*
Indictment	"Zhonghua renmin gongheguo ... tebie jianchating qisushu"
JFJB	*Jiefang junbao (Liberation Army Daily)*
JFRB	*Jiefang ribao (Liberation Daily)*
LSSP	*Lishi de shenpan*
MPS	Ministry of Public Security
NPC	National People's Congress
PLA	People's Liberation Army
PRC	People's Republic of China
PSB	Public Security Bureau
Resolution	"Guanyu jianguo yilai dang de ruogan lishi wenti de jueyi"
RMRB	*Renmin ribao (People's Daily)*
ROC	Republic of China
SPC	Supreme People's Court
TBFTJS	*Zuigao remin fayuan tebie fating shenpan ... jishi*
Verdict	"Zhonghua renmin gongheguo ... tebie fating panjueshu"

Glossary of Key Terms

a	啊	ah (vocative)
bao	报	requital
biran	必然	necessity
cai	才	talent, endowment
cai	材	talent, material
chai	豺	jackal
chenmo	沉默	silence
da cai xiao yong	大材小用	great talents put to petty use
dangshi	党史	party history
dezhi	德治	the rule of virtue
diandao	颠倒	inversion
dinglü	定律	the laws of nature
fa	法	law; standard; method; dharma
fabao	法宝	magic weapon; dharmaratna
falü	法律	law; the statutory laws
fan an	翻案	reversal of verdicts
fandang	反党	antiparty
fawang huihui	法网恢恢	law's net is vast
fazhi	法制	legal system; legality
fazhi	法治	the rule of law
fensui	粉碎	to smash
gan xiao	干校	cadre school
ganxing renshi	感性认识	perceptual knowledge
gongshen dahui	公审大会	public trial rally
guanxi	关系	relationships
guilü	规律	the laws of history
guo chi	国耻	national humiliation
heshang da san	和尚打伞	a monk with an umbrella
jianggao	讲稿	script
jiebo	劫波	apocalypse; kalpa

jilü	纪律	organizational discipline; party discipline
jishi wenxue	纪实文学	documentary literature
laogai	劳改	reform through labor; prison camp
liang an	两案	two cases
liang ge fanshi	两个凡是	two whatevers
lixing renshi	理性认识	rational knowledge
lizhi	礼治	the rule of ritual
lü	律	statute; restraint; codification
pidou	批斗	criticism and struggle
ping minfen	平民愤	to settle the people's righteous indignation
qing suan	清算	to make a clear accounting
qisu	起诉	to indict
ren	人	human
renbenzhuyi	人本主义	humanism
rencai	人才	human resources
rendaozhuyi	人道主义	humanism
renge	人格	personal character
renmin	人民	the people
renqing	人情	human emotions; human circumstances
renxing	人性	human nature
renzhi	人治	the rule of man
shenpan	审判	trial
shenpan guan	审判官	judge
shi	实	substantial; actual; real
shijian	实践	practice
shiqing	事情	circumstances; events
shishi	事实	facts
shishi qiu shi	实事求是	seek truth from facts
shuang da	双打	double strike
si ren bang	四人帮	Gang of Four
suan zhang	算账	to settle accounts
suku	诉苦	to speak bitterness
susong	诉讼	to make a legal complaint
suyuan	诉冤	to seek redress for injustice
tiancai	天才	genius
waishi	外史	unofficial history
wu fa wu tian	无法无天	without law, human or divine

wuqing	无情	without emotion; merciless
xiucai	秀才	elegant talent
xu	虚	empty
xuwei	虚伪	hypocrisy; artifice; phoniness
yao	妖	monster
yi fa ban shi	依法办事	to handle matters according to the law
yi fa zhi guo	依法治国	to govern according to the law
yi fa zhi guo	以法治国	to rule by law
yifen	义愤	righteous indignation; nemesis
yi ren wei ben	以人为本	to take people as the basis
yi yuan bao yuan	以怨报怨	repay injury with injury
yi zhi bao yuan	以直报怨	repay injury with justice
yongcai	庸才	mediocre talent
zao fan you li	造反有理	to rebel is justified
zhengning	狰狞	beastly; hideous
zhengshi	正史	official history
zhengyi	正义	justice; authorized interpretation
zhua jin	抓紧	firmly grasp
zilü	自律	self-discipline; self-regulation
ziwo piping	自我批评	self-criticism
zongpai	宗派	faction

Introduction

The most famous trial in Chinese history took place in Beijing in the winter of 1980–1, four years after the death of Chairman Mao. Ten recently deposed leaders stood before a special tribunal, indicted on charges of orchestrating a counterrevolutionary conspiracy to seize control of the Chinese Communist Party (CCP), its state apparatus the People's Republic of China (PRC), and its military force the People's Liberation Army (PLA). The ten defendants had carried out the radical politics of Chairman Mao's Great Proletarian Cultural Revolution (1966–76), and now stood accused of hijacking the movement as a vehicle to persecute rivals and usurp power.

Among the accused were five military officers implicated in an alleged coup d'état and assassination attempt against Chairman Mao in 1971. The alleged leader of the plot was Lin Biao, then the supreme commander of China's military and Mao's designated successor. (Lin, along with his wife and grown son, died in a plane crash fleeing the country after the plot was hastily aborted.) Also on trial was Mao's former political secretary, Chen Boda, who had been purged in a leadership struggle between radical factions in 1970. Most notorious of all, however, was the "Gang of Four," a clique of radical cultural revolutionaries that fell from power shortly after Mao's death in 1976. It was this small but extraordinary clique – led by Mao's then wife (now widow) Jiang Qing – that gave the trial of the Lin Biao and Jiang Qing counterrevolutionary groups its colloquial misnomer: the "Gang of Four" trial. Absent from the dock, of course, was the late Chairman Mao, whose legacy soon would be dealt with in a separate but related CCP resolution on the history of the party.

The basic facts about the Gang of Four trial were well publicized at the time in China and abroad, and have long been available to Western readers in the Chinese-produced propaganda work, *A Great Trial in Chinese History*.[1] The lengthy indictment, prepared by a special prosecutor, listed

---

[1] *A Great Trial in Chinese History* (Beijing: New World Press; dist. by New York: Pergamon Press, 1981); English reprint edition (Honolulu: University Press of the Pacific, 2003); versions were also published in French, German, and Spanish translation.

forty-eight charges in four categories: (1) the systematic framing and purging of party, state, and military leaders up to the very highest levels; (2) the persecution of more than seven hundred thousand lower-level party cadres and regular citizens, resulting in the unlawful death of nearly thirty-five thousand people; (3) the unconsummated assassination and military coup (in which the Gang of Four proper was not involved); and (4) the Gang of Four's failed plan to stage an armed rebellion in Shanghai during the succession crisis that followed Mao's death. The case was tried by a Special Court, established under the auspices of China's Supreme People's Court. The court worked six days a week for six weeks, from late November to late December, examining the 10 accused, hearing testimony from 49 witnesses, and weighing 651 items of evidence.[2] The defendants were generally compliant, with the notable exception of Mao's widow Jiang Qing, who defended herself vigorously. "To rebel is justified!" she announced in open court, arguing that her actions had taken place in a heroic revolutionary context beyond the reach of legal codes. She also provided the trial's most memorable moments. Describing herself as Mao's dog, she summoned his ghost in her defense: "To vilify me is to vilify Mao!"[3] The verdict, issued in late January following four weeks of deliberations, found all ten defendants guilty. The court imposed sentences ranging from sixteen years of imprisonment to death, though the death sentences for Jiang Qing and one other defendant were suspended and later commuted to life imprisonment. From beginning to end, daily broadcast and print coverage brought the legal drama to a mass audience, providing a curious Chinese public with the most detailed picture yet glimpsed of the destructive political intrigues of the Cultural Revolution.[4]

[2] "Zuigao renmin fayuan tebie fating guanyu shenpan Lin Biao, Jiang Qing fangeming jituan an zhufan de xiaojie" [Brief summary of the trial of the main culprits in the Lin Biao and Jiang Qing counterrevolutionary groups by the Special Court under the Supreme People's Court] (February 9, 1981), *Zhonghua renmin gongheguo zuigao renmin fayuan tebie fating shenpan Lin Biao, Jiang Qing fangeming jituan an zhufan jishi* [Records of the Special Court of the Supreme People's Court of the PRC trial of the main culprits in the Lin Biao and Jiang Qing counterrevolutionary groups] (hereafter abbreviated as *TBFTJS*) (Beijing: Falü chubanshe, 1982), pp. 480–92.

[3] Jiang Qing's most combative testimony does not appear in the redacted transcripts of *TBFTJS*, but can be heard in television footage broadcast overseas. See "Washington Whispers," *US News and World Report* (December 15, 1980), p. 14; John Brecher and Melinda Liu, "Mao's Widow Hangs Tough," *Newsweek* (November 17, 1980), p. 63. The relevant excerpts can be viewed onsite at the Vanderbilt University Television News Archive (Nashville, TN).

[4] Selected English translations of Chinese media coverage can be found in the Foreign Broadcast Information Service (Daily Report) for China (FBIS-CHI). Selections of courtroom testimony from Hong Kong television coverage can be found in David Bonavia, *Verdict in Peking: The Trial of the Gang of Four* (London: Burnett Books, 1984).

The Special Court faced enormous challenges. The trial was expected all at once to model a reformed system of socialist law, determine criminal liability for mass harm, triage open wounds and mend a tattered social fabric, assign meaning to dimly understood historical events, and usher in a new era of sober rationality. The political challenges alone were formidable. It was easy enough to shield Mao from a posthumous legal reckoning, because the late chairman could not be called to testify in court about the events that he had set in motion. But it was impossible to separate the Cultural Revolution from Mao, or Mao from the larger history of Chinese socialism. (A subversive joke from the time of the trial referred to the Gang of Four with four fingers held up and a wiggling thumb outstretched.) During the Cultural Revolution, the floodgates of violence had been opened in the name of "continuing the revolution," and the resulting ruin left the legitimacy of Chinese socialism badly damaged. In the wake of disaster, it was now imperative for Chinese socialism to offer justice. Inevitably, the trial that ensued was inadequate to meet all of these challenges. Nevertheless, the court's orderly legal proceedings posed a stark contrast to both the extensive violence imposed by repressive military and administrative apparatuses and the rough summary justice handed out by unruly mobs during the Cultural Revolution.[5] The trial announced a new political culture and a new way of dealing with the sharpest contradictions in society. Outside the courtroom, this spectacular legal event became the focal point for a larger cultural conversation about history, justice, and the fate of Chinese socialism.

The Gang of Four Trial as History

Although the Gang of Four trial was both the most important legal case and also the most memorable cultural event of the post-Mao transition, its historical significance has gone largely unexamined. In China, the political situation at the time of the trial made it all but impossible to express any view divergent from the official interpretation of the event's meaning. More troubling, historians have limited access to the facts of the case, and those facts available to us have been carefully curated by the Chinese party-state. The most important primary sources relating to the trial that are available are official documents and state media reports. The Research Office of the Supreme People's Court has compiled many official documents from the trial, including photographic reproductions of procedural documents, records of internal court

---

[5] Andrew Walder, "Rebellion and Repression in China, 1966–1971," *Social Science History* 38.3–4 (2014), pp. 513–39.

meetings, and several hundred pages of partially redacted courtroom transcripts.[6] The present study is the first to make extensive use of this valuable and previously classified material. Official documents are voluminously supplemented by Chinese media reports, consisting of print media such as newspapers, popular magazines, and specialized journals, as well as audio-visual materials such as radio and television broadcasts.[7] Unfortunately, researchers do not have access to official archival materials relating to the trial, which are at present secreted away in Beijing's inaccessible Central Archives and most likely will remain so for several decades to come.[8] Therefore, it will not do to simply produce a more detailed chronology of the "facts" as they have been made available. That task is best left to future researchers, who it is hoped will have better materials with which to work.

More recent Chinese accounts belong to the hybrid genre called "documentary literature" (*jishi wenxue*), a distinctly Chinese form of popular nonfiction consisting of insider accounts of actual events presented with varying degrees of literary license. Examples include memoirs by a judge, a prosecutor, and a defense lawyer, as well as several shorter pieces written by other participants in various aspects of the case. These retrospective sources add color and detail to our knowledge of the trial, but rarely diverge from the themes and interpretations first established by official sources and the genre must be used with caution.[9] This historical study mainly analyzes how the trial was presented and received in its own time, and so affords strong preference to contextualized readings of older sources produced contemporaneously with the trial. This is the first book in English to make use of both older and newer Chinese sources on the trial.

---

[6] *Zhonghua renmin gongheguo zuigao renmin fayuan tebie fating shenpan Lin Biao, Jiang Qing fangeming jituan an zhufan jishi* [Records of the Special Court of the Supreme People's Court of the PRC trial of the main culprits in the Lin Biao and Jiang Qing counterrevolutionary groups], Zuigao renmin fayuan yanjiushi, ed. (Beijing: Falü chubanshe, 1982). I am grateful to Professor Tom Bernstein for making a copy available to me.

[7] Some of this material can be found in two published compilations: *Lishi de shenpan: Shenpan Lin Biao, Jiang Qing fangeming jituan an fan jishi*, 2 vols. (orig. 1981 and 1985; reprint edn., Beijing: Qunzhong chubanshe, 2000) (hereafter cited as *LSSP*); and Zhonggong yuanshi ziliao bianji weiyuan hui, ed., *Zhonggong shenpan "Lin Jiang jituan" an*, Zhonggong yuanshi ziliao xuanji zhuanti lei 1, 2 vols. (Taibei: Zhonggong yanjiu zazhi shehui, 1981).

[8] As a relatively recent and politically sensitive event, the Gang of Four trial has the attributes of an inaccessible archival topic. Recent restrictions on previously open archives do not encourage optimism that previously closed archives will suddenly open; see Maura Cunningham, "Denying Historians: China's Archives Increasingly Off-Bounds" (August 19, 2014), http://blogs.wsj.com/chinarealtime/2014/08/19/denying-historians-chinas-archives-increasingly-off-bounds/.

[9] For a critical discussion of Chinese documentary literature, see Mobo Gao, *The Battle for China's Past: Mao and the Cultural Revolution* (Ann Arbor, MI: Pluto Press, 2008), pp. 59–64.

The best scholarly work on the topic consists of a set of essays published a few months after the trial. In his editor's introduction, James C. Hsiung argues that the trial was "probably the most significant political development in China since Mao's death in 1976 and is likely to have far-reaching effects," and that it "symbolized, first of all, the formal reversal of the course into which the People's Republic had been launched since Mao's Cultural Revolution of 1966–1976."[10] The three main essays explore the trial from different angles. H. Lyman Miller assesses the political implications of the trial, seeing it as a way for the Deng Xiaoping regime to restore organizational regularity and to promote all-around modernization.[11] Hungdah Chiu catalogues the many legal problems evident in the conduct of the trial, concluding that it was "essentially a political proceeding and, in fact, an act of vengeance by the officials currently in power against the losers of a political struggle."[12] Lillian Harris further cautions that the trial did not uphold the high standard of individual human rights hoped for by Western liberals, nor even the lower standard of procedural justice set by the socialist state.[13] Hsiung concludes from these essays that "the political significance ... was more important than the legal significance of the trial proceedings."[14] These initial judgments are sound, but by no means do they exhaust the possibilities suggested by Hsiung's introductory premise that "the trial can be studied for its larger meanings."[15] Another notable contribution is found in the conclusion to Ross Terrill's biography of Jiang Qing, which depicts Madame Mao as the flawed protagonist of a tragic drama – a Nora (after the fashion of Ibsen's *The Dollhouse*) – punished for trying to escape a suffocating edifice not of her making.[16] Terrill provides a

---

[10] James C. Hsiung, "Introduction," in James C. Hsiung, ed., *Symposium: The Trial of the "Gang of Four" and Its Implication in China.* Occasional Papers/Reprints Series in Contemporary Asian Studies 40 (Baltimore: University of Maryland, 1981), p. 1.

[11] H. Lyman Miller, "The Cultural Revolution in the Dock: The Trials in Political Perspective," in James C. Hsiung, ed., *Symposium: The Trial of the "Gang of Four" and Its Implication in China.* Occasional Papers/Reprints Series in Contemporary Asian Studies 40 (Baltimore: University of Maryland, 1981), pp. 5–26.

[12] Hungdah Chiu, "Certain Legal Aspects of the Recent Peking Trials of the 'Gang of Four' and Others," in James C. Hsiung, ed., *Symposium: The Trial of the "Gang of Four" and Its Implication in China.* Occasional Papers/Reprints Series in Contemporary Asian Studies 40 (Baltimore: University of Maryland, 1981), p. 38.

[13] Lillian Craig Harris, "Images and Reality: Human Rights and the Trial of the Gang of Four," in James C. Hsiung, ed., *Symposium: The Trial of the "Gang of Four" and Its Implication in China.* Occasional Papers/Reprints Series in Contemporary Asian Studies 40 (Baltimore: University of Maryland, 1981), pp. 40–56.

[14] Hsiung, "Introduction," p. 2.

[15] Ibid., p. 1.

[16] Ross Terrill, *Madame Mao: The White-Boned Demon,* revised and expanded edn. (Stanford, CA: Stanford University Press, 1999), pp. 13–19, 374–94.

salutary reminder that the trial took place within the broader cultural context of twentieth-century China, in which reformers and revolutionaries understood their situation as a struggle to assert agency against the tyranny of existing social structures. Now, more than three decades after the courtroom drama ended, it is possible to reexamine some initial assumptions about the trial and resume the search for larger meanings.

Despite being perhaps the most memorable moment China's post-Mao transition, the trial is not featured prominently in academic studies of modern China. For example, Maurice Meisner's classic history of the PRC, *Mao's China and After*, treats the trial in just one-and-a-half pages.[17] Roderick MacFarquhar and Michael Schoenhals's narrative history of the Cultural Revolution, *Mao's Last Revolution*, devotes only two of its nearly seven hundred pages to the Gang of Four trial.[18] Richard Baum's masterful study of post-Mao politics, *Burying Mao*, gives only a brief overview of the trial.[19] The event barely rates a mention in leading studies of post-Mao legal reform, such as Stanley Lubman's *Bird in a Cage* or Randall Peerenboom's *China's Long March toward Rule of Law*.[20]

In the relative absence of scholarly work on the trial, images crafted by popular media have framed perceptions of the trial. Chinese propaganda lavished praise on the trial uncritically. Chinese media sources cannot be taken at face value, but neither should they be discarded. Contemporary Western media reports were much more skeptical, but these too need to be approached with care. Though well-informed, Western skepticism could be tinged with condescension, as in this postscript to the trial from the pages of *Newsweek*:

> To no one's surprise Jiang Qing [and the others] were convicted. After all, the Chinese are still running a dictatorship. But the trial was a signal that the legal system is important, a reminder that perhaps in China the law can evolve, guaranteeing a modicum of liberty for its citizens. It's not Jeffersonian democracy, but for the people who live there it's no small accomplishment.[21]

For many outside observers, seeing a socialist court press former socialist leaders on charges of counterrevolution recalled the notorious Moscow

[17] Maurice Meisner, *Mao's China and After: A History of the People's Republic* (New York: Free Press, 1986), pp. 461–3.

[18] Roderick MacFarquhar and Michael Schoenhals, *Mao's Last Revolution* (Cambridge, MA: Belknap Press of Harvard University Press, 2008), pp. 454 and 459.

[19] Richard Baum, *Burying Mao: Chinese Politics in the Age of Deng Xiaoping* (Princeton, NJ: Princeton University Press, 1994), pp. 113–16.

[20] Stanley Lubman, *Bird in a Cage: Legal Reform in China after Mao* (Stanford, CA: Stanford University Press, 2000); Randall P. Peerenboom, *China's Long March toward Rule of Law* (New York: Cambridge University Press, 2002).

[21] ARIC Press, "China Lays Down the Law," *Newsweek* (September 7, 1981), p. 47.

Trials of the 1930s and other kangaroo courts. Without a second thought, most critics in the Western media wrote off the trial as a crude Stalinist farce adapted to the Chinese stage – a political show trial. However, this assumption is an analytical black hole: powerfully attractive, but unilluminating.

First of all, it must be emphasized that the political show trial interpretation was and is entirely reasonable. The Gang of Four trial was a purge of disgraced political leaders, a legal spectacle staged by an authoritarian state with a well-deserved reputation for grand political theater. The selective prosecution of politically palatable defendants, the retroactive application of laws, the numerous procedural irregularities, the widespread assumption of guilt, the limited opportunities for defense, the strongly pedagogical tone – these elements rightly contributed to the impression that the Gang of Four trial used the barest of legal trappings to conceal a raw demonstration of political power. Hindsight further confirms the suspicion of contemporary observers that the trial was far less important legally than is was politically. The trial failed to establish a robust and lasting precedent for socialist rule of law, as proponents claimed it would, and criminal prosecution continues to be used in China today as an instrument to suppress political opposition. In all of these ways, the Gang of Four trial typified the type of rough political justice that Otto Kirchheimer famously called "trials by fiat of successor regimes."[22]

Nevertheless, the standard interpretation of the Gang of Four trial as a political show trial, correct as far as it goes, is also severely limited. Unlike the worst of the Soviet show trials, the content of the Gang of Four trial was not "just a show" in the sense of a mere fiction spun by the state. David Bonavia, a journalist who followed the proceedings as closely as any Western observer, concedes in his book-length account that the trial was "[not] even remotely a fair one," but still the show seemed to be "only to some extent stage-managed" and was "rooted in fact, even if tendentiously presented."[23] While the circumstances surrounding the alleged plot to assassinate Mao remain mysterious, much of the trial dealt with very real and painful events in the living memory of the Chinese people.[24] Yet the pejorative "show trial" deems whatever the trial purported to show as unworthy of serious consideration. The implication is that the trial was not a *real* historical event but merely a staged

---

[22] Otto Kirchheimer, *Political Justice: The Use of Legal Procedure for Political Ends* (Princeton, NJ: Princeton University Press, 1961), pp. 304–47.

[23] Bonavia, *Verdict in Peking*, p. 12.

[24] Stephen Uhalley Jr. and Jin Qiu, "The Lin Biao Incident: More Than Twenty Years Later," *Pacific Affairs* 66.3 (Autumn 1993), pp. 386–98.

pseudo-event – that is, a performance "staged or managed (or co-opted) by an existing configuration of power or authority, rather than spontaneously generating any new such configuration."[25] While a staged event is different from a spontaneously occurring one, the action on the stage may still have profound effects on its audience. Even the most clumsily staged trials play out political and cultural values; if anything of historical value is to be learned from such an event, then it is necessary to take the "show" seriously.[26]

These shows can be quite complicated. As historian Lawrence Douglas has observed, trials of the perpetrators of mass violence are intended to carry out a number of important social functions:

Staged as exercises in collective pedagogy, these trials claimed to provide detailed and accurate representations of the larger sweep of historical forces that issues in acts of mass atrocity. In addition, these trials aimed to teach history lessons – they were orchestrated to locate in the historical record clear morals that could serve to shape the terms of collective memory. Finally, these trials aimed more concretely to honor the memory of victims and survivors, by providing a solemn public space in which anguished remembrance could take the form of legally probative testimony.[27]

Whereas Kirchheimer emphasized the destructive goals of victor's justice, Douglas has featured the didactic role that trials play in shaping collective memory of the past. Trials can even be used as a process to decide between competing political visions and interests. Devin Pendas and Jens Meierhenrich have rightly proposed that studies of political trials must be attentive to the dynamic interplay between political power, legal procedure, and cultural performance.[28]

The Gang of Four trial staged new possibilities for the relationship between politics, law, and culture in post-Mao China. The Gang of Four trial was an expression of justice inseparable from its transitional context, the transition from the Cultural Revolution to the post-Mao era. It was a political show trial to be sure, but the historian must take this fact as the impetus for further inquiry and not as the final judgment. To press forward, a more capacious interpretive framework is needed – one that allows us to understand the greater significance of the event in

[25] Scott Newton, "Post-war to New World Order and Post-socialist Transition: 1989 as Pseudo-Event," in Fleur Johns, Richard Joyce, and Sundhya Pahuja, eds., *Events: The Force of International Law* (London: Routledge, 2011), pp. 106–7.

[26] An exemplary study is Elizabeth A. Wood, *Performing Justice: Agitation Trials in Early Soviet Russia* (Ithaca, NY: Cornell University Press, 2005).

[27] Lawrence Douglas, "The Didactic Trial: Filtering History and Memory in the Courtroom," *European Review* 14.4 (2006), pp. 513–14.

[28] Jens Meierhenrich and Devin O. Pendas, "Political Trials in Theory and History," in Jens Meierhenrich and Devin O. Pendas, eds., *Political Trials in Theory and History* (Cambridge University Press, forthcoming), np.

its political, legal, and cultural contexts. That framework – transitional justice – will be introduced further on.

A history dealing with a topic as sensitive as the aftermath of the Cultural Revolution necessarily entails a considerable methodological challenge. Faced with the unavailability of reliable sources and the unreliability of available sources, a conventional approach to the history of the trial is blocked.

This does not mean, however, that it is necessary to abandon the important question of the trial's place in the post-Mao transition. On the contrary, it is the responsibility of historians to pursue problems and questions beyond those deemed safe or acceptable by the state; to act otherwise is to consign history hostage to the demands of political regimes. Of course, the lack of available archival sources does pose a real and formidable obstacle, as it prevents us from answering with confidence some very basic types of questions about the trial. For example, in developing a narrative account of the trial, we can say little about the quality of the evidence produced in court and even less about what really happened behind the scenes. Nevertheless, this frustrating roadblock does not close off all empirical avenues. Those official sources that are available can be subjected to a form of close reading and interpretation.

In socialist China, language was (and to an extent, still is) an indispensable index of political ideology. Beginning in the revolutionary days, Mao shaped the communist party into a discourse community that took language and ideology as the rudiments of identity formation and political power.[29] This language-obsessed regime then established a socialist state that became, in the estimation of Ji Fengyuan, a "laboratory in which Mao conducted easily the biggest experiment in linguistic engineering in world history, and one of the most rigorously controlled."[30] China's communists used language and symbolism purposefully and advisedly to express their ideological views and political aspirations. In this context, all political actions – no matter how seemingly minor, whether constructive policy initiatives or destructive attacks on rivals, and no matter whether motivated by personal, economic, diplomatic, or other goals – had to be justified and explained using the correct terminology and narrative codes before they could be considered legitimate and acceptable. Under

---

[29] David E. Apter and Tony Saich, *Revolutionary Discourse in Mao's Republic* (Cambridge, MA: Harvard University Press, 1994); Franz Schurmann, *Ideology and Organization in Communist China* (Berkeley: University of California Press, 1968); Michael Schoenhals, *Doing Things with Words in Chinese Politics: Five Studies* (Berkeley: University of California at Berkeley, Center for Chinese Studies, 1992).

[30] Ji Fengyuan, *Linguistic Engineering: Language and Politics in Mao's China* (Honolulu: University of Hawai'i Press, 2004), pp. 2–3.

Chinese socialism, and especially during the politically perilous era of the Cultural Revolution, speakers and audiences were constantly alert to the heavy freight of meanings that words (so easily dismissed by outsiders as empty jargon) could convey.[31] Much of our work here on the trial will consist of unpacking linguistic and symbolic freight and examining its hidden contents.

The research in this book is based on two distinct source bases, which are interleaved in the chapters that follow. The chapters directly about the trial are based on sources immediately relevant to the legal trial and its political context. A close examination of formal legal documents and Chinese media accounts will explore official meanings assigned to the trial. Even as these official meanings were being produced and disseminated, however, they were also being framed, interpreted, or contested by other discourses that reflected on China's larger post-Mao predicament. Therefore, the chapters on the trial alternate with chapters based on the only other contemporaneous documents comparable in their liveliness, complexity, impact, and scale: namely, literary works tacitly in conversation with the trial in its broader cultural context. Each of these source bases is problematic in its own way; their full value will emerge only when they are examined closely and in relation to their shared concern for the problem of justice in the post-Mao transition. Analyzing these two very different source bases side by side will answer the central question posed by this book: What did it mean for the Chinese to use a legal trial to address the injustices of the Cultural Revolution? To understand the legal and literary responses to the Cultural Revolution (1966–76), and the relationship of these responses to each other, it is first necessary to understand the events and issues at the heart of that decade-long conflict.

The Core Dilemma

The Cultural Revolution and its aftermath belonged to an age of Chinese revolutions. The conflict was waged as a factional struggle, driven at times by personalities and petty interests, but it was also an attempt at working through a core dilemma of modern Chinese history. Since the late nineteenth century, modernizers in China have launched revolution upon revolution, each with the aim of remediating, deepening, expanding, or

---

[31] Lowell Dittmer and Chen Ruoxi, *Ethics and Rhetoric of the Cultural Revolution*, Studies in Chinese Terminology 19 (Berkeley: Center for Chinese Studies, Institute of East Asian Studies, University of California, 1981). On the continued use of jargon today, see Qian Gang, "Watchwords: The Life of the Party," The China Media Project, http://cmp.hku .hk/2012/09/10/26667/.

improving upon the previous ones – the ultimate goal being the full realization of a distinctly Chinese modernity. A central question attending
China's modernization has been how to attain wealth and power while
still preserving an essential core of cultural values. Despite the bewildering array of political and philosophical views held by China's modern revolutionaries and reformers, most agreed on the need for China's
material development – that is, the development of capacities for extrac-
tion and production, transportation and communication, military force
and political power – so that the feeble "sick man of Asia" could reclaim
its rightful place as one of the world's great civilizations and one of the
engines of the world economy. At the same time, many revolutionaries and reformers stressed the need to nurture spiritual health – that is,
the cultivation of the moral, cultural, and intellectual goodness of the
Chinese people.

This dilemma was central to China's modernization, but it was not
new. Chinese political thought has long concerned itself with how to
balance the instrumental aspects of statecraft with its more human
dimensions. For the better part of the past two millennia the dynastic
state offered a model solution in the dualistic blend of two classical philosophies, Confucianism and Legalism. Confucianism, which provided
the ideology of the dynastic state, held that good government arises
from the virtuous leadership of good rulers and ministers who exercise
moral suasion (*de*: power, virtue) over their subjects, just as good par-
ents foster the growth of their children. This was a humanistic model of
governance committed to the moral cultivation of persons. Legalism,
which provided many of the institutions of the dynastic state, held that
the most effective government depends on the ruthless enforcement
of objectively existing laws and standards. Legalist doctrine was both
highly rational and highly instrumental, taking the power of the state
as the legitimate end of government. The dualistic system balanced the
instrumental rationalism of classical Legalism with the humanism of
Confucianism.

The dynastic system and its dualistic model collapsed early in the twentieth century, but the basic dilemma of statecraft remained. The radicals
and revolutionaries of the twentieth century considered Confucianism and
Legalism to be outmoded philosophies of China's backward past, and yet
this dualism proved remarkably durable, leaving a lasting impression on
modern Chinese political thought. Even as the moderns rejected classical
thought, they restated the classical statecraft positions in new terms: the
"rule of law" and the "rule of man." These capacious terms accommodated a range of meanings in different contexts. The debate was joined
from every part of the ideological spectrum by figures as intellectually

diverse as journalist and reformer Liang Qichao, anarcho-feminist He Zhen, political philosopher Zhang Shizhao, communists Li Dazhao and Chen Duxiu, prominent liberal Hu Shi, rural reformer Liang Shuming, jurist Mei Ju-ao (who represented the Republic of China at the Tokyo War Crimes Tribunal), and sociologist Fei Xiaotong (who served as a judge in the Gang of Four trial).[32] Generally speaking, supporters of the rule of law touted predictable standards, while opponents decried repression; supporters of the rule of man called for moral leadership, while opponents feared autocracy. Thus, while the term *rule of law* entered the modern Chinese political vocabulary through Yan Fu's turn-of-the-century translation of Montesquieu, like so many neologisms this one had a classical Chinese pedigree.[33] Likewise, the term *rule of man* was borrowed from then-current debates in the West, but the concept had deep roots in Chinese history. Taken together, these terms recalled and renewed a long-running dualism within Chinese statecraft between Confucianism and Legalism.

Chinese political thought in the age of revolution was also remarkable for the "depth, intensity, and pervasiveness of scientism," that is, in the belief that "all aspects of the universe are knowable through science."[34] The notion of laws undergirding society came to include not only positive law but also natural laws. Faith in science extended to the perfection of human society, as in this manifesto from the progressive journal *New Century* (1907): "[T]he revolution of the New Century considers that all

[32] Leigh K. Jenco, "'Rule by Man' and 'Rule by Law' in Early Republican China: Contributions to a Theoretical Debate," *Journal of Asian Studies* 69.1 (February 2010), pp. 189–95; Peter Zarrow, "He Zhen and Anarcho-Feminism in China," *The Journal of Asian Studies* 47.4 (November 1988), p. 806; Chen Duxiu, *Chen Duxiu wenzhang xuanbian* [Selected essays of Chen Duxiu] (Beijing: Sanlian shudian, 1984), vol. 1, p. 315; Edmund S. K. Fung, "The Human Rights Issue in China, 1929–1931," *Modern Asian Studies* 32.2 (May 1998), p. 444; Hong-Yok Ip, "Liang Shuming and the Idea of Democracy in Modern China," *Modern China* 17.4 (October 1991), p. 490; Chen Jingliang, "Lun Liang Shuming de fa wen hua guan. Zhongnan caijing zhengzhi daxue, faxue yuan tushuguan," http://fxylib.znufe.edu.cn/new/ShowArticle .asp?ArticleID=4974; Fei Xiaotong, *From the Soil: The Foundations of Chinese Society*, a *Translation of Fei Xiaotong's Xiangtu Zhongguo*, Gary G. Hamilton and Wang Zheng, transl. (Berkeley: University of California Press, 1992), p. 94.

[33] Yan Fu's translation of Montesquieu's *L'Esprit des Lois* (1748) was published as *Fayi* (1904–9). The *locus classicus* of the latter phrase is the Legalist text *Han Feizi*; a recent variation is the less instrumental sounding "rule the state according to law" (also *yi fa zhi guo*). There has been considerable scholarly discussion about whether to measure *fazhi* against a normative Western conception ("*the* rule of law") or on its own terms. This has led to distinctions between "thick" and "thin" rule of law, as well as arguments that the Chinese concept is not rule of law at all, but merely an instrumental "rule *by* law."

[34] D. W. Y. Kwok, *Scientism in Chinese Thought, 1900–1950* (New Haven, CT: Yale University Press, 1965), pp. vii and 3.

that does not conform to the laws of nature is undesirable and must be changed. Not only that, but this revolution will persist, forever nearing the right and the truth. Therefore, this is a relentless and progressive revolution, a revolution that has as its object the happiness of mankind."[35] This desire to model a morally good human society on the dictates of science was entirely representative of the era. Science and Democracy were the watchwords of the New Culture movement of the 1910s and 1920s, which sought a cultural remedy for the imperfections of political revolution that overthrew the dynastic system, and yet which left wholly unrealized so many of the revolutionaries' hopes and desires. It was this intellectual context that gave birth to Chinese socialism, which sought to address the ills of human society through the ostensibly scientific methods of Marxism and Leninism.[36]

The history of Chinese socialism has been defined by the struggle between those who emphasized the constraints imposed by objective history and those who emphasized the possibilities opened by subjective will.[37] The dialectical tension between these two positions forms what Alvin Gouldner calls the "nuclear contradiction" of Marxism.[38] For China's revolutionaries, this was not an abstract philosophical question; it had practical, strategic implications. Emphasis on objective forces called for a scientific, empirically grounded approach to revolution that would produce tangible results, most especially the transformation of economic production. Attention to subjective will stressed that progress in human history arose from our power to reimagine the world, to overcome our present material limitations and strive toward future goals. Chairman Mao, in typically dialectical fashion, espoused the basic truth of both positions:

True, the productive forces, practice, and the economic base *generally* play the principal and decisive role; whoever denies this is not a materialist. But it must

---

[35] Quoted in ibid., pp. 12–13.

[36] For a comparison between traditional Chinese and modern Chinese socialist views of humanity, see Donald J. Munro, *The Concept of Man in Early China*. Michigan Classics in Chinese Studies (Ann Arbor: Center for Chinese Studies, University of Michigan, 2001) and *The Concept of Man in Contemporary China* (Ann Arbor: Center for Chinese Studies, University of Michigan, 1977).

[37] Nick Knight calls this the "core dilemma" of Chinese socialism. See Knight, *Marxist Philosophy in China: From Qu Qiubai to Mao Zedong, 1923–1945* (Dordrecht, The Netherlands: Springer, 2005), p. 32. Frederic Wakeman Jr. calls it "the most significant problematic" in Mao's political thought. See Wakeman, *History and Will: Philosophical Perspectives of Mao Tse-tung's Thought* (Berkeley: University of California Press, 1973), p. xi.

[38] On the "nuclear contradiction," see Alvin W. Gouldner, *The Two Marxisms: Contradictions and Anomalies in the Development of Theory* (New York: Oxford University Press, 1982),

also be admitted that *in certain conditions*, such aspects as the relations of production, theory, and the superstructure in turn manifest themselves in the principal and decisive role.... When the superstructure (politics, culture, etc.) obstructs the development of the economic base, political and cultural changes become principal and decisive.[39]

Mao fully appreciated the need for technical expertise and scientific knowledge, and believed that economic production was the basis for social existence. But he also could see mechanical determinism and economistic analysis as blinkers to creative thought and impediments to social change.

After all, the historical experience of the communist movement had proved time and again that bold revolutionary thinking could help clear seemingly insurmountable obstacles: entrenched landlords and powerful warlords, Nationalist armies and Japanese invaders, the crushing poverty of the China's vast hinterland and the added pressures of foreign imperialism. On the other side of the scale, some of Mao's more audacious attempts to pit human will against material limits – most notably, the Great Leap Forward – had been terrible failures. The pendulum of political fortune swung back and forth between these two positions, with increasingly ambitious political movements put in check by increasingly alarmed bureaucrats. The Cultural Revolution was a forceful swing toward the radical, subjective line, while the post-Mao reforms represent a decisive swing back to the objective, materialist line. The struggle to define the legacy of the Cultural Revolution was a battle for the divided soul of Chinese socialism.

In the later years of the Cultural Revolution, Chinese Marxist historians tread a well-worn path in identifying the struggle between these two positions as the central organizing theme of Chinese history.[40] After the Cultural Revolution, the familiar vocabulary of legality and humanity stood ready to be redeployed in service of reform. Thus, questions of legality and humanity – and by implication their opposites, illegality and inhumanity – remain inextricably intertwined within contemporary China's intellectual world.

---

p. 48. As Gouldner shows, many labels have been given to the two Marxisms: scientific versus utopian, orthodox versus critical, materialist versus idealist, determinist versus activist, fatalist versus voluntarist.

[39] Mao Zedong, "On Contradiction" (1937), www.marxists.org/reference/archive/mao/selected-works/volume-1/mswv1_17.htm.

[40] Tien-wei Wu, *Lin Biao and the Gang of Four: Contra-Confucianism in Historical and Intellectual Perspective* (Carbondale: Southern Illinois University Press, 1983).

China's Cultural Revolution

In October 1949 the CCP founded the socialist state, the PRC. The founding of the new state ended decades of civil war and marked the victorious conclusion of the political revolution. In other ways, though, the founding of the socialist state was only the beginning of the struggle to achieve communism. Completion of the revolution would entail a total structural transformation of Chinese society, from its economic base to its political and cultural institutions, and even to the subjective consciousness of its people. Chairman Mao Zedong accepted Lenin's prediction that the socialist era, as the era of transition from capitalism to communism, would be "a period of unusually violent class struggles in their sharpest possible forms."[41] This meant that under socialism the revolutionary classes must exercise strict dictatorship over the enemies of the people. Thus, on the eve of founding the fledgling state, Mao cautioned his comrades against complacency in victory:

The imperialists and domestic reactionaries will certainly not take their defeat lying down and they will struggle to the last ditch. After there is peace and order throughout the country, they will still engage in sabotage and create disturbances in various ways and will try every day and every minute to stage a comeback. This is inevitable, beyond all doubt, and under no circumstances must we relax our vigilance.[42]

In the years leading up to the Cultural Revolution, Mao perceived the specters of "revisionism" and "capitalist restoration" materializing within the socialist camp, both domestically and overseas. He pointed with alarm to de-Stalinization in the Soviet Union and the retrenchment of agricultural collectivization after the famine caused by the Great Leap Forward in China.[43] Furthermore, Mao suspected that the old guard of Chinese revolutionaries was degenerating into a new privileged class of bureaucrats, and he warned of this danger in a high-level party document issued in January 1965: "[A]fter the socialist transformation of ownership has been basically completed, the class enemies of socialism will use

---

[41] Vladimir Ilyich Lenin, "The State and Revolution," in Henry M. Christman, ed., *Essential Works of Lenin: "What Is to Be Done?" and Other Writings* (New York: Dover, 1987), p. 295.

[42] Mao Zedong, "The Chinese People Have Stood Up!" (Opening address at the First Plenary Session of the Chinese People's Political Consultative Conference, September 21, 1949), www.marxists.org/reference/archive/mao/selected-works/volume-5/mswv5_01.htm.

[43] Roderick MacFarquhar, *Origins of the Chinese Cultural Revolution*, 3 vols. (New York: Columbia University Press for the Royal Institute of International Affairs, the East Asian Institute of Columbia University, and the Research Institute on Communist Affairs of Columbia University, 1974–83).

Figure 1. Cultural Revolution leaders; from left to right: Kang Sheng, Zhou Enlai, Mao Zedong, Lin Biao, Chen Boda, and Jiang Qing. The caption reads, "Forever making revolution with Chairman Mao" (*Genzhe Mao zhuxi yongyuan nao geming*) (1967).
Source: IISH Collection, International Institute of Social History (Amsterdam).

the means of 'peaceful evolution' to seek the restoration of capitalism. This sort of class struggle inevitably will be reflected in the Party."[44] Mao took an increasingly pessimistic view of China's prospects for completing the revolution in his lifetime.

Instead, Mao came to view revolution as a continuous struggle to be fought again and again over a very long period of time.[45] The revolution, if not secured, could be reversed. Now facing the prospect of imminent reversal, the urgent task of the moment was to "grasp the struggle between the two roads of socialism and capitalism" and identify "those in positions of authority in the Party taking the capitalist road."[46] This task – the political and cultural struggle against the restoration of capitalism from within the communist party – was the basic program of the Cultural Revolution. This meant that the Cultural Revolution was a struggle within Chinese socialism, initiated by Chairman Mao against many of his erstwhile comrades. Mao and his allies – including Lin Biao and Jiang Qing – waged a violent, decade-long campaign to attack and purge those who opposed the Chairman's radical vision of Chinese socialism (Figure 1).

[44] CCP Central Committee, "Nongcun shehuizhuyi jiaoyu yundong zhong muqian de yixie wenti" [Some current problems in the rural socialist education movement] (January 14, 1965), http://news.xinhuanet.com/ziliao/2005-02/02/content_2539348.htm.
[45] Nick Knight, *Rethinking Mao: Explorations in Mao Zedong's Thought* (New York: Lexington Books, 2007), pp. 249–69.
[46] CCP Central Committee, "Nongcun shehuizhuyi jiaoyu yundong zhong muqian de yixie wenti."

The Cultural Revolution spanned the decade from 1966 to 1976.[47] Several phases comprised this complex historical period. The most "active" period occurred during the first couple of years, including phases of mass mobilization, the purge of existing leadership structures, the creation of new structures, armed clashes between factions, and mass demobilization. This active period was followed by a consolidation of power, itself marked by a new round of conflicts among the radicals over the spoils of victory. In this period, Mao precipitated the downfall of Chen Boda and the Lin Biao group, and the group that would later become known as the Gang of Four emerged as the standard-bearers of the radical line in Chinese politics. Moderates resurfaced in the party in the mid-1970s and later purged the Gang of Four after Mao's death. The next few pages highlight these main events in the political history of the Cultural Revolution.

The Cultural Revolution began with a party circular dated May 16, 1966. The circular took aim at Mao's perceived enemies in the party, including an informal panel of establishment politicians and intellectuals appointed by the Central Committee in 1964 to oversee the revolution in culture. Several high-ranking officials were exposed as belonging to an "anti-Party clique," and the panel overseeing the revolution in culture was summarily dissolved. The panel was replaced by a more powerful and far more radical body, the Central Cultural Revolution Group (CCRG), to be convened by Premier Zhou Enlai and reporting directly to the Politburo's Standing Committee. Mao's former political secretary Chen Boda headed the new group, whose roster counted Mao's wife Jiang Qing, radical Shanghai politician Zhang Chunqiao, and chief of the national intelligence apparatus Kang Sheng, among others.

Mao had struck the first blow; now he was ready to rally his forces. A June 1 editorial in *People's Daily* called on the Chinese people to "sweep away all monsters."[48] Though Mao had his critics among the top leadership, he enjoyed great prestige among the Chinese people, owing in part to a cult of personality fostered by PLA leader Lin Biao.[49] Soldiers and young people especially admired Mao, as did many common workers and farmers, and some of the more radical intellectuals. Thus was Mao able to rally an unusual but broad coalition of revolutionary forces from outside the party-state apparatus to assail the revolution's supposed

[47] For a standard political history of the Cultural Revolution, see MacFarquhar and Schoenhals, *Mao's Last Revolution*.

[48] Chen Boda, "Hengsao yiqie niugui sheshen" [Sweep away all ox-ghosts and snake-spirits], *Renmin ribao* [People's Daily] [hereafter abbreviated as *RMRB*], June 1, 1966.

[49] Daniel Leese, *Mao Cult: Rhetoric and Ritual in China's Cultural Revolution* (New York: Cambridge University Press, 2013).

enemies. He hailed the younger generation as "revolutionary successors," and over the coming months throngs of students were encouraged to challenge authority at higher and higher levels. From there, the
situation escalated rapidly. Numerous officials were dragged from their
homes and paraded before jeering crowds. Eventually the two biggest
"capitalist roaders" would be revealed as President Liu Shaoqi and
Party Vice-Chairman Deng Xiaoping. In January 1967, a clash between
labor organizations brought down the Shanghai municipal government.
Mao praised this "January Storm" as a seizure of power by the masses,
though in reality it was the military that provided decisive support to
this and similar seizures of power elsewhere across the country. Violent
skirmishes soon became endemic, and it was not always clear to the
military brass which among the many competing rebel groups deserved
their backing. Local armed conflicts grew in intensity, sometimes even
pitting military units against each other. By the summer of 1967, China
teetered on the brink of civil war. It was time to consolidate gains,
declare victory, and bring the "active phase" of the Cultural Revolution
to a close.

The consolidation would take another year and a half of struggle and
bloodshed. Zhou initiated an open-ended campaign to root out trouble-
makers and "purify the class ranks." The campaign would drag on for
years, implicating millions of people. By the end of the summer of 1968,
the new Revolutionary Committees were in place in every province of
China, and normalcy had been restored under de facto martial law.[50]
Millions of radical students and intellectuals were demobilized – exiled
to the countryside, not knowing when they might return. The purge of
party leadership was confirmed in October 1968, when a skeletal party
plenum formally expelled Liu Shaoqi, dismissed Deng Xiaoping from
office, and designated Lin Biao as Mao's future successor. In his summary report at the opening of the Ninth Central Committee in April
1969, Lin Biao declared that although "a great victory has been won in
the Great Proletarian Cultural Revolution," it was "too soon to speak
of final victory." He urged that the study and dissemination of the basic
lessons of the Great Proletarian Cultural Revolution, the history of the
struggle between two lines (capitalism and socialism), and Chairman
Mao's theory of continuing the revolution under the dictatorship of the
proletariat were lessons that would have to be relearned and repeated
"every year, every month, and every day."[51]

---

[50] MacFarquhar and Schoenhals, *Mao's Last Revolution*, pp. 245–6.
[51] Lin Biao, "Report to the Ninth National Congress of the Communist Party of China"
(April 1, 1969), www.marxists.org/reference/archive/lin-biao/1969/04/01.htm.

Almost as soon as victory had been claimed, the radical coalition began to turn against itself. Chen Boda, the head of the CCRG, was the first to fall. The presidency had remained vacant since the purge of Liu Shaoqi. Chen Boda and Lin Biao insisted that Mao should resume the office, which he had held before, while Mao proposed that the post be eliminated. In any case, Mao did not want the largely ceremonial role, which he considered tiresome. Mao resented the hectoring. Lin Biao wanted to add a phrase from his foreword to the Little Red Book, *Quotations from Chairman Mao*, in which he asserted that Mao had developed Marxism-Leninism "with genius, creatively, and comprehensively."[52] Mao countered that genius was a bourgeois concept, and Chen Boda was dismissed as a "phoney Marxist."[53] It was Lin Biao who had put up Chen Boda to pester Mao, and now Mao grew distant from his erstwhile "closest comrade-in-arms." This was a fatal mistake for Lin, who had lost the chairman's trust and confidence. The split between Lin Biao and Mao Zedong set in motion the mysterious events of September 1971, in which Lin died in a plane crash after discovery of an aborted assassination plot against Mao. After his death, Lin Biao was exposed as one half of the "Lin and Chen [Boda] Anti-Party Clique" and later became the central target of the Gang of Four's stultifying campaign to "Criticize Lin and Confucius."[54] In the final years of the Cultural Revolution, the Gang of Four – Jiang Qing, Zhang Chunqiao, Yao Wenyuan, and Wang Hongwen – held firm control of the radical wing of the party, and Wang Hongwen was put forward as a candidate to succeed Mao.

Though Mao became increasingly frail and isolated in his old age, he continued to maintain among the top leadership a delicate balance of power that he could tip to meet his purposes. In 1974, Premier Zhou Enlai recalled to office the moderate (and erstwhile "No. 2 Capitalist Roader") Deng Xiaoping to train as Zhou's successor. Deng lost his patron when Zhou died in January 1976, and Chairman Mao once again singled out Deng for criticism. Popular support for Zhou and Deng swelled in the days surrounding the Tomb-Sweeping Festival (*Qingming*, a traditional holiday of mourning) in April 1976, an event the Gang of Four labeled counterrevolutionary. Thus in the mid-1970s the radicals were held in check by other factions: by occasionally rehabilitated moderates such as

---

[52] Lin Biao, "Foreword to the Second Edition of Quotations of Chairman Mao Tse-tung" (December 16, 1966), www.marxists.org/reference/archive/lin-biao/1966/12/16.htm.

[53] Quoted in Schoenhals and MacFarquhar, *Mao's Last Revolution*, p. 356.

[54] "Circular and Materials of the CCP Central Committee on Organizing the Distribution and Discussion of *The Struggle to Smash the Lin-Chen Anti-Party Clique's Counterrevolutionary Coup* (Materials, Part 1)" (December 11, 1971) [Zhongfa #77 (1971)]; Tien-wei Wu, *Lin Biao and the Gang of Four*.

Deng Xiaoping, of course, but also by supporters of the elder statesman Zhou Enlai; by other senior cadres who had benefited from the turnover in leadership in the late 1960s; and by entrenched interests in strategic economic sectors like the petroleum industry. The Gang of Four members still had Mao's backing as representatives of his radical line, but they otherwise lacked institutional and popular support.

A few months before his death, a frail and ailing Chairman Mao reflected back on his life and counted two great accomplishments. His first great accomplishment, he said, had been to beat back the Japanese invaders and defeat Chiang Kai-shek's Nationalist regime in the subsequent civil war. The second great accomplishment had been to launch the Cultural Revolution. Mao had initiated this second (cultural) revolution in order to safeguard the first, but he had to concede that its greatness was not widely recognized: "Not many people support this thing, and more than a few oppose it. The matter is not yet resolved. It is a legacy to be handed down to the next generation – if not in peace, then in turmoil."[55] Although the Gang of Four was campaigning against the "Right-deviationist reversal of verdicts" issued during the Cultural Revolution (Figure 2), Mao went to his deathbed fearing an end to his continuous revolution. His fear proved prescient.

When Mao died, power initially passed to the capable but colorless Hua Guofeng, a doctrinaire Maoist who represented the senior beneficiaries of the Cultural Revolution. One of Hua's first actions, just weeks after Mao's death, was to "smash" the Gang of Four. The radicals were placed under house arrest and subjected to criticism in a series of political campaigns. Hua Guofeng did not criticize the Cultural Revolution, however. That would be left to the regime of Deng Xiaoping, who outmaneuvered Hua to take control of the party in late 1978. Deng had a reputation as a pragmatist, as well as the résumé of a Long March veteran, deep connections in the military, and the support of other senior leaders who had survived the purges of the past decade. Deng declared the class struggle over and turned to the business of "socialist construction" – the development of productive forces and the social accumulation of material wealth.

Confronting the legacy of the Cultural Revolution, the new regime undertook – just as the radicals had feared – a comprehensive "reversal of false, unjust, and incorrect verdicts." Whereas Mao had believed such a reversal would be a betrayal of the socialist project, the post-Mao

---

[55] This anecdote is oft repeated but not well documented. On attribution of this quote, see Jiang Yihua, "Perspective 1: On Mao Zedong," in Timothy Cheek, ed. *A Critical Introduction to Mao* (Cambridge: Cambridge University Press, 2010), p. 342; Frederick Teiwes and Warren Sun, *The End of the Maoist Era: Chinese Politics during the Twilight of the Cultural Revolution, 1972–1976* (New York: Routledge, 2007), p. 595.

把反击右倾翻案风的斗争进行到底

Figure 2. The radicals feared a reversal of verdicts on the Cultural
Revolution. The caption of the poster reads, "Struggle to the end to
oppose the Right-deviationist trend to reverse verdicts" (*Ba fanji youq-
ing fan'an feng de douzheng jinxing daodi*) (April 1976).
Source: IISH Collection, International Institute of Social History
(Amsterdam).

reformers claimed the reversal to be a redemption of it. At the center of
the reversal of verdicts was the courtroom trial that brought a legal verdict against the most notorious leaders of the Cultural Revolution – and
set the stage for a final, historical verdict on Mao.

Socialist Legality and Transitional Justice

The post-Mao response to the Cultural Revolution can be best understood within the framework of what is now called *transitional justice*. Transitional justice is a field of activity and scholarly inquiry that
"focuse[s] on how societies address legacies of past human rights abuses,
mass atrocity, or other forms of severe social trauma, including genocide or civil war, in order to build a more democratic, just, or peaceful
future."[56] As a field of scholarly inquiry, transitional justice is relatively

[56] *The Encyclopedia of Genocide and Crimes against Humanity* (New York: Macmillan
Reference, 2004), vol. 3, p. 1045.

new.[57] The term first gained currency in the early 1990s as governments and scholars inquired into the process of decommunization in Eastern Europe, often in direct comparison with the collapse of authoritarian regimes in Latin America over the previous decade; it entered common usage in the 2000s in connection with the work of the South African Truth and Reconciliation Commission. Due to the political orientation of the transitions underway when the field of scholarly inquiry took shape, early studies often embraced normative assumptions about liberal democracy, human rights, and the rule of law as the desirable outcomes of transition.[58]

As the field of inquiry into transitional justice has developed, scholars have begun to resist this overly narrow approach.[59] More recent analytical works have used the conceptual framework of transitional justice to inquire retrospectively into a broader field of activity promoting postconflict transitions in many times and places, such as Athens in the fifth century BCE or the Bourbon monarchy in eighteenth-century France.[60] Jon Elster, a leading scholar in the field, has stated flatly that transitional justice "is *not* limited to modern regimes or to democratic regimes."[61] Thus the rather recent field of inquiry has expanded to examine a much older and richer field of transitional justice activity. Expansion of the inquiry has produced the crucial insight that "the particular histories, social norms and cultural practices of affected communities must shape how transitional justice is conceived and will inevitably determine its impact" in real circumstances in specific, diverse, and culturally contingent ways.[62] The Gang of Four trial provides a remarkable example of this fact.

The Gang of Four trial was presented, understood, and evaluated in China as transitional justice, even if commentators of the time did not use that precise term. Media accounts consistently depicted the trial as

---

[57] Neil J. Kritz, ed., *Transitional Justice: How Emerging Democracies Reckon with Former Regimes*, 3 vols. (Washington, DC: U.S. Institute of Peace Press, 1995).

[58] For a normative statement of this type, see Charles D. Smith, Introduction to Kritz, *Transitional Justice*, vol. 1: General Considerations, p. xv.

[59] David A. Crocker, "Reckoning with Past Wrongs: A Normative Framework," *Ethics and International Affairs* 13 (April 1999), pp. 43–64. For more recent critical perspectives, see Phil Clark and Nicola Palmer, "Challenging Transitional Justice," in Nicola Palmer, Phil Clark, and Danielle Granville, eds., *Critical Perspectives on Transitional Justice* (Cambridge: Intersentia, 2012), pp. 5–8; Paige Arthur, "How 'Transitions' Reshaped Human Rights: A Conceptual History of Transitional Justice," *Human Rights Quarterly* 31.2 (2009), pp. 321–67.

[60] See Kritz, *Transitional Justice*, vol. 2: Country Studies. For examples in a broader temporal range, see Jon Elster, *Closing the Books* (New York: Cambridge University Press, 2004); as well as chapters in Carla Hesse and Robert Post, eds., *Human Rights in Political Transitions: Gettysburg to Bosnia* (New York: Zone Books, 1999).

[61] Elster, *Closing the Books*, p. 1, emphasis added.

[62] Clark and Palmer, "Challenging Transitional Justice," p. 8.

a way to address the abuses of the violent past so as to build a more just and peaceful future. Moreover, Chinese authorities had direct experience of postconflict trials and claimed to inherit the legacy of the post–World War II war crimes tribunals at Nuremberg and Tokyo.[63] The language of transition filled the air, albeit inflected with the accents of Chinese socialism. In an editorial published in *People's Daily* just days after the verdict, a judge on the tribunal reflected on the spirit of the moment:

From a historical perspective, this trial signals the ending of a truly unfortunate period in the history of socialist China. When the Gang of Four was smashed in October 1976, the decade of catastrophe ended, as well, but the trial and sentencing of the accused may be seen as the formal ending to that period. In its wake a new period has appeared, a period marked by stability and unity, by democracy and the rule of law, a period in which the nation works together heart and soul for the realization of socialist modernization. We explore and strive so that China's one billion people might build a better society.[64]

These sentiments very clearly express the core ideals of transitional justice: transition to a new era, punishment of wrongdoers, reconciliation and social stability, democracy and the rule of law, and hopes for creating the good society.

It must be emphasized that the transitional justice framework is not incompatible with the show trial or political trial interpretation. Because transitional justice trials aim to make a strong social impact, they necessarily involve politically charged public performance. It would be intellectually lazy to simply use transitional justice as a positively connoted label for those show trials whose political ideologies we find palatable and whose legal outcomes we find agreeable.[65] Of course, some trials hew more or less closely to legally established ideals of substantive and procedural justice. However, the reader should bear in mind that the ideals of justice expressed in this case were not Western liberal ideals but Chinese socialist ideals. Moreover, the Gang of Four trial's failure

---

[63] The nationalist Republic of China (ROC) and the communist PRC states both prosecuted cases against alleged Japanese war criminals in the decade following World War II. Barak Kushner, *Men to Devils, Devils to Men: Japanese War Crimes and Chinese Justice* (Cambridge, MA: Harvard University Press, 2015); Chang Cai, *Trials of Sovereignty: Chinese Nationalist Trials of Japanese War Criminals, 1946–1949*, undergraduate honors thesis, University of California, Berkeley (2010); Adam Cathcart and Patricia Nash, "War Criminals and the Road to Sino-Japanese Normalization: Zhou Enlai and the Shenyang Trials, 1954–1956," *Twentieth Century China* 34.2 (April 2009), pp. 89–111; *Zhongguo qingnianbao*, November 11, 1980; Fei Xiaotong, "Yi ge shenpanyuan de ganshou" [Impressions of a judge], *RMRB*, January 30, 1981.

[64] Fei Xiaotong, "Yi ge shenpanyuan de ganshou."

[65] For a sympathetic but critical discussion of the liberal political ideology underpinning transitional justice, see Judith Shklar, *Legalism: Law, Morals, and Political Trials* (Cambridge, MA: Harvard University Press, 1986).

to perfectly attain these ideals was not in any way exceptional. Indeed, this trial was all the more typical for its failures and limitations – not only for the violations of due process so routinely found in transitional justice trials, but also for the substantial failures to fully redress past injustices or to prevent future ones. It is a tragic fact that the history of transitional justice is a study in contrast between the basest realities and the loftiest ideals – and of the grave difficulties of overcoming the former with the latter. The Gang of Four trial proposed new (or renewed) ideals of justice that were never fully attained in post-Mao China – nor even perfectly realized in the very trial that was meant to exemplify them. This is an important aspect of the trial's shortcomings, but this fact in no way invalidates the historically significant fact that such ideals were so publically championed.

The Gang of Four trial was a discrete historical event that became the focal point on which the issues of transition were momentarily concentrated. The trial was just one part of the Chinese party-state's efforts to confront the harmful legacies of the Cultural Revolution.[66] These efforts included a more comprehensive campaign to reassert legal normalcy under a reformed legal system; criminal trials of scores of Gang of Four accomplices; and lustration, meaning the exclusion from office of political radicals from the government, the military, and the communist party. Deng Xiaoping cautioned that the party should not get bogged down in retribution: "Our ideal is that every wrong should be righted, [. . . but] we cannot possibly achieve – and should not expect – a perfect settlement of every case. We should have the major aspect of each problem

[66] For previous scholarship on transitional justice after the Cultural Revolution, see Amnesty International, *China's Ultra-Left on Trial: Unfair Legal Procedure and Political Imprisonment in the Anti-Gang of Four Purge, 1976–1987* (unpublished manuscript, 1987?), pp. 25–30 and Appendix 2, pp. 58–60; Sue Trevaskes, "People's Justice and Injustice: Courts and the Redressing of Cultural Revolution Cases," *China Information* 16 (October 2002), pp. 1–26; Alexander Cook, "Settling Accounts: Law as History in the Trial of the Gang of Four," in Andrew Lewis and Michael Lobban, eds., *Law and History*, Current Legal Issues 6 (Oxford: Oxford University Press, 2003), pp. 413–32; Thomas Richter, *Strafrecht in Reaktion auf Systemunrecht: Vergleichende Einblicke in Transitionsprozesse 9: China* [China law in reaction to state crime: Insights into transition processes 9: China] (Berlin: Duncker and Humblot, 2006); Susanne Weigelin-Schweidrzik, "Coping with the Cultural Revolution: Competing Interpretations," in Agnes Schick-Chen and Astrid Lipinsky, eds., *Justice Restored? Between Rehabilitation and Reconciliation in China and Taiwan* (Frankfurt and New York: Peter Lang GmbH, Internationaler Verlag der Wissenschaften, 2012); Daniel Leese, "Revising Verdicts in Post-Mao China: The Case of Beijing's Fengtai District," in Jeremy Brown and Matthew Johnson, eds., *Maoism at the Grassroots: Everyday Life in China's Era of High Socialism* (Cambridge, MA: Harvard University Press, 2015), pp. 102–28. Daniel Leese of the Institute of Sinology at the University of Freiburg is presently conducting a major research project funded by the European Research Commission called "The Maoist Legacy: Party Dictatorship, Transitional Justice and the Politics of Truth, 1978–1987."

in mind and solve it in broad outline; to go into every detail is neither possible nor necessary."[67] The basic principles, he said, should be leniency for past mistakes and severity for recidivism, leniency toward the rank-and-file, and severity toward the ringleaders. Moreover, sanctions against wrongdoers were matched by efforts at restorative justice. In the several years following the Cultural Revolution, nearly three million Chinese enjoyed the reversal of unjust cases against them. Victims and their families received restitution of various kinds, including salary adjustments, retirement and death benefits, and improvements in housing allotments. In other words, a history of this kind could not be, and was not, confined to the courtroom. The actual (as opposed to merely judicial) resolution of those issues was a complex and protracted process that played out across society over a long period of time. The Gang of Four trial was only the most visible aspect of transitional justice in post-Mao China.

The main significance of the trial is that it represented law as the key to justice. This claim was important to the legitimacy of the post-Mao socialist state because Marxism-Leninism not only provided a blueprint for modernization; it also promised social justice. Crucially, the revolutionary promise of socialism was by no means limited to legal justice, embracing as it did wide-ranging ideals of retributive, distributive, and productive justice. Retributive justice, or punishment for harms caused to society, was to be exacted against those identified as "enemies of the people." These enemies included both the exploiting classes (rural landlords, the urban bourgeoisie, and the comprador lackeys of foreign imperialism) as well as the adversaries of the socialist state (counterrevolutionaries and political reactionaries, wartime collaborators with foreign foes, traitors and spies). Distributive justice, or the more equitable sharing of wealth in society was to be carried out through programs such as land reform, which expropriated agricultural land from large landowners and granted it to individual farmers or rural cooperatives ("land to the tillers"); nationalization of business and finance, including the seizure of banks, heavy industry, and resource-extraction enterprises ("state ownership"); the payment of wages according to incentivized work-point systems ("from each according to her ability, to each according to her deeds"); and in the large-scale requisition and redistribution of production surpluses. The transition to socialism and on to communism also

---

[67] Deng Xiaoping, "Jiefang sixiang, shishi qiushi, tuanjie yizhi xiang qian kan" [Emancipate the mind, seek truth from facts, and unite as one in looking to the future] (December 13, 1978), *Deng Xiaoping wenxuan* [Selected works of Deng Xiaoping] (Beijing: Renmin chubanshe, 1994), vol. 2, pp. 140–53.

promised a new kind of justice, the justice of production.[68] This ideal arose from Marx's belief in the inherent creativity of human beings. Marx argued that human beings could realize their true humanity, both as individuals and in society, only through their creative remaking of the world through labor – labor free from coercion, exploitation, alienation, and want.

Prior to the Gang of Four trial, law was considered to play a limited and particular role in creating and upholding justice in socialist society. Marxism, especially in Lenin's interpretation, viewed law mainly as an instrument of state power. This meant that law was not inherently just, but rather was the codification of the self-serving norms that the dominant class uses to justify its repression of the dominated class. Just as the Confucian patriarchy and the landed gentry had used the imperial codes to exploit the peasantry and the Western imperialists had used international law as a cudgel to subdue China, so too would the socialist state unapologetically wield law as a tool of the people's democratic dictatorship. Mao was frank and unapologetic about his instrumentalist view of law: "The state apparatus, including the army, the police, and the courts, is the instrument by which one class oppresses another. It is an instrument for the oppression of antagonistic classes. It is violence and not 'benevolence.'"[69] China's socialist state made piecemeal codes and ad hoc institutions as needed, but these were supplemented by informal social practices such as mediation, mutual surveillance, organizational discipline, struggle sessions, and reform through labor, as well as techniques for education, indoctrination, and persuasion. Moreover, the socialist state did not exercise monopoly over the legitimate use of violence. The party, the military, and the masses all used coercive practices to maintain social order, a situation that became most pronounced at the height of the Cultural Revolution.

In the post-Mao era, the party-state looked to strengthen and rationalize its hold over formal, legal institutions. An official party communiqué announced the regime's renewed commitment to socialist legality:

In order to safeguard people's democracy, it is imperative that we strengthen the socialist legal system so that democracy is systematized and codified, and that these democratic institutions and laws possess stability, continuity, and great authority. We must have laws to follow; the laws that we have must be obeyed; enforcement of the laws must be strict; and violations of the law must

---

[68] Robert C. Tucker, *The Marxian Revolutionary Idea* (New York: W. W. Norton and Company, 1970), pp. 48–53.

[69] Mao Zedong, "On the People's Democratic Dictatorship" (1949), www.marxists.org/reference/archive/mao/selected-works/volume-4/mswv4_65.htm.

be investigated. From now on, legislative work should be high on the agenda of the National People's Congress and its standing committees. Prosecutorial and judicial organs must maintain proper independence; they must be faithful to laws and institutions, to the interests of the people, and to the truth; and they must ensure that the people enjoy equality before their laws, and that no person enjoys special authority above the law.[70]

The agenda outlined here meets the essential criteria for the rule of law: law that is systematized in codes and institutions, transparent and accessible to the public, administered and adjudicated by trained professionals, and applied equally and universally to all citizens of the state.[71]

China's post-Mao legal reform belonged to a larger process of reform known in classical sociology as bureaucratic rationalization. This meant the institution of a well-ordered hierarchy of offices, staffed by skilled technocrats capable of efficiently and impersonally executing tasks according to clear rules and procedures. China's post-Mao reformers considered rationalization so important because it meant replacement of arbitrary, charismatic authority with regular, rule-based authority. Rationalization had positive implications for material development, as well. Max Weber in particular saw bureaucratic rationalization as conducive to economic modernization under capitalism, comparing it by analogy to industrialization: "The decisive reason for the advance of bureaucratic organization has always been its purely technical superiority over every other form. A fully developed bureaucratic apparatus stands to these other forms in much the same relation as a machine does to non-mechanical means of production."[72] Legal reform meant rationalization;

---

[70] "Zhongguo gongchandang di shiyi jie zhongyang weiyuanhui di san ci quanti huiyi gongbao" [Communiqué of the Third Plenum of the Eleventh Central Committee of the Chinese Communist Party] (December 22, 1978), http://cpc.people.com.cn/GB/64162/64168/64563/65371/4441902.html.

[71] Tom Bingham, *The Rule of Law*, reprint edn. (London: Penguin UK, 2011), pp. 8 and 37. The World Justice Project, a present-day advocacy group promoting liberal rule of law, lists these four basic principles: "(1) The government and its officials and agents as well as individuals and private entities are accountable under the law. (2) The laws are clear, publicized, stable, and just; are applied evenly; and protect fundamental rights, including the security of persons and property. (3) The process by which the laws are enacted, administered, and enforced is accessible, fair, and efficient. (4) Justice is delivered timely by competent, ethical, and independent representatives and neutrals who are of sufficient number, have adequate resources, and reflect the makeup of the communities they serve." See http://worldjusticeproject.org/what-rule-law. On the distinction between thick and thin definitions of rule of law in relation to China, see Peerenboom, *China's Long March toward Rule of Law*.

[72] Max Weber, "Economy and Society" [1922], in W. G. Runciman, ed.; E. Matthews, transl., *Selections in Translation* (New York: Cambridge University Press, 1978), p. 350. According to Weber, rational institutions better enabled the accurate calculation of cost-benefit calculation (and therefore the likelihood of profitable investment) in economic transactions.

rationalization meant modernization; and modernization meant a better, more prosperous future for socialist China.

Socialist Humanity and the Critique of Instrumentalism

As an official verdict on the past, the conclusions of the trial could not be directly challenged, but its premises did not go uncontested. Operating within the constraints of China's socialist political system, writers of popular literature articulated an alternative diagnosis of the Cultural Revolution. These publically engaged intellectuals were generally sympathetic to the project of reform, but they were not always in unanimous agreement with the dominant views expressed by the official leadership. In the view of these writers, the malady facing Chinese socialism was not merely irrationality, but inhumanity. In this way, popular literature pointed indirectly to the inadequacy of instrumental rationality alone, detached from humanistic values, to guarantee a more just society.[73]

Chinese humanist critiques of instrumental rationality borrowed ideas and terminology from classical sociology, critical theory, and even Maoism. Classical sociologist Max Weber argued that modern bureaucratic rationalization also extended to the realm of subjective thought, to a mind-set that treats all objects, including other people, "as 'conditions' or 'means' to achieve ... rationally pursued and calculated purposes."[74] Weber differentiated instrumental rationality from three other ideal types of reasoning: affective reasoning, which derives from instincts and emotions rather than dispassionate assessment; traditional reasoning, which is habituated by custom rather than purposive calculation; and value-based reasoning, which takes no account of costs in pursuit of some intrinsically valuable goal. Karl Marx, like Weber, had conflicted feelings about rationalization. Both recognized the role played by rational institutions and the rational mind-set in the capacity of modern capitalism to generate unprecedented wealth, but both also warned against the prospect of a wholly instrumental modernity that threatened to debase human life

---

[73] On symptomatic reading, see Louis Althusser and Étienne Balibar, *Reading Capital*, Ben Brewster, transl. (New York: Pantheon Books, 1979); and Fredric Jameson, *The Political Unconscious: Narrative as a Socially Symbolic Act* (Ithaca, NY: Cornell University Press, 1981). On the role of narrative in the ongoing maintenance of ideology as identity, see Etienne Balibar, "The Nation Form: History and Ideology," in Etienne Balibar and Immanuel Wallerstein, eds., *Race, Nation, Class: Ambiguous Identities* (New York: Verso, 1991); and Homi Bhabha, "Introduction: Narrating the Nation," in *Narrating the Nation* (New York: Routledge, 1990), pp. 1–7.

[74] Weber, "Economy and Society," pp. 28–9.

to an abject and alienated existence.[75] Later, critical theorists such as Herbert Marcuse, Max Horkheimer, and Jürgen Habermas continued to examine this fundamental dilemma of modernity, and decried the rise of the technological society (whether capitalist or socialist) in which the only absolute value was instrumentalism.[76] Mao's "cultural" revolution sought to transform the mind-set of modernization. Chinese intellectuals in the post-Mao era took a different path but reached similar conclusions. Reformers representing the party-state sought to scaffold Chinese socialism with rational institutions, and through the Gang of Four trial even presented the renovated edifice of state socialism as a monument to justice. While most intellectuals welcomed the prospect of restored stability, the traumatic experiences of the recent past also contributed to deep misgivings among some about the desirability of accommodating core beliefs of justice to the faceless dictates of instrumental rationalism.

Such alternative views could only be shared obliquely, using highly circumscribed terms of debate. Though Deng Xiaoping had called on the Chinese people to "emancipate their minds" from the formulaic dogma of the Cultural Revolution, he also demanded that public discourse conform to the Four Cardinal Principles: following the socialist path, supporting the dictatorship of the proletariat, following the leadership of the CCP, and upholding the CCP's official ideology. As a result, any critique of the official project had to be systematically distorted to sound like the dominant code. Therefore, as with official sources, alternative views need to be carefully deciphered to unpack their meanings. Culture critic Geremie Barmé finds that *The Velvet Prison* by Hungarian writer Miklós Haraszti provides an apt description of the intellectual scene in post-Mao China, a situation in which the most important conversations took place "between the lines" of the dominant state discourse:

Even the most loyal subject must wear bifocals to read between the lines: this is in fact the only way to decipher the real structure of our culture.... Debates between the lines are an acceptable launching ground for trial balloons, a laboratory of consensus, a chamber for the expression of manageable new interests, an

---

[75] Peter Baeher, "The 'Iron Cage' and the 'Shell as Hard as Steel': Parsons, Weber, and the Stahlhartes Gehäuse Metaphor in the Protestant Ethic and the Spirit of Capitalism," *History and Theory* 40.2 (May 2001), pp. 153–69.

[76] Martin Heidegger, "The Question Concerning Technology" [1954], in *Basic Writings*, Harper Perennial Modern Classics, revised and expanded edn. (New York: HaperCollins, 2008), pp. 307–41; Herbert Marcuse, *One Dimensional Man* [1964)] (Boston, MA: Beacon Press, 1991); Jürgen Habermas, "Technology and Science as 'Ideology'" [1968], in *Toward a Rational Society: Student Protest, Science, and Politics* (Boston, MA: Beacon Press, 1971), pp. 81–122; Max Horkheimer, *The Critique of Instrumental Reason* [1974] (London: Verso, 2013).

archive of weather reports. The opinions expressed there are not alien to the state but perhaps simply premature.[77]

To understand the real structure of Chinese culture in this moment of dynamic change – that is, to see the play of possibilities and potential – the reader will need to wear bifocals. Or better yet (to adjust Haraszti's metaphor slightly), the reader will need to take a stereoscopic view, examining a single phenomenon through two separate lenses. In practice this means that this book's analysis of justice during the post-Mao transition will draw the Gang of Four trial into focus, chapter by chapter, alongside another set of images not typically associated with the trial – those found in literary accounts produced outside the courtroom. Viewing these images together will add depth to our perception of the post-Mao transition.[78]

The propaganda cartoon in Figure 3 provides an example of just such a double image. The drawing depicts the post-Mao Chinese socialist fantasy of modernization through law.[79] The title of the cartoon is a line from a famous poem composed by the late Chairman Mao. The top half of the drawing illustrates the ideal modern society in which science, technology, and engineering are harnessed to master the physical and social environment. The bottom half is a variation on an iconic traditional image, a scene from the classic adventure *Journey to the West* (*Xi you ji*) in which the heroic Monkey (Sun Wukong) sweeps away the evil White-Boned Demon. In the legend, Monkey accompanies a Buddhist monk on a pilgrimage to retrieve sacred texts, such that Monkey can be seen as an agent of "law" (Chinese *fa*, Sanskrit *dharma*) bringing enlightenment to China. In this modern cartoon version, Monkey banishes those villainous enemies of modernization, the Gang of Four.

Monkey is perhaps the most popular character in traditional Chinese fiction, and he was certainly a favorite of Mao. The daring and irascible Monkey embodied the spirit of revolution and was elevated to the status

---

[77] Miklós Haraszti quoted in Geremie Barmé, *In the Red: On Contemporary Chinese Culture* (New York: Columbia University Press, 1999), pp. 5–6.

[78] Martha C. Nussbaum takes a similar approach, using tragic poems to better understand Greek philosophy in *The Fragility of Goodness: Luck and Ethics in Greek Tragedy and Philosophy* (New York: Cambridge University Press, 1986), pp. 1–23.

[79] Jiang Fan, "Yuyu dengqing wanli ai" [Ten thousand miles of dust cleared from the Palace of Heaven], in Zeng Jinshun, ed., *Lishi de shenpan: jiepi "Sirenbang" manhua xuan* [History's trial: Selected cartoons criticizing the Gang of Four] (Shanghai: Shanghai renmin meishu chubanshe, 1979), no page number. A slightly different version appeared in the newspaper article by Hua Junwu, "Manhua: Bai hua zhi yi hua" [Cartoons: One flower among one hundred], *RMRB*, June 4, 1978.

Figure 3. Monkey sweeps away the Gang of Four under the caption, "Build a powerful, modernized, socialist nation."
Source: Jiang Fan, "Ten thousand miles of dust cleared from the Palace of Heaven" (1978).

of a deity in socialist arts and literature.[80] However, Monkey's rebellious energy was not indomitable; the cartoon pictures the magical diadem placed around the Monkey's head by the Goddess of Mercy in order to control his impulsive and potentially self-destructive ways. If Monkey is the totem for China's socialist project, then the diadem represents the channeling of revolutionary spirit by the guiding hand of the CCP and the salvational constraint imposed by a higher law. In this scenario, the powerful but disciplined Monkey has swept away the ghosts and demons and ushered in a "powerful, modernized, socialist nation."

This is the intended meaning of the cartoon, but another, very different reading is possible. For, in this utopian dream of modernization, there

[80] Rudolf G. Wagner, "Monkey King Subdues the White-Bone Demon: A Study in PRC Mythology," in *The Contemporary Chinese Historical Drama: Four Studies* (Berkeley: University of California Press, 1990), pp. 139–235.

is something missing. The ideal society in the top half of the drawing is apparently devoid of people, while in the bottom half, to a non-human subject exorcizes the only visible humans: the Gang of Four (literally, the "four-person gang"). The turn to a rational, objective, depersonalized, and law-based system of rule implied a troubling admission that individual human beings were inherently unreliable agents of historical progress. Both scientism and humanism sought "to fill the intellectual vacuum left by the Cultural Revolution," but scientism became the dominant mode of official discourse.[81]

The humanistic mode, though overshadowed and swept aside by official scientism, demands attention. Literature in particular has been the preferred medium of politics throughout Chinese history, and no serious study of Chinese politics in any era, much less the modern era, can afford to ignore it. For post-Mao Chinese intellectuals, literature was still the obvious venue in which to mount a serious critique of rational instrumentalism. Moreover, compared to the arid and detached writings found in specialized academic journals and polemical party rags, popular literature had the capacity to touch on politics through the vivid depiction of human experience, lived and imagined. In post-Mao China, all aspects of public communication were monitored and regulated to some degree, but the literary press was granted unusual license to explore topics, perspectives, and voices simply not found in other media. Through popular literature, an author could hope to reach the broadest possible audience and, therefore, have the greatest social impact. In the pages of widely circulated literary works, writers were able to probe with relative freedom the moral complexities, ethical dilemmas, personal contradictions, and emotional ambiguities that attended the crisis of Chinese socialism. In so doing, literary works set the stage for reception of and reaction to the trial, and offered alternative responses to the vitally important question posed by the Cultural Revolution and answered by the trial – the question of justice.

Just as no trial could hope to address the entirety of the Cultural Revolution, neither could any repertoire of literary works. This study does not aim for a comprehensive survey of the post-Mao literary scene. In order to intensify rather than dilute the analysis, the chapters concentrate on a small number of authors and texts. To leverage the advantages of literature in this political context, each chapter on the trial will be paired with a chapter organized around a single literary text: Liu Binyan's long-form reportage *Between Man and Monster* (1979), Dai Houying's novel

---

[81] Shiping Hua, *Scientism and Humanism: Two Cultures in Post-Mao China (1978–1989)* (Albany: State University of New York Press, 1995), p. 42.

Humanity, Ah Humanity! (1980), and Yang Jiang's memoir *Six Records of a Cadre School* (1981), respectively. All three texts approached the theme of socialist humanity, but each from a different angle. Liu Binyan, writing from the position of an activist public intellectual, employed literary forms and theoretical conceits of Mao-era socialism to raise the issue of human nature. Dai Houying, a popular writer inspired by Western literary modernism and critical Marxism, explored the irreducible complexity of the subjective human condition. Yang Jiang, a respected senior scholar from the world of high culture, took inspiration from more traditional literary forms and ethical values to examine the perennial problem of human resources, or how to make use of human talent for the good of society. These intellectuals professed socialist leanings and were generally sympathetic to the party-state's reform project, but their writings drew strength from a robust variety of intellectual traditions.

These works were selected from among those produced at the same time that the Gang of Four trial was conceived and presented, ranging from the initial planning for the trial in 1979 to shortly after its final verdict in 1981. Like the trial, these works deal with events of the Cultural Revolution period, narrated retrospectively from the beginnings of the post-Mao transition. The condition of this retrospection – its rawness and immediacy – matters a great deal for us, because it intensified the literary inquiry into justice at a formative historical moment. In a rapidly changing China, the passage of even a few years radically changed the sociopolitical and cultural scene. In certain ways, then, it might have been more gratifying from a literary perspective to spotlight the more daring and sophisticated works of the period that followed in the mid-1980s. What might be gained in artistic richness, though, would be lost in the insight afforded by historicity. The legal and literary narratives chosen here, produced contemporaneously inside and outside the courtroom, were vitally connected to each other, and to the pulse of the historical moment.

The trial of the Gang of Four was a media spectacle, consumed by newspaper publics and radio and television audiences throughout China, and indeed around the world. It was not a private or circumscribed reflection upon the "decade of chaos," but one undertaken under the blazing heat of studio lights. Likewise, the three literary works presented here faced intense public scrutiny. All three were widely popular in their own time and recognized for their artistic merit by contemporaries. In addition, these works are all of sufficient length and complexity to sustain close readings of the same depth and intensity as the analysis to be performed vis-à-vis the trial.

These three literary texts will provide three vantage points from which to cross-examine the trial proceedings. The trial was meant to exemplify a historical transition to a new era embodying ideals of rational legality. The well-worn "show trial" critique shows that this official narrative was marred by the manifestly irrational aspects of the trial; this critique, grounded as it is in familiar liberal conceptions of the rule of law, will come to the reader quite naturally. However, contemporaneous Chinese literature reveals another, wide-ranging critique – one less intuitive to the Western reader but arguably more trenchant and vexing to the socialist state providing the leading diagnosis of the Cultural Revolution. According to the official interpretation, subjective forces wreaked havoc on the development of objective conditions. Undue emphasis on revolutionary consciousness led to the pathological destruction of institutional norms, lent credence to unfounded judgments, and invested power in unaccountable individuals. Consequently, it was possible for counterrevolutionaries to carry out illegal activities in the name of revolution. Meanwhile, the objective forces of production were appropriated, neglected, or destroyed. The gains of the socialist revolution were lost, and China failed to continue on the path of modernization. This line of reasoning implied that the failures of the Cultural Revolution arose from an approach to history and revolution that was sadly "all too human." The corrective response, according to the reformist party-state, must be a return to a more rational and scientific form of socialism.

In contrast, the literary turn to humanism posited that the Cultural Revolution had not been all too human, but all too *inhuman*. Endless struggles had reduced the people to inhuman monsters, demons, freaks, and slaves. The humanist critique did not necessarily preclude desires for legal accountability, social order, or economic development, but it did reject the continued evacuation of human values from politics. The cold sterility of instrumental rationality alone could not be the basis for the good society. Societal rationalization could provide the necessary means to modernization, but it should not be an end in itself. Following this line of critique, our analysis will contrast tidy, rational ideals of commensuration, containment, and comprehension found in works about the trial with more troubling themes of monstrosity, emotional trauma, and vanity found in literature. Moving back and forth between the worlds of law and literature, the analysis will bring into view both sides of a dilemma facing Chinese socialism in the wake of the Cultural Revolution.

1   Indictment

The Gang of Four trial was initiated by an indictment – a text whose very creation and presentation to the public was meant to exemplify the state's claim for law as a rational way of pursuing justice. As a way to end the chaotic cycles of recrimination and revenge that had characterized the Cultural Revolution, this more rational and orderly approach to justice took on the force of a moral imperative. In contrast to the unaccountable political violence of the past, the indictment lodged its accusations of wrongdoing according to clearly defined legal standards, bringing its claims before a legitimate authority that could make an objective finding of facts, assess harm, and mete out punishment appropriately. This document set the stage for the trial. Its form symbolized a new approach to justice; its contents established the parameters of the courtroom inquiry, helping to shape interpretations of the Cultural Revolution even today; and its reading in the courtroom constituted a physical and symbolic space where new institutional and social ideals could be performed. The very act of indictment manifested the ideal of pursuing legal accountability, an act that Chinese commentators described using the accounting metaphor of "settling accounts" (*suan zhang*): calculating a ledger and closing the books.

Settling Accounts: Legal Accountability

On November 20, 1980, four years after the end of the Cultural Revolution, state prosecutors presented to the Special Court their indictment against ten defendants of the Jiang Qing and Lin Biao groups. "Today's indictment," read one report in the *Guangming Daily*, "represents an indictment by the people of the entire nation, and today's public trial represents a public trial by the people of the entire nation."[1] The

[1] Wu Kailiu, "Renmin de shenpan, lishi de shenpan" [The people's trial, history's trial], *Guangming ribao* [hereafter cited as *GMRB*], November 21, 1980.

35

reporter went on to describe the "profound significance" of the event in an article titled, "The People's Trial, History's Trial":

This moment has profound significance, as a summary to one aspect of the "Cultural Revolution" and as an important sign that our nation is entering an era of "ruling the nation by law." It is bound to spur the development of our nation's stability and unity and to fire the determination of the people of the nation in their struggle for the Four Modernizations.[2]

As this account from the official media makes clear, it was not solely the trial that was heavily freighted, but also the act of indictment. This pointedly *legal* mode of inaugurating an inquiry into the injustices of the Cultural Revolution was carefully chosen and was intended as a break with precedents of the recent past.

The act of indictment was presented in contrast to the more disruptive modes of accusation practiced during the Cultural Revolution. Even after many courts were reestablished in the early to mid-1970s, the official prosecuting authority – the people's procuratorate – remained defunct. Accusations were handled by ad hoc, extralegal, or informal authorities. Moreover, valuing class struggle over social order, the Cultural Revolution radicals had adapted rhetorical strategies from the era of socialist revolution and applied them to the era of state socialism. These rhetorical strategies included "criticism and struggle" (*pidou*) and "speaking bitterness" (*suku*).

Criticism and struggle began as a method of intraparty discipline, developed for party members to help each other raise their ideological consciousness and improve their style of work.[3] In group-study meetings called *struggle sessions*, comrades were singled out one by one and subjected to constructive criticism by their peers. The target of the session was then expected to restate the criticism as a self-criticism (*ziwo piping*), indicating that the critique had been accepted and internalized. Thereupon the targeted cadre was welcomed back into the fold as a reformed and improved member of the party. During the course of the socialist revolution, however, the scope of criticism and struggle changed. Struggle sessions were employed with increasing frequency in political campaigns directed at class enemies *outside* the party. As a result, more people were "struggled against" and fewer of them earned redemption. During the Cultural Revolution, these sessions became a ubiquitous aspect of everyday life, fueling widespread social conflict.

[2] Ibid.
[3] The schematic description of criticism and struggle in this paragraph draws on Lowell Dittmer, "The Structural Evolution of Criticism and Self-Criticism," *China Quarterly* 53 (March 1973), pp. 708–29.

Because criticism often took aim at the target's subjective consciousness, there was no objective way to prove one's sincere conformity to the ideological standard. Moreover, the standards of political correctness could and did change rapidly during this period, as once authoritative theories and interpretations were overturned. The standards of the moment were often applied retrospectively, so that one could be criticized for having once held an idea that was considered correct at the time but no longer accepted. Consequently, as Lowell Dittmer has observed, "[T]he indeterminacy of [Mao Zedong Thought] as a calculus of innocence or guilt meant that criticism had no intrinsic limits."[4] Criticism and struggle became a dangerously irrational and unaccountable form of accusation.

In this atmosphere of pervasive struggle, another form of revolutionary rhetoric called "speaking bitterness" put accusatory power in the hands of the common people. This formulaic discursive practice was developed during violent land reform campaigns, when it was intended to promote class identity and heighten the revolutionary consciousness of the masses. Party cadres would encourage and guide the speaker (often an illiterate peasant or menial worker) to publically narrate his or her personal experience of the old society, recounting injustices suffered at the hands of the exploitive classes.[5] The rhetoric of revolutionary class struggle was reprised after the revolution, in the early 1960s, when people were asked to "recall the bitterness [of the old society] and reflect on the sweetness [of the new society]" (yiku sitian) – so they might better appreciate life under the socialist state. During the Cultural Revolution the radicals shifted the temporal frame, once again emphasizing the lingering bitterness of class struggle in the present day. They insisted that bitterness belonged to the masses of the people, and it was cause for continuing the revolution under socialism, with the slogan, "To rebel is justified" (zaofan you li).

In this way, the revived rhetoric of the socialist revolution fed the volatile and dangerous conditions of the Cultural Revolution. Radicals incited the people to "take clear account" (qing suan) of their enemies and to "settle old accounts" (suan jiu zhang), sometimes through violent retribution.[6] The Gang of Four became synonymous with such campaigns (Figure 4). Endemic political violence, including personal vendettas carried out in the name of politics, became a social force

---

[4] Ibid., p. 724.
[5] Ann Anagnost, *National Past-Times: Narrative, Representation, and Power in Modern China* (Durham, NC, and London: Duke University Press, 1997), pp. 1–27.
[6] Lowell Dittmer and Chen Ruoxi, *Ethics and Rhetoric of the Cultural Revolution.* Studies in Chinese Terminology (Berkeley: Center for Chinese Studies: 19, Institute of East Asian Studies, University of California, 1981), p. 19.

Figure 4. Allegorical depictions of the Gang of Four, including Zhang Chunqiao at bottom left using an abacus to settle accounts. Zhang's last name, meaning "account," appears on the back of his robe.
Source: Hand-painted poster displayed outside the Canton Trade Fair in early November 1976, photograph by Judith Lubman.

"unleashed from all countervailing moral restraints."[7] By the end of this rancorous decade, many people were weary of "settling accounts," so much that the *New York Times* reported that in the late 1970s some Chinese refused to use this common phrase even for settling restaurant tabs.[8] Likewise, writer Liu Zhixia told his fellow cultural producers at the Fourth National Conference on Literature and the Arts in 1979, "The more one calculates old scores (*suan jiu zhang*), the more one becomes depressed and divided; the more one talks about unity, the more one feels warm and unified."[9]

The Gang of Four trial redeemed the concept of "settling accounts" by making it a function of law. The law represented a rational way to settle accounts, replacing violent personal retribution with an orderly way to

[7] Richard Madsen, "The Politics of Revenge in Rural China during the Cultural Revolution," in Jonathan N. Lipman and Stevan Harrell, eds., *Violence in China: Essays in Culture and Counterculture* (Albany: State University of New York Press, 1990), p. 183.
[8] "China Reports Plot by Four to Seize Power 'Shattered' by Hua; Mao's Widow Named in Group," *New York Times*, October 22, 1976.
[9] Quoted in Dittmer and Chen, *Ethics and Rhetoric of the Cultural Revolution*, p. 16.

assess wrongdoing and provide commensurate remedy. Building on the double meaning of the Chinese character for law (*fa*), which also means a way or method, it can be said that the new legal system sanctioned new ways of thinking law, speaking law, and performing law (*xiangfa*, *shuofa*, and *zuofa*). The slogan "handling matters according to law" (*yifa banshi*) pointed to a new *banfa*, or way to solve problems. In the case of the Gang of Four trial, the act of legal indictment was a way to present the accusations of the state within the normative framework of the law.

As a "way of speaking" the act of bringing a legal case (*susong*) is comparable to that of speaking bitterness (*suku*). Both are discursive practices that seek redress for injustice (*suyuan*) – they are both ways to *su* (recount a personal experience) in order to sue for justice. To be effective as a speech act, such an appeal must be stated in the proper way, at the proper time, and in the proper place. It also must be addressed to a body that has the authority to recognize the claimed injustice and provide redress. The rhetorical strategy used in an appeal for justice is therefore rooted in assumptions about audience and context.[10] In this regard, a legal plaint is very different from a complaint of bitterness. Indictment differs from speaking bitterness in the authority to which the speech act is directed and in the normative order to which it refers. Speaking bitterness is a call for justice made in reference to *moral* values that may transcend the existing legal order of the state. That is the basis for the revolutionary potential of speaking bitterness. The fact that it has become necessary to seek redress for injustice on extralegal moral grounds implies that the existing state has lost the capacity to administer the morally good community. For this reason, the appeal is being made to an authority (the party) that can bring about a moral, just, but as-yet-unrealized legal order; that is, an appeal to a revolutionary force. In contrast, a legal complaint is, by definition, made in reference to the existing legal order. The legal order is established and enforced by the existing state, in affirmation of the state's exclusive claim to the legitimate use of punishment and even violence to deliver justice.

Indictment takes the power of accusation out of the hands of individuals and puts it under the roof of institutions. To begin with, indictment is brought in the collective name of the people to an impersonal legal apparatus staffed by disinterested professionals and bureaucrats. The document is filed according to set procedures, using standardized language. It makes claims in reference to statutory laws rather than fungible

---

[10] On speech acts, see J. L. Austin, *How to Do Things with Words* (London: Oxford University Press, 1962); and John L. Searle, *Speech Acts: An Essay in the Philosophy of Language* (New York: Cambridge University Press, 1989).

ideological interpretations, pointing to crimes that are objective actions that can be factually established rather than subjective attitudes that cannot. Indictment is a method of accusation that is, in a word, *rational*. This, at least, was the promise of settling accounts by law.

"Smashing" the Gang of Four

The indictment made its accusations in reference to a legal system whose main components had either ceased to function normally or did not yet exist at the time that the Gang of Four was toppled from power. The four years leading up to the trial were a liminal period in which the legal system, the laws, and even the expectation of legal accountability all had to be made to order. Preparation for the trial required far-reaching legal reforms, including reconstruction of dismantled legal institutions such as courts; rehabilitation of purged legal professionals such as lawyers and judges; and even creation of the first comprehensive legal codes in the history of the People's Republic of China (PRC). It also demanded new ways of thinking about law and justice under Chinese socialism. These reforms did not happen overnight. The institutional context of the post-Mao legal reforms is well known.[11] The changing situation of the defendants during these four years offers a different angle from which to view the reforms, helping us to understand the expectations of the public that would become the audience for the trial.

Jiang Qing and her political allies were toppled from power on October 6, 1976, less than a month after the death of Mao on September 9. The "smashing" (*fensui*) of the Gang of Four, as the event was called at the time, was no regular legal arrest; it had all the hallmarks of a Cultural Revolution–style purge. The Gang of Four was ousted by political rivals, detained and investigated by secret police, and vilified in a series of mass campaigns. Most of the popular anti-Gang imagery from this time was crude and violent, typified by Figure 5, a hand-painted poster portraying the Gang of Four as inhuman creatures roasting on a spit. At the same time, there is evidence of an enduring legal consciousness, as seen in Figure 6, a poster imagining Jiang Qing and the rest of the Gang of Four facing trial. At that moment, however, China's post-Mao regime lacked the institutions for pursuing legal accountability. The decision to try the Gang of Four in a court of law – to indict them legally rather than purge

---

[11] Two surveys of post-Mao legal reform are Stanley Lubman, *Bird in a Cage: Legal Reform in China after Mao* (Stanford, CA: Stanford University Press, 1999); and Zhang Youyu and Wang Shuwen, eds., *Zhongguo faxue sishi nian* [Forty years of PRC legal studies, 1949–1989] (Shanghai: Shanghai renmin chubanshe, 1989).

Figure 5. The Gang of Four as creatures on a roasting spit.
Source: Hand-painted poster displayed outside the Canton Trade Fair in early November 1976, photograph by Judith Lubman.

them violently – was several years away and by no means a foregone conclusion.

The purge of the Gang of Four was orchestrated by Mao's handpicked successor Hua Guofeng, who planned the move in concert with Defense Minister Ye Jianying, veteran party leader Li Xiannian, and head of the Central Security Bureau (CSB; the leadership's special security detail) Wang Dongxing.[12] On the evening of October 6, less than a month after the death of Mao, Hua Guofeng convened a special meeting of the Politburo, ostensibly to arrange for publication of the latest volume of Mao's *Selected Works*. The meeting was a trap.[13] Agents of the CSB captured Zhang Chunqiao, Wang Hongwen, and Yao Wenyuan immediately

---

[12] Keith Forster, "China's Coup of 1976," *Modern China* 18.3 (July 1992), pp. 263–303; Yin Yungong, "Lun chenggong fensui 'sirenbang' de guanjian qunti" [On the key group that successfully overthrew the Gang of Four], paper presented at the International Forum on the Contemporary History of China (Beijing, September 2004).

[13] Wu Jicheng and Wang Fan, *Hongse jingwei: Zhongyang jingweiju yuan fujuzhang Wu Jicheng huiyilü* [Red sentry: Memoir of Wu Jicheng, former deputy chief of the Central Security Bureau] (Beijing: Dangdai zhongguo chubanshe, 2003), pp. 356–97.

Figure 6. The Gang of Four imagined on trial before a People's Court. Though Jiang Qing is most prominent in the picture, the accused are listed by party rank.
Source: Hand-painted poster displayed outside the Canton Trade Fair in early November 1976, photograph by Judith Lubman.

upon arrival. Jiang Qing was nabbed even before leaving her residence in the leadership compound. It has been reported that Hua Guofeng read out a list of charges against the four at the time of their capture; if so, historians have no access to such a warrant.[14] In any case, the arrest was carried out like a coup d'état. By the following morning, the Beijing Garrison Command had moved to secure cultural and media institutions in the capital, including the official Xinhua News Agency, radio and television broadcast stations, and radical strongholds at Qinghua University and Peking University in Beijing.[15] Meanwhile, the People's Liberation Army (PLA) carried out coordinated actions in other major cities such as Tianjin, Shenyang, and especially Shanghai, where an unknown number

[14] Wu Jianhua, "Jiang 'Sirenbang' yajie Qin Cheng shilu" [Account of escorting the Gang of Four to Qincheng prison], *Shiji* [Century] (March 2002), pp. 5–6.
[15] Jin Chunming, Huang Yuchong, and Chang Huimin, eds., *"Wenge" shiqi guaishi guaiyu* [Strange events and terminology of the Cultural Revolution period] (Beijing: Qiushi chubanshe, 1989), p. 207; Chi Hsin [pseudo.], *The Case of the Gang of Four* (Hong Kong: Cosmos Books, 1977), p. 42.

of Gang of Four backers were suppressed.[16] Rumors of the purge circulated domestically and among foreign diplomats. Then, signs and posters sprang up attacking Jiang Qing and Zhang Chunqiao by name, building into "spontaneous" public demonstrations in support of Hua Guofeng and to celebrate the radicals' demise.[17] These activities culminated in a massive rally in Tiananmen Square on October 24, reportedly attended by more than one million people.

The case against the Gang of Four began to take shape. On October 18, a Central Directive accused the Gang of Four of committing a series of "extremely serious anti-party, power-usurping conspiratorial activities and crimes."[18] The scope of this document is much narrower, both substantively and chronologically, than the legal indictment that would emerge four years later. Nearly all the specific charges in the directive relate to misrepresenting or misdirecting Chairman Mao's intentions in order to attack political rivals, and the examples are mostly limited to 1974–6. At this early stage of the post-Mao transition, the regime did not renounce the Cultural Revolution. In fact, Hua Guofeng attacked the Gang of Four as enemies of the Cultural Revolution, which he continued to defend. He consistently held the line against reversal or reform, saying, "We must continue the campaign to criticize Deng [Xiaoping] and beat back the right-deviationist reversal of verdicts. We must take a correct attitude toward the Great Cultural Revolution, toward the masses, and toward ourselves."[19] The directive did establish a principle that would be followed later by the Deng Xiaoping regime in bringing the Gang of Four to trial, namely to focus on the crimes of the few rather than the mistakes of the many: "We must not get tangled up in history's old accounts."[20]

In the official political judgment of the Hua Guofeng regime, Mao and the Cultural Revolution were on the side of the good, in opposition to the Gang of Four. The late chairman was said to have coined the "Gang of Four" moniker, demonstrating the continued weight of his personal authority. An article on the front page of the October 25, 1976 edition of *People's Daily* detailed Mao's suspicions of the four disgraced

[16] Chou Yunzhou, "Xiang 'Sirenbang' yudang duoquan: Su Zhenhua jieguan Shanghai," *Bainian chao* (May 2002), pp. 4–11.

[17] Li Kuaicai, ed., *"Wenge" midang* [Secret files of the Cultural Revolution], 6 vols., Zhonghua ernü jiemi xilie, Zhonghua ernü zazhishe haiwai ban (Hong Kong: Xianggang Zhonghua wenhua chubanshe, 2003), vol. 6, pp. 2023–5.

[18] "Wang Hongwen, Zhang Chunqiao, Jiang Qing, Yao Wenyuan fangeming jituan zuizheng (cailiao 1)" [Evidence against the Wang Hongwen, Zhang Chunqiao, Jiang Qing, Yao Wenyuan counterrevolutionary group (materials part 1)] (October 18, 1976). Zhongfa [Central Directive] [1976], No. 16.

[19] Ibid.

[20] Ibid.

leaders, now referred to publicly for the first time as the Gang of Four. According to the report, Mao first called out Jiang Qing and her associates on July 17, 1974, saying, "She is planning a Shanghai gang! Take heed: don't form a four-person clique."[21] With this colorful reference to Jiang Qing's roots in the old gangster town of Shanghai, Mao warned that factional cliques (*xiao zongpai*) threatened party unity. He repeated this sentiment in his second admonition on December 24, 1974: "Don't form a faction (*zongpai*). Those who form factions will take a fall."[22] Mao first spoke the phrase "gang of four" at a Politburo meeting on May 3, 1975, where he warned, "Don't form a gang of four – don't do it! Why go about things the same old way? Why not unite with the two hundred-plus Central Committee members? Forming a minority is bad; all throughout history it's been bad." In each of these posthumously reported examples, the "gang" is not characterized as an incorrigible counterrevolutionary criminal syndicate but as a wayward party faction that might yet be brought back into the fold of the party. Accordingly, the case against the Gang of Four began as a matter of party discipline, not law. Official sources consistently listed the Gang of Four in order of *party* rank as the "Wang, Zhang, Jiang, Yao antiparty group" (see Figure 7). It would not be until four years later, only after their formal indictment in September 1980, that the Gang of Four members' names would be listed as they still are today, according to the severity of their alleged crimes: the "Jiang, Zhang, Wang, Yao counterrevolutionary group."[23]

Long before the Gang of Four faced indictment, its members were convicted in the party's manufactured court of public opinion. Although the Gang of Four was spared the humiliation of being paraded in dunce caps and browbeat at mass rallies, as so many of their Cultural Revolution victims had suffered, nevertheless the Gang of Four members were investigated by an extralegal, Cultural Revolution–style Special Case Group reporting to the party's Politburo.[24] The Special Case Group issued materials documenting the Gang of Four's crimes in three stages: in

---

[21] Jin, Huang, and Chang, "*Wenge*" shiqi guaishi guaiyu, pp. 157–8; See also Dittmer and Chen, *Ethics and Rhetoric of the Cultural Revolution*, p. 53.

[22] "Relie huanhu Hua Guofeng tongzhi wei women dang de lingxiu, fennu shengtao 'si ren bang' fandang jituan taotian zuaxing" [Comrade Hua Guofeng enthusiastically cheered by our party leaders, "Gang of Four" angrily denounced for heinous antiparty crimes], *RMRB*, October 26, 1976.

[23] Jin, Huang, and Chang, "*Wenge*" shiqi guaishi guaiyu, p. 158; Wu Xiuquan, *Wangshi cangsang* [Vicissitudes of bygone days] (Shanghai: Shanghai wenyi chubanshe, 1986), p. 319.

[24] On the history of Special Case Groups, see Michael Schoenhals, "The Central Case Examination Group, 1966–1979," *China Quarterly* 145 (March 1996), pp. 87–111.

坚决打倒王张江姚反党集团！

Figure 7. "Resolutely overthrow the Wang, Zhang, Jiang, Yao anti-party group!" (October 24, 1976) (*Jianjue dadao Wang Zhang Jiang Yao fandang jituan!*).
Source: IISH Collection, International Institute of Social History (Amsterdam).

December 1976, March 1977, and September 1977.[25] Some of these early charges would make their way into the legal indictment, but these "criticism" dossiers were not legal documents enumerating evidence of listed crimes. Jiang Qing was accused of eating and drinking too lavishly while Chairman Mao was on his deathbed, for example, and Wang Hongwen of inappropriately commissioning a portrait of himself. The second set of materials in particular contains invented, exaggerated, or

---

[25] "Wang Hongwen, Zhang Chunqiao, Jiang Qing, Yao Wenyuan fangeming jituan zuizheng (cailiao zhi yi, er, san)" [Evidence against the Wang Hongwen, Zhang Chunqiao, Jiang Qing, Yao Wenyuan counterrevolutionary group (materials parts 1, 2, 3)] (October 18, 1976; March 3, 1977; September 23, 1977). Zhongfa [Central Directive] [1976] No. 16, [1977] No. 10, [1977] No. 37.

irrelevant attacks on the unsavory class backgrounds of its targets: Zhang Chunqiao is revealed to have been a "special agent" for the Nationalists (Kuomingtang [Guomindang], or KMT); Jiang Qing is said to be a traitor raised by a landlord family; Yao Wenyuan is exposed as an "alien class element"; and Wang Hongwen is declared a representative of the "new capitalist class" under socialism.[26] These sorts of dubious claims about saboteurs, spies, and shape-shifting demons hiding among the party leadership were commonplace during the Cultural Revolution – in official proclamations, public criticism sessions, and works of popular fiction. Chinese audiences understood that before an evildoer faced punishment, he or she had first to be revealed as an inhuman enemy of the people. Having been so revealed, these arch counterrevolutionaries were vilified in the press and expelled from the party. All of this is to say that the initial purge of the Gang of Four did not introduce to the public any fundamentally new conception of justice.

Without institutions for a legal trial, or even necessarily the intention to hold one, the Gang of Four remained in a state of legal limbo. For the first six months after their capture, the Gang of Four was detained by the CSB at a secret facility near the capital. Living conditions there were humane: Jiang Qing's suite was appointed with a bed, writing desk, sofa, carpeting, climate control, and a private washroom with bathtub and Western-style toilet. She was even permitted to wear her own clothes and enjoyed full meals delivered daily by car from the central leadership compound at Zhongnanhai.[27] Nevertheless, the four were subjected to relentless criticism and struggle by their former staff, including secretaries, chauffeurs, and physicians.[28] In April 1977, after half a year under house arrest, the Gang of Four was transferred into custody of the Ministry of Public Security (MPS). They were secretly transported by armored car to Qin Cheng, the infamous maximum-security prison in the suburbs of Beijing where the remnants of the Lin Biao group were housed and where many high-profile victims of the Cultural Revolution had been locked away.[29] Conditions at Qin Cheng were more like a regular prison: each defendant was housed in a spartan cell with a tatami-style

---

[26] "Wang Hongwen, Zhang Chunqiao, Jiang Qing, Yao Wenyuan fangeming jituan zuizheng (cailiao zhi er)" [Evidence against the Wang Hongwen, Zhang Chunqiao, Jiang Qing, Yao Wenyuan counterrevolutionary group (materials part 2)] (March 3, 1977). Zhongfa [Central Directive] [1977], No. 10.

[27] Wu, "Jiang 'Sirenbang,'" pp. 4–5.

[28] Wu and Wang, Hongse jingwei.

[29] Wu, "Jiang 'Sirenbang,'" pp. 6–7. The five Lin Biao group defendants also ended up at Qin Cheng, though little is known about the conditions of their detention over the previous several years.

bed mat, toilet, and washbasin.[30] At this stage, the investigation of the Gang of Four was still considered a matter of internal party discipline, outside the purview of the law. The party formally expelled the Gang of Four in July 1977. At the same meeting, the party officially ratified Hua Guofeng as its new chairman and restored to office several previously disgraced targets of the Cultural Revolution, including Deng Xiaoping.

The authoritarian political culture of the Mao era continued under Hua Guofeng, though the sometimes strident tone of the Cultural Revolution was softened. Hua Guofeng's legitimacy derived largely from the late Chairman Mao's personal authority. Mao Zedong had handpicked Hua Guofeng to be his successor, but the latter lacked deep institutional and factional ties. Seeking to inherit Mao's charismatic power, Hua Guofeng fostered a rather mild-mannered cult of personality around himself. He also fortified himself with prestigious titles, becoming the only paramount leader of China to hold simultaneously the three top offices in the party, state, and military. By no means did Hua Guofeng repudiate the legacy of the Cultural Revolution, either. On the contrary, he accused the Gang of Four of harming the Cultural Revolution and declared that additional cultural revolutions would be necessary in the future. From beginning to end, the faithful successor professed steadfast loyalty to the late chairman with a political orientation of orthodox or conservative Maoism: "Whatever policy decisions Chairman Mao made, we must resolutely uphold; whatever instructions Chairman Mao gave, we must unswervingly follow."[31] The Gang of Four was "smashed," but the ideology and institutions of the Cultural Revolution remained largely intact.

Preparation of the Legal Context

The post-Mao transition took a new turn in late 1978, two years after the death of Mao and the ouster of the Gang of Four. As recently rehabilitated victims of the Cultural Revolution returned to office, they rallied around China's erstwhile "No. 2 Capitalist Roader" Deng Xiaoping, who soon outmaneuvered Hua Guofeng to become the new de facto

---

[30] Jiang Hua and Zuo Mingxing, "Yige ceng kanya Jiang Qing de nübing huiyi Jiang Qing yuzhong rizi" [A female guard recalls Jiang Qing's time in custody], *Wode beijilu* (mymemo. cn99.com), excerpt from *Nanfang zhoumo* [Southern Weekly] (May 10, 1995), http:// xingguolian.com/mymemo/article/211.htm; Li Haiwen and Wang Yanling, eds., *Shiji duihua: yi Xin Zhongguo fazhi zunjiren Peng Zhen* [A century of conversations: Remembering Peng Zhen, the key figure in New China's legal system] (Beijing: Qunzhong chubanshe, 2002), pp. 90–1.

[31] "*Xue hao wenjian zhuazhu gang*" [Study the documents well and grasp the key link], joint editorial of *RMRB*, *Hongqi* [Red Flag] [hereafter abbreviated as *HQ*], and *Jiefang ribao* [Liberation Daily] [hereafter abbreviated as *JFRB*], February 7, 1977.

leader of China. These politically moderate returnees pushed an agenda of ideological deradicalization and institutional reform. The reformers' ideological and institutional programs would set the stage for the legal trial of the Gang of Four. As has usually been the case among China's communists, ideological justification was articulated prior to and prepared the ground for institutional change. The ideological sea change valued economic development over political and cultural revolution, the objective material foundations of socialism rather than its subjective spiritual manifestations, and the stability of law and order over the raw vitality of mass movements. Legal reform was an important component of this change, both in ideology and in its implementation in practice.

In terms of ideology, the reformists promoted socialist rule of law and denigrated Cultural Revolution radicalism as the rule of man. The political culture of the Cultural Revolution was criticized as authoritarianism, an outmoded vestige of the Oriental despotism from China's feudal past.[32] The reformers argued that the lack of rational norms and institutions (especially the lack of a functioning legal system) had enabled Mao to rule the socialist state as a sort of Red Emperor.[33] Relying on his personal charismatic authority, Mao circumvented institutions of collective leadership in order to advance his radical agenda of continuing the revolution against the party and state.[34]

Mao's charismatic authority was developed and mobilized through a cult of personality.[35] Prior to the outset of the Cultural Revolution, Lin Biao forged a cult around Mao in which his utterances were treated as sacred scripts.[36] As the Cultural Revolution took shape, Mao was worshiped as a quasireligious figure and his very image idolized.[37] Even after the fall of Lin Biao and the dismantling of the cult of personality, the Gang of Four used specious historical analogies to continue to support

---

[32] On reception of the theory of Oriental despotism, Alexander Day, *The Peasant in Post-Socialist China: History, Politics, and Capitalism* (New York: Cambridge University Press, 2013), p. 34.

[33] For a critical assessment of this trope, see Geremie R. Barmé, "For Truly Great Men, Look to This Age Alone: Was Mao a New Emperor?," in Timothy Cheek, ed. *A Critical Introduction to Mao* (New York: Cambridge University Press, 2010), pp. 243–72.

[34] Tang Tsou introduced this idea into the English-language historiography on China with his essay, "Back from the Brink of Revolutionary-'Feudal' Totalitarianism," in *The Cultural Revolution and Post-Mao Reforms: A Historical Perspective* (Chicago: University of Chicago Press, 1986), pp. 144–88.

[35] Daniel Leese, *Mao Cult: Rhetoric and Ritual in China's Cultural Revolution* (New York: Cambridge University Press, 2013).

[36] Ban Wang, "Conclusion: In the Beginning Is the Word," in Alexander Cook, ed., *Mao's Little Red Book: A Global History* (New York: Cambridge University Press, 2014), pp. 266–77.

[37] Michael Dutton, *Streetlife China* (New York: Cambridge University Press, 1999), pp. 238–71.

Mao's authoritarian power. For example, the political campaign to "criticize Lin Biao and criticize Confucius" praised classical Legalism to liken Chairman Mao to China's autocratic first emperor, the Legalist-advised Qin Shihuang.[38] The post-Mao reformers rejected the cult of personality and its authoritarian implications, a position that was equally useful for attacking the Cultural Revolution as for discrediting Hua Guofeng. In the eyes of the post-Mao reformers, Chairman Hua was an unimaginative and hidebound functionary incapable of making the changes that China needed to truly modernize. They criticized Hua's avuncular cult of personality and derided his uncritical devotion to the "two whatevers" of whatever policies and instructions were devised by Mao. According to the reformers, the scientific kernel of Mao Zedong Thought lay in the dialectical application of Marxism-Leninism to Chinese conditions. The correctness of Chinese socialism did not reside in the person of the party chairman, nor should his words and theories be imbued with unimpeachable truth. For the people to project power on a quasireligious authoritarian leader was nothing more than "modern superstition" and the basis for political alienation.[39] Overcoming the false consciousness behind political alienation required a new Enlightenment to objective, scientific thought and the practical, material basis of truth.[40]

First, a new epistemological slogan, "practice is the sole criterion of truth," weakened the hold of Mao's personal authority as well as Hua's claim to Maoist orthodoxy. The reformers preemptively fended off the possibility of revisionism by cleverly cribbing the slogan from Mao's own seminal essay "On Practice" (1937). This rather bland-sounding slogan summarized a basic position of dialectical materialism: that knowledge emerges from our interaction with the material world through labor, social practice, and scientific experimentation. In terms of divining truth, neither religious dogma nor abstract theory could compare with practice. The supposedly epochal importance of the slogan was dramatized most colorfully in a "philosophical fantasy" called "Religion, Reason, and Practice: Visiting Three 'Courts' of Truth in Three Different Ages."[41] This fantastical tale, printed in the reformist-leaning newspaper *Guangming*

---

[38] Tien-wei Wu, *Lin Biao and the Gang of Four: Contra-Confucianism in Historical and Intellectual Perspective* (Carbondale: Southern Illinois University Press, 1983).

[39] For examples from popular media, see *Pochu Lin Biao, "Sirenbang" de xiandai mixin* [Do away with Lin Biao and the Gang of Four's modern superstition] (Beijing: Renmin chubanshe, 1978).

[40] See Huaiyin Li, "Challenging the Revolutionary Orthodoxy: 'New Enlightenment' Historiography in the 1980s," in *Reinventing Modern China: Imagination and Authenticity in Chinese Historical Writing* (Honolulu: University of Hawai'i Press, 2013), pp. 170–203.

[41] Yan Jiaqi, "Zongjiao, lixing, shijian: fang sange shidai guanyu zhenli wenti de sange 'fating' (Zhexue huanxiang xiaoshuo)" [Religion, rationality, practice: Paying a visit to three

Daily, developed a legal metaphor for discovering truth. The narrator is a reporter who travels in a time machine to witness three "courts": Galileo's trial before the feudal papal court (representing the persecution of science by ideologues), a conversation in a salon with famous bourgeois philosophers of the Enlightenment court of reason (representing the fallacy of abstract theory detached from social reality), and finally the court of practice in a futuristic Beijing in 1994 (which very much resembles the ultramodern city in the Monkey cartoon found in the introduction to this book). In this future world, the reporter locates an expert on the determination of truth – significantly, a trial judge – who explains that China's rapid modernization since the smashing of the Gang of Four is due to the Chinese people reasserting the authority of practice in the age of socialism: "In the end the people used the 'court of practice' to pronounce a death sentence on the 'Gang of Four.'"[42] When this article was published, concrete plans for the Gang of Four trial had not yet been made and the event was still more than two years away. Yet already this fantasy expressed hopes for the rule of law to usher a just historical transition, with falsehood put on trial and truth vindicated.

Academic essays soon elaborated a second point: the argument that the emergence of the rule of law was a positive marker of progressive historical transition. The newly established Chinese Academy of Social Science Institute of Law published a collection of these essays in September 1980, the same month that the Special Court was established.[43] Although the collected essays cover a range of specific topics and express a variety of views, they support a general historical argument. The essays focus almost exclusively on eras identified in Chinese Marxian historiography as periods of historical transition: the transition from slave society to feudalism in the ancient Warring States period, the emergence of the domestic "sprouts of capitalism" in the Ming-Qing transition, the growth of semicolonial capitalism in the first half of the twentieth-century, and the subsequent defeat of semifeudal, semicolonial forces by the socialist revolution. The essays distinguish between "rule of law" and "rule of man" concepts from different historical periods, but in each period the rule of law is situated as progressive relative to the rule of man. According to this

---

'courts' of truth in three different ages (A philosophical fantasy)], in *Pochu Lin Biao, "Sirenbang" de xiandai mixin* [Do away with the modern superstition of Lin Biao and the Gang of Four] (Beijing: Renmin chubanshe, 1978), pp. 42–66; revised, originally published in *GMRB*, September 14, 1978. The "court of reason" alludes to the introduction to Engels's *Anti-Dühring* (1877).

42 Ibid., p. 61.

43 *Fazhi yu renzhi wenti taolun ji* [Collected theses on the rule of law and the rule of man], China Forum on the Rule of Law, reprint edn. [1981] (Beijing: Shehui kexue wenxian chubanshe, 2003).

model, at each stage of historical development the rule of man must be overcome by the rule of law. Thus the emergence of socialist rule of law in the reform era signaled a progressive transition from what the reformers called the "undeveloped" or "primary" stage of socialism to a more mature form of socialism. This theoretical argument added a deeper historical dimension to the claim of "transitional" justice.

Institutional reforms implemented the imperative for transitional justice. The reformists successfully asserted their agenda at the Third Plenum of the Eleventh Central Committee of the Chinese Communist Party (CCP) held in December 1978. The reformists were so successful that this plenum is regarded as the beginning of Deng Xiaoping's reign as paramount leader, even though Hua Guofeng retained his lofty official titles. The meeting wrapped up the campaign against the Gang of Four, which had been Hua Guofeng's major political accomplishment, and resolved to turn the party's attention to economic construction as the material basis for socialist modernization. The plenum adopted as its top priority the Four Modernizations, meaning material development of four main sectors: industry, agriculture, science and technology, and national defense. The plenum also approved reversals of several specific past judgments. As mentioned previously, the party had already reversed negative judgments against the most prominent political victims of the Cultural Revolution, both living and dead, including Deng Xiaoping. Now the party moved beyond redeeming individual cases and averred that the Gang of Four's campaign against "the Rightist trend to reverse correct verdicts" was an unjust "inversion of history that must once again be set right."[44] The plenum resolved to exonerate a much larger number of specific political victims, setting in motion a general process that over the next few years would reverse "unjust, false, and incorrect verdicts" against some 2.9 million people.[45] Although the party put off overall assessment of the Cultural Revolution until an unspecified "appropriate time," the plenum made preparations for systemic, institutional changes. First, the party immediately revived its dormant organs for internal discipline inspection. Second, although the Hua Guofeng regime had already ratified a revised and expanded state constitution less than a year prior, the party again made plans to revise the state constitution. Third, the party urged judicial and procuratorial organs to "maintain proper

---

[44] "Zhongguo gongchandang di shiyi jie zhongyang weiyuanhui di san ci quanti huiyi gongbao" [Communiqué of the Third Plenum of the Eleventh Central Committee of the Chinese Communist Party] (December 22, 1978), http://cpc.people.com.cn/GB/64162/64168/64563/65371/4441902.html (accessed July 9, 2012).

[45] He Zai, ed., *Yuan jia cuo an shi zheyang pingfande* [This is how unjust, false, and wrong cases were reversed] (Beijing: Zhonggong zhongyang dangxiao chubanshe, 1999), p. 3.

independence" and used provisions in the existing constitution to authorize reform of the legal system.

The recently rehabilitated Peng Zhen, one of the first political targets of the Cultural Revolution, was appointed to oversee comprehensive reform of the socialist legal system. Legal reform entailed bureaucratization and regularization of police, prosecutorial, and judicial organs; popular education and professional training in legal thought; and creation of the first complete criminal code and procedural code in the history of the socialist state.[46] These were important changes from the practices of the Cultural Revolution period, when police, prosecution, and court institutions were disrupted, and when cases were initiated, investigated, and adjudicated on an ad hoc basis by an irregular assortment of state, party, military, leadership, and mass organizations.

The purpose of legal reform was to make criminal law a more rational and effective instrument of state power. Law claimed for the rational bureaucratic state a monopoly over the legitimate exercise of violence and the regulation of social order. The resulting stability was seen as a prerequisite to foster development, but socialist modernization did not imply a move toward liberal democracy and rule of law. Another important trial from this period ensured that Chinese citizens had no illusions on this point. In October 1979, a socialist court imposed a harsh sentence on Wei Jingsheng, a grassroots political activist who had posting an essay calling democracy the much-needed Fifth Modernization. The harsh sentencing of Wei Jingsheng signaled clearly that the law was a weapon that would be used without compunction against those who violated the Four Cardinal Principles of upholding the socialist path, the people's democratic dictatorship, the leadership of the CCP, and the ideology of Marxism-Leninism and Mao Zedong Thought. That weapon was about to bear on the Gang of Four.

Preparation of the Indictment Text

Plans for the Gang of Four trial were in the works from the very beginning of legal reform and gave urgency to that aspect of modernization.[47] In November 1979, scholars from the newly established Institute of Law of the Chinese Academy of Social Science came on board to assess

---

[46] Zhang and Wang, *Zhongguo faxue sishi nian*; Randall P. Peerenboom, *China's Long March toward Rule of Law* (New York: Cambridge University Press, 2002); Lubman, *Bird in a Cage*.

[47] Tumen and Xiao Sike, *Tebie shenpan: Lin Biao, Jiang Qing fangeming jituan shoushen shilu* [Special trial: True account of the trial of the Lin Biao and Jiang Qing counterrevolutionary groups] (Beijing: Zhongyang wenxian chubanshe, 2002), pp. 132–5.

the investigation of the Lin Biao and Jiang Qing groups by the Central Commission for Discipline Inspection (CDI). They made several suggestions. First, to bring the Gang of Four case forward, it was necessary to establish a clear rationale distinguishing legal crimes from political errors. Second, the investigation should focus as narrowly as possible on concrete evidence of specific criminal activities. Third, it would be desirable to work out ahead of time any legal issues likely to arise at trial.[48] The new *Criminal Law* promulgated on January 1, 1980 contained provisions to address crimes characteristic of the Cultural Revolution period, such as mob activity, incitement of violence, unlawful detention, torture, and frame-ups.[49] Likewise, the new *Criminal Procedure Law* set limits on evidence collection, stressed the reliability of material evidence over personal accusations, and carefully qualified the use of confessions. The new laws narrowed the scope of political activity that could be criminalized and rationalized the standards for establishing legal facts. With the ideology and institutions for legal reform now in place, it was possible to produce an indictment against the Gang of Four.

In February 1980, Peng Zhen convened an ad hoc Committee on the Trial of the "Two Cases" – short hand for the cases of the Lin Biao and Jiang Qing counterrevolutionary groups. This powerful committee reported directly to the Secretariat of the CCP and consisted of Peng Zhen (secretary of the Central Commission for Politics and Law); Jiang Hua (chief justice of the Supreme People's Court, later named president of the Special Court); Huang Huoqing (chief of the Supreme People's Procuratorate, later named Chief of the Special Procuratorate); Zhao Cangbi (minister of public security); Wang Heshou (deputy secretary of the Central Commission for Discipline Inspection); Peng Chong (a politburo member who had directed the purge of Gang of Four allies from Shanghai in 1976); and Wu Xiuquan (a central committee member with experience in diplomacy and military affairs, later named a vice president of the Special Court and chief judge of its military tribunal).[50] In March 1980, the secretariat of the CCP, acting on the advice of the ad

---

[48] Wu Jianfan, "Wode yanjiu zhi lu (3)" [The course of my research (Part 3)], Chinese Academy of Social Sciences Institute of Law web site (2003), iolaw.org.cn/shownews. asp?id=2705. Two of the legal scholars, Wu Jianfan and Liu Hainian, reiterated these concerns in an interview with the author on September 30, 2003. See also Wu Jianfan and Ouyang Tao, "Lun shenpan Lin Biao, Jiang Qing fangeming jituan de jige falü wenti" [Discussion of a few legal questions in the trial of Lin Biao and Jiang Qing counterrevolution groups], *Faxue yanjiu* [Research in jurisprudence] (June 1980), pp. 1–5.

[49] Harold M. Tanner, *Strike Hard! Anti-Crime Campaigns and Chinese Criminal Justice, 1979–1985* (Ithaca, NY: Cornell University East Asia Program, 1999), pp. 14–19.

[50] Li and Wang, *Shiji duihua*, pp. 89–90. PLA Chief of Staff Yang Dezhi may have joined the committee at a later date.

hoc committee, formally recommended a trial to be conducted according to the newly enacted legal codes.[51] According to this initial recommendation, the trial would be held in secret with the results to be publicized at its conclusion.[52] The secretariat specifically cautioned that the Gang of Four trial should not be a flimsy show trial:

The case – the indictment and evidence and so forth – must be irrefutable and stand firmly on its own feet, so it can be passed on to posterity and never be overturned. If done in this way, the trial will have the positive effect of strengthening government unity and help us to implement the Four Modernizations with one heart and one mind. It will also have a good influence on our international standing.[53]

In April 1980, as a matter of procedural regularity, Peng Zhen insisted the case files be transferred from the party's CDI to state organs, namely the MPS and the Supreme People's Procuratorate.[54] The party investigation had collected evidence from more than one million documents and 178,000 persons, and had whittled down a list of five hundred suspects to just eleven names.[55] Ten of these eleven names would appear in the Special Procuratorate's indictment.[56] The basic outline of the case had already taken shape; the main points established by the party's pretrial investigation would be reviewed through normal police and prosecution channels. Now the case had formally entered the legal system.

State organs concluded their review of the case files in September 1980 and prepared a document of "Written Suggestions on the Prosecution of the Lin Biao and Jiang Qing Counterrevolutionary Groups." Huang Huoqing, chief of the Supreme People's Procuratorate, presented the report before the Standing Committee of the National People's Congress and recommended the indictment of ten main conspirators: five surviving members of the alleged Lin Biao conspiracy,

---

[51] Wu and Ouyang, "Lun shenpan," pp. 4–5.

[52] Xiao Sike, *Chaoji shenpan: Tumen jiangjun canyu shenli Lin Biao fangeming jituan qin liji* [Super trial: A personal account of the trial of Ling Biao counterrevolutionary groups], 2 vols. (Jinan: Jinan chubanshe, 1992), vol. 1, pp. 197–9; Tumen and Xiao, *Tebie shenpan*, pp. 135–6.

[53] Quoted in Tumen and Xiao, *Tebie shenpan*, p. 135.

[54] Li and Wang, *Shiji duihua*, p. 90.

[55] The party's investigation is detailed in Wang Wenfeng, *Dou Mo: Mian dui mian shencha Jiang Qing fangeming jituan qin liji* [Battling demons: Personal memoirs of investigating the Jiang Qing counterrevolutionary group face-to-face] (Beijing: Zhongguo shehui kexue chubanshe, 2000). Wang was then head of the CDI's "Two Case" Investigatory Small Group No. 2 Office, which handled the Gang of Four case. For the figures cited, see ibid., pp. 96–7 and 88.

[56] The eleventh name was Wang Weiguo, a member of the Lin Biao group who was tried and convicted in 1982 by the Court Martial of the PLA, and sentenced to a term of fourteen years (with credit for eleven years of time served); see *LSSP*, vol. 2, pp. 332–46.

Figure 8. Defendants before the military tribunal of the Special Court;
from left to right: Huang Huoqing, Wu Faxian, Li Zuopeng, Qiu
Huizuo, and Jiang Tengjiao.
Source: China Pictorial, April 1981, p. 31.

Mao's former political secretary Chen Boda, and of course the Gang of
Four (Figures 8 and 9).[57] Just as important as the names listed for prosecution were the names that were not. First, the procuratorate suggested
that key accomplices be tried later in separate trials. Second, it recommended against posthumous prosecution of six deceased main conspirators. The deceased conspirators posed a particular difficulty because
they had played important roles in the alleged crimes. Kang Sheng, who
died of cancer in December 1975 while still a vice-chairman of the CCP,
had headed China's security and intelligence apparatus. He had framed
up cases against the party leadership, sometimes setting in motion large-
scale purges. Kang Sheng was arguably at least as responsible as the
Gang of Four for the political violence of the Cultural Revolution. He
also worked closely with alleged conspirator and fellow member of the
Cultural Revolution Group, Minister of Public Security Xie Fuzhi, who
died in 1972. The other four deceased conspirators were clearly the

[57] *Law Annual Report of China 1982/3* (Hong Kong: Kingsway International, 1982), p. 179;
entry for September 27, 1980 in *TBFTJS*, p. 70. Deputy Secretary of the CCP Central
Commission for Discipline Inspection Wang Heshou and Deputy Chief of the Ministry
of Public Security Ling Yun also made presentations at the meeting, which was headed
by NPC Standing Committee Deputy Committee Head Peng Zhen (*RMRB*, September
28, 1980). The full text of Chief Huang Huoqing's report can be found in *LSSP*, vol. 1,
pp. 14–16.

Figure 9. Defendants before the civilian tribunal of the Special Court; from left to right: Zhang Chunqiao, Chen Boda, Wang Hongwen, Yao Wenyuan, Jiang Qing.
Source: China Pictorial, April 1981, p. 30.

key players in the Lin Biao case. They were Lin Biao, his wife Ye Qun, their son Lin Liguo, and Lin Liguo's aide Zhou Yuchi. The five military defendants slated to face trial were considered active members of the Lin Biao conspiracy, but they were not its ringleaders.

On September 29, 1980 the National People's Congress (NPC) responded to the procuratorate's suggestions by establishing a Special Procuratorate to prosecute the case and a Special Court to hear the case.[58] The Special Court will be introduced later in this chapter. As for the Special Procuratorate, it was very large: consisting of a chief procurator, two deputy chiefs, and twenty-one leading procurators representing different regions. They were assisted by more than four hundred public security officials from every corner of the nation.[59] Many of the

[58] "Di wu jie quanguo renmin daibiao hui changwu weiyuanhui guanyu chengli zuigao renmin jianchayuan tebie jianchating he zuigao renmin fayuan tebie fating jiancha, shenpan Lin Biao, Jiang Qing fangeming jituan an zhufan de jueding" (September 29, 1980) [Resolution of the Standing Committee of the Fifth National People's Congress Regarding Establishment of the Special Procuratorate of the Supreme People's Procuratorate and the Special Court of the Supreme People's Court to Investigate and Try the Main Culprits of the Lin Biao and Jiang Qing Counterrevolutionary Groups], in *TBFTJS*, p. 1.

[59] Wu Xiuquan, *Wangshi cangsang* [Vicissitudes of bygone days] (Shanghai: Shanghai wenyi chubanshe, 1986), p. 312; Li and Wang, *Shiji duihua*, p. 90.

prosecutors were victims of the Cultural Revolution, including Chief Procurator Huang Huoqing, who had been purged in 1967 for "counterrevolutionary revisionism." This was the group that would bring what the newspapers had called "the indictment by the people of the entire nation."[60]

The NPC resolution stated that the trial would be conducted openly, with exceptions for testimony touching upon state secrets. This entailed some risk. A public trial might give a platform to the defeated radicals, and there was always a danger of tarnishing the reputations of Mao and other leaders who were not on trial. However, the moral imperative for justice meant that the greater risk was to do nothing. As several politicians argued, the new regime could not "hesitate to strike at rats for fear of breaking the dishes."[61]

The indictment that initiated the trial was a technical legal document, but it was also a work of history. The counts constituted an empirically grounded story about the Cultural Revolution, and this version of the story would be the foundation for the testimony and verdict to follow. As such, the indictment was worded meticulously: more than thirty draft revisions were completed before the document reached its final form.[62] The Special Procuratorate completed its indictment on November 2, submitted it to the court on November 5, and presented it to the defendants on November 10.[63] The full text was later publicized in *People's Daily* in four installments on November 16–19, and finally read aloud in open court on the first day of the trial, November 20.

Indictment as Historical Account

The indictment carries the formal title, "Indictment of the Special Procuratorate under the Supreme People's Procuratorate of the People's Republic of China" (Special Procuratorate Document No. 1) (November 2, 1980).[64] The text consists of forty-eight counts enumerated in four

---

[60] Wu Kailiu, "Renmin de shenpan."

[61] Tumen and Xiao, *Tebie shenpan*, p. 156; Jin, Huang, and Chang, "*Wenge*" shiqi guaishi guaiyu, p. 199. This aphorism was attributed to both Deng Xiaoping and Ye Jianying.

[62] Wu, *Wangshi cangsang*, p. 318. On the direct involvement of Peng Zhen, see Li and Wang, *Shiji duihua*, pp. 92–3.

[63] "Zuigao renmin jianchayuan tebie jianchating jueding dui Lin Biao, Jiang Qing fangeming jituan an shi ming zhufan tiqi gongsu zhi zuigao renmin fayuan han" [Letter to the Supreme People's Court from the Special Procuratorate of the Supreme People's Procuratorate Resolving to Seek Public Prosecution of the Ten Main Culprits of the Lin Biao and Jiang Qing Counterrevolutionary Cases] (Supreme People's Procuratorate Criminal Case Letter #59 (80), dated November 5, 1980), *TBFTJS*, p. 436.

[64] "Zhonghua renmin gongheguo zuigao renmin jianchayuan tebie jianchating qisushu" (November 2, 1980) [Indictment by the Special Procuratorate of the Supreme People's

main parts, along with an introduction and a conclusion. The first and second parts describe a broad plot to seize power, looking first at the persecution of top party and state leaders and then at the persecution of people at lower levels. The third and fourth parts focus more narrowly on two specific attempts, one by the Lin Biao group and another by supporters of the Gang of Four, to engage in actual armed rebellion.

From start to finish, the indictment presents a dramatic history of conspiracy and intrigue. The temporal scope of this story is inseparable from our current definition of the Cultural Revolution as an historical era running from 1966 to 1976. This official periodization of the "ten-year cultural revolution," coincides exactly with the charges listed in the indictment, implying that the defining feature of the historical era was the abnormal political situation that emboldened the defendants' counterrevolutionary plot to seize power. This periodization should not be applied too literally, however.[65] Significantly, the indictment charges are not distributed evenly over the decade. Nearly all the charges in the first two parts of the indictment relate events from the "two-year Cultural Revolution," from Mao's mobilization of the masses in 1966 through the violent internecine conflicts of 1968. The additional charges extend the temporal scope in fits and starts toward the end of the ten-year Cultural Revolution. The third part of the indictment, dealing with the Lin Biao conspiracy, relates a separate period of conflict between the radicals over the spoils of victory in 1970–1. The fourth part of the indictment jumps to 1976, when the Gang of Four allegedly made preparations to consolidate power after the eventual death of Chairman Mao. Though the indictment places all of these episodes together in a single narrative, it is not at all obvious that they fit together in a single coherent era. Recent scholarship has begun to find continuity across the purported ruptures at the beginning and end of the Cultural Revolution, as well as ruptures within its apparent continuity. Alternative periodization schemes can be devised, defined by different features of the era. For example, if the Cultural Revolution is defined by the continuous-revolution-within-state-socialism theory of

Procuratorate of the PRC, Special Procuratorate Document No. 1], *TBFTJS*, pp. 3–39; henceforth abbreviated in the notes as Indictment. Compare English translation in *A Great Trial in Chinese History* (Beijing: New World Press; distributed by New York: Pergamon Press, 1981), pp. 149–98.

[65] Lowell Dittmer, "Rethinking China's Cultural Revolution amid Reform," in Woei Lien Chong, ed., *China's Great Proletarian Cultural Revolution: Master Narratives and Post-Mao Counternarratives* (New York: Rowman and Littlefield, 2000), p. 12; Susanne Weigelin-Schweidrzik, "Coping with the Cultural Revolution: Competing Interpretations," in Agnes Schick-Chen and Astrid Lipinsky, eds., *Justice Restored? Between Rehabilitation and Reconciliation in China and Taiwan* (Frankfurt and New York: Peter Lang GmbH, Internationaler Verlag der Wissenschaften, 2012), pp. 25–72.

"class struggle as the key link," then the beginning could be pushed back to 1962 and the end extended forward to 1978. Another sensible beginning date could be 1964, the year Lin Biao gave Jiang Qing a platform to propose a radical new cultural agenda.[66] It also seems that some of the post-Mao reforms actually started in southern China in the mid-1970s.[67] The success of the 1966–6 periodization, in both academic writing and, of course, in official historiography, demonstrates the extent to which the crimes outlined in the indictment have been cast as historical milestones. By helping to create and solidify the historiographical convention of the ten-year Cultural Revolution, the Gang of Four trial has had a lasting – and politically charged – impact on the historical field.

Taken together, the charges amount to a case of counterrevolutionary treason. The introduction to the indictment presents the case as a conspiracy to usurp state power and overthrow the dictatorship of the proletariat. The sixteen "principal culprits" of the Lin Biao and Jiang Qing counterrevolutionary groups – including both the ten living defendants and the six deceased alleged conspirators – are accused of colluding to seize power.

[T]aking advantage of their positions and the power at their disposal, [they] framed and persecuted communist party and state leaders in a premeditated way in their attempts to usurp party leadership and state power and overthrow the political power of the dictatorship of the proletariat. They did this by resorting to all kinds of intrigues and using every possible means, legal or illegal, overt or covert, by pen or by gun.[68]

This introductory section concludes decisively, "The Lin Biao and Jiang Qing counterrevolutionary groups brought untold disasters to our country and nation." Due to the conspiratorial nature of the case, the indictment organizes its forty-eight counts around particular crimes committed by one or more defendants, rather than defendant by defendant. The charges are further grouped into four main parts.

Part I of the indictment, comprised of twenty-three counts, details "the frame-up and persecution of party and state leaders in a plot to

[66] Kam-yee Law, ed., *The Chinese Cultural Revolution Reconsidered: Beyond Purge and Holocaust* (New York: Palgrave Macmillan, 2003); the essays in Joseph W. Esherick, Paul G. Pickowicz, and Andrew G. Walder, eds., *The Chinese Cultural Revolution as History* (Stanford, CA: Stanford University Press, 2006).

[67] Odd Arne Westad, "The Great Transformation: China in the Long 1970s," in Niall Ferguson, Charles S. Maier, Erez Manela, and Daniel J. Sargent, eds., *The Shock of the Global: The 1970s in Perspective* (Cambridge, MA: Belknap Press of Harvard University Press, 2010); Sebastian Heilmann and Elizabeth J. Perry, eds., *Mao's Invisible Hand: The Political Foundations of Adaptive Governance in China*, Harvard Contemporary China Series 17 (Cambridge, MA: Harvard University Press, 2011).

[68] Indictment in *TBFTJS*, p. 3.

overthrow the political power of the dictatorship of the proletariat." The first count establishes the intent of the two groups to seize power. On January 22, 1967 Zhang Chunqiao allegedly said, "Our aim in the Great Proletarian Cultural Revolution has always been to seize power, from the grass roots to the central organizations, including the powers of the party and the state, as well as fields such as finance and culture." The count alleges that the next day Lin Biao also said, "All power, be it at the top, middle, or lower levels, should be seized. In some cases this should be done sooner, in others later."

The second count details the persecution of Liu Shaoqi, who was the president of the PRC and concurrently a vice-chairman of the CCP. This is the longest single count in the indictment, in part because it established the *modus operandi* employed in the commission of many of the other crimes alleged in Parts I and II. In August 1966, Lin Biao allegedly had an underling concoct charges against Liu Shaoqi and sent the material to Jiang Qing for her to "consider forwarding" to Mao; in December 1966, Zhang Chunqiao urged Qinghua University students to demonstrate against Liu Shaoqi and Deng Xiaoping; in July 1967 a member of the Cultural Revolution Group organized a rally where Liu Shaoqi and his wife were dragged from their home and physically harassed. Beginning in May 1967, Jiang Qing, Kang Sheng, and Xie Fuzhi personally directed the Liu Shaoqi and Wang Guangmei Special Case Group to unlawfully imprison and extract statements from at least eleven of the couple's employees and associates, three of whom died during interrogation; victims were prevented from later rescinding false accusation made under duress. Liu Shaoqi was expelled from the party, stripped of his posts, and placed under house arrest, where he was severely neglected and denied medical care for complications arising from chronic diabetes. He died in custody in November 1969.

The next several counts in the indictment repeat this pattern of conspiratorial plotting against political rivals, using trumped up charges, unlawful detention, denunciations at mass rallies, and eventual expulsion from power. Together the charges lay out a far-reaching conspiracy to purge the party, state, and military leadership of so-called counter-revolutionaries, antiparty elements, renegades, traitors, scabs, enemy agents, compradors, capitalist roaders, and so on. Counts 3–4 accuse Kang Sheng and Jiang Qing of bringing false charges against ninety-three members and alternate members of the Eighth Central Committee of the CCP, some of whom were implicated by Chen Boda and Wu Faxian in the fabricated case of the "Extraordinary Central Committee of the Communist Party of China (Marxist-Leninist)." Counts 5–7 concern the compilation in late August 1968 of falsified reports on the political background of members of three important bodies: the Central Control Commission, which was the precursor to the Central Commission for Discipline Inspection, naming 37 of its 60 members; the Standing Committee of the Third National People's Congress, naming 60 of 115 its members; and the Standing Committee of the Fourth People's Political Consultative Congress, naming 74 of its 159 members. Counts 8–18 detail the frame-up and persecution of the most prominent of these targeted leaders: Zhou Enlai, Zhu De, Deng Xiaoping, Chen Yi, Peng Dehuai, He Long, Xu Xiangqian, Nie Rongzhen, Ye Jianying, Lu Dingyi, and Luo Ruiqing. Count 19 lists additional victims – all of them leading members of party, state, and military organs.

The next four counts (20–23) turn to the conspirators' purge of various apparatuses of control. Count 20 describes the purge of the Central Organization Department of the CCP, the organ that monitors and implements high-level personnel appointments to the party, the state, and strategic sectors of the economy. Count 21 describes the gutting of the state's coercive apparatuses, including public security, procuratorial, and judicial organs at all levels. Count 22 describes the Lin Biao group's purge of the headquarters of the PLA General Staff and its Political Department. Count 23 outlines the defendants' seditious manipulation of mass media. The count begins with Chen Boda's incendiary article "Sweep Away All Monsters and Demons" at the start of the Cultural Revolution; surveys the Gang of Four's use of shadowy writing groups to smear enemies; and jumps ahead to the Gang of Four's attempt in April 1976 to misrepresent public mourning for the recently deceased Premier Zhou Enlai as a "counterrevolutionary" incident organized by their rival Deng Xiaoping.

In summary, the purges described in Part I of the indictment reached the highest levels of power. Its victims included the president of the state, the premier and eight vice-premiers, the chairman and a majority of the members of the Standing Committee of the Third National People's Congress, five vice-chairmen of the Central Military Affairs Commission, the chief of the PLA General Staff, two vice-chairmen and the general secretary of the CCP, two-thirds of the Standing Committee of the Politburo of the Eighth Central Committee of the CCP, the chief justice of the Supreme People's Court, the chief procurator of the Supreme People's Procuratorate, the minister of public security, the directors or deputy directors of various central party committees, and numerous high-ranking officers of the PLA.[69] At the very top of the

[69] Zhang Zhanwu, ed., *Zhengzhi fazhan yu dangdai Zhongguo* [Political development and contemporary China] (Changchun: Jilin wenshi chubanshe, 1990), pp. 123–8.

leadership structure, only the chairmanships of the CCP and its Central Military Affairs Commission – both posts occupied by Mao – remained untouched.

Part II of the indictment lists fifteen counts of the "persecution and suppression of numerous cadres and the masses." Following in numerical order from Part I, Counts 24 and 25 describe the use of trumped up charges to systematically gut the municipal governments of Beijing and Shanghai in January 1968. Counts 26–30 allege that Kang Sheng, Xie Fuzhi, and Chen Boda took leading roles instigating large-scale purges in eastern Hebei, Yunnan, Inner Mongolia, Xinjiang, and Manchuria. (Yunnan and Xinjiang are border territories with large ethnic minority populations; the other three hosted Japanese puppet governments during World War II.) These purges were the bloodiest incidents of the Cultural Revolution. The indictment discloses that 346,000 people were persecuted in Inner Mongolia, 16,222 of whom died. Eighty-four thousand were persecuted in eastern Hebei, 2,955 of whom died. Another fourteen thousand died in Yunnan.

The charges continue to mount. In Count 31, members of the Lin Biao and Jiang Qing groups are also charged with baselessly investigating the activities of underground communist organizations during the war years, falsely implicating more than seven thousand people in Guangdong alone as "enemy agents" and "spies." According to Count 32, the Lin Biao group framed and persecuted more than eighty thousand members of the PLA, resulting in the death of 1,169. The four named defendants carried out purges of the Guangzhou units of the PLA, the air force, the navy, and the PLA General Logistics Department. Counts 33 and 34 describe specific incidents in 1967 when Gang of Four members engineered violent attacks on mass organizations. Wang Hongwen directed attacks against a faction called the Workers' Red Detachment at Kangping Road in Shanghai and against another workers' alliance at the Shanghai Diesel Engine Plant. Zhang Chunqiao and Yao Wenyuan supported an episode of violent suppression in Jinan by the Shandong Provincial Revolutionary Committee. These three incidents resulted in the injury or imprisonment of more than eleven hundred people. Count 35 describes how in October 1966, Jiang Qing collaborated with Lin Biao's wife Ye Qun and defendant Wu Faxian to dispatch defendant Jiang Tengjiao to ransack the homes of writers and artists in Shanghai, in order to collect and destroy personal information about Jiang Qing. This was one of the few counts in the indictment that showed how members of the two groups allegedly worked together.

Count 36 states that in 1967 and 1968, Zhang Chunqiao deployed a counterrevolutionary secret service organization in Shanghai, code named the You Xuetao Group or simply "244," which gathered or fabricated evidence used to persecute 183 people. Count 37 states that, from 1974 to 1976, the Gang of Four used Qinghua University as a base to collect intelligence and publish defamatory materials against leaders in Beijing. Finally, Count 38 provides a catchall summary of "ubiquitous" frame-ups and persecution of people in the democratic (i.e., noncommunist) political parties and in various people's organizations, workers in various fields, returned overseas Chinese, and "innumerable cadres and other people working in party, state, and military organs, in enterprises and business establishments, in rural communes, production brigades, and teams, and in urban neighborhood work units throughout the country." Some notable victims are named as examples, including scientists, sports coaches, school teachers, and even a celebrated model worker whose job was to collect human waste for fertilizer. Along with the names are estimated numbers of victims in various fields: 142,000 people in education, 53,000 in science and technology, 2,600 in literature and the arts, and so on.

Summing up, Part II of the indictment expands the scope of the defendants' alleged crimes from the upper echelons of power down to the common people, cementing the impression of the Cultural Revolution as an Olympian battle waged on high that visited disaster on those below. The indictment tally of 729,511 people persecuted and 34,800 people killed acknowledges the victimhood of the masses. Still, the vast majority of victims remain nameless and faceless numbers in the indictment. Only 417 victims are mentioned specifically, and of these only 36 were not well-known personages. Moreover, because the indictment is limited to crimes committed by a small number of conspirators, the total figures do not account for untold numbers of other lives disrupted or destroyed during the Cultural Revolution. This part of the indictment tells of a war between the powerful, with the masses as fodder. Though the indictment was presented in their name, "the people" are the victims rather than the masters of this history.

Part III details in six counts the most sensational and mysterious event of the Cultural Revolution, the Lin Biao group's alleged "plot to assassinate Chairman Mao Zedong and engineer an armed counterrevolutionary coup d'état" in September 1971. Count 39 explains that in October 1969 defendant Wu Faxian, then Commander of the PLA Air Force, unlawfully and without regard for the chain of command put that branch of the military directly under the control of Lin Biao's son Lin Liguo. The Lins, father and son, subsequently assembled a clandestine "joint fleet" of military officers personally loyal to them. According to Count 40, in March 1971 the "joint fleet" sketched out plans for a coup d'état called *Outline of "Project 571"* (that number being a pun for "armed uprising"). Count 41 details the alleged movements of the Lin Biao group in early September 1971. On September 6, Lin Biao and his wife Ye Qun resolved to assassinate the chairman and carry out the coup d'état. Defendant Huang Yongsheng, then chief of the General Staff of the PLA, transmitted the plan to the coconspirators. Defendant Jiang Tengjiao, at the time political commissar of the air force units in Nanjing, took charge of the operation to attack Mao's train near Shanghai. Proposed methods included flamethrowers to assault the train, bombs to sabotage a trestle or a trackside oil depot, or an assassin onboard the train. However, Mao's train departed Shanghai ahead of schedule, before the plan could be enacted. The window of opportunity was closed and now the conspirators feared their plot would be discovered.

The next several counts address the sequelae to this failed plot. According to Count 42, on September 11 Lin Biao, his family, and several of the defendants discussed setting up a rebel government in Guangzhou, hoping to enlist Soviet military support. When these contingency plans were foiled, the conspirators attempted to flee. Just before midnight on September 12, Lin Biao, his wife Ye Qun, and his son Lin Liguo made a rushed takeoff from the airport at Shanhaiguan, the famed strategic pass northeast of Beijing where centuries earlier General Wu Sangui had betrayed the Ming Dynasty to the Manchus. Allegedly they planned to defect to the Soviet Union. The Lins' plane crashed in Mongolia in the early hours of September 13, killing all on board.[70] Meanwhile, conspirator Zhou Yuchi attempted to flee Beijing by helicopter and committed suicide after he was forced to land. Count 43 returns to the scene of the airfield at Shanhaiguan, where defendant Li Zuopeng, acting as deputy chief of the PLA General Staff, had intentionally scuttled Premier Zhou Enlai's order to keep Lin Biao's plane grounded and later falsified the logbook to cover up his crime. Count 44 notes that defendants Wu Faxian, Huang Yongsheng, and Qui Huizuo hastily destroyed evidence of their involvement in the ill-fated plot. So concludes the indictment's account of the infamous September 13 or 9/13 Incident.

Part IV rounds out the indictment with four counts that describe the Gang of Four's "plot for armed rebellion in Shanghai" at the end of the Cultural Revolution. Lacking firm control of the military

---

[70] Wang Haiguang, *Zhe ji chen sha Wendu'erhan* [Crash in the sands of Öndörkhaan] (Beijing: Jiuzhou chubanshe, 2012).

nationally, the Gang of Four planned to build a local stronghold on their home turf. Count 45 lists statements by Zhang Chunqiao and Wang Hongwen regarding their intention to form an irregular people's militia under the control of the Shanghai Municipal Party Committee. Count 46 says that in August 1976 defendant Yao Wenyuan approved a laudatory newspaper article on the workers' militia in order to prepare public opinion in Shanghai for armed rebellion against possible violent suppression of the radicals by the so-called bourgeoisie inside the party. According to Count 47, in that same month the head of the Nanjing regional units of the PLA warned radical Shanghai mayor Ma Tianshui and other Gang of Four associates that he had no direct control over the several military divisions poised outside Shanghai. In response, the mayor distributed 74,220 rifles, 300 artillery pieces, and more than 10 million rounds of ammunition to the local militia. Learning of these preparations after the fact, some two weeks after the death of Chairman Mao and amidst the concealed power struggle for succession, defendants Zhang Chunqiao and Wang Hongwen cautioned their Shanghai allies: "Be on guard, for the struggle isn't over yet. The bourgeoisie within the party will not be reconciled to defeat. Someone or other is sure to try to reinstate Deng Xiaoping."[71] Just two weeks later, Hua Guofeng moved to smash the Gang of Four. Count 48 alleges that the Shanghai radicals responded to the fall of the Gang of Four by mustering forces, distributing arms, and making plans to blockade the city. The planned uprising failed and the Gang of Four's bid for power was over. So ends the list of charges.

After enumerating all the counts, the indictment lists the ten individual defendants according to the extent of their alleged criminal liability: the Gang of Four is listed first, namely Jiang Qing, Zhang Chunqiao, Yao Wenyuan, and Wang Hongwen; followed next by Chen Boda; and then finally the surviving Lin Biao group members, namely Huang Yongsheng, Wu Faxian, Li Zuopeng, Qui Huizhou, and Jiang Tengjiao. For each defendant in custody, the indictment indicates their age, native place, and any state, party, or military titles held at the time of arrest. The indictment concludes by affirming that in accordance with Article 115 of the Criminal Procedure Code, the six other deceased conspirators would not be prosecuted, while the numerous additional accomplices named in the indictment would be tried separately before the Special Court.

---

[71] Indictment in *TBFTJS*, p. 36.

Figure 10. The judges of the Special Court.
Source: China Pictorial, April 1981, p. 30.

Indictment by the People, Courtroom of the People

The Special Court was established by the NPC to be broadly representative of society, so that the case could be judged symbolically by the
whole of the people. As a result, the Special Court's panel of judges was
unusually large (Figure 10). Under the socialist legal system, a typical
case would be tried by one to three judges and audited by two to four
common people called assessors, but the Special Court had a president,
three vice-presidents, and a blue-ribbon panel of thirty-one lay judges
selected from diverse backgrounds.[72] The Special Court divided into
two tribunals: the First Tribunal to try the five civilian defendants and
the Second Tribunal to try the five military defendants. Presiding over
the full court was Jiang Hua, president of the Court and concurrently
chief justice of the Supreme People's Court. He was assisted by three
vice-presidents: Huang Yukun, concurrently major general and deputy
director of the Political Department of the PLA; Zeng Hanzhou, vice-
president of the Court and associate justice of the Supreme People's
Court, who would serve as chief judge of the First Tribunal; and Wu
Xiuquan, vice-president of the Court and deputy chief of Staff of the

---

[72] "Quanguo renda changweihui guanyu chengli tebie fating gei zuigao renmin fayuan de
tong zhi" [Notification by the Standing Committee of the National People's Congress
Given to the Supreme People's Court Regarding Establishment of the Special Court]
(Standing Committee of the National People's Congress Document No. 27) (September
29, 1980), *TBFTJS,* p. 433.

PLA, who would serve as chief judge of the Second Tribunal. Two to five of the lay judges were assigned to focus on each defendant, with the two female judges among the five assigned to the only female defendant, Jiang Qing.[73] Unlike the assessors usually found in the people's courts, the lay judges of the Special Court could and did participate actively and lead court inquiry.[74]

The panel of judges included representatives from all eight minority political parties, as well as diplomats, jurists, and experts on party and military discipline. Scientists, industrialists, agriculture experts, and military personnel personified the regime's commitment to the Four Modernizations. Though it is obvious the panel was chosen to be representative, the NPC offered no explanation of how it selected the individual judges. Some of the judges were fairly prominent in their fields, and others seem to have been more or less common people. One of the more prominent judges, who emerged to become a sort of informal public spokesman for the court, was Fei Xiaotong, a leading sociologist. Like several other judges on the Special Court, he had been branded a "Rightist" in the late 1950s and then persecuted during the Cultural Revolution. Similarly, the president of the Special Court was a victim named in the indictment, and his wife had died from mistreatment at the hands of her political persecutors. One of the vice-presidents of the court had spent seven years as a political prisoner. These judges were not recused, on the logic that nearly everyone had suffered during the Cultural Revolution; on the contrary, the inclusion of these judges seemed that much more just, because through them other victims could vicariously fulfill their desire to condemn their tormentors. This inclusiveness was important symbolically: the Special Court would be a court of the people.

Even the address of the Special Court was symbolic: No. 1 Justice Road. The building that housed the courtroom was actually the MPS's Ceremonial Hall, located on the grounds of the police headquarters in a restricted-access area just east of Tiananmen Square. This large hall had

---

[73] "Zuigao renmin fayuan tebie fating guanyu shenpan renyuan fengong de yijian" [Suggestions of the Special Court of the Supreme People's Court Regarding Division of Work among Judges (Passed by the First Meeting of the Special Court of the Supreme People's Court, dated 6 November 1980)], *TBFTJS*, pp. 455–6. Gan Ying and Liu Liying were both members of the Central Commission for Discipline Inspection. Liu Liying went on to become a famous jurist. See Li and Wang, *Shiji duihua*, p. 94; Liu Guohang, "Yu Jiang Qing da san nian jiaodao 'nü baogong' Liu Liying chenzhuo yingdui feibang" [Three years of dealings with Jiang Qing, female "Judge Bao" Liu Liying handled slander with calm] (December 11, 2002), http://news.tom.com/Archive/1002/2002/12/11-38889.html.

[74] The Special Court held its first organizational meeting on November 6, where it established the special rules and procedures by which the indictment would be examined and adjudicated. Entry for November 6, 1980 in *TBFTJS*, pp. 70–3.

Figure 11. Layout of the Special Court.
Source: China Pictorial, January 1981, p. 14.

more suitable facilities than the nearby Supreme People's Court building; however, Peng Zhen was concerned that using a police building might compromise the appearance of judicial autonomy. He suggested therefore that the location simply be described as "Justice Road," because a service entrance to the building did open onto that street. Ren Lingyun, deputy chief of the MPS also a lay judge on the Special Court, erroneously reported the address to the media as No. 1 Justice Road (the service entrance was actually at No. 7).[75] Once reported, the name stuck in the public imagination: "What profound significance!" observed *People's Daily* reporter Hu Sisheng, "We have taken many twists and turns; now at last we walk the road of upholding justice!"[76]

The courtroom's interior was a symbolic space for China's transition to legal modernity (Figure 11). The courtroom was designed by special legal advisor to the court Qiu Shaoheng (Henry Chiu), who held degrees in both law and literature and served as a delegate to the Far Eastern War

[75] Ren Lingyun as quoted in Li and Wang, *Shiji duihua*, p. 94. Two photographs of the courthouse are reproduced in the frontispiece to *LSSP*, vol. 1.
[76] Hu Sisheng, "Kaiting zhi ri" [Opening day of court], *RMRB*, November 21, 1980.

Crimes Tribunal in Tokyo in April 1946.[77] Reporter Wu Kailiu described the impressive effect of the room. He wrote, "The first thing to catch your eye was, in the very center of the bar, a brightly colored national emblem hanging high upon the curtain. Below the national emblem was the bench, formed of a stepped platform arrayed with two sets of crimson upholstered seats.... Red carpeting adorned the aisles of the bench, and the entire bar looked particularly solemn and imposing in the brilliant lights."[78] A deep red velvet curtain, interwoven with golden thread, set the backdrop to the bar.[79] This sea of red and velvet conveyed the majesty of the Special Court in the symbolic color of Communism. The national emblem heralded the power of the state.

As in the stylized performance of Chinese opera, each role on the stage had a conventional costume and place. Members of the Special Court and the Special Procuratorate addressed the audience and defendants from the authority of a raised dais. An aisle divided the platform, with Chief Justice Jiang Hua flanked by the three associate justices and Chief Procurator Huang Huoqing by his two deputy chiefs. The remaining judges and procurators were arrayed in rows behind them. A metal-railed dock for the defendants sat recessed in the orchestra pit, divided into ten stalls and furnished with wooden chairs and green carpeting. Thus defendants occupied the lowest position in the Special Court, with their backs turned to the people assembled in the gallery. Wooden placards with black lettering designated their seating areas within the courtroom. In this staging, the inclusion of the procurators on the platform with the judges signaled their close relationship as unified representatives of the people and the state. By contrast, locating the defense on a lower level and off to the side set them apart. The clothing worn by the court personnel and the accused established similar distinctions. The judges wore black uniforms, the clerks and procurators dark grey, and the defense light grey. The defendants wore clothes of their own choosing. In the weeks leading up to the trial, the Special Court had held several dress

---

[77] Qiu Shaoheng was brought on as an advisor in mid-September 1980. See Ma Lingguo, "Tebie Fating de falü guwen Qiu Shaoheng" [Special Court legal consultant Henry Chiu], *Shiji* [Century] (September 1999), pp. 18–21.

[78] Wu, "Renmin de shenpan, lishi de shenpan."

[79] Ma, "Tebie Fating de falü guwen Qiu Shaoheng," p. 19. The curtain is described as silver-grey in Sun Haogang and Qian Gang, "Kaiting di yi tian" [First day of trial], *Jiefang junbao* [Liberation Army News], November 21, 1980; perhaps this report is based on a black and white photograph? Most Chinese would have viewed the trial on black and white television sets and in black and white print news. However, the events were filmed and photographed in color, and print reports did take care to describe colors when significant. Seating layout based on photographs and video and descriptions in Hu, "Kaiting zhi ri," and Wu, "Lishi de shenpan, lishi de shenpan."

rehearsals, sometimes with mock defendants. Through these practice sessions, the judges learned to anticipate and handle many situations that might arise during this unprecedented trial.[80] Now the real trial was set to begin.

On November 20, 1980 the courtroom was ready to open with real defendants in the dock. In mid-afternoon, ticketed audience members and reporters filed into the courtroom gallery, which could accommodate more than 880 spectators at a sitting. The spectators were carefully selected and included representatives from every province, provincial-level municipality, autonomous region, political party, people's organization, CCP Central Committee organ, national-level state organ, and the PLA. Also present were the widows of prominent Cultural Revolution victims such as President Liu Shaoqi.[81] Shortly before 3:00 PM, a series of electronic bells toned, alerting the audience to take their seats in silence and signaling court personnel to take their positions. Court police in smart blue uniforms took their positions at either side of the dock. The clerks of the court entered, followed by the prosecution and the acting counsel for the defense. When all had been seated, Clerk Guo Zhiwen read aloud the regulations of the Special Court. Finally, the justices and judges were announced by name as they entered. The clerk notified the chief justice that the Special Procuratorate was on hand to initiate public prosecution against the ten defendants held in custody.[82]

At 3:00 PM sharp the bell toned again and the room was flooded with lights. Reporters Sun Haogang and Qing Gang described the moment for readers of the *Liberation Army News* as if it were a theatrical production:

Suddenly the mercury-vapor stage lamps were illuminated and the atmosphere turned solemn. The movie and television cameras hissed and hummed in unison. With this dazzling flash of light, the ten defendants of the Lin Biao and Jiang Qing counterrevolutionary groups were led in custody onto the scene of this historic trial, and one by one they came into focus.[83]

In the glow of the lights, Chief Justice Jiang Hua called the Special Court into session. The chief justice summoned defendant Wang Hongwen, handing a billet to the clerk of court. This was passed to an officer of the court police, who went to the holding room to fetch this disgraced former vice-chairman of the CCP. At 3:03 PM the court

---

[80] Lu Hong, *Zhonggong zhengzhi wutai shang de "Fu Jiang": Wu Xiuquan chuanqi* ["Lucky General" on the government stage: The legend of Wu Xiuquan] (Beijing: Zhongguo qingnian chubanshe, 2000), pp. 215–16.

[81] Wu, "Renmin de shenpan, lishi de shenpan."

[82] Entry for November 20, 1980 in *TBFTJS*, pp. 79–80.

[83] Sun and Qian, "Kaiting di yi tian."

police returned and led the first defendant down the middle aisle of the gallery. It had been more than four years since the Gang of Four had appeared in public, and even longer for Chen Boda and the Lin Biao group. Everyone was curious to see them. In a hush, the spectators craned to look.[84]

One at a time, ten former party leaders and military officials were called by the chief justice and paraded into the courtroom in manacles. First Wang Hongwen and Yao Wenyuan were summoned, followed by each of the five Lin Biao defendants and Mao's personal secretary Chen Boda. Finally, the chief justice called the two most important defendants, Zhang Chunqiao and Jiang Qing. One of the few ways the defendants had to present themselves was through their personal bearing and dress. However, the state had the advantage of interpreting the scene to the public. The official papers glommed onto every detail of each the defendant's appearance, never shying away from using figurative descriptions to editorialize on their characters.

The youngest defendant, Wang Hongwen, entered first. As a factory worker, Wang had led his peers to overthrow bureaucratic managers and eventually the whole Shanghai Party apparatus. He had come to represent the young upstart faction of the CCP. On this day he was visibly thinner, looking humbled and forlorn. The once energetic Wang sat motionless in his chair for the reading of the indictment.[85] Reporters Sun Haogang and Qing Gang captured the contrast between "Wang Hongwen, rebel" and "Wang Hongwen, defendant" in their description. They wrote, "Wang Hongwen wore a grey pantsuit with crew-cut hair and a jaundiced complexion, his two listless eyes blinking mechanically. The confident swagger of the Shanghai Bund's erstwhile 'Rebel Commander' had dissipated, leaving only the residue of his native mediocrity."[86] By exposing Wang Hongwen's illusory swagger, the description implied he was part of a dysfunctional political system that had failed to nurture real talent and instead promoted criminals.

Propagandist Yao Wenyuan entered next. Presentation did not work in his favor. If the vicissitudes of time revealed a telling change in Wang Hongwen's outward appearance, Yao looked much the same as always: toady and squat, with large watery eyes. The papers took pains to note that Yao had lived well off the fruits of his writings, which had caused suffering and starvation for so many others. Only since receiving

---

[84] Composite description based on reports from Hu, "Kaiting zhi ri"; Sun and Qian, "Kaiting di yi tian"; and Wu, "Renmin de shenpan, lishi de shenpan."

[85] Hu, "Kaiting zhi ri."

[86] Sun and Qian, "Kaiting di yi tian."

the indictment had his hearty appetite for sleep and food finally waned.[87] Again, *Liberation Army News* provided a particularly colorful description, noting, "Yao Wenyuan was bald as ever, and fat made his fish-eyes seem to bulge out even more. He could be seen to put on a sanctimonious and dignified appearance, even remembering to clip a fountain pen into his shirt pocket when in court. But his eyes revealed trepidation and dejection."[88] Perhaps the pen was intended to remind us that whatever his crimes, the wordsmith had never wielded an actual sword. But the newspapers played up his haughty carriage, stout frame, and ridiculous visage.

The military defendants, all now elderly, had close-cropped hair and one of them, Huang Yongsheng, wore a green military-style uniform stripped of insignia. Mao's former political secretary Chen Boda looked weak and ashen, needing assistance to walk to the dock. Grizzled old theoretician Zhang Chunqiao shuffled into the courtroom wearing a grimy shirt hanging loose at the collar. Throughout the session he sat silent and despondent, his unshaven jaw and sagging eyelids betraying impatience, boredom, or annoyance in turn. *People's Daily* described his bizarre behavior:

Zhang Chunqiao, who plotted all sorts of tricks during the ten years of chaos, today continually bobbed his head about – if not to this side, then to that – never once keeping still. His lips curled downward, eyes darting left and right, [he looked] the very image of the masses' epithet: 'the traitorous official.' ... Several times he supported his body with the back of the chair, dumbstruck as a wooden chicken, ... and though he wore only a thin Chinese-style placard shirt with the collar hanging open, sweat gathered continuously on his face.[89]

His attitude would be interpreted later as an act of defiance, but at this stage in the trial the media saw Zhang Chunqiao as defeated and disengaged.

Finally, at 3:15 PM, the star of the show made her much anticipated entry. Jiang Qing, Chairman Mao's widow and alleged ringleader of the Gang of Four, wore a conservative, ankle-length, long-sleeved gown. She did not appear in the jaunty cap and scarf that had been her sartorial trademark during the Cultural Revolution, nor in the elaborate royal finery of the "female emperor" Empress Wu Zetian, the model for Jiang Qing's depiction in propaganda posters after her downfall.[90]

---

[87] Hu, "Kaiting zhi ri."
[88] Sun and Qian, "Kaiting di yi tian."
[89] Hu, "Kaiting zhi ri."
[90] Jiang Qing's sartorial tastes were much criticized in the years leading up to trial. Her alleged sketch of a model "Jiang Qing suit" (in the spirit of Sun Yat-sen's Zhongshan suit or its progeny, the Mao suit) was seen as presumptuous in the extreme, while her

Nevertheless, the newspapers persisted in describing her as a conniving female usurper, writing, "Two female court police brought into the courtroom the fanatic Jiang Qing, in her own mind a 'female emperor.' Today she wore a black outer-garment and black cotton-upper flats. Her hair as always was combed to glossy sheen, and on the bridge of her nose sat a colorful pair of wide-rimmed tortoise-shell glasses."[91] The *People's Daily* emphasized Jiang Qing's careful accoutrement, including expensive eyewear and carefully coifed hair. This description was typical in its insistent reminder that Jiang Qing was above all else an *actress* – spry and wily, and in her younger days even charming enough to beguile the chairman. But today in court, her affected manner held no charms. The report continues, "With her every movement she maintained her customary arrogant posture. Still employing performance techniques from her time as a movie actress, she deliberately cocked her head and advanced with slow paces under everyone's eyes, in a manner that made you sick."[92] Reporter Shi Hongdao of the *Beijing Daily* echoed this crude reaction to Jiang Qing's insincerity, "Seeing her performance really made you want to vomit."[93]

By 3:17 PM all ten defendants were standing in the dock, separated from the gallery by a cordon of court police. Jiang Qing put in a hearing aid and listened intently. Chief Justice Jiang Hua, with his close attention to procedure, instructed the defendants to be seated and informed them that the trial would begin. After calling the roll of court personnel, the chief justice invited the chief procurator to read the indictment aloud. It took several hours to read the document in its entirety, and at 5:20 PM court was adjourned. This public reading of the indictment added nothing from a textual standpoint, but the performance and especially the media coverage of it created an audience and a model response. The next morning's newspapers ran several reaction pieces featuring prominent victims' family members, including an interview with the widow of Marshal Peng Dehuai – the modern paragon of the virtuous official, who had earned Mao's wrath by speaking out against the Great Leap Forward, and who was the subject of the historical allegory that set off the Cultural Revolution. "This is a trial by the people, history's trial," reported Marshal Peng's widow, "I'm thrilled to see [the defendants]

adoration of capable empresses was supposed to reveal her autocratic imperial ambitions. See *Liang Xiao zuizheng cailiao* [Material on the crimes of the Liang Xiao group] (Beijing: Liang Xiao Special Case Group, unpublished, 1978), pp. 116–18.

[91] Hu, "Kaiting zhi ri."

[92] Ibid.

[93] Shi Hongdao, "Lishi de shenpan, renmin de shengli" [History's trial, people's victory], *Beijing ribao* [Beijing Daily], November 21, 1980.

with my own eyes being led in shackles to the dock, and now I can console Old Peng's spirit in heaven."[94]

The performance also engaged the desire for justice of those assembled outside the courtroom, according to *People's Daily* reader Li Demin. He watched the opening session of the trial from the packed television lounge at his office and described the reactions of his fellow viewers in a "Daily Chat" column called, "In Front of the Television Set, Viewing the People's Hearts." "'See! The wicked Jiang Qing is a shameless actress.' 'Zhang Chunqiao looks like he's been exhumed from a tomb.' 'Look at that Wang Hongwen – where is the authoritative air of the Rebel Commander?'"[95] These published responses modeled judgments for other members. "In front of that glowing screen, it felt like we ourselves were sitting on the judges' bench."[96] As *Liberation Daily* reported, in that moment the people began to form their own verdict. "History has firmly nailed [the defendants] into the pillory; no matter how they dissemble and connive, they will never be set free."[97]

The indictment provided the outline for the opening act of a carefully staged but loosely scripted drama. Media coverage prejudged the case and short-circuited the ability of the public to give a fair hearing, so that the guilt of the defendants was largely a foregone conclusion. Yet the legal indictment was intended to initiate an objective and rational way of settling accounts with the Cultural Revolution. The key to this apparent contradiction lies in the concept of justice embraced by the narrative form of the indictment. The indictment set in motion a type of narrative that resonated with deeply held ideals of justice; specifically, the indictment initiated a type of narrative that the Chinese cultural tradition trial calls a "requital" (*bao*) story.

Justice as Commensuration: A Requital Narrative

The Chinese concept of requital is based on the idea that social relationships are reciprocal, such that all actions demand commensurate reaction to maintain a harmonious and equitable balance of payments. Lien-sheng Yang's study of the term shows that in Chinese culture requital is the basic glue of social relations and a dominant concept of

---

[94] Ibid.

[95] "Dianshiji qian kan minxin" (In front of the television set, watching the people's heart), *RMRB*, November 23, 1980.

[96] Ibid.

[97] Sun and Qian, "Kaiting di yi tian." Similar rhetoric is repeated in Social Commentary editorials for November 21, 1980 such as: "Renmin de shenpan, lishi de shenpan" [The people's trial, history's trial], *Gongmin ribao* [Workers' Daily]; "Zhengyi de shenpan, renmin de xinyuan" [Justice's trial, the people's aspiration], *Jiefang junbao* [Liberation Army News]; and "Jiuyi renmin de shenpan" [Nine hundred thousand people's trial], *RMRB*.

justice.[98] Karl S. Y. Kao agrees that requital is "a code underlying most areas of human conduct, either observed explicitly, as in legal exchanges, or implicitly, as in ethics and family relationships."[99] Requital is a common theme in Chinese philosophical, political, religious, and literary texts since very early times. The concept is evident in the classical ethical teachings of Confucianism and Daoism, and was strongly reinforced in medieval times by the Buddhist concept of *karma*.[100] The idea of commensurate repayment is one of the most fundamental and universally held concepts of justice in all of Chinese culture.

Requital is a basic normative frame structuring Chinese social experience. Not surprisingly, then, it is also a basic normative frame structuring Chinese storytelling. Requital is central to a wide range of literary and dramatic genres, as Kao has shown, but nowhere is its operation more obvious than in tales of crimes and punishment. Most Chinese people have little direct experience with courts of law, and indeed try to avoid entanglement in litigation if at all possible, and so the popular understanding of criminal trials has been shaped by fictional accounts. Naturally, Chinese audiences expect real life trials to meet expectations established in popular and mass media such as opera, drama, literature, television, and film: And Chinese crime stories, unlike Western detective stories, make no mystery of who the culprit is. Robert van Gulik's explanation of audience expectations for traditional Chinese crime stories holds true for modern cultural productions, as well:

First of all, the criminal is, as a rule, introduced formally to the reader at the very beginning of the book, with his full name, an account of his past history, and the motive that led him to commit the crime. The Chinese want to derive from the reading of a detective novel the same purely intellectual enjoyment as from watching a game of chess; with all the factors known, the excitement lies in following every move of the detective and the counter measures taken by the criminal, until the game ends in the unavoidable check-mate of the latter.[101]

As a cultural production in its own right, the Gang of Four trial faced similar audience expectations. The legal indictment fulfilled the same narrative purposes as the opening to a detective novel: it introduced the

---

[98] Lien-sheng Yang, "The Concept of Pao [Bao] as a Basis for Social Relations in China," in John K. Fairbank, ed., *Chinese Thought and Institutions* (Chicago: University of Chicago Press, 1957), pp. 291–309.

[99] Karl S. Y. Kao, "Bao and Baoying: Narrative Causality and External Motivations in Chinese Fiction," *Chinese Literature: Essays, Articles, Reviews* 11 (1989), p. 120.

[100] Regina Llamas, "Retribution, Revenge, and the Ungrateful Scholar in Early Chinese Southern Drama," *Asia Major* 2 (2007), p. 94.

[101] Robert van Gulik, *Celebrated Cases of Judge Dee; Dee Goong An: An Authentic Eighteenth-Century Chinese Detective Novel* (New York: Dover Publications, 1976), p. iii.

criminals, established the rules of the game, and set the chess match underway. In this genre, due process is meant to ensure fair play but guilt is assumed from the start: a trial could be a satisfying requital story only if, in the end, the criminals got their just deserts.

In this cultural context, law makes its claim to justice as a vector for requital. The legal trial is a method (*fa*) to calculate and deliver just deserts. The indictment sets in motion a process that leads to a proper substantive outcome – a requital of injury with a commensurate measure of redress. The properly calculated ratio of exchange, of redress for injury, undergirds the metaphor of "settling accounts" (*suan zhang*). Law allows a more rational exchange than do primitive methods of requital, such as vengeance, because law depersonalizes the exchange relationship and abstracts the currency of exchange.[102] Thus while the ancient *Book of Rites* says to "repay injury with injury" (*yi yuan bao yuan*), Confucius later advises that it is better to "repay injury with justice" (*yi zhi bao yuan*).[103] This rationalization of punishment out of the hands of the victim and into a more abstract form befits a civilized society governed by rules, at least according to one medieval Chinese moral treatise: "to repay injury with justice is public-spirited."[104]

The Gang of Four trial acted out the familiar story of repaying injury with a commensurate measure of legal justice. Settling accounts in a rational and evenhanded way would close the books without producing new excesses and debts. As Deng Xiaoping put it, "The purpose of summing up the past is to encourage people to close ranks and look to the future."[105] Yet even as the state attempted to deliver justice and close the books on the Cultural Revolution, this ideal – justice as commensuration – created a new set of dilemmas. In the aftermath of a societal disaster on this scale, was it really possible to stage a commensurate exchange that would close the books?

Chinese literature of the post-Mao transition approached this unsettling question with ambivalence. The first major literary movement of

---

[102] In Western civilization, this difference can be seen in the shift from the Old Testament ideal of exact retribution in kind ("an eye for eye, a tooth for a tooth") to the Roman law of just compensation (*lex talionis*), in which injury is tallied and repaid in some abstract commodity like time, money, or floggings. For further discussion of this concept in Western culture, see William Ian Miller, *An Eye for an Eye* (New York: Cambridge University Press, 2007).

[103] Yang, "The Concept of Pao [Bao]," p. 293.

[104] Quoted in ibid., p. 294.

[105] Deng Xiaoping, "Talk with some leading comrades of the Central Committee (March 19, 1980): Remarks on Successive Drafts of the *Resolution on Certain Questions in the History of Our Party since the Founding of the People's Republic of China* (March 1980–June 1981), http://english.peopledaily.com.cn/dengxp/vol2/text/b1420.html.

the post-Mao era was called "scar literature."[106] Published in mainstream journals in the late 1970s, these stories supported the agenda of the state: they criticized the Gang of Four, called for the reversal of unjust verdicts, and adhered to the doctrine of socialist realism, which demanded optimism about the future.[107] Yet the very name of the movement hinted at the lingering, residual effects of the Cultural Revolution, of wounds that might be closed but would never fully heal. However compelling the concept of commensurate requital, it has inherent limitations. Literary scholar Wai Chee Dimock provides a useful language for describing this problem in her study of how Western literature has problematized the ideal of justice as "a dream of objective adequation" and the "reification of commensurability itself."[108] It is worth paying heed to the "residues of justice" that indelibly remain after the settling of accounts.

The Chinese word for *settling* (*suan*: to calculate) carries contradictory connotations. On the one hand, it can mean to settle a bill or a score – to get even. On the other hand, it can mean to let pass or forget – to move on. The common expression *suan le* ("never mind") uses the grammatical particle *le* to signal a change in temporal aspect, transforming the verb from a transitive sense (to settle it) to a putative one (to consider it settled). The indictment and trial of the Gang of Four was supposed to transform the constant and divisive accounting of the past into a final and decisive reckoning, allowing the nation to close the books and move on. Chapter 2 situates the official party-state effort at "settling accounts" more closely within the cultural context of the post-Mao transition, exploring an example of how Chinese literature tried to account for the residues of justice. Liu Binyan's famous reportage piece *Between Man and Monster* illustrates how committed socialist intellectuals struggled to come to terms with those injustices that defy commensurate redress.

---

[106] For an extended discussion of the Scar Literature genre, see Richard King, "'Wounds' and 'Exposure': Chinese Literature after the Gang of Four," *Pacific Affairs* 54 (January 1981), pp. 82–99.

[107] Yu Zongqi, *Zhongguo wenxue yu zhongguo falü* [Chinese literature and Chinese law] (Beijing: Zhongguo zhengfa daxue chubanshe, 2002), p. 248.

[108] Wai Chee Dimock, *Residues of Justice: Literature, Law, Philosophy* (Berkeley: University of California Press, 1996), p. 6.

2   Monsters

Liu Binyan's *Between Man and Monster* (1979) is still today China's most famous piece of investigative journalism.[1] The piece takes its title from the opening line of a classical-style poem by Guo Moruo, the polymath Marxist who served as president of the Chinese Academy of Sciences from 1949 until his death in 1978.[2] Guo Moruo's poem, "On Viewing *Sun Wukong Thrice Strikes the White-Boned Demon*," was a response to an opera he had seen performed in Beijing in October 1961. The opera recounts a famous episode from the legend of Monkey (*Journey to the West*), in which the evil White-Boned Demon repeatedly disguises herself in human form. Each time she appears, Monkey perceives her true form and strikes her down, but his companion the Buddhist monk intercedes with an incantation that tightens the golden band around Monkey's head and allows the demon to escape. The poem sharply criticizes those who, like the hapless monk, fail to see the monsters in their midst: "Confounding men and monsters, muddling right and wrong, / Merciful to enemies and troublesome to friends. / [. . .] / May a thousand cuts dismember the monk's flesh, / [. . .] / Even Pigsy had more wisdom than that fool."[3] Chairman Mao responded shortly after with his

[1] Liu Binyan, "Ren yao zhi jian" [Between man and monster], *Renmin wenxue* [People's literature] 240 (September 1979), pp. 83–102. Parenthetical references in this chapter refer to page numbers in the original Chinese edition. The work is available in English translation as Liu Binyan, "People or Monsters?," James V. Feinerman with Perry Link, transl., in *People or Monsters? And Other Stories and Reportage from China after Mao*, Perry Link, ed. (Bloomington: Indiana University Press, 1983), pp. 11–68.

[2] Aside from the title, the phrase juxtaposing "man and monster" appears just a single time in the main text of Liu Binyan's report, using the same four-character construction as the opening to Guo Moruo's poem: "*ren yao dian dao*" (98), indicating an improper inversion of opposing categories. Man and monster are opposites that have been mistakenly transposed or confused.

[3] Guo Moruo, "Kan Sun Wukong san ci da Bai Gu Jing" and Mao Zedong, "He Guo Moruo tongzhi," in *Mao zhuxi shici xuexi xiaozu, Mao zhuxi shici qianshi* [Classical Poetry of Chairman Mao] (Guangdong Yueju xuexiao, 1988), p. 231; with background and textual analysis by Jin Fang in Su Gui, *Mao Zedong shi ci dadian* [Compendium of Mao Zedong's poetry] (Nanning: Guangxi renmin chubanshe, 1993), pp. 227–35. For an extended discussion of the two poems, see Rudolph G. Wagner, "Monkey King

own verse written in the same highly technical style, "To Comrade Guo Moruo," a line from which gives the title to the cartoon shown in the introduction to this book. Mao's poem interprets the lesson of the opera differently, concluding, "The Monk was a foolish person but could still be taught" – apparently meaning that those in the middle of the struggle between heroes and monsters would be better educated and converted into allies than destroyed as enemies.

Before analyzing the imagery of this exchange and its relevance to the Gang of Four trial, it is worth pausing for a moment to note the deep and layered interplay of literature and politics on evidence here. In a piece of long-form journalism intended for a general audience is found an allusion to a political debate waged in the form of a classical-style poem written by a head of state in response to another poem about an opera based on a traditional novel recounting an episode from a popular folk legend. Such a profoundly literary exchange is nigh unimaginable in contemporary Western politics, but was so normal and indeed character-istic of the political culture of socialist China that the allusion needed no explanation to resonate meaningfully with Chinese readers. So, what did this phrase, "confounding men and monsters," mean to a Chinese reader in post-Mao China?

Guo Moruo's poem took on a prescient tone after the Cultural Revolution, when Jiang Qing came to be identified with the White-Boned Demon. In the same way that the fictional demon had threatened to destroy Monkey and his fellow pilgrims in their allegorical quest for *dharma* (*fa*), so too did real-life "monsters" like Jiang Qing and Wang Shouxin, the villain of *Between Man and Monster*, threaten to destroy the Chinese people in their modernizing quest for law (*fa*). In this crucial historical moment and in this particular cultural context, Liu Binyan's allusion to Guo Moruo's strident poem – rather than to Mao's mild response – admonishes those who have failed to recognize and vanquish the monsters in their midst.

Liu Binyan's *Between Man and Monster* details massive official cor-ruption committed during and continuing after the Cultural Revolution at a state-run coal enterprise in China's far northeastern province of Heilongjiang. It was written and published a year before the trial of the Gang of Four took place and itself resulted in a famous criminal trial. The published exposé and subsequent trial focused on local party boss Wang Shouxin, a female cadre member who bore more than a passing

Subdues the White-Bone Demon: A Study in PRC Mythology," in *The Contemporary Chinese Historical Drama: Four Studies* (Berkeley: University of California Press, 1990), pp. 143–58.

resemblance to Jiang Qing. As director of the coal enterprise, Wang Shouxin sat at the center of a complex web of embezzlement, bribery, and theft – purported at the time to have been the biggest corruption case in the history of the People's Republic of China. This chapter will develop a reading of *Between Man and Monster* as a sort of "literary indictment" to be viewed in parallel with the legal indictment against Jiang Qing and the other defendants before the Special Court. This parallel reading will allow us to reconsider the implications of the Chinese state's use of a legal indictment to interpret and intervene into history.

Literary Indictment

Between Man and Monster first appeared in the September 1979 issue of China's foremost literary journal, *People's Literature* (*Renmin wenxue*). A publication of the prestigious Chinese Writers Association, *People's Literature* boasted a monthly circulation of 1.4 million copies and reached a huge audience. The story was endorsed in *People's Daily* and actively promoted elsewhere in the official press, being reprinted in at least seven different regional newspapers and broadcast on at least three radio stations.[4] The article was also posted widely in the communal spaces of work units and public markets throughout China (still a common practice today), and easily could have reached a hundred million readers.[5] The lurid content, presented with great literary skill, created a popular sensation. The success of the work was also due in part to the reputation of its author, Liu Binyan. The publication of *Between Man and Monster* announced the stunning return to the literary scene of socialist China's most respected – and most criticized – investigative journalist. The work garnered critical acclaim, as well; several decades later, *Between Man and Monster* is still considered the epitome of long-form journalism in socialist China.[6]

At the time of the report, some basic facts about the Wang Shouxin case were already known to the public. However, Liu Binyan's article dug much deeper. A year before he began his journalistic investigation,

[4] Liu Binyan, "Guanyu 'Ren yao zhi jian' da duzhe wen" [Answers to readers' questions about *Between Man and Monster*], *Renmin wenxue* [*People's Literature*], January 1980.

[5] Reader comments were published in an editorial endorsement of the work, "Jiji ganyu shenghuo, tuidong shehui qianjin: tujian Liu Binyan de texie 'Renyao zhi jian'" [Actively delve into life, promote social advancement: Recommending Liu Binyan's special report "Between Man and Monster"], in *RMRB*, October 9, 1979.

[6] It is specifically an example of the special report (*texie*) form. See Rudolf G. Wagner, "Liu Binyan and the *Texie*," *Modern Chinese Literature* 2.1 (Spring 1986): pp. 63–98; Thomas Elton Moran, "True Stories: Contemporary Chinese Reportage and Its Ideology and Aesthetics," PhD diss. (Cornell University, 1994), pp. 222–3 and 57–168 *passim*.

local Bin County authorities had targeted Wang Shouxin's coal operation in the "Double Strike" (*shuang da*) anticorruption campaign. As the staggering extent of malfeasance came to light, the district committee formed an official investigation team in conjunction with the party commission for discipline inspection, the public security bureau, the district procuratorate, and the district court. Scores of forensic auditors, eventually numbering more than two hundred, were assigned to examine the operation's transactions dating from November 1971 to June 1978. Wang Shouxin and her associates were arrested and subjected to mass criticism at a rally in December 1978. The provincial newspaper *Heilongjiang Daily* (*Heilongjiang ribao*) publicized details of the case in March and April 1979, and the story was picked up nationally by *People's Daily*.[7] Liu Binyan, acting as a special reporter for *People's Daily*, traveled to Bin County in July 1979 to investigate further. He wanted to go behind the scenes to find out not only *what* had happened, but to understand *how* and *why* it had happened. The resulting report ran thirty thousand Chinese characters and densely packed twenty journal-sized pages. *Between Man and Monster* was not simply a sterile list of charges; it intimately described the lives of the people living in a corrupted world.

In the month following the publication of *Between Man and Monster*, Wang Shouxin and her associates faced trial. During October 18–20, in a public proceeding attended by more than two thousand spectators, the Songhuajiang District Intermediate People's Court in Harbin determined that Wang Shouxin and her codefendants had embezzled precisely RMB 500,770.02.[8] This amount was nearly double the value of the fixed assets of the company, and about nine hundred times the average annual wages of a Chinese worker in the mid-1970s. The court sentenced the assistant director of the coal enterprise, Ma Zhanqing, to fifteen years imprisonment. Six other codefendants, including Wang Shouxin's

---

[7] "Heilongjiang Sheng pohuo yiqi yanzhong tanwu jituan anjian" [Heilongjiang Province uncovers serious corruption group case], *RMRB*, April 23, 1979; "Yansu dangji guofa; hen daji tanwu fan: duzhe fenfen laixin, dui Wang Shouxin de fanzui xingwei biaoshi jida fenkai, yizhi yaoqiu yifa yancheng" [Stern discipline and law; severe crackdown on corruption: Flood of reader letters express utmost indignation at the crimes of Wang Shouxin and unanimously demand serious legal punishment], *RMRB*, May 17, 1979; Chumu jingxin faren shenxing: da tanwu fan Wang Shouxin weishenme you name da de shentong? [Shocking and thought-provoking: How did the corrupt Wang Shouxin attain such supernatural powers?], *RMRB*, August 16, 1979.

[8] "Jingtun guojia ju kuan de 'Binzhou meiba' shoudao guofa zhicai; da tanwu fan Wang Shouxin bei panchu sixing yu gai an youguan de qita zuifan Ma Zhanqing deng fenbie panchu tuxing" [Bin County Coal Tyrant who devoured state funds is subjected to legal sanction; Major embezzler Wang Shouxin sentenced to death; Ma Zhanqing and other defendants in the case sentenced to imprisonment], *RMRB*, October 25, 1979; based on reports from *Heilongjiang ribao* [Heilongjiang Daily].

brother, sister, two sons, and a daughter-in-law received prison terms ranging from two to seven years. Finally, the court sentenced the "Bin County Coal Tyrant," as Wang Shouxin was called, to death.[9] A *People's Daily* summary of the trial reported that "the people could not help but applaud with joy" to see "the parasites who had jeopardized the people's interests and harmed the Four Modernizations" get their just deserts.[10] In a very real sense though, *Between Man and Monster* was the public indictment of Wang Shouxin – much more so than the legal indictment presented in the district courtroom. Like the Gang of Four trial, it was an indictment by proxy of the entire Cultural Revolution.

The author positioned *Between Man and Monster* as a sort of literary indictment, famously calling on his fellow writers to be "advocates for the people" in the "courtroom of history." The legal metaphor is apt, as there are striking parallels between this literary work and the legal indictment presented to the Special Court. First, the two texts are roughly contemporaneous: Liu Binyan began his investigation the same month that Chinese leaders resolved to hold a trial against the Gang of Four, and he published his report just a year before the legal indictment against the Gang of Four was completed. Second, like its courtroom counterpart, Liu Binyan's report filed an accusation of wrongdoing supported by forensic investigation of facts and presented for judgment. Third, *Between Man and Monster* exemplifies an exceptionally stable and formulaic literary genre, and so like a legal indictment pressed its charges according to established rules.[11] Fourth, the specific criminal conduct alleged

---

[9] "Wang Shouxin tanwu an gongkai shenpan gao jieshu" [Public trial of Wang Shouxin corruption case concluded], *Heilongjiang ribao* [Heilongjiang Daily], October 21, 1979. The death sentence issued by the lower court was approved on review by the provincial High People's Court and the national Supreme People's Court.

[10] "Jingtun guojia ju kuan de 'Binzhou meiba.'" A follow-up report was published alongside Liu Binyan's speech "Listen Carefully to the Voice of the People," as "Jiuchu tanwu fan, qiye huo xinsheng: bei Wang Shouxin panju shi nian zhi jiu de Bin xian ranliao gongsi jingguo yi nian de zhengdun, meitan gouxiao gongzuo zhua de jin, gongzuo zuofeng da bianyang" [Embezzlers excised, enterprise given new life: Bin County fuel company occupied for a decade by Wang Shouxin undergoes a year of retrenchment, work of buying and selling coal is grasped firmly and work style changes greatly], *RMRB*, November 26, 1979.

[11] The stability of the genre makes *Between Man and Monster* an ideal starting point for our examination of justice in the legal and literary realms. In this chapter I will use the terms *purpose*, *authorial position*, *methods*, and *truth claims* to distill Rudolph G. Wagner's analysis of the nine generic characteristics of the *texie* (special report) reportage form. My term *purpose* encompasses Wagner's terms *functionality*, *militancy*, and *modernity*; *method* encompasses *discovery* and *sociological analysis*; *truth claims* encompasses *immediacy* and *authenticity*; and *authorial position* encompasses *morality* and *ironic distance*. See Rudolph G. Wagner, *Inside a Service Trade: Studies in Contemporary Chinese Prose*. Harvard-Yenching Institute Monograph Series 34 (Cambridge, MA: Harvard University Council on East Asian Studies, 1992), pp. 243–376. According to Zhang Yinjing, these stable genre characteristics highlight the inherent ideological content of

in Liu Binyan's report indirectly shed light on the systemic corruption of the Cultural Revolution period. Fifth, *Between Man and Monster* and the Gang of Four trial both focused on a small but powerful group of perpetrators led by a "ruthless" woman. Finally, like a real legal indictment, Liu Binyan's literary indictment ultimately resulted in a spectacular court case and criminal conviction.

These similarities set in relief some major differences. The most obvious and basic difference is that a literary indictment lacks the legal authority of the state. Under the sign of the monster, Liu Binyan instead frames his case as a matter that transcends legality and illegality and cuts to the moral core of the society. The title intimates that the fate of Chinese socialism is really a question of humanity and inhumanity. This rhetorical move enables the author to bypass the legal authority of the state and instead appeal directly to the moral authority of his audience, the people. This extralegal approach has important implications. Each of the following sections explores a different aspect of *Between Man and Monster* as a literary indictment: the author's conception of the socialist writer as an advocate for the people; his investigative approach as a socialist scientist discovering the facts of the case; the report's diagnosis of the Cultural Revolution as a figurative rule of monsters; identification of the underlying cause as a dehumanizing system of exchange; and the proposed remedy – to activate the people as true human subjects in the courtroom of history. The conclusion to the chapter will reflect on some troubling features that this literary indictment shared with the Special Court's legal indictment.

Advocate for the People

In a high-profile speech given in November 1979, shortly after the publication of *Between Man and Monster* and the conclusion to the Wang Shouxin trial, Liu Binyan used a legal metaphor to describe the ideal role for the socialist writer: "In the courtroom of history, we [writers] have no right to sit by as auditors. The people are the judges, and the ones who bring suit; we must provide them with scripts."[12] Writers – like

---

the form. See "Narrative, Ideology, Subjectivity: Defining a Subversive Discourse in Chinese Reportage," in Liu Kang and Tang Xiaobing, eds., *Politics, Ideology, and Literary Discourse in Modern China* (Durham, NC: Duke University Press, 1993), p. 212.

[12] The speech was given to the Third Congress of the Chinese Writers Association, which met in conjunction with the Fourth Congress of Literature and Art Workers. See Liu Binyan, "Qingting renmin de shengyin" [Listen carefully to the voice of the people], *RMRB*, November 26, 1979. This version is available in English translation by Kyna Rubin and Perry Link in Link, ed. *People or Monsters? And Other Stories*, pp. 1–10. A longer version of the speech was published in the November–December 1979 issue of *Wenyi bao* [Literary gazette] under the title "*Shidai de zhaohuan*" [Call of times],

lawyers – are educated professionals with the specialized rhetorical skills and technical training to articulate claims in persuasive and appropriate language. In a society beset by injustice, the "people's writer" (Liu Binyan's term) is morally and professionally obligated to help the plaintiffs of history – the people – to file grievances and seek redress. "[Our readers] especially need writers who will serve as spokesmen for the people, writers who will answer their questions and express their demands by confronting the major issues of the day."[13] *Between Man and Monster* was a model of the literary work as indictment, a prosecutorial "script" (*jianggao*) provided to help the plaintiffs (*yuangao*) state their case and win justice.

Outside the institutional context of a courtroom, though, what is the usefulness of such a prosecutorial script? To appreciate the efficacy and authority of Liu Binyan's literary work, it is necessary to first understand the complex relationship of its author to the state and his place in socialist society. Liu Binyan's reportage established him as a sort of socialist public intellectual, neither fully of the state nor fully autonomous from it. Like any citizen he was completely dependent on the party-state for his livelihood and even his basic freedoms, yet his chosen occupation was to point out and criticize the flaws of socialist society. This put him in a precarious position. Literature, perhaps even more than other intellectual fields in socialist China, was subject to highly elastic and rapidly changing cycles of relaxation and repression. Liu Binyan at times enjoyed institutional support, political patronage, and professional stature. These provided him an audience, but by no means immunized him from harm. The vicissitudes of his career – before, during, and after publication of *Between Man and Monster* – illustrate the opportunities for, and the limitations of, critical intervention by a socialist writer in the courtroom of history.[14]

Liu Binyan grew up amidst the warfare of the first half the twentieth century, in the heavily industrialized northeastern region formerly known as Manchuria. The son of a railway worker, Liu Binyan was born in 1925 in the rail car manufacturing city of Changchun and spent most of his childhood in the hub city of Harbin, where the Trans-Manchurian

also available in English translation by John Meyer in Howard Goldblatt, ed., *Chinese Literature for the 1980s: The Fourth Congress of Writers & Artists* (Armonk, NY: M. E. Sharpe, 1982), pp. 103–20.

[13] Liu Binyan, quoted in Link, ed. *People or Monsters? And Other Stories*, p. 9.

[14] For biographical details, see: Liu Binyan's autobiography, *A Higher Kind of Loyalty: A Memoir by China's Foremost Journalist [Liu Binyan zi zhuan]*, Zhu Hong, transl. (New York: Pantheon Books, 1990); Anna Doležalová, "Liu Binyan's Comeback to the Contemporary Chinese Literary Scene," *Asian and African Studies* (Bratislava) 20 (1984), pp. 81–100.

Railway connects Beijing and the rest of China to the Trans-Siberian Railway. Japan invaded Manchuria in 1931, a precursor to the all-out invasion of China in 1937, and Liu Binyan came of age during the Japanese occupation. Liu Binyan's father had been stationed in Russia during World War I, and under his influence the younger Liu learned the Russian language. Although he abandoned his formal studies after completing middle school, he continued to be an avid reader in both Russian and Chinese. As a teenager, Liu Binyan joined the underground communist resistance movement against Japan. He continued to support the communists in the civil war that followed, and in 1949 he took a post with the Chinese Socialist Youth League (the precursor to the Communist Youth League). In 1951, he became a reporter for that organization's widely circulated newspaper, *China Youth Daily* (*Zhongguo qingnian bao*), touting the promise of the new socialist state.

Liu Binyan's experience under state socialism was fraught with difficulty, however. In the Hundred Flowers movement of the late 1950s, Chairman Mao invited intellectuals to offer constructive criticism of the communist party and socialist state. In this spirit, Liu Binyan published two scathing investigative reports on bureaucratic corruption and interference. These reports instantly won him national prominence, but were subsequently deemed too dark, unconstructive, and even seditious. In the Anti-Rightist repression that crushed the Hundred Flowers movement, Liu Binyan was denounced, stripped of his party membership, and exiled for "reform by labor" from 1958 to 1962. Labeled a Rightist again during the Cultural Revolution, he toiled in a labor reform (*laogai*) camp for an even longer spell, from 1969 to 1977.[15] Hu Yaobang, a Deng Xiaoping protégé and leading reformist – who also happened to have been First Secretary of the Communist Youth League during Liu Binyan's time there – took a personal interest in the disgraced writer's predicament. His was one of many prominent cases reversed in the winter thaw of 1978–9. The intrepid reporter, now well into middle age, assumed a new post at the Institute of Philosophy, a division of the state-run Chinese Academy of Social Sciences (CASS) in Beijing.

Almost immediately upon his return, Liu Binyan released a pent-up programmatic statement called On *"Writing about the Dark Side" and "Intervening into Life."*[16] This strongly worded manifesto staked out his

[15] On the institution of the labor reform camp, see James D. Seymour and Richard Anderson, *Old Ghosts, New Ghosts: Prisons and Labor Reform Camps in China*, Socialism and Social Movements (New York: Routledge, 1999).

[16] Liu Binyan, "Guanyu 'xie yin'an mian' he 'ganyu shenghuo,'" [On "writing about the dark side" and "intervening into life"], *Shanghai wenxue* [Shanghai literature], March 1979.

position in the debate over the nature of socialist realism, a debate that had raged in China for more than half a century.[17] The central question was how to balance the two main purposes of socialist realism: to expose hardships and agitate for change, on the one hand, and, on the other hand, to promote the past and future victories of socialism. The radical literary theorists of the Cultural Revolution period, led by the Gang of Four, advocated a romanticized realism in the style of the "six mores" – after Mao's statement in the canonical "Yan'an Talks" (1942) that "literature and art can and ought to be on a higher plane, more intense, more concentrated, more typical, nearer the ideal, and therefore more universal than actual everyday life." The model works of the Cultural Revolution created a heroic distillation of revolution that sometimes bore little resemblance to present-day reality. Liu Binyan's manifesto, in contrast, called for writings that were more raw, more timely, and more faithful to lived experience. He wanted writing that was so unflinchingly realistic that it could shed its artistic falsity and occupy "the intermediate stages between life and a literary work."[18] *Between Man and Monster* was a way to expose the dark side of socialist society and make a positive intervention. His goal was to advance an indictment with such clarity and forcefulness that the reader (and by extension society) would be pressed to judgment.

It must be emphasized that Liu Binyan was an ardent socialist. His purpose in criticizing the reality of socialism was not to destroy it but to improve it. However, for Liu Binyan, socialism entailed a lifelong commitment to the people, a commitment that trumped his loyalty to any particular leaders, institutions, or policies of the party-state. His uncompromising principles won him the admiration of his fellow writers; in 1985, the membership of the Chinese Writers Association elected him as their vice-chairman. But commitment to principles also brought his downfall. Liu Binyan remained a visible and outspoken agitator for political reform, but when the interests of the people came into conflict with the interests of the reformist party-state, he once again ran afoul of the system. When the "people's writer" threw his support behind the student demonstrations that erupted on college campuses across China

---

[17] Marston Anderson, *The Limits of Realism: Chinese Fiction in the Revolutionary Period* (Berkeley: University of California Press, 1990); Kirk A. Denton, *Modern Chinese Literary Thought: Writings on Literature, 1893–1945* (Stanford, CA: Stanford University Press, 1996).

[18] Liu Binyan, "Guanyu 'xie yin'an mian' he 'ganyu shenghuo.'" In a lecture at Columbia University in 1988, he went so far as to declare that "reportage literature is not literature" (*baogao wenxue bu shi wenxue*); quoted in Charles A. Laughlin, *Chinese Reportage: The Aesthetics of Historical Experience* (Durham, NC: Duke University Press, 2002), p. 264n1.

in December 1986, he crossed an invisible line. This event led to the demotion of his patron Hu Yaobang from his post as party secretary, and cost Liu Binyan his party membership.[19] In 1988, the author left China to take up a temporary teaching fellowship in the United States, but the eruption of protests in Tiananmen Square in 1989 condemned him to permanent exile.[20] These protests had been inspired in part by the death of Hu Yaobang, and Liu Binyan could not help but decry the bloody crackdown. Liu Binyan was no longer welcome in his home land; he died in the United States in 2005, having never returned to China.

To the end, Liu Binyan fancied himself a champion of the people in the populist (nonauthoritarian) mold of Maoism. He was not afraid to "speak truth to power" and considered it his duty to do so. Like a prosecutor bringing an indictment, he took aim at evildoers and spoke on behalf of the people in their search for justice. Unlike a typical prosecutor, however, his legitimacy derived not from the state, but from the moral authority invested in him by his patrons, sponsors, and readers. Ultimately, this authority derived from his willingness to investigate and disclose the truth.

The Rule of Monsters

Although Liu Binyan was sympathetic to the agenda of legal reform, his analysis began from a very different premise. While the legal response to the Cultural Revolution assumed that the rule of law provided a corrective to the rule of man, the premise of Liu Binyan's dramatic reportage was that the problem of the Cultural Revolution was not the rule of man, but the rule of inhuman monsters. The remedy was to cultivate the rule of true human beings.

Liu Binyan reports on the crimes of metaphorical (not literal) monsters. To Western ears it may sound strange to hear an author evoke in serious tones the specter of alien and deformed enemies of the people. What role could monsters play in a rational inquiry? To a Chinese audience, though, it did not sound odd at all. An array of monsters and demons populate the pantheons of Daoism, Buddhism, and folk belief, staffing supernatural

---

[19] Julia Kwong, "The 1986 Student Demonstrations in China: A Democratic Movement?," *Asian Survey* 28.9 (September 1988), pp. 970–85. Other notable intellectuals expelled from the party included astrophysicist Fang Lizhi, writer Wang Ruowang, and director of the CASS Institute of Marxism Su Shaozhi.

[20] Liu was granted leave to teach one course as a visiting scholar at the University of California in Los Angeles and then take up a Nieman Fellowship in Journalism at Harvard University. David Holley, "Chinese Journalist Punished in Crackdown to Teach at UCLA," *Los Angeles Times*, March 18, 1988.

bureaucracies, holding human transgressors to account, and aiding reflections on justice. No traditional Chinese crime story is complete without some ghost stepping forward to give testimony in the temporal world, or a vivid description of the punishments meted out in some circle of hell. In these stories, nonhuman agents normally intervene to correct injustices in the human realm. Liu Binyan's writing belongs to a modern inversion of that trope, in which human beings prosecute monsters and demons and exorcise them from the human community. This inversion is what Barend J. ter Haar has called the "demonological paradigm" of Chinese socialism; it reached a fever pitch during the Cultural Revolution.[21] For example, Special Court defendant Chen Boda famously ignited the firestorm against "revisionists" and "capitalist roaders" with the incendiary newspaper headline, "Sweep Away All Ox-Ghosts and Snake-Demons." In the fallout of the Cultural Revolution, it remained to define who was or was not to be a member of the human community. Just as the public identified Jiang Qing as the evil White-Boned Demon and the deceased Lin Biao as the incompetent Dog-Headed General, enemies of the people were by definition not truly human. In a recent article, former Minister of Culture Wang Meng reflected back on this aspect of the appeal of Liu Binyan's writing in the disorienting moment of post-Mao transition:

What readers most wanted to understand clearly was this: who are the good guys and who are the bad guys; who are the reformers and who are the conservatives against reform; who are the people and who is out to oppose, suppress, and harm the people ... ; lastly, who are the human beings like you and me, and who are the ox-ghosts and snake-demons, the specters and wraiths, the goblins and ghouls?[22]

Liu Binyan answers these questions and more, by taking the position of a genuine human looking for the truth among dissembling monsters. Liu Binyan's unforgiving delineation of humans and monsters is not concerned with a morally complex "gray" area. The situation in Bin County may be complicated, but the author has no doubts about right and wrong: where there are monsters in human form, they must be destroyed.

The problem and the urgent need for intervention seemed obvious to Liu Binyan, and he could not understand why others failed to recognize the demons who threatened socialism and the people. In his memoir, Liu

---

[21] Barend J. ter Haar, "China's Inner Demons: The Political Impact of the Demonological Paradigm," in Woei Lien Chong, ed., *China's Great Proletarian Cultural Revolution: Master Narratives and Post-Mao Counter-Narratives* (Oxford: Rowman and Littlefield, 2002), pp. 27–68.

[22] Wang Meng, "Yi wei xiansheng yu tade da fangxiang" [One gentleman and his path], in *Wang Meng zizhuan* [Autobiography of Wang Meng] (Guangzhou: Huacheng chubanshe, 2007), vol. 2, p. 132.

Binyan recalled two reasons for choosing to investigate the corruption in
Bin County.

One was the fact that all the culprits were Chinese Communist Party members.
The second was the fact that although Wang, the leader, was already under arrest,
she had not really been discredited – she was still affectionately called 'Old Mrs.
Wang' by the locals, while the people who had helped to uncover the crime were
treated like dirt.... What was the secret behind this strange state of affairs?[23]

As he dug into the history of the county, he came to see that personnel
changes made at the beginning of the Cultural Revolution were like the
rising of an evil moon, a baleful sign of lycanthropy that went unheeded
at the time. "Tian Fengshan was toppled and Commissar Yang rose up;
Zhang Zhixin left the Party and Wang Shouxin entered. In its implications for the CCP organization, were these just insignificant accidents?
Another ten years would pass before such inversions could even be called
into question" (86). Thus the human beings in Liu Binyan's world are
like the naïve Buddhist monk in Guo Moruo's poem, afflicted with blindness, indecision, and trepidation in the face of danger. Take, for example,
Liu Binyan's characterization of the local official in charge of party discipline. He describes her as a well-intentioned person who despised corruption. "But even this good comrade 'failed to see' that she would have
to step forward and struggle in order to 'solve this problem.' She was
self-effacing, meticulous, diligent, conscientious, persevering, and plain-
living; aside from her unwillingness to struggle she fit perfectly the model
of a 'good cadre'" (95).

   Liu Binyan emphasizes that such spinelessness is not an innate pathology, but an acquired malady he calls "the disease of the times" (94).
He muses on another, particularly obsequious party secretary, Liu asks,
"Was he born with this sort of nature? Not necessarily. If we say it's
nature, then how can it be so coincidental, so concentrated, that all three
current members of the County Secretariat are widely known to be 'slip-
pery' and 'treacherous'?" (94). Reflecting on this question in an interview for *People's Literature*, Liu Binyan supposed that the pathology of
corruption had its origins in the external, objective conditions of society:

After the Gang of Four was eliminated, people said that the continued and pernicious influence [of the radicals] was merely an ideological and moral problem.
But where do people's ideological and moral problems come from? The fate of an
individual may rise or fall on subjective will, but we cannot explain the decline of
a larger group of people by looking at subjective factors alone.[24]

---

[23] Liu Binyan, *A Higher Kind of Loyalty*, pp. 133–4.
[24] Liu Binyan, "Guanyu 'Renyao zhijian' da duzhe wen," pp. 99–101.

In this spirit, *Between Man and Monster* builds a sociological explanation for the problem of monsters. Like the legal indictment, the argument of Liu Binyan's literary indictment accords with the principle of requital (*bao*). He argues that the regulating social mechanisms of commensurate exchange have been crippled by an irrational socialist economic system and an irrational mode of traditional interpersonal relations. This compelling argument at the heart of Liu Binyan's very well-known essay has gone unnoticed, or at least unremarked. Let us now open the argument for inspection.

Author as Social(ist) Scientist

The indictment against the Gang of Four was supposed to embody the reformist slogan "seek truth from facts." It presented allegations based on facts for adjudication into a truthful verdict. This simple insistence on truth and facts was a corrective to the unhinged political life of the Cultural Revolution, where "truths" were based on paranoia, distortion, fantasies, and lies. The post-Mao reformers concluded that the crisis of Chinese socialism stemmed from an ignorance – sometimes a willful ignorance – of real social conditions. Liu Binyan agreed. The remedy, he said, was to rebuild scientific knowledge of society:

One serious problem is that we still lack an accurate understanding of our own society. Our efforts to understand it have been suspended for many years. In recent years we have not had any sociology, political science, legal or ethical studies worthy of the name "science." The kind of investigative research that Chairman Mao used to advocate has been shelved for many years. A vast unknown world lies before us.[25]

Liu Binyan set out to explore this world.

Liu Binyan adopted the role of a "socialist scientist." His writings were a finding of facts based on investigation and research, to be used to better socialist society. It was important that the socialist scientist fit the Maoist mold of "Red" and "expert": a skilled cadre member who stays close to the people, having the proper ideological standpoint as well as good technical expertise.[26] Only a writer possessing this special combination of outlook and skills could advocate effectively for the people.

"The investigative research that Chairman Mao used to advocate" was practical field work carried out by party cadres embedded in society. Mao

---

[25] Liu Binyan, "Listen carefully," *RMRB*, November 26, 1979; quoted in Link, *People or Monsters?*, p. 8.
[26] Maurice Meisner, "Marx, Mao, and Deng on the Division of Labor in History," in Arif Dirlik and Maurice Meisner, eds., *Marxism and the Chinese Experience: Issues in Contemporary Chinese Socialism* (Armonk, NY: M. E. Sharpe, 1989), pp. 79–116.

Zedong's 1927 report on the peasant situation in Hunan, which awakened Chinese communists to the potential for rural revolution, exemplifies the tradition. Like Liu Binyan's reportage, Mao's report is a polemic that crackles with fiery language and telling detail. Mao argued that revolutionary strategy and tactics could succeed only if based on empirical knowledge of local conditions and tested in actual practice. Book learning was no substitute for fieldwork, and empty theoretical speculation was inadmissible: "Unless you have investigated a problem, you will be deprived of the right to speak on it. Isn't that too harsh? Not in the least. When you have not probed into a problem, into its present facts and its past history, and know nothing of its essentials, whatever you say about it will undoubtedly be nonsense."[27] This meant that true knowledge was grounded in human experience. "Do [correct ideas] drop from the skies? No. Are they innate in the mind? No. They come from social practice, and from it alone; they come from three kinds of social practice: the struggle for production, the class struggle, and scientific experiment."[28] Liu Binyan subscribed to the Maoist belief in social practice as the root of knowledge, and to the reformers' belief that airy, nonsensical theories had inflicted much unnecessary suffering.

Liu Binyan had experienced this suffering first hand. His years of reeducation in the labor reform camp, sharing hardships with the most miserable of China's rural poor, taught him the vital importance of improving the living conditions of the people. It was obvious to him that the material needs of these communities were strikingly different from the abstract ideals depicted in the radical leadership's propaganda. Faced with the "two diametrically opposed 'truths'" of reality-as-it-is and reality-as-it-should-be, Liu Binyan concluded, "There is no avoiding the fact that objective, material things are more powerful than subjective, spiritual ones."[29] Therefore, the vanguard of revolution was out in the field. Drawing inspiration from his friend and comrade, the pioneering Soviet writer Valentin Ovechkin, Liu Binyan envisioned the investigative

---

[27] Mao Zedong, "Oppose Book Worship" (1930), www.marxists.org/reference/archive/mao/selected-works/volume-6/mswv6_11.htm.

[28] Mao Zedong, "Where Do Correct Ideas Come from?" (1963), www.marxists.org/reference/archive/mao/selected-works/volume-9/mswv9_01.htm. And again: "You can't solve a problem? Well, get down and investigate the present facts and its past history! When you have investigated the problem thoroughly, you will know how to solve it. Conclusions invariably come after investigation, and not before. Only a blockhead cudgels his brains on his own, or together with a group, to 'find a solution' or 'evolve an idea' without making any investigation."

[29] Liu Binyan quoted in Link, *People or Monsters?*, p. 3. On fieldwork methodology in twentieth-century China, see Yung-chen Chiang, *Social Engineering and the Social Sciences in China, 1919–1949* (New York: Cambridge University Press, 2001).

reporter as an "advance scout" for socialism – an autonomous researcher free to roam, feet on the ground, eyes and ears attentive to contradictions and conflicts in society.[30] This is why it was so important for Liu Binyan to be on the scene in Bin County, where he could observe conditions, review local documents, receive visitors, and seek out interviewees. *Between Man and Monster* was his report from the field.

By taking to the field, a news reporter is able to make stronger truth claims than normally afforded to writers of literature. It allows the writer to "intervene into life" in a more direct, timely, and effective way. In this spirit, Liu Binyan has described his reportage literature as a liminal form of writing that is "intermediate between journalism and literature, science and literature, and politics and literature."[31] It must be emphasized, however, that *Between Man and Monster* makes free use of literary devices such as reconstructed dialogue, figurative description, composite characters, psychological insight, interiority, and dramatic irony.

Liu Binyan's presentation of the facts follows a method that Rudolph G. Wagner calls "discovery." This is an appropriate characterization of Liu Binyan's literary approach because it is also a legal term; Liu Binyan's writing puts the evidence before us. The discovery process produces a pointillist picture, a constellation of facts susceptible to sociological analysis, extrapolation, and generalization.[32] This examination of the evidence is no longer restricted to the state or its legal agents (police, prosecutors), and now is joined by the enterprising investigator and his readers. The reporter, and vicariously the reader, then connects the dots to form hypotheses and eventually conclusions.

Wondrous Exchange: The Perversion of Justice

Liu Binyan seeks out the cause for the "great inversion" of humanity and inhumanity, the confusion between man and monster. His essay describes the mechanism in economic terms, as the inverse of rational commensuration. The root of injustice in socialist China is a system of irrational, incommensurate exchange – a system he sardonically calls "wondrous exchange" (86). Liu argues that the corruption of human nature is

---

[30] Rudolf G. Wagner has argued that "*physiologie / oçerk / literarische Reportage / texie* evolved as the documentary counterpart of the fictionalized novel into a minor genre of world literature"; Wagner, p. 373.

[31] Quoted in Michael Duke, *Blooming and Contending: Chinese Literature in the Post-Mao Era* (Bloomington: Indiana University Press, 1985), p. 118. Liu has also described his writing as a *diaocha baogao* ("findings report"); see Doležalová, "Liu Binyan's Comeback," p. 91n41.

[32] Wagner, "Liu Binyan and the *Texie*," pp. 66–7.

further facilitated by the irrational system of interpersonal relationships (*guanxi*) common to both traditional and socialist China. Not coincidentally, one of the most influential theorists of this topic was tribunal member Fei Xiaotong. In his seminal sociological work first published in the 1940s, Fei argues that China's traditional rural society is organized according to a "differential mode of association," wherein each person is the center of numerous, hierarchically differentiated social circles. (This is contrasted with the "organizational mode of association" supposedly characteristic of modern Western society.) The *guanxi* or interpersonal "ties" between people are prescribed by Confucian beliefs about ordering the community through morally binding duties and responsibilities – they are the ligatures of the rule of man. For those tied to the same social circles, *guanxi* may serve a rationalizing function similar to law, reducing transaction costs by establishing trust and predictability.[33] However, because interpersonal relationships are not universal, formal, or isolated from other structures of social power, both Fei Xiaotong and Liu Binyan see them as impediments to building a community that is fully just and rational in the Weberian sense. As a practical matter, the complexity of interpersonal relationships may foster favoritism, cronyism, and illegal economic activities. Corruption creeps in, abetted and concealed by "degeneration of social morality, gradual legalization of criminal activities, and inurement to ethical ruin" (97). Unconscionable monsters rise to power preying on their fellows' sense of humanity (friendship, deference, filial piety, etc.), while those who cannot be cowed into submission and complicity can be demonized and destroyed. And the inversion is complete.

In the context, the villain Wang Shouxin is more than a formidable individual; she represents pernicious "social force" (102). *Between Man and Monster* likens the web of *guanxi* to an electrical force field. As one local informant explains, "In Bin County, it's difficult to sort out the connections between people. It's as if they have a special switch on them: you bump into this one person and it unwittingly trips off a reaction in many other people" (97). For Liu, *guanxi* possesses the deadly and vaguely numinous power of electricity, and it is the complexity and redundancy of the *guanxi* circuitry that generates such paralyzing force. "Relationships between man and man – intricate and complex, layered and overlapping – formed a thick, dense network. The moment any Marxist-Leninist principle or Party policy bumped into the network, it would seize up as

---

[33] Albert H. Y. Chen, "Toward a Legal Enlightenment: Discussions in Contemporary China on the Rule of Law," *UCLA Pacific Basin Law Journal* 17.125 (Fall 1999/Spring 2000), pp. 125–65.

if electrocuted" (98). The coursing power of *guanxi* seems to strike down human beings and to animate inhuman monsters. Like that other quintessentially modern literary exploration of the relationship between man and monster, Mary Shelley's nineteenth-century classic *Frankenstein: A Modern Prometheus*, Liu Binyan's reportage warns modern man against tapping into powerful currents not susceptible to rational control.

Management principles of self-reliance and local initiative meant little effective oversight of state-run enterprises; certainly Wang Shouxin had great latitude in running the coal factory under her control. With cadres allocating scarce goods as they saw fit, good connections (*guanxi*) were essential, and greasing the skids became an indispensable management skill. Wang was able to work her scheme through simple embezzlement and accounting fraud: she kept two sets of accounting books, skimming profits off the sale of coal to use as lending capital. She also appropriated coal and other public property to lend out. In this way she assumed the role of creditor, later reaping repayment in cash, goods, or personal favors. She amassed a monetary fortune for herself, but also a stockpile of luxuries – meat, cooking oil, liquor, cigarettes, sweets – necessary to transact business in lean times. This was business as usual at all levels of government: Jiang Qing likewise rewarded close associates with mangoes, winter melon, eggplant, millet, wine, and desserts.[34] Wondrous exchange was the new norm. "Wang Shouxin's mind was at ease. Everything she did was 'for the public good'" (90). After all, her illegal activities kept the coal factory afloat and her employees fed.

The author notes bitterly that embezzlement of public property soon became the defining feature of the new socialist economy, where public property is confounded with private property: "This kind of 'socialist' exchange does indeed evince a certain 'superiority' over capitalist exchange: neither party to the exchange needs any capital of their own, there is no need to transact any private possessions, there is no risk of loss or bankruptcy, and each side gets what they want" (88). The conflation of public and private property allowed dishonest cadres to accumulate power as a kind of commodity or social capital. "Indeed, in the above examples the trade of goods was realized through the exchange of power," says Liu Binyan (87). Power over the flow of people and goods assumed so much value in this society that Wang Shouxin preferred *not* to be repaid in cash – figuring it better to hold other cadres in debt for favors. In Bin County, as in so many other places, unchecked access to public property had become an exchangeable commodity. The elimination of

[34] See *Liang Xiao zuizheng cailiao* [Material on the crimes of the Liang Xiao group] (Beijing: Liang Xiao Special Case Group, unpublished, 1978), pp. 32–5.

private property should have eliminated such alienating exchanges from socialist society; instead, the power to control the flow of state property gave rise to a new and wondrous exchange, undermining the socialist economy, party discipline, and the legal system. But the exchange had an even more profound effect on the people who practiced it, transforming them from humans into an alienated race of inhuman monsters: "[I]n the midst of these sorts of endless exchanges, Party and state cadres themselves gradually molted into parasites, devouring the fruits of the people's labor and nibbling away at the socialist system. Relations between the Party and the masses deteriorated accordingly" (88). As the parasites filled their bellies on public property, they grew larger and more powerful. Another incommensurate situation arose: what the Chinese call "petty people managing big affairs." Rather than relying on experts and professionals, or on rational legal standards, the corrupted CCP allowed unqualified cadres to take charge of important jobs. The nearly illiterate Wang Shouxin insinuated herself into a leadership position, inducted her riff-raff relatives into the party, and eliminated those honest and talented people who might threaten her hold on power.

It is curious that the two monsters identified so far – Wang Shouxin in Liu's literary indictment and her counterpart Jiang Qing in the legal indictment – are not true "men" in another sense: both happen to be women. *Between Man and Monster* focuses its accusations on a corrupt female cadre member whose appearance, biography, and *modus operandi* all closely resemble Gang of Four leader Jiang Qing. Chinese studies of Jiang Qing invariably detail how this former actress (a title tantamount to prostitute) exploited her sexual relationship with Mao Zedong to seize power. This rumor of opportunistic sexual promiscuity was subtext for the indictment charge that she had former colleagues' houses ransacked to recover personal items dating back to her theater days in Shanghai. Liu Binyan makes a similar charge when he recounts Wang Shouxin's rise to power as County Commissioner Yang's mistress. Indeed, Liu's description of Wang Shouxin's ascension to the political "stage" might easily be mistaken for a description of Jiang Qing: "Wang Shouxin was up on stage, her hair cut short and tucked behind her ears, shiny and black. Although she did not apply so much rouge since declaring herself a rebel, the fair complexion of her face was lively and pretty, and not like that of a forty-five year old woman" (84). Liu Binyan reports, through the mouths of his informants, various misogynistic descriptions of Wang Shouxin's reputation: "old biddy gossip," "hussy," "worn shoe" (i.e., a slut) (84).

His decision to focus on a Jiang Qing–type character and his unblushing use of harsh invective against her suggest that Liu Binyan's "monster" may be a gendered term. Just as monster seems to be the species opposite of man, so too could woman be considered the gendered opposite of man. This reading is supported by the Chinese character for monster (*yao*), which is classified by its component radical, woman. Granted, Liu Binyan insinuates that if women like Jiang Qing and Wang Shouxin are more susceptible to corruption, it is due less to natural endowment than to social circumstances. Monsters are not born, but created by material and social conditions. Specifically, Liu Binyan attributes Wang Shouxin's monstrous character to her to upbringing:

Wang Shouxin's life had been a very bumpy road.... But, relying on her womanhood, a measure of good looks, and a complete lack of shame, she did have some weapons for self-defense and for attack. In this environment she learned to not be shy around strangers and was willing to make contacts with people of much higher social status. She had no fear of hardship, could endure inhuman conditions, and got along well with people living in the very lowest stratum of society. All of these things were very useful to her in the 1970s, when her environment underwent a radical transformation. (89)

Wang Shouxin's biography evokes Jiang Qing's own hardscrabble childhood and ambitious rise to power. Both are depicted as conniving usurpers, who rose to power not on their own merits but rather through feminine wiles. Traditional Chinese historiography reserves special venom for so-called female emperors such as Lü Zhi, Wu Zetian, and Cixi, who despite their demonstrated abilities are vilified for their (alleged) inhuman cruelty, savage ambition, and sexual depravity. With few other opportunities, such women shamelessly grasp the weapons and strategies that society allows them. "It is in the most impoverished and uncultivated soil it seems that the flowers of authority bloom, enticing with their fragrance and color" (85). Liu Binyan seems to recognize that Chinese society denies opportunities to women and then blames them for being objects of desire, yet his own analysis is not able to transcend these misogynistic attitudes. It would be unfair, though, to judge him too harshly; authors cannot be expected to dramatize, let alone illuminate, just solutions to all the deep structural problems besetting their own historical moment.

The Courtroom of History: A Space for Intervention

Liu Binyan's inductive method is to focus steadily and vividly on what may be learned about Chinese socialism from close attention to a particular place. He fashions that place as a privileged location in which to file an indictment in the "courtroom of history." *Between Man and Monster* transports its readers to the coal-mining outpost of Bin County to investigate and press the people's case against corruption. In so doing, the reportage also constructs an imagined social space for inquiry, indictment, and ultimately for. A sense of place is established in the opening passage, where the author sets the scene by describing a change in the physical and social space.[35] The reader can almost see and feel the place where the corruption takes root; the place will color the action with an ominous quality:

> The courtyard of the Bin County Party Committee has always been the center of attention for the people of the entire county. In the ten years or so following land reform, people came and went almost as casually as if they were dropping in on relatives.... After a time, however, the courtyard walls seemed to grow slowly taller and thicker, so that when common folks passed by or popped their heads in for a look, they were touched with mystery and awe. (83)

The description – which is not only physical, but also figurative ("the walls seemed to grow") and psychological ("they were touched with mystery") – creates a palpable sense of the transformation from an inviting and familiar public space to a distant and imposing fortress. The passage then turns to the bodily and sensual experience of the hungry locals in the lean years after the Great Leap Forward: "By the early 1960s, when people who hurried past the main gate could smell enticing odors of meat, cooking oil, and steamed bread wafting from the committee's dining hall, they were left with a bad taste; their mouths would contort into bitter smiles: being an official is not a bad way to live" (83). The immediacy produced by such vivid description is crucial to the effectiveness of reportage. As literary giant Mao Dun explained in his early writing on the genre, a "full and well-rounded" account "bring[s] to life both the environment in which a given event occurred and the characters involved in that event, so that the reader can experience the incident and come to understand, from the specific slice of life in question, the more general point the author is making."[36] Liu Binyan's story is grounded in a real place. His literary skill transports us there to experience the hard reality of life in Bin County.

The writing creates another kind of space, as well – a discursive space shared by the author and his readers.[37] This discursive space has the

---

[35] Reportage is topical in the dual sense of establishing a *topos* (place) and delivering news about current events.

[36] Mao Dun, "On Reportage," quoted in Moran, "True Stories," p. 7. This is an example of the rhetorical device *ekphrasis*; see Janice Hewlett Koelb, *The Poetics of Description: Imagined Places in European Literature* (New York: Palgrave Macmillan, 2006).

[37] Charles A. Laughlin says that reportage functions through the "literary construction of social space"; Laughlin, *Chinese Reportage*, p. 26.

potential to function as an imagined social space where real intervention into politics is possible. In the context of an authoritarian party-state, civil society was too well policed to be considered truly autonomous.[38] But however closed and regulated, the social space was neither immutable nor airless. Competing factional interests opened cracks in the totalitarian party-state edifice, and it was possible to intervene from *within* these liminal spaces. Liu Binyan epitomized this model of change from within. The backing of personal and institutional patrons allowed him the freedom to test the boundaries of public debate, or at least mitigated the risk of doing so. He opened a space for change and invited his audience into that space to participate in the transformation of society. He sought to use his writing not only to advocate for the people in their role as plaintiffs, but also to mobilize his readers to accept their role as judges (*shenpan guan*).

In January 1980, shortly after the conviction of the "Bin County Coal Tyrant" Wang Shouxin and a year before the Special Court verdict, writer Liu Binyan fielded readers' questions about *Between Man and Monster* for the journal *People's Literature*. Asked why he took up the Bin County corruption case in his writing, he responded with some questions of his own. Regarding the Four Cardinal Principles – the historical pursuit of socialism, the establishment of the state as a people's democratic dictatorship, the leadership of the CCP, and the ideology Marxism-Leninism-Mao Zedong Thought – he asked,

What do [these principles] mean in a place like Bin County? After ten years of destruction at the hands of Lin Biao and the Gang of Four, are there no scars still left behind? In a short span of two years [since the arrest of Wang Shouxin] have all the wounds healed over, such that the people no longer need to emancipate their minds, promote democracy, and reflect on central issues of vital interest to themselves?[39]

These were rhetorical questions. Liu Binyan's reportage left no doubt that the wounds of the Cultural Revolution were not yet healed, and he harbored no illusion that recovery would be fast or easy. Figurative demons and monsters had wrought great destruction on the human community, and it would not suffice for the party-state to offer up some ready-made solution. A true reckoning with the past would have to come from the people, thinking with their own minds and acting of their own volition to protect their own shared interests.

---

[38] For a fuller discussion of Chinese reportage and the controversial question of civil society in modern China, see Moran, "True Stories," pp. 388–459.

[39] Liu Binyan, "Guanyu 'Renyao zhi jian' da duzhe wen," p. 100.

The Violence of Interpretation

The concluding section of *Between Man and Monster* quotes at length a "most beneficial and useful" big-character poster.[40] According to Liu Binyan, this poster was affixed to the wall of the Bin County Party Committee building in September 1978, calling for a full investigation of the Wang Shouxin case. Aping the radicals' bluster about "the superiority of Chinese socialism," the poster mordantly praises Wang Shouxin as China's *Sputnik*:

In the twentieth century, in the decade of the seventies, leaders of the Bin County party committee achieved a great success for our nation's social science. They launched as a satellite a member of the "social bourgeoisie" [jargon for the new propertied class under socialism]. Besides providing valuable data for the Chinese Academy of Social Sciences, she can also serve as a reference material for the other socialist nations of the world.... I suppose there must be a scientific explanation for the creation and development of this Wang Shouxin, otherwise she simply could not exist. Dissecting and analyzing this specimen will promote the development of human society and the advancement of the social sciences, and I beseech those with knowledge of the case to report everything to the county and central committees in a "seek truth from facts" manner, so we may summarize the lessons to be learned. (100)

The poster is an indictment and ostensibly not a final verdict – remanding the case for adjudication in a court of law, the court of public opinion, or the courtroom of history. But this profusion of courts is potentially subversive, suggesting that the legal state is neither identical to the people nor the only agent of historical justice. Like a legal indictment of criminality, Liu's social-scientific inquiry into inhumanity initiated a longer process in the search for justice. There remained two more stages before justice could be found: testimony and verdict. To bring all the facts out, people must come forward and tell their stories; to grasp the lessons to be learned, a judgment must be reached.

The writer as advocate initiates the case with an indictment, but then the people must take the stage as the actors in history.[41] The work to be done is indicated in the text's "anticathartic" nature, a lack of narrative

---

[40] The big-character poster (*dazibao*) is a remarkable choice of medium with which to close the story, as it illustrates Liu Binyan's attachment to Cultural Revolution modes of thought and discourse. The big-character poster was one of four great modes of popular democratic expression protected as basic rights in the radical Constitution of 1975 and preserved in the Hua Guofeng regime's conservative Maoist Constitution of 1978 – a right soon expunged by Deng Xiaoping's reformist regime.

[41] Zhang, "Narrative, Ideology, Subjectivity," pp. 212 and 230–1.

closure intended to spur the reader to action and completion.[42] *Between Man and Monster* ends with a remarkably Maoist-sounding call for continued struggle:

The Wang Shouxin corruption case is cracked. But how many of the social conditions that gave rise to Wang Shouxin have changed? Are there not Wang Shouxins of every size burrowed into every nook and cranny – pests who gnaw away at socialism and corrode the Party organization and who even now evade punishment by the dictatorship of the proletariat?

Ah, people, be vigilant! It is not yet time to celebrate victory. (102)

By calling out to his audience, the author invites the reader to respond, to self-identify as a human subject capable of speaking up and effecting change. The author is an exemplar, a courageous and publicly engaged individual encouraging other individuals to take action against ideological distortion and bureaucratic intransigence, to destroy corruption and achieve collective identity as the agents of history – to become human once again. *Between Man and Monster* was both a heartfelt literary indictment and – to the extent that the desired humanization of socialist society has not yet occurred – a troubling model script for future official indictments.

Wang Shouxin faced trial in October 1979, more than a year before the beginning of the Gang of Four trial in November 1980. In tone and procedure, her trial closely resembled several contemporaneous trials of Gang of Four accomplices, held in 1978 and 1979. These earlier trials show Liu Binyan's script as a work in progress and help us understand what a Chinese audience, primed by reportage, expected from a trial of counterrevolutionaries in post-Mao China.

There are several notable differences between the conduct of these earlier trials and the conduct of the Gang of Four trial. To begin with, the earlier trials proceeded on a different legal basis. The new legal codes (*Organic Law of the People's Courts, Criminal Code*, and *Criminal Procedure Code*) did not take effect until January 1, 1980. In some cases, the court offered no specific statutory basis for its verdict.[43] In other cases, the court applied the Regulations for Punishment of Counterrevolutionaries (1951) and Articles 8 and 18 of the state constitution of 1978.[44] The Special Court and later trials, of course, followed the new codes. Another

---

[42] Laughlin, *Chinese Reportage*, p. 275. As Anna Doležalová observes, "Liu Binyan's positive characters do not surrender, but neither do they ever win"; see "Liu Binyan's Comeback," p. 82.

[43] E.g., "Henan sheng Zhengzhou shi zhongji renmin fayuan xingshi panjue shu" [Verdict of the Henan Province Zhengzhou City Intermediate People's Court, Criminal Division Document No. 50] (December 4, 1979), *LSSP*, vol. 2, pp. 387–9.

[44] On stated legal basis for convictions, see e.g., "Zhejiang sheng Kangzhou shi zhongji renmin fayuan xingshi panjue shu" [Verdict of the Zhejiang Province Kangzhou

important difference is that the earlier trials were conducted as "public trial rallies" (*gongshen dahui*) reminiscent of the Cultural Revolution–era mass rallies to denounce counterrevolutionaries. Although the Special Court accommodated a large gallery of more than eight hundred spectators at a time, still this was orders of magnitude less than (to take two examples) the four thousand–seat gymnasium used by the Jiangsu Province Suzhou City Intermediate People's Court for the trial of three defendants on December 28, 1978 or the one hundred thousand–seat stadium used by the Zhejiang Province Kangzhou City Intermediate People's Court for the trial of a single defendant on August 13, 1978. In media depictions these early trials seem much more raucous than the self-consciously solemn atmosphere of the Special Court. Upon announcement of the verdict to the stadium crowd in Kangzhou, for example, the crowd reportedly "erupted in thunderous applause and chanted, 'Resolutely crush counterrevolution!' and 'Struggle to expose and criticize the Gang of Four to the very end!'"[45] Compared with these theatrics, the Gang of Four trial seems a model of judicial decorum.

Wang Shouxin's death sentence was carried out on February 28, 1980.[46] A public sentencing was made at the Harbin Workers Stadium in front of nearly five thousand people. Then Wang Shouxin was driven to the execution ground. Published photographs showed a scene far removed from the lighted velvet majesty of the Special Court. Wang Shouxin – the *ersatz* Jiang Qing – knelt in a snowy, barren field, her arms bound behind her back. A judicial police marksman fired a single bullet into the back of her head.[47] This final act of violence concluded the state's case against Wang Shouxin.[48]

City Intermediate People's Court, Criminal Division Document No. 27] (August 13, 1978), *LSSP*, vol. 2, pp. 453–5. Full text of the "Regulations for Punishment of Counterrevolutionaries" (1951) can be found at http://chinacopyrightandmedia.wordpress.com/1951/02/20/regulations-on-the-punishment-of-counterrevolutionaries-of-the-peoples-republic-of-china/.

[45] "Zhejiang sheng Kangzhou shi yifa kangbu Zhang Yongsheng, panchu Weng Senhe wuqi tuxing" [Zhejiang Province's Kangzhou City arrests Zhang Yongsheng and sentences Weng Senhe to life imprisonment according to law], *Zhejiang ribao* [Zhejiang Daily] (August 14, 1978), *LSSP*, vol. 2, pp. 442–6.

[46] "Da tanwu fan Wang Shouxin fufa" [Corruption criminal Wang Shouxin executed], *RMRB*, February 29, 1980.

[47] "Qishi niandai zuida nü tanwu fan zhixing sixing quancheng" [Full story of the execution of the greatest female embezzler of the 1970s], http://legal.gmw.cn/2013-04/30/content_7482682.htm (accessed February 17, 2014). The unnamed author of the article attended the sentencing and execution as a photographer for *Heilongjiang Daily*.

[48] The criminal trial was followed in March 1980 by a purge of the local party apparatus by the provincial commission for discipline inspection. The commission investigated 153 people from 71 work units implicated in the Wang Shouxin case, meting out penalties

Wang Meng's recent essay criticizing *Between Man and Monster* takes Liu Binyan to task on several counts, most strongly for trying Wang Shouxin in the court of public opinion and for possibly even contributing to her execution:

> It is obvious that no author can judge independently whether a crime has been committed, the severity of a crime, or what the standard of punishment for it should be. To initiate a case and conduct an investigation, to bring an indictment and conduct a court inquiry, to argue the merits and render a verdict – it is not possible for reportage to undertake all of these tasks.[49]

Acting on the moral authority invested in his person through no formal process, Liu Binyan catalyzed a sort of public prosecution. The dark and violent end to the Wang Shouxin case showed just how difficult it could be to draw clear lines between the rule of law, the rule of man, and the rule of monsters.

---

from docked pay to expulsion from the party. The newspapers noted that the purge helped to "ease the people's outrage," "to improve party work style and social morality," and "to strictly enforce party discipline and national law." *RMRB*, March 28, 1980.

[49] Wang, "Yi wei xiansheng," p. 137.

3   Testimony

Although most observers presumed the accused to be guilty, indictment was only the beginning of the Gang of Four trial. The accusations would have to be elaborated, substantiated, and contested before the judges of the Special Court. Following the public reading of the indictment on November 20, 1980, the court recessed for several days to prepare for testimony. Testimony was elicited in two stages, court inquiry and court debate, following the inquisitorial approach found in Japan and much of continental Europe. During the court inquiry, the judges worked in concert with the prosecutors to pursue questions related to allegations raised in the indictment. The judges entered physical and documentary evidence into the trial record and directly examined witnesses and defendants from the bench. Court debate allowed the prosecution to summarize its case in light of the inquiry and also provided oppurtunity for the defendants to address the charges in a more general manner.

Testimony began on Sunday, November 23, 1980. The Second (Military) Tribunal opened its inquiry on that day, and the First (Civilian) Tribunal began the next day. Afterward, the two tribunals worked concurrently, usually with one meeting in the morning and the other in the afternoon. The Special Court kept a rigorous schedule: from November 23 through December 13, the court conducted inquiry nearly every day, Monday through Saturday, from roughly 9:00 AM to 5:00 PM. Court debate, the phase set aside for defense statements and procuratorial rebuttal, commenced on the morning of December 18 and continued for one week. The debate was punctuated by a recess of several days, with an extra session added on December 29. In the space of thirty-seven days the Special Court conducted a total of 42 sessions, heard testimony from 49 witnesses, and examined 651 pieces of evidence.[1] The testimony and

---

[1] "Zuigao renmin fayuan tebie fating kaiting shenwen shi ming beigao ren chushi zhengju zongji biao" [Statistical chart of the presentation of evidence in sessions of the Special Court of the Supreme People's Court of the PRC's trial of the main culprits in the Lin Biao and Jiang Qing counterrevolutionary groups], *TBFTJS*, p. 452.

evidence produced in these sessions would form the basis for the Special Court's verdict – a resolution to the legal case that would also be the post-Mao state's first official verdict on the Cultural Revolution.

To successfully promote its narrative of transitional justice, the trial had to enlist public participation and support. It needed to manifest what Etienne Balibar has called "the projection of individual existence into the weft of a collective narrative."[2] By incorporating witnesses and victims as well as defendants into the process of narrative building, the criminal trial makes them parties to the final, authorized account of the verdict; this participation is essential to the public trial's political power. The social symbolism of the courtroom was reproduced in media reports.

Mass media projected the symbolic courtroom drama to the largest possible audience and magnified its impact. Those not fortunate enough to secure a seat in the courtroom gallery observed the trial through saturation coverage in print media, radio reports, and broadcast television. Throughout the trial, state-run Central China Television (CCTV) broadcast six minutes of highlights from that day's testimony on its nightly *Network News* program and often an hour-long *Special Report* covering the previous day's events. These programs, reaching a viewership of at least two hundred million people, heralded the emergence of television as a new mass medium in China.[3] Television was a major advance over print and sound media as a tool for propaganda, giving credence to the theory that television's small-screen simulacrum of "real-life" social interactions can exert a strong normative influence on viewers. The Gang of Four trial certainly made an impression on its viewers, who received constant audience-response cues from the interactions of the judges, prosecution, defense, and live courtroom audience, not to mention a chorus of reporters and commentators. Group viewing habits further amplified this effect. Watching the trial was a social occasion, because most Chinese people would watch television

[2] Etienne Balibar, "The Nation Form: History and Ideology," in Etienne Balibar and Immanuel Wallerstein, eds., *Race, Nation, Class: Ambiguous Identities* (New York: Verso, 1991), p. 93.

[3] Xinhua wire report, November 19, 1980. CCTV reached an estimated audience of 210 million viewers in 1980 and 270 million in 1981, up from just 18 million in 1975. In 1981, 57 percent of urban households had television sets, compared to less than 1 percent in rural areas. See Jingyu Lu, "The Structure and Function of Chinese Television, 1979–1989," in Chin-chuan Lee, ed., *Voices of China: The Interplay of Politics and Journalism* (New York and London: The Guilford Press, 1990), pp. 73–4. For a brief analysis of televised coverage of the trial, see Mary Farquhar and Chris Berry, "Speaking Bitterness: History, Media, and Nation in Twentieth Century China," *Historiography East and West* 2.1 (2004), pp. 116–43.

on a set shared by their family or even by an entire neighborhood work unit.[4] In this author's experience, almost every Chinese who had access to a television at that time will vividly remember viewing and discussing at least some portion of the trial. This fact attests to how skillfully the state deployed the new mass medium of television, in conjunction with print and radio, to shape personal testimony into public experience, and if possible into a fully shared narrative. This ostensibly rational approach to developing testimony was supposed to satisfy and settle the wounded public's desire for retribution, and to set the nation on the path to recovery.

Inquiry

The inquiry did not simply reproduce the indictment, moving deliberately from one count to the next. Instead, this phase of the trial was characterized by multivocal messiness, choppiness, and even incoherence. While the opening ceremony of the Special Court had been closely scripted and rehearsed, the courtroom inquiry weaved in and out of the indictment, seeming to move pell-mell from charge to charge, making false starts and later tracking back, belaboring some issues while seeming to ignore others. As the inquiry progressed, the neatly wrapped narrative first offered in the indictment unspooled into a tangle of overlapping and competing accounts. The court took advantage of its authority to set arbitrary parameters, and defendants understandably balked at following the court's seemingly haphazard narrative path. Defendant Yao Wenyuan found the process bewildering and unfair: "It's not in the same order as the indictment!?" he protested, "I haven't had a chance to say all the things I planned to say!"[5] Such incoherence marks a phenomenon that legal scholar Robert A. Ferguson has called the "natural proliferation of stories at trial."[6] It is characteristic of testimony, where each side works to undermine one narrative and substitute another. Eventually these proliferating accounts must be settled into a single narrative: the verdict.

In the meantime, however, during this intermediate stage of the trial, courts typically exercise strategies of containment to promote their side of the justice equation and to control what kinds of testimony may be

---

[4] Tumen and Xiao Sike, *Tebie shenpan: Lin Biao, Jiang Qing fangeming jituan shoushen shilu* [Special trial: True account of the trial of the Lin Biao and Jiang Qing counterrevolutionary groups] (Beijing: Zhongyang wenxian chubanshe, 2003), p. 354.

[5] Quoted in Tumen and Xiao, *Tebie shenpan*, p. 211.

[6] Robert A. Ferguson, "Untold Stories in the Law," in Peter Brooks and Paul Gewirtz, eds., *Law's Stories: Narrative and Rhetoric in the Law* (New Haven, CT: Yale University Press, 1996), p. 86.

given in court. The state prosecution employed and unfolded its interpretation of the violent past within the bounds of legal discourse. The
Gang of Four and the other defendants, with their lives at stake, worked
within and sometimes against the strictures of law to tell their own stories about the Cultural Revolution. This regulated push and pull is the
fundamental structure of legal storytelling.

Legal storytelling is both a constrained and constraining discourse.
The law constrains the types of knowledge and experience that may be
articulated and recognized in court: "the law and its institutions establish
form and substance requirements for stories that claim rights and express
needs. Elements include a specified vocabulary for invoking claims, a
paradigm of argumentation, formulae for proof, and narrative conven-
tions for reconstructing individual and collective stories."[7] Other elements include social rituals, cultural mores, professional standards, and
ethical assumptions about causation and culpability. Such constraints
are designed into the very space and protocol of any courtroom, helping
to channel and delimit how stories are told, how evidence is exhibited,
and who is permitted to speak and how.

The *Regulations of the Special Court* provided constraints in the form of
the order in this particular court and in the process of narrative construction that could occur at this trial.[8] For example, Article 2 granted the
president of the court final authority over content, stating, "Participants
in the trial shall require the permission of the President of the Court to
speak, make arguments, or give statements in court. The President of
the Court may prevent speech, arguments, and statements not germane
to the case or intended to unreasonably prolong the trial."[9] Article 5
vested the court with coercive powers to control, admonish, restrain, and
exclude witnesses, arguments, and evidence. Articles 3 and 4 reserved
control over communication and information, limiting the participation
of audience and media. For example, reporters were allowed to take photographs but were prohibited from making audio recordings of the trial.
These regulations gave the Special Court close control over the "text"

---

[7] Christopher P. Gilkerson, "Poverty Law Narratives: The Critical Practice and Theory of
Receiving and Translating Stories," *Hastings Law Journal* 43 (April 1992), p. 872.
[8] "Zhonghua renmin gongheguo zuigao renmin fayuan tebie fating guize" [Regulations
of the Special Court of the Supreme People's Court of the People's Republic of China]
(Passed by the first meeting of the Special Court of the Supreme People's Court,
November 6, 1980), *TBFTJS*, p. 453. On November 13, the Special Court formal-
ized rules for its judicial police. "Zuigao renmin fayuan tebie fating sifa jingcha gongzuo shouze" [Rules and regulations for judicial police work of the Special Court of the
Supreme People's Court] (Court Oversight Group, October [*sic*] 13, 1980), *TBFTJS*,
pp. 457–8.
[9] "Zhonghua renmin gongheguo zuigao renmin fayuan tebie fating guize," p. 453.

of the testimony during its production and the final word on the verdict. Moreover, once the court of the people had spoken, there could be no appeals.[10]

The inquiry proceeded according to a narrative logic of its own, related to but not identical with that of the indictment.[11] Although researchers lack sources to explain how the judges determined the sequence of their inquisition, it is possible to infer the overall narrative arc from a statement written by Special Court judge Fei Xiaotong at the conclusion of the trial:

Imagine that China is a large ship advancing at high speed along a course of socialism but the navigator makes an error and the ship enters hazardous waters, where there are treacherous shoals. At this moment, some of the people in charge of the ship clandestinely get together, form cliques, commit murder, resort to various foul means to seize the ship and turn the several hundred million on board into their slaves.[12]

Generally speaking, the inquiry progressed from top to bottom, according to the status of the victims, establishing the impact of the Gang of Four's counterrevolutionary conspiracy. Despite the inherent drama of the charges, much of the inquiry and debate was tedious and undramatic, with considerable time spent reading documents and depositions into evidence. Testimony detailed and elaborated upon the indictment, filling the courtroom with mounds of evidence and competing voices.

Fei Xiaotong's imaginative metaphor of "treacherous shoals" maps well onto the actual case laid out in the courtroom inquiry. The case begins with Mao Zedong being duped by the Changsha Incident ("the navigator makes an error"). The Gang of Four members conspire ("clandestinely get together, form cliques") to eliminate their moderate rivals in the party. The radicals denounce Premier Liu Shaoqi and persecute him to death ("commit murder"), knocking off high-ranking state and party officials one after another. Through frame-ups, personal attacks, inciting violence, and manufacturing propaganda ("various foul means"), the Gang of Four is able rise to the top ("seize the ship"). In the process, the great masses of the Chinese people ("the several hundred million on board") are forced to suffer. This is the allegorical account of the Cultural Revolution presented by the trial.

[10] Entry for November 6, *TBFTJS*, pp. 71–3.
[11] "Zuigao renmin fayuan tebie fating kaiting shenpan Lin Biao, Jiang Qing fangeming jituan an zhufan gaikuang biao" [Overview chart of sessions of the Special Court of the Supreme People's Court of the PRC's trial of the main culprits in the Lin Biao and Jiang Qing counterrevolutionary groups], *TBFTJS*, pp. 439–51.
[12] Fei Xiaotong, "Yi ge shenpanyuan de ganshou."

The two tribunals of the Special Court opened their separate inquiries into two seemingly unrelated charges. The military tribunal spent its first four days investigating the Lin Biao group's alleged plot to assassinate Chairman Mao in 1971 (November 23, 25, 26, and 27). Meanwhile, the civilian tribunal devoted its first three sessions to the Gang of Four's alleged conspiracy to make slanderous insinuations to Mao about their chief rivals Zhou Enlai and Deng Xiaoping in 1974 (November 24, 26, and 27). The plot to kill Mao was the most sensational and mysterious charge before the court and its significance is obvious. However, the relatively mild slander of Zhou Enlai and Deng Xiaoping at Changsha was a historical footnote compared to some of the other charges against the Gang of Four. Why did inquiry begin with these two charges?

Defendant Wang Hongwen appeared first in the dock before the civilian tribunal and recounted the Gang of Four's secret plot to dispatch Wang to Mao's country villa near the capital of his home province (the incident later became known as the Changsha Incident). Next the court heard the deposition of Mao's personal secretary Zhang Yufeng, who was present at the resultant meeting: "At the conclusion of their talk, Chairman Mao said to Wang Hongwen, 'That's fine. When you get back, confer some more with the Premier [Zhou Enlai] and comrade [Ye] Jianying. Don't get mixed up with Jiang Qing; keep an eye on her.'"[13] The court painstakingly replayed the evidence (including Wang Hongwen's courtroom confession) for each defendant in turn, spending more time on the Changsha Incident than nearly any other charge in the indictment. Yet ultimately this portion of the inquiry served no legal purpose: the incident was determined not to be a crime and does not appear in the verdict. Nevertheless, the inquiry served crucial narrative purposes. Starting with the most compliant defendant and applying his testimony as a fulcrum against the more recalcitrant ones, the court showed a specific instance of the Gang of Four conspiring together ("some of the people in charge of the ship clandestinely get together, form cliques"). Most important, the incident demonstrated Mao's suspicions of Jiang Qing and his support of Zhou Enlai and Deng Xiaoping. It effectively separated Chairman Mao from the Gang of Four.

Next the court focused on the Liu Shaoqi and Wang Guangmei Special Case Group (inquiry on November 28; December 3 and 5). The alleged conspiracy in 1967–8 to fabricate evidence and frame a case against the

---

[13] Entry for November 24, *TBFTJS*, p. 95. For English translation of some testimony on the Changsha Incident, see David Bonavia, *Verdict in Peking: The Trial of the Gang of Four* (London: Burnett Books, 1984), pp. 73–4.

Figure 12. Witnesses testify before the Special Court.
Source: China Pictorial, April 1981, p. 33.

president of the state and his wife revealed the Gang of Four's counterrevolutionary ambitions to make the Cultural Revolution "a change of
dynasties." From there the inquiry looked at the persecution of other
high-ranking party and state officials (inquiry on November 27 and 28;
December 4, 6, 8, 10, and 12). The Gang of Four's witch hunts to identify spies and capitalist roaders in the party extended to numerous top
leaders, including Zhu De, Chen Yi, and the entire Shanghai Municipal
Committee. This showed the wide extent of the Gang of Four's plot.
Several sessions also examined the Lin Biao group's efforts to slander and
defame their rivals (November 29; December 3, 4, 5, 8, 9, 10, and 12).

The next step in the inquiry looked at efforts to mobilize counterrevolutionary forces to incite mass violence (inquiry on November 29;
December 4, 6, and 8). According to the evidence presented, the Gang
of Four organized a secret police force called the You Xuetao Group and
enlisted cronies such as Lu Ying and Kuai Dafu to set off violent clashes,
including the Ji'nan Military Incident and the Kangping Road Incident.
Mass media propaganda fanned the flames. Thus the Gang of Four's
counterrevolutionary plot was put into effect as a mass movement.
Another session on December 13 considered the charge of plotting an
armed insurrection in Shanghai. It was alleged that in order to secure
their succession to power the Gang of Four had established an irregular
military presence in their political base of Shanghai, which they intended
to mobilize in late 1976.

The Gang of Four also stood accused of persecuting the masses of
regular people (inquiry on December 3, 9, and 23). These sessions provided the trial's most emotional exchanges, as victims faced their accusers in open court (Figure 12). One session examined the impact that the
persecution of Liu Shaoqi had on his household staff. Two other sessions
looked at the persecution of well-known personages in the Shanghai art
scene, who accused Jiang Qing of having their homes ransacked and families harassed. On December 12, the court called witness Liao Mosha, a

journalist who had been persecuted for publishing a criticism of Mao in a series of articles called "Three Family Village":

LIAO: I underwent criticism and struggle several hundred times. On top of that [begins sobbing], in the prison they carried out cruel physical maltreatment. All my teeth have been knocked out and I have false ones. It wasn't only I who suffered cruel persecution....

JIANG: Don't pretend! Weren't you in on the "Three Family Village" business? Why –

JUDGE: [shouting] You're not allowed to speak!

JIANG: I had the right to expose you to the Chairman!

JUDGE: [hammering the table and shouting] You're not allowed to speak! Accused Jiang Qing, you're not allowed to speak!

JIANG: If I do, what will you do?

JUDGE: If you go on committing crimes –

JIANG: You're the one who's committing crimes! [Laughs.] You call these renegades and rotten eggs here to speak, and I want to make it quite clear that – [14]

Anytime a witness took the stand, there was a danger that the sober and rational proceedings could devolve into a shouting match.

The preceding exchange illustrates that judges did not produce the legal narrative on their own. The trial was an interactive ritual and a contest designed to appropriate testimony and evidence into the production of a narrative.[15] The court, in reclaiming for the socialist state the special authority to create and interpret historical narratives, opened itself to testimony that it could control only imperfectly. Participants might hope to appropriate the narrative to their own purposes. This helps to explain why the Special Court relied so heavily on documentary evidence and depositions and called potentially volatile witnesses so sparingly. No appropriation was more critical than the enrollment of the alleged perpetrators. If this trial was to bring closure to the events of the recent past, it could only do so by eliciting a defense – at the same time that the trial's structure contained it.

Defense Strategies

The defendants used strikingly different strategies for defense, each with different implications for building the legal narrative. The courtroom drama developed along four distinct trajectories, as the discursive contest

---

[14] Bonavia, *Verdict in Peking*, pp. 21–2. The exchange is redacted from the entry for December 12 in *TBFTJS*, p. 347.

[15] Ferguson, "Untold Stories," p. 95.

played out between prosecution and defense. As two scholars of another trial have put it, the contestants engage in a forensic battle wherein testimony is encoded with normative values and assumptions: "All trial records can be read as an interlocking set of codes. Each side possesses the key to its own code and understands the rules of the game."[16] Within this legal arena, Wang Hongwen, Yao Wenyuan, and most of the other defendants adopted conventional strategies of two kinds: confession and contestation. Conventional strategies observe the rules of the contest. Wang Hongwen, who along with several others adopted a strategy of confession, complied with the prosecution against him and begged the mercy of the court. Yao Wenyuan, by contrast, contested the charges, making full and creative use of the limited rights and opportunities afforded to him by the rules. In contrast, defendants Zhang Chunqiao and Jiang Qing essayed two unconventional strategies: silence and transcendence. Zhang Chunqiao maintained a stubborn silence throughout the entire trial, utterly refusing to engage in any way. His strategy was to refuse to engage directly with the opponent. Jiang Qing, for her part, sought to transcend the courtroom battle through extralegal appeals to the logic of history and revolution. This sort of extralegal textual strategy targeted the vulnerability inherent in the participatory nature of trials. Robert Ferguson, a scholar of how trials create narratives, has observed that "the elaborate give-and-take of legal procedures leaves numerous opportunities for breakdown, and the antagonistic participant, one who also has courage, can achieve a profound level of disruption by violating the fragile decorum and sense of ritual in the sequence of question and answer."[17] With Jiang Qing, it was not simply a matter of ruining the efficacy of the courtroom ritual by disrupting its performance; her defense challenged the very idea of the trial as a legitimate contest. With their unconventional defense strategies, the two most important defendants threatened to evade containment in the state's legal narrative.

The criminal law codes and the procedural rules of the court limited the forms in which a defense could be mounted. The new *Criminal Procedure Law* of 1979 provided that "defendants have the right to obtain defense, and the people's courts have the duty to guarantee that defendants obtain defense."[18] Articles 26–30 enumerated the following rights of the defendants: the right to defend themselves, assisted by counsel

---

[16] Barbara A. Hanawalt and Susan Noakes, "Trial Transcript, Romance, Propaganda: Joan of Arc and the French Body Politic," *Modern Language Quarterly* 57.4 (December 1996), p. 613.

[17] Ferguson, "Untold Stories," p. 95.

[18] *Criminal Procedure Law of the People's Republic of China* (1979), Article 8.

should they wish; the right to choose their own counsel or have counsel designated by the court; and the right to change or refuse counsel during the course of a trial.[19] Article 28 summarized the basic role of the defense in a criminal trial: "The responsibility of the defense is to safeguard the lawful rights and interests of the defendant by presenting materials and opinions on the basis of facts and the law proving that the defendant is innocent or their crime is less severe, or that the defendant should receive mitigation of or exemption from punishment or criminal responsibility."[20] However, the codes were vague about what constituted "legitimate" rights and interests or how these might be preserved. Nevertheless, various procedures granted the defense basic protections, such as the opportunity for defense counsel to meet with the defendant and view case materials (Article 29); the right to view the indictment several days before trial (Article 110); the opportunity to cross-examine witnesses (Articles 36 and 115); the right to view, identify, and comment upon material and documentary evidence presented in court (Article 116); the right to request that the court call new witnesses and evidence (Article 117); and the right to participate in court debate and make a final statement (Article 118). In practice, the defendants were granted limited exercise of these rights.

First, the defendants could not select their own lawyers and they were not offered legal counsel until very late in the process. Original pretrial preparations for a secret trial did not mention defense lawyers at all. Even after appointment of personnel to the Special Court and the Special Procuratorate in March 1980, there were still no concrete plans to include defense lawyers in the proceedings.[21] This meant that the defendants did not have the benefit of counsel during pretrial investigation. Moreover, the defendants were encouraged to make self-incriminating statements without advice from counsel, as laid out in the secretariat's proposal to hold a trial: "3. Begin pretrial preparations. Allow the defendants to speak and defend themselves so we can figure out their thinking and better hit the target; 4. Before the proceedings distribute the indictment to the defendants in hopes that they not only submit to the law but also come forward to give evidence."[22] Defense counsel was eventually

---

[19] *Criminal Procedure Law of the People's Republic of China* (1979).
[20] Ibid.
[21] Tumen and Xiao, *Tebie shenpan*, pp. 254–5. General Tumen was a member of the Special Procuratorate and participated in the pretrial investigation. He says it was Peng Zhen who insisted that the defendants receive counsel.
[22] Quoted in Xiao Sike, *Chaoji shenpan: Tumen jiangjun canyu shenli Lin Biao fangeming jituan qin liji* [Super trial: A personal account of the trial of the Lin Biao counter-revolutionary group], 2 vols. (Jinan: Jinan chubanshe, 1992), vol. 1, pp. 197–9.

assigned from a pool of eighteen veteran lawyers specially selected by the Ministry of Justice in October 1980.[23] This restriction caused some difficulty for Jiang Qing, who initially requested representation by renowned female legal scholar Shi Liang. Jiang Qing's request was refused, and she was told that the eighty-year-old lawyer was too feeble to appear in court.[24] After additional requests were rebuffed, Jiang Qing consented to meet with lawyers appointed by the court, but ultimately declined their services when she learned they would not be allowed to testify or answer questions in her place.[25] Zhang Chunqiao also refused counsel when served the indictment, reportedly growling: "I do not agree to it. I do not accept it. I do not want it. I fundamentally refuse to accept your indictment – what the hell do I want lawyers for? Nonsense!"[26] Wang Hongwen also declined his right to legal representation. Yao Wenyuan, Chen Boda, and several of the Lin Biao group's defendants did accept defense counsel appointed by the court.[27]

The defense counsels were not exactly delighted to be assigned to represent the Gang of Four, as lawyer Han Xuezhang explained in a post-trial interview:

Frankly, when I was appointed to be Yao Wenyuan's lawyer, I wasn't sure I could bring myself to do it. The great crimes and extreme evil perpetrated by these horrible counter-revolutionaries were completely indefensible. However, I realized that as a people's lawyer my duty was to strive for a sound socialist legal system, and this meant that cooperating with the court as the defense counsel in this case

---

[23] Tumen and Xiao, *Tebie shenpan*, pp. 256–7.

[24] Ibid., p. 256. Shi Liang was a prominent Leftist, active leader of the Democratic Alliance (*Minzhu tongmen*) of noncommunist political parties, and the PRC's first Minister of Justice – a post she held until her dismissal as a "Rightist" in 1958. Despite her advanced age, she had recently fulfilled Deng Xiaoping's personal request to review a draft of the Special Procuratorate's indictment in July 1980, and she continued to serve on the Standing Committee of the National People's Congress and as vice-chair of the multi-party Chinese People's Political Consultative Congress.

[25] "Jieshou Lin, Jiang fangeming jituan wu ming beigao de weituo shi ming lüshi jiang chuting bianhu" [Accepting the commission to represent five of the accused in the Lin and Jiang counterrevolutionary groups: Ten lawyers to appear in court for the defense], *RMRB*, November 20, 1980. The attorneys who met with Jiang Qing were Zhang Sizhi, Zhu Huarong, and Fu Zhiren. Zhang Sizhi provides an account of the meeting in Zhang Sizhi, "Wo ceng bei zhiding zuo Jiang Qing de bianhu lüshi" [I was once appointed to be Jiang Qing's defense lawyer], in Wang Fan, ed., *Muji lishi: guanyu dangdai Zhongguo dashi weiren de koushu shilu* [Witnessing history: Oral accounts by great people of major events in contemporary Chinese history] (Changsha: Hunan wenyi chubanshe, 2008), pp. 339–64.

[26] Quoted in Tumen and Xiao, *Tebie shenpan*, p. 261.

[27] "Zuigao renmin fayuan tebie fating he Beijing shi falü guwenchu guanyu wei beigaoren zhipai bianhu lüshi de laiwang xinhan" [Correspondence between the Special Court of the Supreme People's Court and the Beijing Legal Consultancy regarding assignment of defense lawyers to the defendants], *TBFTJS*, pp. 459–62.

would have immense political significance, with an impact even on the reputation of the nation.[28]

The assumption of guilt was strong – again, the preceding are the sentiments of an attorney *assigned to the defense*. The procedural necessity of providing counsel meant that these lawyers would have to contain their personal feelings about the case and perform their collegial function in the court.

The defense faced many obstacles. To begin with, neither Chinese legal tradition nor the new collegial system of the people's courts valued a strong, adversarial defense. Chinese culture has traditionally held a negative view of litigation and a special contempt for the supposedly disingenuous sophistry of lawyers – so much so that imperial law proscribed professional legal representation.[29] For a public poorly versed in modern legal process, defense of the hated Gang of Four might seem like approval of their alleged crimes. The purpose of defense, as stated in the *Criminal Procedure Law*, was "to safeguard the legitimate rights and interests" of the accused – and nothing more. Just as the defendants were reluctant to retain counsel lest they appear too combative, the lawyers were reluctant to appear too vigorous in their defense of counterrevolutionaries.[30] Lawyer Han Xuezhang met with Yao in prison:

Talking with Yao Wenyuan was not so easy. He kept on giving sophistic arguments, singing the same three tunes: one, changing something into nothing; two, changing major into minor; three, changing crimes into errors. He acknowledged errors but not crimes, pleading over and over, "I've made mistakes and want to give a self-criticism. I want to apologize and ask forgiveness from the victims." Then I said to him sternly, "Your crimes are severe. A lawyer's responsibility is to defend on questions of guilt or severity based solely on facts and law; [I] certainly cannot invert black and white, muddling right and wrong."[31]

Han Xuezhang's reluctance was thus understandable. Defending the Gang of Four would be unpopular and difficult, but nevertheless essential. On the other side of the coin, defendants worried that having a lawyer might compromise their pleas for leniency.[32] Further complicating the picture for the defense was the fact that some defendants declined

---

[28] Shang Yiren, "Fang Han Xuezhang lüshi" [Interview with lawyer Han Xuezhang], *Minzhu yu fazhi* [Democracy and legal system] (May 1981), p. 13.

[29] The prohibition on lawyering did not eliminate the demand for legal services, as Melissa Macauley shows in *Social Power and Legal Culture: Litigation Masters in Late Imperial China* (Stanford, CA: Stanford University Press, 1998).

[30] Tumen and Xiao, *Tebie shenpan*, pp. 254–5.

[31] Shang Yiren, "Fang Han Xuezhang lüshi," p. 13.

[32] This concern was voiced by Lin Biao group defendant Huang Yongsheng; see Tumen and Xiao, *Tebie shenpan*, p. 262.

counsel altogether: they would have to negotiate all the unknowns of the trial on their own.

By far the most serious difficulty was time pressure. Defense counsel had little opportunity to review the massive case files before mid-October, and they did not see the indictment until mid-November – just days before the trial was set to begin. There was simply not enough time to prepare proper defenses. The defendants also had little time to review the specific charges against them, notwithstanding their long pretrial incarceration. On the evening of November 17, three days before the opening session, official couriers delivered summonses to the defendants. In a preview of his defense strategy, the intransigent Zhang Chunqiao refused to initial and date the document to acknowledge receipt.[33] Jiang Qing put on a brave face, but the newspapers said it was just an act: her hand shook nervously as she signed and she mistakenly reversed two digits in the date.[34] Just before midnight on November 19, armed guards transferred the defendants from Qin Cheng prison to holding cells at the Special Court in anticipation of the trial the following day.[35] Now it would be well to examine how the defendants deployed four types of defense strategy: confession, contestation, silence, and transcendence.

Confession

A majority of the defendants submitted completely to the mercy of the court. Wang Hongwen set a clear example. Throughout the trial, he freely confessed to numerous crimes, appeared as a witness for the state, and matter-of-factly implicated his alleged coconspirators in the Gang of Four. In court debate on December 20, Procurator Jing Yusong restated the case that Wang Hongwen was a main conspirator in the Jiang Qing group who actively participated in their counterrevolutionary crimes over the course of many years. Moreover, he had taken the lead role in the violent suppression of the masses and in plotting an armed insurrection in Shanghai.[36] The prosecution needn't have bothered. When asked what he had to say for himself, Wang replied, "None of my actions merit

[33] Entry for November 17, *TBFTJS*, pp. 76–9.

[34] "Zai beigao zhushang" [In the defendants' seats], *RMRB*, November 21, 1980.

[35] Jiang Hua and Zuo Mingxing, "Yige ceng kanya Jiang Qing de nübing huiyi Jiang Qing yuzhong rizi" [A female guard recalls Jiang Qing's time in custody], *Wode beijilu* (mymemo.cn99.com), excerpt from *Nanfang zhoumo* [Southern Weekly] (May 10, 1995), http://xingguolian.com/mymemo/article/211.htm, p. 6.

[36] Entry for December 20, *TBFTJS*, pp. 384–5.

defense."[37] After the prosecutor's lengthy closing statement, Wang again threw himself on the mercy of the court. Restating his crimes in his own words, he asked for an opportunity to redeem his humanity:

I acknowledge my guilt, here, before the whole Party, the whole military, and the people of the entire nation. Having fallen so deeply into the pit of the Lin Biao and Jiang Qing counter-revolutionary groups and having committing such serious crimes, I know I will have a long way to go to change my ideological stand. Nevertheless I am determined to change my standpoint and reform myself. It is my heartfelt hope that the government will give me an opportunity to reform myself and become a new person.[38]

Wang's rhetoric exemplified the call-and-response style of Chinese communist "criticism–self-criticism." "Criticism–self-criticism" promised reform of the subject's very humanity through the dialectic of "unity-struggle-unity" or "criticism-struggle-transformation," in which personal salvation was found in submission to and identification with the collective narrative. Willing participation in self-criticism allowed wayward individuals to isolate and renounce incorrect thoughts and opened the possibility, after sanction and reform, of reintegration into the group.[39] In the contest that was the trial, Wang Hongwen's confession was an act of full submission to and identification with his opponent.[40] The defense and prosecution "codes" did not merely interlock; they were the same.

Several other defendants offered more or less unconditional confessions. For example, in court debate on December 18, head of the Central Cultural Revolution Small Group Chen Boda confessed completely: "I plead guilty. I have nothing to say in my defense." Later that day, former Deputy Chief of Staff of the People's Liberation Army (PLA) and Air Force Commander Wu Faxian subjected himself to self-flagellation before the court: "I hate myself. I hate the traitor and renegade Lin Biao."[41] (His defense counsel did point out that Wu had no knowledge of Lin Biao's plot to kill Mao, however.) Defendant Qiu Huizuo, former PLA deputy chief of staff and director of general logistics, bent over backward to get his confession onto the public record: he concluded his

[37] Ibid., p. 385.
[38] Ibid., p. 386.
[39] Li Jie, "Confessions and Denunciations of the Cultural Revolution: The Practice of Everyday Graphomania," unpublished paper.
[40] Through the work of defense counsel assigned to the case (but not acting under Wang Hongwen's direction), he was found not guilty for his role in the so-called Changsha Report. See Tumen and Xiao, *Tebie shenpan*, p. 209.
[41] *A Great Trial in Chinese History* (Beijing: New World Press; dist. by New York: Pergamon Press, 1981), p. 115.

oral confession on December 20 by submitting an unsolicited written confession, as well.[42] Jiang Tengjiao, former political commissar of the PLA Air Force (Nanjing Unit), the only defendant with prior knowledge of Lin's plot against Mao, said in his closing statement: "I have nothing to say in my defense. My crimes are piled high and the evidence is like an iron mountain. I really and truly bow my head in acknowledgement of my crimes, prostrate myself before the law, and will accept whatever punishment is due."[43] In each case, these defendants' narratives became identical with that of the state.

Confession had an important narrative function in traditional Chinese law. For example, an examination of magistrates' reports on criminal cases reveals a great deal of *verbatim* repetition, in which defendant confessions were made identical to accuser and witness statements.[44] In real criminal cases, as well as traditional courtroom dramas and detective stories, it was imperative that the defendant admit his or her guilt to achieve narrative closure. Resolution was unthinkable without a full confession, even if extracted by elaborate physical torture. This is why the whodunit aspect of Western crime dramas was of little interest to Chinese audiences, who expected guilt to be established at the beginning of the narrative, not the end; in the Chinese version of the genre, the dénouement was the torture and confession of the bad guys, often described in grisly detail.[45] This traditional emplotment played out in the Gang of Four trial as well, in the sense that the case had been prejudged in the official media and popular imagination, and was reaffirmed in defendant testimony before the Special Court.

Unlike traditional law or drama, however, the new socialist legal system was supposed to eschew confessions in favor of evidence. This stance fit with the state's new emphasis on objective, empirical knowledge, and rejected the Cultural Revolution practice of coerced confessions. Article 32 of the *Criminal Procedure Code* explicitly forbade the extortion or coercion of confessions, and Article 35 of the *Criminal Procedure Code* decreed:

In judging all cases, stress shall be laid on the weight of evidence and on investigation and research; one should not readily give credence to confessions. When there is only a confession and no other evidence, the defendant should not be

---

[42] Entry for December 20, *TBFTJS*, p. 392.

[43] Entry for December 1, *TBFTJS*, pp. 192–3.

[44] Robert Hegel, *True Crimes in Eighteenth-Century China: Twenty Case Histories* (Seattle: University of Washington Press, 2009).

[45] Robert van Gulik, *Celebrated Cases of Judge Dee; Dee Goong An: An Authentic Eighteenth-Century Chinese Detective Novel* (New York: Dover Publications, 1976), pp. ii–iv and xviii.

considered guilty or sentenced. When there is no confession, but evidence is ample and reliable, the defendant may be found guilty and sentenced.[46]

A confession would not be accepted in lieu of evidence, but neither was a confession necessary to close the case.

Why, then, did Wang Hongwen and the others confess? Their confessions were admissible because they were said to be backed by evidence and to have come voluntarily. It should be noted, however, that the distinction between coerced and voluntary confessions is problematic.[47] The absence of torture does not remove the subtler coercive power of legal interpretation. Robert M. Cover, building on the work of Elaine Scarry, has argued that all forms of defendant cooperation, from outright confession to mere observance of courtroom procedures, occur under the threatening penumbra of penalty. As Cover says, "It is, of course, grotesque to assume the civil façade is 'voluntary' except in the sense that it represents the defendant's autonomous recognition of the overwhelming array of violence ranged against him, and of the hopelessness of resistance or outcry."[48] The potentially violent forces arrayed against a defendant may lead to hopelessness and provide strong motivation to comply with the court, especially when cooperation may increase the likelihood of a mitigated sentence. At least two defendants said they had come to terms with their crimes during their lengthy incarceration, but there is no evidence, either in the available documents or in Wang Hongwen's shallow personality, to suggest he arrived at his confession through a searching self-examination in the manner of Nikolai Bukharin's elaborately conceived philosophical confession presented in his Stalin-era show trial.[49] It is known that Wang Hongwen and the others who confessed avoided death sentences. The defendants' confessions anticipated the verdict by creating narrative closure *in their own words*; thus the final outcome became a shared reality for all – even the defendants.

Contestation

Defendant Yao Wenyuan persisted in a different strategy, one used more sparingly by the other defendants. He partook of the legal contest,

---

[46] *Criminal Procedure Law of the People's Republic of China* (1979).

[47] An excellent discussion of confessions as problematic narratives is found in Peter Brooks, "Storytelling without Fear? Confession in Law and Literature," in Peter Brooks and Paul Gewirtz, eds., *Law's Stories: Narrative and Rhetoric in the Law* (New Haven, CT: Yale University Press, 1996), pp. 114–34.

[48] Robert M. Cover, "Violence and the Word," *Yale Law Journal* 95.8 (July 1986), p. 1607.

[49] Jochen Hellbeck, "With Hegel to Salvation: Bukharin's Other Trial," *Representations* 107 (Summer 2009), pp. 56–90.

contesting in accord with the established "rules of the game." On the morning of December 19, the procurator summarized the case against Yao Wenyuan.[50] Now at last, with the case presented in an orderly fashion, Yao made use of the extensive notes he had written in his defense.[51] He unfolded the wadded sheets he had guarded on his person throughout the trial and began to read: "I still accept those facts that I have already acknowledged and explained. I will not argue those points again."[52] However, he asserted, several of the charges against him were simply not in accord with the facts. In addition to disputing facts, Yao Wenyuan proceeded to demonstrate his understanding of the legal issues at hand. Yao launched a brief litany of arguments, exploiting numerous weaknesses in the special procurator's case. His defense may be summarized as follows: First, he was simply not a member of the Lin Biao and Jiang Qing counterrevolutionary groups. He had no connection whatsoever with Lin Biao. And while it was indisputable that he had manipulated public opinion during the Cultural Revolution, he did so in service of the Chinese Communist Party, not Jiang Qing. Second, the intent of Yao's actions had not been counterrevolutionary. For example, his essays criticizing "capitalist roaders" and "bourgeois democrats" were directed at specific leaders and not, as was alleged, at cadres in all levels in the party, state, and military. The motivation behind certain actions, such as the decision to send Wang Hongwen to report on Deng Xiaoping and Zhou Enlai to Chairman Mao in Changsha, had been totally mischaracterized in the indictment. Third, many of the alleged crimes were actually political errors. Yao was merely following the orders of superiors to carry out actions that seemed ideologically justified at the time. Fourth, there was often no demonstrable casual connection between Yao's political writings and the violent events that followed. Finally, in those instances where Yao was culpable for crimes, he played a secondary role to the ringleaders. For example, Yao admitted a degree of responsibility for slandering the mayor and members of the Shanghai Municipal Committee in 1968, but it was his superior, Zhang Chunqiao, who had played the decisive role in the persecution to death of committee member Chen Diqiu.

---

[50] Full Chinese text of the Special Procuratorate's closing statement against Yao Wenyuan can be found in *LSSP*, vol. 1, pp. 83–5.

[51] After receiving the indictment, Yao Wenyuan began to plan a defense, complaining: "To say that I'm one of the ten main culprits of the Lin and Jiang counterrevolutionary groups – to tie me in with Lin Biao! – I can't let that pass. I won't conceal my point of view. I'm in the midst of writing some things down; I'll mainly rely upon myself for my defense." Quoted in Tumen and Xiao Sike, *Tebie shenpan*, p. 211.

[52] "Special Court Commences Court Debate on the Facts of Yao Wenyuan's Crimes," Xinhua News Agency wire report, December 19, 1980.

The lawyers for both sides spoke next.[53] Lead defense counsel Han Xuezhang argued that the court should distinguish between ringleaders, main culprits, and accomplices, noting the specific role and function of each party to the conspiracy. She depicted Yao Wenyuan as one of several main culprits acting under the direction of their ringleader, Jiang Qing.[54] Procurator Wang Wenlin's rebuttal asserted the value of evidence over disputation: "The facts are very clear. In his defense speech defendant Yao Wenyuan is playing with ornate speech, flowery words, and foxlike sophistry to deny criminal liability. He is denigrating and abusing his legally provided right to defense."[55] When it came time for Yao Wenyuan to make a final statement, he said, "What I had originally planned to talk about are the points I've just covered. I'm not prepared to make a hasty statement right now.... If I have further comments after reading the court records, then I will add them in an addendum. I have nothing more to say here."[56] With that, his defense concluded.

Yao Wenyuan's defense was competent and multifaceted. He focused on causality and intent, the two aspects of his alleged crimes most difficult to establish. He introduced mitigating factors, accepting responsibility for minor crimes while disclaiming responsibility for major crimes. Lastly, Yao's references to the "unprecedented historical circumstances" of the Cultural Revolution appealed to the confusing distinction between errors and crimes: Yao had made errors in revolutionary strategy that violated the objective laws of historical development, but he had not committed crimes in violation of any existing criminal law. Yao Wenyuan understood the rules of the game and mounted the best defense he could within those constraints.

Two other defendants argued their cases on similar grounds. In three sessions spanning December 18–20, former General Chief of Staff of the PLA Huang Yongsheng denied being a "prime culprit" in the Lin Biao group, saying he did not know about, much less participate in, many of Lin Biao's counterrevolutionary activities.[57] (In response, the

---

[53] The complete defense statement by Han Xuezhang and Zhang Zhong was reprinted in *Zhongguo fazhi bao* [Chinese legal system], December 26, 1980.

[54] To prove her argument, Han Xuezhang pointed out three more examples in which Yao had played a limited role: Yao Wenyuan did not help Zhang Chunqiao and Wang Hongwen plan for an armed uprising in Shanghai; Yao helped slander the Shanghai Municipal Committee, but it was Zhang Chunqiao who played the major and decisive role in the persecution to death of committee member Chen Diqiu; and Zhang Chunqiao bore main responsibility for the suppression of demonstrators in Ji'nan in May 1967.

[55] Entry for December 19, *TBFTJS*, p. 379. That night Xinhua News Agency wire reports published Procurator Wang Wenlin's detailed refutation of Yao's defense.

[56] Ibid., p. 380.

[57] *A Great Trial in Chinese History*, p. 117; Entry for December 18, *TBFTJS*, p. 375.

prosecution noted it was Huang's phone call that tipped off Lin Biao to the fact that the plot against Mao had been discovered.) In court debate on December 22, former Deputy Chief of Staff of the PLA Li Zuopeng admitted his role in framing leaders such as He Long, Ye Jianying, and Luo Ruiqing, as well as in persecuting top navy officials, but he also noted that the historical circumstances surrounding these crimes were "complicated."[58] (The available records do not elaborate on this claim.) Li also argued that he altered the order from Zhou Enlai to keep Lin Biao's plane grounded, thereby allowing the would-be assassins of Mao to escape; however, he maintained that he had not been involved in the planning of Project 571. Yao Wenyuan and the others all conceded at least some of the charges against them, and their defense counsel, working collegially with the court, acknowledged the strength of evidence against them. Although their stories diverged from the official account in some respects, they defended themselves according to the codes of law and the rules of the court.

Silence

Defendants such as Wang Hongwen and Yao Wenyuan used confession and contestation in hopes of avoiding or mitigating punishment. Their narrative strategies, whether cooperative or confrontational, relied on weaving their own stories into the fabric of the larger trial narrative. The two most important defendants, Jiang Qing and Zhang Chunqiao, adopted strategies that rejected the trial narrative whole cloth.

Defendant Zhang Chunqiao remained silent throughout the entire trial. He simply stood or sat in a shabby padded jacket, his head tilted, unshaven, mouth agape, eyelids sagging.[59] Despite repeated assurances from the court that his rights would be preserved, and increasingly impatient prodding either to assume responsibility for his crimes or to contest the evidence against him, Zhang refused to speak. The Special Court stressed to its mute defendant that the need for confessions was obviated by the presentation of factual evidence.[60] The reason for Zhang's silence was cause for much speculation. The official Xinhua News Agency posed some possibilities in its report on Zhang's first day of testimony:

Through one hundred minutes of court inquiry today, Zhang Chunqiao kept his lips sealed and did not speak a single word. Was it that he had no answer, or

---

[58] *A Great Trial in Chinese History*, pp. 122–3.

[59] Description following Wu Xiuquan, *Wangshi cangsang* [Vicissitudes of bygone days] (Shanghai: Shanghai wenyi chubanshe, 1986), p. 317.

[60] Entry for November 27, *TBFTJS*, p. 132.

that he refused to answer, or that he tacitly acknowledged his crimes? Whatever his motivation, he cannot change the iron-clad facts found in depositions and testimony. Whatever ruse he plays, in the end he cannot escape the people's vast net of law.[61]

People's Daily took a different angle, opining that there was simply nothing Zhang *could* say to answer for his crimes.[62] Others suggested he was resigned to the inevitability of a guilty verdict and a death sentence, as "dead swine fear not the scalding pot" (*sizhu bu pa kaishui tang*).[63] Speculation that Zhang was prepared to die were further encouraged by his poor appearance and rumors that he suffered from cancer.[64] Another possibility, not entertained in the official press, was that Zhang was no longer competent to testify: perhaps four years in prison had addled the old man's mind. Such a suggestion would have undermined the credibility of the proceedings, and there is good reason to doubt it: an important coconspirator in the case, Ma Tianshui, already had been declared legally incompetent to stand trial. In the end, Zhang Chunqiao's silence was deemed unimportant, because his cooperation was not necessary for legal resolution of the case.

Nonetheless, it is possible to detect efforts to make Zhang Chunqiao "speak" through his silence. Chief Judge of the Second Tribunal Wu Xiuquan was quick to point out in his memoirs that he observed (by closed-circuit television) that Zhang Chunqiao furtively read the indictment in his prison cell.[65] The implication was that Zhang's disinterested silence was an elaborate and deliberate ruse, an expressive act. Another example is a newspaper account of Zhang's court appearance, entitled, "The Face of Grand Conspirator Zhang Chunqiao," which explains how Zhang's "hideous face" (*zhengning zuilian*) "spoke" for itself.[66] The prosecution's closing argument also tried to make the silent Zhang speak in his own words, reading from evidence the defendant's prior statements of counterrevolutionary intent: "the Great Proletarian Cultural Revolution, from beginning to end, is a seizure of power"; "from the

---

[61] Xinhua wire report, November 27, 1980.

[62] "'Gaichao huandai' zhi meng de pomei" ['Change of dynasty' dream destroyed], *RMRB*, November 28, 1980.

[63] This phrase was widely used. See caption to photograph on tenth page of front materials to Xiao, *Chaoji shenpan*, vol. 1.

[64] Rumors of Zhang's cancer appeared in a Reuters report filed December 20, 1980.

[65] Wu Xiuquan, *Wangshi cangsang*, p. 314.

[66] The expression draws its imagery from the *zheng*, a legendary creature described in the classical bestiary *Shan hai jing* as an animal that "resembles a red leopard with five tails and a single horn. It makes a sound like stones striking together." Richard E. Strassberg, ed. and transl., *A Chinese Bestiary: Strange Creatures from the Guideways through Mountains and Seas* [A translation of the *Shan hai jing*] (Berkeley: University of California Press, 2002), p. 110.

lowest levels to the Central Committee, including the power of the Party, of the government, of finance, of culture, and other power"; his boast that the Cultural Revolution was "a change of dynasty"; and his complaint of older cadres that "there's nothing good about them" and that "none will be spared."[67] After reviewing the rest of the evidence, the prosecutor concluded:

> The above-mentioned facts all show that Zhang Chunqiao personally committed counter-revolutionary crimes, under odious circumstances and with serious results, visiting profound disaster on the nation and the people.... Through the course of the trial his attitude has been recalcitrant, and in the face of overwhelming evidence he has refused to accept criminal responsibility. We request the court to punish him severely.[68]

Twice, Chief Judge of the First Tribunal Zeng Hanzhou reminded Zhang of his right to make a statement or mount a defense. After two minutes of silence elapsed, the Chief Judge announced: "The defendant Zhang Chunqiao has not made a statement or a defense. Let it be noted in the records."[69] The prosecution had nothing further to add, and so the chief judge announced: "The court debate is concluded. Zhang Chunqiao, you have the right to make a final statement." None was forthcoming. Finally, the chief judge announced, "The defendant Zhang Chunqiao has made no final statement. Let it be noted in the records. Defendant Zhang Chunqiao, you will await announcement of the verdict. Take Zhang Chunqiao away. Court is adjourned."[70]

The official press saw fit to speculate on the motive for Zhang Chunqiao's silence, and the historian may also hazard a guess. Zhang Chunqiao seems to have used his silence to open a space – a sort of ideological no man's land – from within the script. Unlike either traditional Chinese justice or the Maoist confessional ritual of self-criticism, the new legal system claimed no need for the defense to compete or submit. The recalcitrant defendant leveraged the new system to remove a time-honored structural element from the trial's apparatus of narrative construction. Invoking a right to avoid self-incrimination can be jarring enough in the United States, where such silence is constitutionally protected; in a Chinese cultural context, where the defendant is expected to accept the judge's authorized account, such calculated silence was downright alien and unnerving. Faced only with silence, "judges are left

---

[67] *LSSP*, vol. 1, pp. 80–2; Entry for December 20, *TBFTJS*, p. 386; *A Great Trial in Chinese History*, p. 109.
[68] Entry for December 20, *TBFTJS*, p. 387.
[69] Ibid.
[70] Ibid.

with naked power in the place of consensual, validating process," says Ferguson, and Zhang Chunqiao's silence exposed the violence behind the polite rituals of the court.[71]

Transcendence: Beyond Law and Heaven

In contrast with Zhang Chunqiao's silence, Mao's wife Jiang Qing put forth an active and energetic defense. She effectively seized control of the narrative even as it was taking shape, interrupting the proceedings with disruptive comments, troubling questions, and incisive sarcasm. Most important, Jiang Qing attempted to elude the legal process of narrative containment by making an appeal from *within* the legal narrative to an authority *without*. In so doing, Jiang Qing dared to violate the most fundamental rule of the game, which is to win the agreement of the judge. Her defense testimony introduced an entirely different ideology or system of belief – a different conception of justice. The result was not merely disagreement, but antinomy. Defense and prosecution codes could *not* interlock but instead could only grind down or spin free from each other. Antigone's appeal to divine law over human law is the classical example in the Western tradition, as the irresolvable clash between normative systems forms the basis for tragedy. Likewise Joan of Arc's appeal to religious authority, which carried no legal weight but nevertheless impressed the pious public. To be successful, such strategies must engage those in the audience who share the key to that other code – in this case, those true believers willing to see Jiang Qing as a martyr to an unjust law. Only then does antinomy threaten to destroy the totality of the dominant code.

The potentially devastating effectiveness of this strategy had much to do with the new medium, television. The new television medium opened possibilities to defendants with few legal rights. An experienced actress, Jiang Qing seemed to understand the new form best of all. Unlike the pantomime and exaggerated emotions of the traditional stage, television is "a medium of faces, close-ups, reactions, domestic interiors, with human emotions being explored through the facial muscles."[72] With tidy clothes and shiny hair, she appeared nonchalant – even confident – in the courtroom.[73] She listened attentively to the indictment, but blunted damaging testimony by claiming to have trouble hearing the strongest

---

[71] Ferguson, "Untold Stories," p. 95.
[72] Anthony Smith, "Introduction," *Television: An International History*, 2nd edn. (Oxford: Oxford University Press, 1998), p. 5.
[73] Wu, *Wangshi cangsang*, p. 317.

accusations. When she spoke, Jiang Qing exuded confidence on the stand, breaking from the script to tell a story very different from that of the indictment.

She described a Cultural Revolution fostered by Chairman Mao and carried out by many of the same leaders persecuting her now. She believed herself to be the defender of the correct political line, originating from Mao. "Everything I did, Mao told me to do. I was his dog; what he said to bite, I bit."[74] She was the target of a veiled attack on Mao, the victim of an ancient historiographical tradition of vilifying women in power.[75] "Arresting and trying me is a defamation of Chairman Mao Zedong," she said.[76] If the trial was conceived as a platform to denounce the Gang of Four, Jiang Qing was nevertheless determined to use that stage to present her final soliloquy. The Special Court's published transcripts gloss over her most outrageous courtroom antics, blandly noting that the defendant disrupted the order of the court. Ross Terrill's biography *Madame Mao: White-Boned Demon* (1984) characterizes her behavior as a final dramatic performance:

She did not look as if she belonged in the pinched, staged ritual that began to unfold in the Ceremonial Hall. She seemed to be appearing before a crowd of millions in Tiananmen Square, watching for cues, alert to the camera's position, making an appeal to some absent, suprapolitical force that could acknowledge her for what she believed herself to be.[77]

The intended audience for Jiang Qing's defense was not the legal authority of the bench, but rather the viewing public – or perhaps more abstractly, a personified History. Jiang Qing's deftly executed apostrophe to History substituted for direct address to the court.[78]

Even when Jiang Qing did address the bench directly, it was to shame the judges before the wider audience. For example, on the question

---

[74] Ross Terrill, *Madame Mao: The White-Boned Demon*, revised and expanded edn. (Stanford, CA: Stanford University Press, 1999), p. 15.

[75] For an analysis of Jiang Qing's courtroom testimony as a gendered performance, see Chen Xiaomei, *Acting the Right Part: Political Theater and Popular Drama in Contemporary China* (Honolulu: University of Hawai'i Press, 2002), pp. 215–34.

[76] Quoted in Xinhua wire report, December 29, 1980, and reprinted in *Zhonggong shenpan "Lin Jiang jituan" an* [Communist China's trial of the Lin and Jiang groups], 2 vols., Zhonggong yuanshi ziliao xuanji zhuanti lei 1 (Taibei: Zhonggong yanjiu zazhi shehui, 1981), vol. 1, p. 163.

[77] Terrill, *White-Boned Demon*, p. 15.

[78] "The diversion of our words to address some person other than the judge" is Quintilian's classical definition of apostrophe (*aversio*); see Douglas J. Kneale, "Romantic Aversions: Apostrophe Reconsidered," *ELH* 58.1 (Spring 1991), p. 143; Jonathan Culler, "Apostrophe," *diacritics* 7.4 (Winter 1977), pp. 59–69.

of persecuting party leader Liu Shaoqi to death, she met charges with countercharges:

> Most members of the present Central Committee of the Party, and most of our government leaders, including you, [Chief Justice] Jiang Hua, *competed* with each other to criticize Liu Shaoqi. If I am guilty, *how about you all?*'
> "Shut up, Jiang Qing! *Shut up!*'" the judges yelled back in chorus.[79]

Jiang Qing's arguments sought to reframe the legal case against the historical context of the Cultural Revolution. She appealed to a morality and logic that transcended the bounds of statutory law. The Cultural Revolution radicals had operated in a revolutionary context that challenged the very definitions of law and criminality: Who (she asked) could retroactively apply legal jurisdiction to a revolution?[80] Moreover, Jiang Qing reminded the audience that all of society had taken part in the Cultural Revolution. Who, recalling their own shameful deeds or unacknowledged suffering, could happily pass judgment and then move on? By turning away from the bench, Jiang Qing challenged the Special Court's authority to declare a definitive narrative resolution. It is unlikely that her extralegal authority won over new converts, but it did put the project of closure at risk.

The formal moment for defense came on the morning of Wednesday, December 24. Special Procurator Jiang Wen gave a lengthy prosecution statement, recounting the case against Jiang Qing and pressing for a harsh sentence.[81] He cited her conduct before the court as an aggravating factor:

> In court, defendant Jiang Qing has obstinately stuck to her counter-revolutionary standpoint, saying "I don't know" or "I don't remember" or passing blame around, refusing to acknowledge her crimes. She has even gone so far as to publicly slander national leaders in court, to attack and vilify the court and its personnel, to disrupt court procedures, and to continue committing new offenses.... Her danger to the nation and the people is especially grave and the circumstances of her crimes are especially odious, and she should be punished severely in accordance with Article 103 of the Criminal Code.[82]

Now it was Jiang Qing's turn to make her case. Published records omit the content of her statement, because it fell "outside the scope of the trial." But the records note that "in her defense statement, Jiang Qing

---

[79] Terrill, *White-Boned Demon*, p. 382.

[80] Li Gengchen, "Rebutting Jiang Qing's Theory of Legal Illegality" [*Chi Jiang Qing de fanfa hefa lun*], *JFRB*, December 28, 1980.

[81] Jiang Wen, "Dui beigaoren Jiang Qing suo fan zuixing de fayan" [Statement on defendant Jiang Qing's criminal conduct] (December 24, 1980), *LSSP*, vol. 1, pp. 67–70.

[82] Ibid., p. 70.

did not defend herself against the criminal accusations in the Special Procuratorate's indictment, and instead used the opportunity to continue her assaults on national leaders."[83]

The presiding judge, Associate Justice and Chief Judge of the First Tribunal Zeng Hangzhou, warned Jiang Qing to stick to the case at hand in her final statement. As usual, Jiang Qing got the best of the exchange, making a mockery of the scene. A testy exchange ensued, as reported by Jiang Qing biographer Ye Yonglie:

JIANG QING: Go ahead and name my crimes by the basis you have set. I've listened to your trial. This is just your way of dragging me off to Tiananmen Square for a public hearing and execution by firing squad!

ZENG HANZHOU: Whether or not you are executed is a matter the court will judge based of the facts of your crimes and according to the law.

JIANG: Don't bother puffing yourself up to strike a pose. Without me as your prop, this drama of yours would never come off! You should have the courage to ask your director backstage to come out front. I'd like to confront him face to face.

ZENG: I'm warning you! I won't allow you to denigrate the law....

JIANG: I'm beholden to no law, human or divine. I'm not afraid of you! I wasn't afraid of Liu Shaoqi or Lin Biao, how could I be afraid of you?

Several times Jiang Qing described herself as "a monk with an umbrella" (*heshang dasan*).[84] This curious image refers to a shaven-headed monk seeking shelter from the rain, with the rejoinder: "without hair or sky" (*wufa wutian*) – a pun meaning "without human or divine law." The newspapers had used the rejoinder to describe the Cultural Revolution as a period of lawless chaos, but Jiang Qing adopted the symbolic role of the religious devotee in the initial phrase, signifying that she was forsaken by justice. How, she asked, could she be held to anachronistic legal and moral standards that had not prevailed (and indeed had been emphatically renounced) under the iconoclastic historical conditions of the time? She was not the White-Boned Demon of legend, but the pious monk – or better yet, at one with Mao as the Monkey King:

ZENG: The court has investigated a great many facts and given you ample time for defense, but instead you use the court to spread your counter-revolutionary propaganda....

JIANG: *You* are the counter-revolutionary!

ZENG: You are in contempt of court; that is yet another crime. . . .

JIANG: You can do nothing more than kill me. I am the Monkey King. However many heads you lop off, I just grow another.

---

[83] Entry for December 24, *TBFTJS*, p. 407.

[84] Jiang Qing used this phrase several times; see, e.g., entry for December 29, *TBFTJS*, p. 412.

ZENG (ringing the bell): If you disrupt the court again, you will forfeit your right to a defense.

JIANG: I'm sorry; may I be excused to use the bathroom?

ZENG: Take the defendant to use the bathroom.

JIANG: Never mind, I don't have to go. I'd like to read you something I wrote called "My Viewpoint." I suppose you have no objection?[85]

Her "viewpoint" was a two-page poem written in pencil; the original document has not been made available, but we can be sure its content was not a legal argument. When asked if she had anything more to add, Jiang Qing simply replied, "I'm exhausted; let's end here."[86]

It did not end there, however. Her defense had been sufficiently disruptive to cause a hasty cancellation of television coverage that night, and the newspaper accounts suddenly turned cursory. Though the full content of her defense has not been published, its substance can be inferred from the extra session of court debate scheduled five days later, on the morning of Monday, December 29. The Special Procuratorate issued a second statement, wired across the country by the official Xinhua News Agency under the title "Refuting Jiang Qing's Shameless Sophistry." The three main headings of this rebuttal indicate just how successful Jiang Qing was at shifting the conversation from legal disputation to the larger context of the Cultural Revolution: "Jiang Qing's vain attempt to project her own crimes onto the person of Chairman Mao is absolutely untenable"; "Jiang Qing calling herself a representative of the people is a public insult to one billion"; and "Jiang Qing counting herself an anti-Lin Biao hero is an outrageous lie."[87]

Jiang Qing's defense seemed to be addressed to history, as if a personified History might be the judge that would somehow vindicate her.[88] Jiang Qing's apostrophe only underscored that the court was historically situated and ideologically charged. Her narrative of the Cultural Revolution was not well contained, and defied incorporation into the authorized account. She belonged to a different, jarring world that still had a word

---

[85] Ye Yonglie, *Jiang Qing zhuan* [Biography of Jiang Qing], Sirenbang quan zhuan (Urumqi: Xinjiang renmin chubanshe, 2000), pp. 880–1. Ye Yonglie provides a few lines of the poem, but with no original source given. Jiang Qing, "Wo de yi dian kanfa" [My viewpoint] (dated October 26, 1979, revised October 9, 1980).

[86] Entry for December 24, *TBFTJS*, p. 408.

[87] "Bochi Jiang Qing wuchi guibian" [Refuting Jiang Qing's shameless sophistry], Xinhua wire report reprinted in *Zhonggong shenpan "Lin Jiang jituan" an*, vol. 1, pp. 160–8; *LSSP*, vol. 1, pp. 70–8.

[88] "[Apostrophe] takes the crucial step of constituting the object as another subject with whom the poetic subject might hope to strike up a harmonious relationship" (Culler, "Apostrophe," pp. 63–4).

or two to say. It would be overstating the case to say that Jiang Qing's appeals won over her audience. She remained a wildly unpopular figure. But anecdotally, many admit a begrudging respect for her defiant stand and acknowledge the validity of her claims: the Cultural Revolution was not perpetrated by just a few carefully selected ringleaders without the complicity of others, and it could not be settled in a court of law.

Settling Accounts: Justice as Containment

The court's final containment tool was ideological. To gain some purchase on this aspect of the state's narrative strategy, it is instructive to apply to the trial testimony Fredric Jameson's notion of narrative as a "strategy of containment." In *The Political Unconscious*, Jameson sets forth a synthesis of literary criticism, Marxist theory, and psychoanalysis that describes how narrative may operate on multiple levels at once. For Jameson, literary theory tells us that the creation of coherent narratives must involve a flattening of reality.[89] This is not only because social reality is irreducibly complex, but also because it is rife with contradictions. Specifically, from a Marxian perspective, social reality is a nightmare of human suffering and alienation founded on an exploitative mode of production and its attendant contradictions. Psychological repression is an unconscious defensive mechanism to block out this unbearable knowledge that would otherwise threaten to crush the psyche.[90] Jameson then applies these observations to his study of nineteenth-century novels to show how fictional accounts employ symbolic "strategies of containment" to magically resolve and repress real contradictions in the societies they describe. Whereas Jameson confines his argument to fiction, his intervention is all the more applicable to the narratives produced by courts, where symbolic resolution is accompanied by the material resolution of an individual case. Legal trials, like literary works, also attempt symbolic resolutions to real social problems. This is especially true of transitional justice trials. Following episodes of mass violence, in order to sooth the lingering

---

[89] Fredric Jameson, *The Political Unconscious: Narrative as a Socially Symbolic Act* (Ithaca, NY: Cornell University Press, 1981); see also William C. Dowling, *Jameson, Althusser, Marx: An Introduction to "The Political Unconscious"* (Ithaca, NY: Cornell University Press, 1984).

[90] On the relationship between, repression, narrative, and identity, see Ian Hacking, *Rewriting the Soul: Multiple Personality and the Sciences of Memory* (Princeton, NJ: Princeton University Press, 1998).

trauma of past horrors, legal responses may blot out the underlying social contradictions that give rise to conflict.

As the psychological metaphor suggests, such repression can be a deeply emotional – and not entirely rational – process. While law may claim to be a reasoned and objective field of discourse, the legal process makes room for emotional testimony, impassioned pleas to the bench, and the sympathy or disdain of the audience. As Martha Nussbaum has observed, "Law without appeals to emotion is virtually unthinkable.... The law ubiquitously takes account of people's emotional states."[91] In societies recovering from mass violence, where all sorts of unbearable contradictions have recently surfaced, the prospect of containment enjoys particular psychological appeal and grants political power to those who promise to deliver it. Postconflict societies are precisely the ones most likely to seek sweeping resolutions to the nightmare of history. The need to contain raw and festering realities demands recourse to powerful and binding narratives. This explains why legal narratives have been pressed into service, again and again, for duties they are ill-equipped to perform: retribution, societal healing, and historical reckoning. This perspective sheds light on the push and pull in the inquiry and the debate phase of the trial of the Gang of Four where argument of fact acquires emotional depth for the defendants and for the society. There is a persistent, roiling undertow of ideological conflict beneath the surface of the Gang of Four trial's narrative.

In the Gang of Four trial, narrative repression also had a sublimating function. The aesthetic of the sublime, with its pervasive confusion of the human and the transcendent, was a central motif of Mao's revolution.[92] Not surprisingly, it also became a critical motif in the trial. Part of the purpose of the back and forth of the testimonial phase was to narratively contain the legacy of Mao's revolution. In the course of channeling individual retellings of the Cultural Revolution into a collective narrative, the trial was meant to manage the trauma of the past, by harnessing the potentially destructive emotional energies of the present and redirecting them toward the state's sublime and utopian project of modernization. One important task of testimony was to elicit accounts that could settle the emotional forces unleashed by the Cultural Revolution and sublimate or redirect these energies toward building the future of socialist China.

Official rhetoric referred to "settling the people's [righteous] indignation," a phrase that appeared immediately after the Gang of Four's

[91] Martha Nussbaum, *Hiding from Humanity: Disgust, Shame, and the Law* (Princeton, NJ: Princeton University Press, 2004), p. 5.
[92] Ban Wang, *The Sublime Figure of History: Aesthetics and Politics in Twentieth-Century China* (Stanford, CA: Stanford University Press, 1997).

downfall and a phrase that continued to attend media coverage of their trial. Although "settling the people's indignation" was not a formal legal concept, it articulated a claim about the relationship between law and justice in the post-Mao transition. The term *people's indignation (minfen)* is a contraction of the phrase *renmin de yifen,* which attributes to the collective subjectivity of the people *(renmin)* the emotion of righteous indignation *(yifen).*[93] The people *(renmin)* is a term of modern vintage, emerging as part of the rise of Chinese nationalism and later taking on a class character under Chinese communism.[94] *Righteous indignation (yifen)* by contrast is a classical term at least two and a half millennia old with a long history in Chinese legal and ethical thought.[95] To understand the juxtaposition of modern and ancient terms in this contraction, it will be necessary first to examine the place of righteous indignation in traditional Chinese thinking on justice, and then to explore the troubling implications of ascribing this emotional state in modern times to the people as a whole.

Righteousness *(yi)* is a sense of personal morality manifested in the conduct of interpersonal relationships. Righteousness may also be thought of as a sense of dutifulness or justice because this is the principal that compels one to requite an injustice *(bao yuan)* on behalf of a third party who has been wronged. Righteousness is highly valued in the Confucian tradition, where it was considered to help bind hierarchical family and social relationships, and also in the Chinese tradition of chivalry, where it was seen to uphold social justice whether inside or outside the law. Indignation *(fen)* in this context refers to the enmity that a righteous person feels toward the perpetrator of an injury or injustice to a third party. By the logic of requital *(bao),* indignation at injustice will motivate a righteous person to exact revenge. The two commonly discussed scenarios in legal settings are a son taking revenge on the killer of his father and a husband killing his adulterous wife and her lover. Chinese law has long recognized righteous indignation as a special kind of motive, though regimes through the ages have taken different stances on whether it should be accepted as an exculpatory or mitigating

---

[93] In the early newspaper *Shen bao (Shanghai News)* the earliest example of the phrase *ping minfen* dates to the mid-1870s, but the phrase was first used frequently in coverage the May Fourth [1919] student movement; see, e.g., "Beijing xuesheng shijian" [Beijing student incident], *Shenbao,* May 8, 1919.

[94] See discussion of the term *renmin* at Michael Y. M. Kau and John K. Leung, *Writings of Mao Zedong, 1949–1976,* vol. 2: January 1956–December 1957 (Armonk, NY: M. E. Sharpe, 1992), p. 341.

[95] Michael Dalby, "Revenge and the Law in Traditional China," *The American Journal of Legal History* 25.4 (October 1981), p. 272.

factor.[96] This legal question is no mere relic of ancient dynastic codes, either; as recently as 1930s the criminal code of the modern Republic of China recognized pleas of righteous indignation.[97]

A literary device crucial to narratives of righteous indignation is *nemesis*.[98] The classical Greek *nemesis* constitutes the inevitable and impersonal force leading to retributive justice, and it has a strong conceptual affinity to the Chinese *ping minfen*. Northrop Fyre has described *nemesis* this way:

> The righting of the balance is what the Greeks called *nemesis*: again, the agent or instrument of *nemesis* may be human vengeance, ghostly vengeance, divine vengeance, divine justice, accident, fate or the logic of events, but the essential thing is that *nemesis* happens, and happens impersonally, unaffected, as *Oedipus Tyrannus* illustrates, by the moral quality of human motivation involved.[99]

Likewise, in the Chinese phrase, verb *ping* evokes the "balancing of scales," and the abstraction of *minfen* ensures that the redress of injustice occurs without regard for individual motivation.[100] Moreover, this counterbalancing is described as an inevitable manifestation of some transcendent force or law, in this case the unstoppable train of History. Finally, the emotional content of righteous indignation is abstracted such that justice is meted out impersonally yet mercilessly.[101] In this view History is nothing short of Nemesis, rendering its verdict through humankind in ways that call to mind Marx's declaration: "History itself is the judge, and the proletariat the executioner."[102] The discursive transformation

[96] Dalby, "Revenge and the Law in Traditional China," pp. 267–307; Marinus J. Meijer, *Murder and Adultery in Late Imperial China: A Study of Law and Morality*. Sinica Leidensia 25 (New York: E. J. Brill, 1991), pp. 55–6.

[97] Such a plea by the female assassin of the warlord Sun Chuanfang sparked a public ethical debate. See Eugenia Lean, *Public Passions: The Trial of Shi Jianqiao and the Rise of Popular Sympathy in Republican China* (Berkeley: University of California Press, Los Angeles, 2007).

[98] David Konstan, *The Emotions of the Ancient Greeks: Studies in Aristotle and Classical Literature*. Robson Classical Lectures (Toronto: University of Toronto, 2007), p. 120.

[99] Northrop Frye, *Anatomy of Criticism: Four Essays* (Princeton, NJ: Princeton University Press, 1957), p. 209.

[100] Jon Elster, in his discussion of emotional motivations for transitional justice, has distinguished between Cartesian indignation, which is directed at those who have unjustly caused harm to others, and Aristotelian indignation, which is directed at one who enjoys undeserved good fortune. See Elster, *Closing the Books*, pp. 229–30.

[101] On nemesis/Nemesis: "Both as an impersonal and personified power, she is merciless." *Oxford Classical Dictionary*, 3rd edn., 1996, p. 1034.

[102] Quoted, e.g., in "Huo guo yang min, guo fa bu rong" [Calamity for the nation, prohibited by law], *GMRB*, September 30, 1980; cf. Karl Marx, "Speech at the Anniversary of the People's Paper" (April 14, 1856), www.marxists.org/archive/marx/works/1856/04/14.htm.

of *yifen* into *minfen* mirrors the ancient Greek transition from *nemesis* to *dike*, or justice according to customs and laws. Northrop Frye notes that while *nemesis* had been one of the most rudimentary and enduring mechanisms of Greek drama, "tragedy seems to lead up to an epiphany of law, of that which is and must be."[103] It is Aeschylus's classical tragedy *The Eumenides* (the conclusion of the *Oresteia* trilogy) that marks the symbolic transition from a primitive society ruled by vengeance to an advanced civilization ruled by law. In similar fashion the Gang of Four trial supposedly marked the end of "a tragedy that cannot be repeated" and the beginning of a new era of law. As a transition from vengeance to law, the Gang of Four trial represented not merely the correction of particular injustices, but more importantly part of the inevitable historical progression toward the future Communist utopia, toward "that which must be." Building on this teleological faith in the ultimate justice of History, socialist legal reforms tried to pattern human law (*falü*) on the supposed laws of historical development (*guilü*). Thus Frye's description of *dike* applies well to China's socialist rule of law: "In such a world-view nature is seen as an impersonal process which human law imitates as best it can."[104]

Ah, History – Merciless Judge

A succinct statement of the correspondence between human laws and the laws of history is found in a poem written about the trial as it was being conducted. The poem "Ah History - Merciless Judge," was published in the January 1981 issue of *People's Public Security*, a journal sponsored by the Ministry of Public Security and dedicated to professionalization in law enforcement.[105] Founded in 1952, this leading journal of a central government ministry had just recently resumed publication after being suspended for eight years during the Cultural Revolution. The poem is remarkable for the mixture, so typical in Chinese culture, of poetry and politics in a medium concerning law. In traditional China, law was the ambit of scholar-officials trained primarily in the literary arts.[106] In socialist China, arts and literature were a ubiquitous part of everyday life

---

[103] Frye, *Anatomy of Criticism*, p. 208.
[104] Ibid.
[105] Li Yonghai, "A, Lishi – wuqing de faguan" [Ah, History – merciless judge], *Renmin gong'an* [People's Public Security] 269 (January 1981), p. 33.
[106] T. H. Chen, "Law and Poetry in Ancient China," *Asian Culture Quarterly* 16.4 (Winter 1988), pp. 39–54. The connection is most obvious in the case of Chinese "regulated verse" (*lü*), a term that also means legal statutes.

and certainly not confined to exclusive venues of "high" culture. Thus the readers of a magazine written for police officers would not be surprised to find cultural productions ranging from calligraphy to woodcut prints featured alongside articles on suspect interrogation and the latest techniques in fingerprint analysis. This poem takes up the theme of how the subjective and emotional content of legal testimony are contained and settled by the rational and objective process of a trial where History is the presiding judge.

The first word of the title (a vocative equivalent to the English poetic "O") is a lyrical outpouring of emotion. Calling out "ah" asserts the poet as a speaking subject and also hails the addressee as another subject with whom the poet hopes to speak. In this case, the addressee is a personified History.[107] The lyrical outpouring of the poet is contrasted with the stolid equanimity of History, who is characterized as a merciless or "emotionless" (*wuqing*) judge.

The poem is a trial writ small, consisting of three short stanzas that correspond to the phases of indictment, testimony, and verdict. The first stanza presents the indictment. Just as the indictment against the Gang of Four was described as "an indictment by the people of the entire nation" for "a trial by the people of the entire nation," likewise this poetic indictment identifies the courtroom with the geography and population of the entire nation: "Whoever saw such a large courtroom? / – Nine million six hundred thousand square kilometers; / Whoever saw so many accusers? / – Nine hundred million men and women, young and old!" In the second stanza the reader is an observer to the testimony: "A thousand rivers rush with ten years' resentment, / Ten thousand mountain peaks bristle with furious pens, / The vast expansive earth bares inexhaustible evidence, / The boundless firmament holds a monster-reflecting mirror." The emotional tone of the poet is matched by the indignant fury of the testimony, and even heightened by the rhetoric of the sublime, which conflates the human and the natural. The earthly landscape gives testimony and the heavens reveal the truth of horrible crimes.[108] In the third stanza, the dispassionate judge, History, sorts out the facts and delivers a just verdict: "Ah, History – merciless judge, / Just

---

[107] Barbara Johnson has argued for the Western cultural context that law and lyric are both "law-abiding" genres that construct subjectivity in remarkably similar ways. See Barbara Johnson, "Anthropomorphism in Lyric and Law," in Tom Cohen et al., eds., *Material Events: Paul de Man and the Afterlife of Theory* (Minneapolis: University of Minnesota, 2001), pp. 201–25.

[108] "The conferring of speech on nature ... implies that the poet calls on these natural objects to have them *testify*, to make them 'responsive to his call' or invocation." Kneale, "Romantic Aversions," p. 157.

righteousness, stern words, without a whit of bias." Thus History condemns the would-be empress Jiang Qing, the fallen general Lin Biao, and their villainous lackeys: "The 'empress' and the 'general' struck with awe, / For the crimes of these villains and traitors, the accounts will be settled by law!"

Testimony before the Special Court introduced facts and evidence, but also stories and emotions. On the one hand, legal structures served to constrain and contain these potentially volatile stories and emotions within the stable confines of the courtroom and the trial transcript. On the other hand, the Chinese state's elaborate efforts at containment sometimes were subverted – and what is more, subverted before a public audience who had been invited to project themselves into the drama unfolding in the courtroom. The task remained for the state to carry out its object: a legal and historical narrative produced through testimony that could be received and experienced by the people of China as an emotionally or psychologically "settling" account. Saying that the trial would "settle the people's indignation" implied that the state acknowledged the reality of past injustices, validated the shared sense of indignation, and legitimated the people's desire for retribution. It would, moreover, be necessary that retribution take a form of violence that reinforced the social order, and that the agency for retribution be assigned to a collective social institution: the court. Thus the individual, emotional, and subjective would become collective, rational, and objective. In this way, the state promised that the Gang of Four trial would achieve historical and psychological closure on the past through the well-modulated expression and containment of emotion. In order to understand this affective side of the state's aspiration to settle accounts, it is desirable to probe more deeply into the emotions actually felt as "the people's indignation" and how the trial might have been imagined to settle it. This is the topic of Chapter 4.

4   Emotions

Media coverage of the Gang of Four trial portrayed History as a just and merciless judge. In this view, the ineluctable progression toward the justice of communist utopia is to be welcomed and even expedited if possible, but the actual process advances mercilessly, "without emotion" (*wu qing*). In November 1980, just as the Gang of Four trial got underway, an unknown author named Dai Houying published a novel called *Humanity, Ah Humanity! (Ren A, Ren!)*.[1] This remarkable work of fiction contested the conception of a rational, impersonal, and objectively existing force of justice. Despite the obscurity of its author, the book's initial printing sold out almost immediately and was reprinted four more times in two and a half years.[2] The novel was so successful because it tapped into a sentiment widely shared among her Chinese audience – that the mechanical determinism of history was no guarantee of justice. Contrary to official proclamations, justice could not be reduced to anything so simple as "settling the people's indignation." Through the course of her writing, the author concludes that individual life experiences simply cannot be contained by the state's grand narrative of a just and merciless History. Rather, a truly just reckoning with the past must take full account of the complexity and individuality of human emotions.

Dai Houying's novel stands as a form of personal, literary testimony with which to reconsider legal testimony given before the court. Building

---

[1] Parenthetical page references refer to the complete and unabridged Hong Kong edition: Dai Houying, *Ren a, ren!* [Humanity, Ah Humanity!] (Hong Kong: Xiangjiang youxian chubanshe, 1996). An English translation by Frances Wood is available (with some omissions) under the title, *Stones of the Wall* (London: Michael Joseph, 1985).

[2] The initial run of 121,000 copies was fairly large, especially for a relatively unknown author. In 1980, print runs from major literary publishers (excluding Beijing's People's Literature Publishing and China Youth Publishing) rarely exceeded two hundred thousand copies. See Perry Link, "Fiction and the Reading Public in Guangzhou and Other Chinese Cities, 1979–1980," in Jeffrey C. Kinkley, ed., *After Mao: Chinese Literature and Society, 1978–1981* (Cambridge, MA: Harvard University Council on East Asian Studies, 1985), pp. 229–30. The novel was first printed in November 1980, and then reprinted in May 1981, January 1982, April 1982, and May 1983. After a pause, printing then resumed a few years later.

on the question of human nature raised by Liu Binyan's reportage "Between Man and Monster," Dai Houying's novel pursued the theme of human emotions (*renqing*). While Liu Binyan's reportage extrapolated a real-life instance of inhuman behavior into a sociological indictment of a corrupt system, Dai Houying's fiction is less concerned with generalizable knowledge about society and more concerned with the irreducible complexity of subjective experience. By exploring the narrative possibilities of testimony, she argues for a more considered and humanly inflected understanding of the past.

The novel also introduced its wide readership to a compelling alternative interpretation of Marxism that previously had been confined to closed academic circles: Marxist humanism. The author incorporates Marxist humanism into her text to interrogate some of the assumptions underlying the state project of socialist legality. By incorporating humanistic elements of Marxism into readable fiction, she created a popular work of literary testimony that reached well beyond the boundaries of fiction as entertainment to problematize the notion of justice as the rational containment of personal, subjective humanity. Dai Houying's theme is that a healthy society must respect the irreducible complexity of human social relations and give free expression to each individual's emotions.

Personal and Literary Testimony

The novel, set in the historical present, follows various characters' efforts to reconcile personal and professional relationships in the aftermath of the Cultural Revolution. The complex web of characters centers on a group of intellectuals, mostly former college classmates and current co-workers in a university literature department. As the story unfolds, the reader learns of the intentional and unintentional injuries, betrayals, and humiliations the characters inflicted on each other during the tumultuous past decade. They struggle to recover some sense of normalcy in their personal and professional lives, and along the way they encounter the difficulties of moving beyond a past that is not easily forgotten.

The action centers on a literature professor named Sun Yue, a fictional character who closely resembles the real-life author Dai Houying. At work, Sun Yue seeks to restore a productive relationship with her departmental colleagues, all of whom have troubled histories with each other. Most pointedly, she tries to broker an agreement between the department's intransigent party secretary and a recently rehabilitated colleague who has written a politically controversial manuscript on Marxist humanism. Sun Yue herself has a complicated personal relationship with this colleague, a close friend who had a romantic interest in her back when they were students. At home, Sun Yue also weighs a potential reconciliation between her estranged ex-husband and their daughter, even as she searches for her own understanding with the unhappy young girl. Through the complexity of these relationships, Dai Houying portrays the ubiquitous, lingering tensions of the post-Mao period – day-to-day personal and professional tensions that cannot be resolved by spectacular legal interventions or political proclamations.

Dai Houying's novel is highly autobiographical. Though only thirteen years younger than Liu Binyan, Dai Houying's experiences during and after the Cultural Revolution were representative of a new generation of intellectuals who had come of age during the radicalization of Chinese socialism in the 1960s.[3] She was born in 1938 to a poor family in an agricultural county on the Huai River in Anhui Province, a few hundred miles west of Nanjing and Shanghai. A product of the socialist education system, she was the first member of her family to finish primary school. She took an interest in reading and proved to be a gifted student. After graduating with a degree in Chinese literature from Shanghai's East China Normal University in 1960, Dai Houying worked for nearly two decades at the Shanghai Writers Association's Institute for Literary Research. She was not happy in that position, however, and has described her work there as that of a hack critic and essayist. Dai Houying also had a turbulent personal life during those two decades. She gave birth to a daughter in 1964 but divorced in 1970. In 1971 her lover, the writer Wen Jie, committed suicide. This traumatic suicide inspired her first attempt at writing a novel, *Death of a Poet* (*Shiren zhi si*), written in 1978 but withheld from publication for several years. In 1979, with that first manuscript still in limbo, Dai Houying left her unsatisfying post at the Shanghai Writers Association. She took a position as a lecturer in the department of Chinese literature at Shanghai's prestigious Fudan University, where she taught courses in literary criticism and critical theory. It was at this time that she wrote *Humanity, Ah Humanity!*, the novel that would bring her widespread criticism and acclaim.

Humanity, Ah Humanity! sold well more than half a million copies in its first three years. This sudden success placed Dai Houying at the center of the Chinese literary scene. Dai Houying's fortunes took a turn for the worse in late 1983, when the party launched a campaign to "eliminate spiritual pollution." The campaign aimed to clean up a wide variety of troubling social ills that the party attributed to "bourgeois liberalization"

[3] Biographical information in this section based on Wang Yiyan, "Dai Houying," in Lily Xiao, Hong Lee, and A. D. Stefanowska, eds., *Zhongguo funü zhuanji cidian* [Biographical Dictionary of Chinese Women] (Armonk, NY: M. E. Sharpe, 2003), vol. 2, pp. 120–3.

in Chinese culture, ranging from unkempt hairstyles and revealing clothing to the spread of unorthodox political theories. Dai Houying was one
of several writers singled out for criticism because her novel had done
so much to promote discussion of humanism and alienation among the
general reading public. This time of intense criticism was a difficult one
for Dai Houying, but the outcome of the campaign was not entirely negative. As both Perry Link and Geremie Barmé have pointed out, a measured dose of official criticism has helped many a writer in socialist China
to promote their works and to solidify their reputations.[4] Dai Houying's
newfound status as an important writer was confirmed by her admission to the Chinese Writers Association in 1985. In her middle age, Dai
Houying finally achieved the stable and comfortable lifestyle that had
eluded her for so long. She even managed to send her daughter to university in the United States. Dai Houying continued to publish commercially successful novels, novellas, short stories, sketches, and essays. Then
in 1996 Dai Houying suffered a tragic and violent death. She and her
nineteen-year-old niece were murdered in their Shanghai apartment by a
burglar who turned out to be a troubled young man from her home town.
Today Dai Houying is best remembered for *Humanity, Ah Humanity!* and
its contribution to the post-Mao exploration of socialist humanity.

   Humanity, Ah Humanity! takes up the author's personal testimony and
translates events from her own autobiography into realistic prose.[5] Dai
Houying's lengthy postscript to the novel further confirms the place of
personal testimony in her writing. The rhetoric of the postscript is very
much in keeping with the Cultural Revolution practice of self-criticism:

Twenty years ago, I graduated early from Shanghai's East China Normal
University and stepped into a stormy and calamitous literary world. Blindness
and ignorance gave me strength. I thought I had already grasped the fundamental principles of Marxism-Leninism and correctly understood society and human
beings. I stood up on stage and shouted out scripts cribbed from the party leadership, criticizing the humanism espoused by my teachers. I said: "I love my
teachers, but I love the truth even more!" The applause in the crowded hall made
me drunk; I thought I had become a "warrior" and swelled with pride.

---

[4] See Perry Link, *The Uses of Literature: Life in the Socialist Chinese Literary System* (Princeton,
  NJ: Princeton University Press, 2000); and Geremie Barmé, *In the Red: On Contemporary
  Chinese Culture* (New York: Columbia University Press, 1999). Publication was halted
  during the period of political criticism beginning in late 1983, but soon resumed full
  steam with three more reprints in June 1986, November 1986, and March 1987.
  Numerous other editions and reprints followed, and the book remains in print today.
[5] The events were fictionalized and the prose embellished with the stylistic flourishes of
  literary modernism, yet even these techniques were intended to heighten the novel's realism; see postscript, pp. 352–4.

Today, twenty years later, I've written some novels. What I want to advocate in these novels are some of the very things I criticized in the past; what I want to bring out in these novels are the very "human emotions" I worked so hard to control and reform in the past. (347)

After this confessional passage about her reversal, she goes on to describe *Humanity, Ah Humanity!* as a "settling of accounts" with those past beliefs (348–9). Dai Houying's phrasing here echoes Marx's explanation of why he and Engels had set to work on *The German Ideology*, a key text of Marxist humanism. As Marx explains it, he and Engels had set out "to settle accounts with [their] erstwhile philosophical conscience," coming to terms with the past by engaging a failed ideological inheritance.[6] For Chinese intellectuals such as Dai Houying, indignation at the dehumanizing experiences of the Cultural Revolution invited them to reexamine the theoretical basis of their thought. As Bill Brugger and David Kelly put it, in post-Mao China "an alienated Marxism was becoming conscious of its own alienation."[7] Critical interest in Marxist humanism on the part of Dai Houying and her fellow intellectuals was part and parcel of their attempts to come to terms with the crisis of Chinese socialism. Dai Houying's postscript *mea culpa* establishes her personal authority as a firsthand witness to and participant in those dehumanizing experiences. In the novel, she transfers this authority to multiple narrators.

The formal device of multiple narrators emulates courtroom testimony, where various witnesses are called to describe the same events. Courtroom testimony is used to establish facts, substantiate claims, document the past, and assess criminal responsibility. The people giving testimony to the court, just like the characters in a novel, can be evil, deluded, or mendacious. Some are more sympathetic or trustworthy than others. Truth is supposed to emerge organically or meta-textually, from the interaction of diverse subject perspectives. Through the course of the novel, each character struggles to be heard and understood. The reader experiences the value of testimony here, and by extension in the courtroom, by struggling to choose between the competing versions of events. Each reader, each person who hears or reads the competing accounts, is drawn into the circle of responsibility for deciding which version is valid. However, there is an important difference. Dai Houying and her readers are free from the responsibility of the court to actually reach

---

[6] Karl Marx, preface to *A Contribution to the Critique of Political Economy* (1859), quoted in Robert C. Tucker, ed., *The Marx-Engels Reader*, 2nd edn. (New York: Norton, 1978), p. 5.

[7] Bill Brugger and David Kelly, *Chinese Marxism in the Post-Mao Era* (Stanford, CA: Stanford University Press, 1990), p. 146.

a final judgment that "contains" or "resolves" the issues introduced by the indictment and debated through testimony. Whereas legal testimony must find closure in a verdict, literary testimony may remain open-ended.

Dai Houying's multiple storytellers shift irregularly throughout the twenty-seven chapters, which are grouped into four sections. The three characters who narrate the first three chapters are the most prominent; together they narrate sixteen of the chapters, and individually each narrates a chapter in all four sections. The three main character-narrators are Sun Yue, a university professor of Chinese literature who is also her academic department's party secretary; Zhao Zhenhuan, a newspaper journalist who is the ex-husband of Sun Yue and father to their daughter; and He Jingfu, a scholar who was cast out of the academy during the Cultural Revolution and has recently been reinstated. In the remaining chapters, secondary character-narrators offer different perspectives on the two main dramatic conflicts of the novel: He Jingfu's frustrated attempts to publish his politically controversial manuscript on *Marxism and Humanism* and Sun Yue's troubled efforts to repair damaged relationships with her family, friends, and colleagues.

Dai Houying's writing focuses on the inner world of her characters to make her case for honoring subjective human emotion in any just and meaningful resolution of conflict. Thus, explains Carolyn Pruyn, it does not much matter that the conflict over publication of He Jingfu's manuscript goes unresolved: "In fact, we see that this is not essential to the novel, for in these particular lives a *psychological* resolution has occurred. It is the characters themselves who constitute the major elements of the 'plot.'"[8] Narrative experimentation with interiority was a hallmark of Western literary modernists writing in the first half of the twentieth century, such as James Joyce, William Faulkner, and Virginia Woolf. Their techniques had been influential in China at the time, but fell into ideological disfavor with the promotion of socialist realism in the 1930s and 1940s. By the end of the Cultural Revolution, popular works of Chinese fiction tended to be long on sound and fury, but short on psychological complexity. In the late 1970s, Chinese writers again turned to questions of individual human character. Dai Houying's revival of modernist techniques was well suited to this goal, restoring to Chinese socialist fiction a psychological realism that had been lost for decades.

The novel's popularity demonstrated the power of fiction as an occasion for nuanced and unaccustomed reflections on the most serious

---

[8] Carolyn S. Pruyn, *Humanism in Modern Chinese Literature: The Case of Dai Houying*. Chinathemen 35 (Berlin: Bochum, 1988), pp. 48–9 (emphasis added).

issues besetting Chinese society. The author's attempt to represent emotion reasserted the existence and validity of an autonomous inner life – a private subjectivity separate from the social life of the collective. As a psychological novel, *Humanity, Ah Humanity!* posits the individual as a subject, undermining the socialist ideal of collective subjectivity. Lest there be any doubt about the author's intention, Dai Houying explicitly states her theme in the epigraph to Part 1 of the novel: "In each person's mind is stored a piece of history, each with its own way of living" (1). Her chapters grant each character's history a life of its own within the text, embedded in the histories of the others.

The closest thing to an omniscient narrator in the novel is a character identified only as The Novelist. This Novelist resembles Dai Houying in many ways and comments on the action with a tone of authority, but she is not a simple mouthpiece for the author. The character of the Novelist serves to explain the themes of the novel to its readers. The literary techniques used in the novel illustrate the central theme that everyone deserves a say, or a day in court – even those people too low in the scheme of things to be called to the docket in a major trial. Reviewing her story, the Novelist observes, "Each person was a type, and each of their experiences could be written as a novel. But there must be hundreds of millions of people like them in China" (185). Later on, The Novelist states that each character fulfills a necessary role in the great cosmological drama of life: "If one of these people were missing, the situation would be much simpler. But which one should be missing? We can't do without any of them" (324). If every person's story is a necessary element of the whole, then there is no single, privileged viewpoint from which to narrate a synoptic and comprehensive account of the past. Dai Houying insists that individuals must assume responsibility for themselves and settle accounts with history. Settling accounts cannot be done by proxy through a trial.

Dai Houing's modernist focus on subjective interiority was intellectually provocative and emotionally evocative – not to mention politically daring. Her novel's multivocal approach runs completely counter to the Leninist ideal of a disciplined party voicing a unified and definitive line. To appreciate the role of *Humanity, Ah Humanity!* in unsettling the Leninist ideal, it is instructive to look more closely at the reception of the novel. Quite aside from the controversial humanist content of the novel, the literary form was equally disturbing. Attention to interiority and the use of multiple narrators challenged established notions of knowledge production in socialist China. The Maoist "mass line" was supposed to fulfill the Leninist ideal of "democratic centralism": the party listened to the cacophony of voices produced by the masses (democracy) and crystallized it into a clear and authoritative voice (centralism). The realization of the people's historical destiny depended on the second part of this process, on the transformation of their inchoate hopes and ambitions into a single correct "line" to enact in revolutionary practice. Dai Houying's novel was pointedly lacking in this regard.[9] As one reviewer for a popular Chinese literary magazine complained, Dai Houying's innovative use of narrative devices ultimately comes to no great end: "Can we count such a work a novel? Its plot is disjointed, with no clear or distinguishable 'beginning' and no satisfactory or conclusive 'ending.' The chapters amount to nothing more than the inward mutterings of all different people, resembling a collage of diary pages drawn from multiple protagonists."[10]

Western literary critics took a different tack, arguing that Dai Houying's narrative experimentation had not pushed far enough. For example, Michael Duke takes Dai Houying to task for tying up loose ends too neatly. Discussing Dai Houying's treatment of dream imagery and symbolism, Duke laments that "[i]n the course of the novel one or another of the characters reveals the true meaning of nearly every possibly ambiguous figurative usage that might give rise to multiple interpretation and lively intellectual debate."[11] David Wang offers a similar complaint. He says that while the text's multiple characterizations of history "tantaliz[e] us with a possible heteroglossia," in the end Dai Houying "has not done away with the lure of totalizing human experience."[12] Ultimately, Dai Houying's strong authorial point of view undercuts the experimental side of her novel. Wang concludes – with obvious disappointment – that "as stunning as her skepticism on the official definition of history may first appear, her answers turn out to be very weak."[13] For the postmodern Western critic, Dai Houying's attempt at literary modernism fell a half-measure short.[14] For Chinese readers, though, her writing widened the circle of testimony about the Cultural Revolution and raised questions left hanging by the official judgments of the party-state.

[9] Sabina Knight, *The Heart of Time: Moral Agency in Twentieth-Century Chinese Fiction.* Harvard East Asian Monographs 276 (Cambridge, MA: Harvard University Press, 2006), pp. 33–44 and 171–85.

[10] Wang Xingzhi, "Wo du *Ren a, ren!*" [My reading of *Man Ah, Man!*], *Dushu* (November 1981), p. 40.

[11] Michael Duke, *Blooming and Contending: Chinese Literature in the Post-Mao Era* (Bloomington: Indiana University Press, 1985), p. 151.

[12] David D. W. Wang, "Tai Hou-ying, Feng Chi-ts'ai, and Ah Ch'eng: Three Approaches to the Historical Novel," *Asian Culture Quarterly* 16.2 (Summer 1988), pp. 75–6.

[13] Ibid., p. 75.

[14] Duke, *Blooming and Contending*, pp. 149–53. Pruyn, *Humanism*, pp. 43–4. For a more positive assessment, see Knight, *Heart of Time*, pp. 171–85.

Figure 13. Wang Keping, "Silence" (*Chenmo*), sculpture in stained wood, 40 cm. (1979).
Source: Photograph by Adam Dean.

Inadmissible Testimony? The Politics of Publishing

Just as evidentiary rules, legal procedures, and the discretion of the judge can be used to deem some speech irrelevant or inadmissible in the courtroom, testimony outside the courtroom can also be excluded from the public record. The idea of silenced or inadmissible testimony was an emotionally powerful and politically dangerous theme in post-Mao China, as vividly illustrated by Wang Keping's controversial sculpture *Silence* (1979) (Figure 13).[15] Like other artists and intellectuals who lived through the Cultural Revolution, Dai Houying knew from personal experience that the publication of literary testimony in socialist China was subject to political, economic, and institutional controls.

---

[15] Martina Köppel-Yang, *Semiotic Warfare: A Semiotic Analysis, the Chinese Avant-Garde, 1979–1989* (Hong Kong: Timezone 8, 2003), pp. 127–30.

Freedom of expression was not to be taken for granted in post-Mao China, either, as illustrated by Dai Houying's own difficulties with publication. The author wrote *Humanity, Ah Humanity!* in the midst of a maelstrom surrounding her first, unsuccessful attempt to publish a different novel, called *Death of a Poet*.[16] Due to Dai Houying's active support of the radical literary line during the Cultural Revolution, she had personal and political enemies in the Shanghai publishing world. Her manuscript for *Death of a Poet* had been accepted for publication, but the author's opponents managed to halt the process several times. Even after the work was typeset, it was blocked from printing.[17]

Dai Houying managed to get *Humanity, Ah Humanity!* published only after escaping the personal politics of the Shanghai publishing world and sending the manuscript far away to the Guangdong People's Publishing House (later renamed the commercial Huacheng Publishing House) in that southern metropolis near Hong Kong where many of the post-Mao reforms got started. The press in Guangdong had actually contacted Dai Houying to inquire about publishing *Death of a Poet*, but she submitted *Humanity, Ah Humanity!* instead. Despite continued attempts at interference from Shanghai, the publishers in Guangdong stood firm in support of Dai Houying's novel: unless they received a formal letter rescinding her legal right to publish, they would move forward.[18] With the green light in Guangdong, the writing and publishing processes progressed quickly. Dai completed the entire manuscript in about a month, in May 1980. She submitted the manuscript for publication in late June, and it was accepted in July; she made extensive revisions in July and August, and the book was finalized in September of that year. The first edition

---

[16] This episode is detailed David Der-wei Wang, *The Monster That Is History: History, Violence, and Fictional Writing in Twentieth-Century China* (Berkeley: University of California Press, 2004), pp. 224–61.

[17] Du Jiankun, "Wo wei Dai Houying bianji" [I was Dai houying's editor], in Wu Zhongjie and Gao Yun, eds., *Dai Houying ah Dai Houying* [Dai Houying, ah, Dai Houying] (Haikou: Hainan guoji xinwen chuban zhongxin, 1997), p. 197. Du Jianku refers obliquely to the "complex personal relations" governing the Shanghai publishing world, without explaining specifically who opposed Dai Houying or why.

[18] According to the retrospective accounts of her publishers in Guangdong, influential opponents in Shanghai tried to block publication, putting pressure on the publishing house and filing complaints with the Guangdong Provincial Publishing Division. The Shanghai camp even threatened a campaign of ideological criticism against the book – the text of which they had never seen. See Du Jiankun, "Wo wei Dai Houying bianji," p. 197; Wang Man, "Women cengjing yiqi zhandou" [We fought a battle together], in Wu Zhongjie and Gao Yun, eds., *Dai Houying ah Dai Houying* [Dai Houying, ah, Dai Houying] (Haikou: Hainan guoji xinwen chuban zhongxin, 1997), pp. 209–10.

of *Humanity, Ah Humanity!* came to press in November 1980, the same month that the Gang of Four trial began.[19]

Dai Houying's personal difficulties in the publishing world offer another point of entry into the novel as a reflection on the Cultural Revolution, for fictional publishing troubles are presented in the story as conflict between the rule of law and the rule of man. In one episode, an instructor in the Chinese literature department learns that the university's party secretary, who had been publicly humiliated during the Cultural Revolution by this particular instructor, intends to blacklist him from publishing articles. The instructor confides in the reader, "I didn't understand why I couldn't write articles. No one ever notified me that 'By law you are stripped of the freedoms of press and speech.' But this comrade meant well, and I nodded. The transition from rule of man to rule of law is necessarily slow and cannot be rushed" (38). In a later chapter, the instructor's resignation turns to frustration. He speaks directly to the words already spoken by the party secretary, and defends himself from the earlier narrator. He says, "We hear every day that the legal system is stronger now, but as far as we know here at the University, the law is whatever comes out of [Party Secretary] Xi Liu's mouth" (327). In the novel, the rule of man is an obstacle to freedom of expression, and the rule of law is a possible but thus far ineffectively administered antidote.

The issue of publication comes up again when the university party secretary conspires to block publication of another teacher's manuscript, He Jingfu's provocatively titled *Marxism and Humanism*. At a committee meeting, the party secretary teams up with his wife and a subordinate to criticize the book's "revisionism" and "bourgeois humanism" – even though the critics are unable to articulate coherent definitions of these terms. The accusations of the party secretary and his wife are opposed by several sympathetic characters who speak about the unfairness of blocking this controversial book. The cynical party secretary's idealistic son Xi Wang (whose name is a homonym for "hope") writes a protest on the department blackboard under the heading, "Rule of Law or Rule of Man? – Thoughts on our Freedom to Publish after the Setbacks to Teacher He's Book" (325).

In her own narrative, the main character Sun Yue also attributes these setbacks to the persistence of the rule of man, the habituated acceptance of autocratic power. "What has more strength and authority than habit? People's eyes are always trained upward. A person's value, including the

[19] Du Jiankun, "Wo wei Dai Houying bianji," pp. 197–9; Ye Yonglie, *Mingren fengyun lu* [How famous people weathered the storm] (Nanjing: Jiangsu wenyi chubanshe, 2002), pp. 74–6.

value of their words, varies according to status. An eminent person's words are treasured; an insignificant person's words are ignored. This is not truth, but it is a fact. And facts are usually more persuasive than the truth" (293–4). The fact of the party secretary's power trumps the truth of the teacher's ideas. What's more, Dai Houying's fictional party officials are not necessarily motivated by ideological purity nor even by personal grudges. In many cases, they are simply unwilling to risk any association with a potentially controversial book. Party Secretary Xi Liu's name means "flow of the stream" and his subordinate You Ruoshui's name means "swim like water"; lacking personal integrity, they are afraid to make waves or rock the boat. There is even a student who circulates a mocking cartoon depicting You Ruoshui as a headless body floating between the rocky banks of a river. In fact, in the chapter narrated by You Ruoshui he admits that he secretly admires He Jingfu's book, but cannot summon the courage to formulate an opinion or take a stand. He has a telling dream in which his headless body sprouts the heads of various party officials. Dai Houying's point is obvious: the pliant subordinate enables the rule of man; the rule of law depends on personal integrity and critical thinking.

Later in the book, the character called The Novelist speaks about the censorship of He Jingfu's book as a symptom of systemic failure in the party. While rule of law is needed, it is not sufficient in the absence of cultivated human beings who are willing and able to implement it. The Novelist's critique likens organizational failure to organ failure:

Is this what they call an "inner wound"? There's no wound visible on the surface, but the internal organs are failing. If we don't enact rule of law, how can we conquer this sort of phenomenon? Conversely, if we don't conquer this sort of phenomenon, how can we truly enact rule of law? (328)

Even after the downfall of the Gang of Four and the apparent healing of the party, rule of man continued to cause a potentially lethal inner wound. The Novelist is not at all sure that treatment can be administered successfully. The hemorrhage may be concealed and contained within the body politic, but this is not the same as a cure.

The issue of the integrity of the writer comes up in another subplot of the novel. In this case, a newspaperman named Zhao Zhenhuan finds his fundamental humanity in the assertion of professional integrity.[20] His

---

[20] A negative example is presented in Zhao's colleague at the newspaper, Wang Panzi. Although Zhao defends Wang Panzi's right to publish against the attacks of their editor, Wang completely betrays Zhao's friendship and loyalty. By the end of the novel, we learn that Wang has secretly disavowed Zhao's complaint about the editor to the party office, accepted the editor's corrupt assignment, framed Zhao for adultery, and run off with Zhao's new wife. The crooked reporter ends up with a promotion.

voice argues that humanity can be rebuilt through personal and professional integrity. When his unscrupulous editor wants to tamper with the credits for a revised edition of *The Development of Revolutionary Journalism*, Zhao objects. He argues that the editor-in-chief should not remove another writer's name because of his political background, nor should he add his own name to work he did not do (95–6). Later in the novel, when the editor asks Zhao to criticize a stage play for the paper, it turns out that the editor had willingly helped the Gang of Four by publishing such unmerited attacks in the past, and that Zhao had agreed to write them. By accepting these assignments, Zhao says, "I'd slowly buried the sense of responsibility and honor of a 'people's reporter'. I had buried the self-respect and self-confidence of a human being. I became a soulless tool and completely lost myself" (204). Zhao resembles Liu Binyan's ideal "people's writer," linking professional and personal integrity with a sense of basic humanity. This time Zhao refuses to do his boss's dirty work. Presenting the Cultural Revolution and its aftermath as worlds apart, he tells the reader, "In a world ruled by demons [i.e., during the Cultural Revolution], I couldn't demand to be a person. But in a world of human beings, of course I want to be one" (203). But Zhao Zhenhuan turns out to be a victim of dramatic irony, as Dai Houying complicates the idealized distinction between a past world of demons and a present world of human beings. Although Zhao has taken a stand to defend Wang Panzi's right to publish against the attacks of their editor, Wang completely betrays Zhao's friendship and loyalty. By the end of the novel, the reader learns that Wang has secretly disavowed Zhao's complaint about the editor to the local party office, accepted the editor's corrupt assignment, framed Zhao for adultery, and run off with Zhao's wife. To add final insult to injury, the crooked reporter is awarded a promotion. This terrible scenario recalls the alienated society described in Liu Binyan's "Between Man and Monsters," where inhuman villains slowly and systematically destroy their human adversaries. Dai Houying's response also recalls Liu Binyan's idea of the principled "people's writer" as a champion for human values.

Admissible Testimony? Humanism and Emotion

Dai Houying's novel uses its narrators and their conflicts to expand the range of testimony that could be admitted into the public conversation about the injustices and legacies of the Cultural Revolution. The conversation was constrained by several factors: by the lingering trauma of a past that many wished could be forgotten; by the current political line that determined what could or could not be criticized; and by the fear of reprisals as judgments were subject to future revision or reversal. There was no surefire safe way to escape these constraints, but Dai Houying was determined that the conversation be heard. The crucial content that she felt needed to be voiced, that had been brushed aside in the rush to rationality, was emotion. Her strategy was to use the language of the party-state – the language of socialism – to explore the human condition in post-Mao China, speaking from a critical position called Marxist humanism. Was this strategy analogous to legal defense by the rules – working out an alternate position by staying inside the system and following the established rules of testimony? Or was it an appeal to the gallery instead of the judge? Was the emotional content of her statement acceptable to the court, or was it based on a discredited, irrelevant, or inadmissible worldview? As demonstrated by the difficulty surrounding publication of her novel, and also by its great commercial success, these questions had not yet been settled. Against the constraints of rules and procedures, and before the final closure of the verdict, the testimony phase is a moment of possibility. Dai Houying's *Humanity, Ah Humanity!* pushed insistently at the limits of what was possible.

Dai Houying's writerly testimony was deeply informed by Marxist humanism, a strain of Marxian theory concerned with the nature of humanity and its realization in society. Much of Marxist humanist thought in the West is based on the early philosophical works of Marx, most notably his *Economic and Philosophical Manuscripts* (1844), "Theses on Feuerbach" (1845), and *The German Ideology* (1844–5), written before Marx turned his attention to the systematic critique of political economy in *Capital* (first volume published 1867). There is some considerable debate among Marxists about whether there is a sharp break between these early texts and Marx's later works and, if so, whether the early writings expound an immature and outmoded philosophy. The humanist position is that there is no break: the early works provide the philosophical underpinnings for Marx's interest in political economy and dialectical materialism. Until the middle of twentieth century, though, these earlier works were not widely known outside the intellectual circles of critical Marxism in Western Europe; Marx's *The German Ideology*, for example, was not even published in Russian until 1932 or in English until 1964. Chinese interest in Marxist humanism was much retarded by censorship, and did not develop until the late 1970s.[21]

In post-Mao China, Marxist humanism initially was a concern of specialists in political philosophy such as Ru Xin and Li Zehou. This Marxist

---

[21] Ding Xueliang, "Xin Makesizhuyi dui Zhongguo delu de yingxiang" [Influence of Neo-Marxism on the Chinese mainland], in Chen Guide, ed., *Zhongguo dalu dangdai wenhua bianqian (1978–1989)* [Changes in mainland Chinese contemporary culture] (Taipei: Guiguan, 1991), pp. 115–44.

humanism soon found influential sponsors among leading opinion makers like *People's Daily* editor Wang Ruoshui and culture czar Zhou Yang.[22] Works like Dai Houying's novel brought the conversation into the popular mainstream. In early 1983, *People's Daily* reported that nearly three hundred different periodicals had published a total of 422 articles on humanism over the previous three years.[23] During this period Chinese engagement with existing theories of Marxist humanism was frequently superficial, tangential, or crude.[24] Most importantly, in China the more specific topic of Marxist humanism slipped easily into the more general question of "man" (*ren*: the human) under socialism. As He Yuhuai has put it, " 'man' became unquestionably the central topic in every field of human sciences."[25] Marxist humanism was not a touchstone of received wisdom for the Chinese, but merely a stepping-off point for an inquiry into the human condition under Chinese socialism – an inquiry that the Chinese would undertake in their own terms.

The slow and troubled transmission of these critical Marxist texts and ideas into China helps explain the remarkable reception of Dai Houying's *Humanity, Ah Humanity!* For most readers, the novel provided them their first vivid and sustained exposure to a new, more humanistic vision of Marxism. Dai Houying presents an emotionally charged story as a framing vehicle for the novel's philosophical content. Yet her take on Marxist humanism is groping and unsystematic, and the presentation is sometimes artless. The fictional plot device of the unpublished manuscript called *Marxism and Humanism* allows Dai Houying's characters to quote passages from key Marxist humanist texts that are clumsily nested

[22] See David A. Kelly, "The Emergence of Humanism: Wang Ruoshui and the Critique of Socialist Alienation," in Merle Goldman et al., eds., *China's Intellectuals and the State: In Search of a New Relationship* (Cambridge, MA: Council on East Asian Studies, Harvard University, 1987), pp. 159–82. Wang Ruoshui was deputy editor-in-chief of *RMRB* from July 1978 to late 1983, and a member of the party's inaugural Committee on Discipline Inspection from December 1978 to September 1982. Wang Ruoshui's theories of humanism and socialist alienation received a strong and very conspicuous endorsement from Zhou Yang, president of the All-China Federation of Literary and Art Circles, at the CASS centennial observance of Karl Marx's death the spring of 1983. For the text of Zhou Yang's speech, see *RMRB*, March 16, 1983. In turn, Wang Ruoshui featured Zhou Yang's speech in the pages of *People's Daily*.

[23] He Yuhuai, *Cycles of Repression and Relaxation: Politico-Literary Events in China, 1976– 1989*, Chinathemen, Serie Europäisches Projekt zur Modernisierung in China 6 (Bochum: N. Brockmeyer, 1992), pp. 230–1 and 231n11: figure reported in *RMRB*, January 11, 1983.

[24] Brugger and Kelly, *Chinese Marxism in the Post-Mao Era*, p. 17. The best general discussion of humanism as a theoretical issue in post-Mao China is Brugger and Kelly, *Marxism in China*, pp. 139–70. He Yuhuai has surveyed how the humanism and alienation debates played out in the literary world: He, *Cycles of Repression and Relaxation*, pp. 229–78.

[25] He, *Cycles of Repression and Relaxation*, p. 231.

within the story. As an illustration, here the character He Jingfu closely paraphrases a famous passage from Marx's *The German Ideology*:

[I]n communist society, where nobody has one exclusive sphere of activity but each can become accomplished in any branch he wishes, society regulates the general production and makes it possible for me to do one thing today and another tomorrow: to hunt in the morning, to fish in the afternoon, to rear cattle in the evening, and to engage in literary criticism after dinner, just as I have a mind to do, without ever becoming hunter, fisherman, shepherd or critic. (279)[26]

These passages convey important concepts associated with Marxist humanism, such as Marx's theory of alienation and his explanation of human actualization through labor. However, Dai Houying does not engage, and is understandably not conversant with, how these ideas have been elaborated in the Western field of critical Marxism. Indeed, isolation from Western Marxists may have served her fiction well. For, in three hundred pages of moving prose she builds a dramatic and accessible argument for a compelling alternative to scientific socialism rooted in the specific cultural and historical experiences of modern China.

Overall, Dai Houying's intellectual position is not so distant from the declaration for humanism present in Liu Binyan's reportage. The words of her narrators echo Liu Binyan's call for a socialism in which "man is the aim, man is the center." But where Liu was interested principally in the distortions that produced alien monsters, Dai Houying was mainly troubled by the everyday alienation experienced by society's genuine human beings. Socialism was supposed to end the alienation of people from the products of their labor, from their essential nature as creative producers, and from their fellow human beings; yet here were socialist writers and philosophers ruminating on the persistence of alienation under socialism.[27]

This sort of testimony implied a damning indictment of Chinese socialism, not just during the Cultural Revolution but in the historical

---

[26] My translation from the Chinese, closely following Tucker's translation of Marx in *The Marx-Engels Reader*, p. 160.

[27] This was a question of whether ideological development matched material development (or if a discrepancy were even possible). In 1979 Marxist theorist and champion of wholesale reform Su Shaozhi argued that China was in a transitional phase of "undeveloped socialism." Though this theory was initially rejected by moderate reformists such as Deng Xiaoping and Hu Qiaomu, it nevertheless held currency in academic circles. By 1987, the basic idea was adopted into official ideology under the name "the primary stage of socialism." See Kalpana Misra, *From Post-Maoism to Post-Marxism: The Erosion of Official Ideology in Deng's China* (New York: Routledge, 1998), pp. 91–116; Brugger and Kelly, *Marxism in China*, pp. 19–44. This socialist alienation took form as ideological and political alienation: fetish of dogma alienated people from official ideology; personality cult, rule of man alienated people from the political leadership of the party.

present. It is not surprising, then, that *Humanity, Ah Humanity!* fell victim to a swiftly turning tide against Marxist humanism. In October 1983 Deng Xiaoping personally kicked off the campaign against "spiritual pollution" by denouncing theories of humanism and socialist alienation.[28] Dai Houying and her book were singled out for criticism in the press – ironically ensuring the book's continued commercial success.[29] Though in the end her testimony was struck down, crucially she had already had her say in the court of public opinion. What was it about this novel that connected so intimately with so many Chinese readers? The answer is emotion.

"History is just, and it is merciless."[30] This trope found in official coverage of the Gang of Four trial portrayed the justice of history as rational and merciless – literally, "without emotion" (*wuqing*). The affective state that was validated and addressed by the court was not a personal emotion, but the collective indignation of the Chinese body politic. The people's indignation (*minfen*) was claimed to be a nigh-cosmological expression of historical necessity, an impersonal force that would deliver retribution with deterministic certainty and balance the scales of justice with merciless efficiency. Dai Houying's novel rebuts this claim. In the words of the sympathetic character He Jingfu, the author of the manuscript of *Marxism and Humanism*, history may seem inscrutable, but it is just and has emotions: "History is like a reserved and introverted person who does not easily show his true feelings. But someday you will see, it is just" (42). This theme is reprised in the densely meaningful epigraph to the fourth and final part of the novel: "This sort of weather should be considered normal: the sun comes out in the East; in the West it's raining. It seems the sky won't clear, and yet it clears" (271). In traditional Chinese culture, the clear sky signifies an incorruptible magistrate who will tirelessly

---

[28] On the 1983 campaign against spiritual pollution in literature, see Wendy Larson, "Realism, Modernism, and the Anti-'Spiritual Pollution' Campaign in China," *Modern China* 15.1 (January 1989), pp. 37–71; and Thomas B. Gold, "'Just in Time!' China Battles Spiritual Pollution on the Eve of 1984," *Asian Survey* 24.9 (September 1984), pp. 947–74. For a review of official criticism against Dai Houying in particular, see also Pruyn, *Humanism in China*, pp. 53–67 and (up to 1982) *China News Analysis*, No. 1231. The definitive official statement against was Hu Qiaomu, "On the Question of Humanism and Alienation," *Hongqi* [Red flag] (February 1984), pp. 2–28.

[29] All told, the book sold out at least ten printings in the People's Republic of China, totaling more than one million copies. Domestic publication figures from Du Jiankun, "Wo wei Dai Houying bianji," p. 199. These figures do not include numerous editions and reprints published in Hong Kong and Taiwan, or translations into at least seven foreign languages. For Dai Houying's take on the connection between the criticism and her book's popularity, see Ye Yonglie, *Mingren fengyun lu*, pp. 74–92.

[30] To give just one example: "Lishi wuqing, renmin liliang bu ke shengli" [History is merciless and the people's strength is invincible], *RMRB*, January 28, 1981.

solve every case. Thus the metaphor could be interpreted: "Amidst the storm of injustices, there will yet be justice." When this line appears in the text proper, it is spoken by The Novelist, a proxy for Dai Houying. Here, the addition of a single word in parentheses adds another layer of meaning. After the Chinese character for clear sky (*qing*) appears its homonym emotion (*qing*), giving us an alternate, parenthetical reading: "It seems to be merciless, and yet there is emotion" (324). So, instead of the official trope, "History is just, and it is emotionless," the reader once again gets Dai Houying's view: "History is just, and it is *emotional*."

Thus Dai Houying's vision of justice is very different from that of the socialist legal project: history is just precisely to the extent that it is *not* merciless. For her, the threat of injustice arises when humanity abandons the emotional subjectivity that gives rise to moral judgment and social progress. History is not the ineluctable, mechanical train of progress, pressing ever forward to no end. For Dai Houying, history holds the promise of human salvation, and its motive force is found in our innate and common humanity – that is to say, in the equation of "human circumstances" with "emotions," the two meanings of *renqing*.

Dai Houying's literary testimony and the trial's legal testimony differ in their evaluations of *renqing*, which is a multivalent term that could refer to either internal emotions or external conditions. The purpose of legal testimony is to establish the objectively existing facts and circumstances of the case, while subjective emotion is a superfluous factor to be contained and pacified. Dai Houying's literary testimony, however, is little concerned with hard facts – it is after all a fictional account, and one in which plot is secondary to psychological interiority. Rather, the novel establishes human emotion as the principle and decisive factor. There are no real factual contradictions among the various narrators' accounts, only differences of affect and perspective. These characters share a history, but they do not share some uniform, collective feeling about the past. Again: "This kind of weather *should be considered normal*: the sun is coming out in the East; in the West it is raining" (271). The ambiguity of the external meteorological condition is a figure for the arguably more important and complex psychological condition.[31] Dai Houying is not asking her readers to judge the case on the facts, but to hear the internal motivations and subjective feelings of her characters in all their multivocal complexity.

---

[31] On sympathetic fallacy and the pairing of *qing* and *jing* in Chinese literature and philosophy, see Curie Virag, "'That Which Encompasses the Myriad Cares': Subjectivity, Knowledge, and the Ethics of Emotion in Tang and Song China," PhD diss. (Harvard University, 2004), pp. 4–5.

The Gang of Four trial and *Humanity, Ah Humanity!* are contrasting stories about justice, and the contrast is typically Chinese. The trial was a story of requital (*bao*), while Dai Houying's novel is a story of human emotions or circumstances (*renqing*). *Renqing* narratives emerged in early modern times as an alternative to the rigid morality of requital narratives, and were based on a more nuanced and ambivalent understanding of human circumstances. Like Dai Houying's modern foray into the genre, these *renqing* stories were attentive to the contingencies of human action and the psychology of human actors. "Unlike narratives that illustrate the straightforward application of *bao* as a structuring and ideological principle," explains Daniel Youd, "legal fictions that prioritize issues of *renqing* often involve a much greater tolerance of moral ambiguity."[32] Because truth emerges from multiple perspectives, a society interested in truth must allow people to tell their stories. Most of the author's other arguments follow as corollaries of this main point. Dai Houying was cautiously optimistic that socialist rule of law could help guarantee a hearing for multiple perspectives, and thereby move society closer to the truth. The excesses of the Cultural Revolution painfully demonstrated the fallibility of human knowledge, the unreliability of human emotions, and the destructive potential of unchecked subjective judgments. Despite all this, Dai Houying maintained that objective facts alone cannot fully account for the truth. The truth must also encompass the subjective reality – the fact – of human emotion, both as a universal social condition and an inalienable inheritance of human nature.

Humanity, a Complicating Factor

Looking back late in the novel, The Novelist reflects on the publishing controversy at the core of the plot, saying, "If someone were to ask me, 'How did a simple issue become so complicated?' I'd reply without hesitation that the main factor is man" (324). The Novelist is the speaker most concerned with the increasingly intricate relationships between people and issues raised by the controversy. Dai Houying reinforces the voice of The Novelist, using various characters to bolster her argument for the irreducible complexity of human relationships. Using the multiple narrators to explore the pros and cons, the right and wrong of differing perspectives, she affirms the value of testimony and the importance of questioning the capacity of transitional justice to safely close off and contain the past with

---

[32] Daniel M. Youd, "Beyond Bao: Moral Ambiguity and the Law in Late Imperial Chinese Narrative Literature," in Robert E. Hegel and Katherine Carlitz, eds., *Writing and Law in Late Imperial China: Crime, Conflict, and Judgment* (Seattle: University of Washington Press, 2007), p. 229.

a totalizing narrative. As the character of the humanist scholar, He Jingfu, says, "I don't think you can understand man's essential nature by consulting a textbook on *The General Principles of Social Relations*" (49).

Rather, the certainty presented by the totalizing social scientific worldview is inherently limited and should be countered with critical doubt. Because truth only begins to emerge from the convergence of multiple subjectivities, each person's limited knowledge is defined by gaps and fractures. In the novel, negative space simultaneously holds us together and keeps us apart. That space is none other than the simultaneously interior and interstitial realm of emotion. The novel champions greater openness to subjective emotion as the necessary complement to objective knowledge, by exposing the limitations of the narrators who cannot arrive at this openness. The strengths of the narrators who engage emotion, and the failings of those who do not, show that if history is to be just it cannot be "merciless" as suggested by the legal model. Subjective human emotion is integral to the justice of history.

Various characters speak to the claim that human relations form a complex system. In one scene, Sun Yue's daughter Hanhan cannot concentrate on her geometry homework knowing that her estranged father, whom she has not seen in years, is visiting nearby. As she thinks of her broken family, each person indelibly complicates the picture in a geometrical progression:

The simplest is a single point. Two points join to make a line, like Mom and me. But add another point – just one more – and inexplicably you have two more lines, and these again form a triangle and now a plane. How much more complicated! Should I rub out this last point? – but a Dad cannot be erased. All the world is this complicated: given X, prove Y. What a headache. (241)

In frustration, Hanhan realizes that human relationships defy the deductive analysis that one might apply to geometrical proofs. Her voice becomes more unsettled as she struggles to decide what to do: "Given, given! The given is that Dad is at Uncle He [Jingfu]'s house. But does that prove I should go see him there or not? Who can say?" (241).

Later in the chapter, in conversation with He Jingfu, the scholar extends the girl's metaphor of crossing and converging lines to describe the complexity of human history. He describes to her the myriad converging lines that result in a very different vision from the party's insistence on a single, unified revolutionary line marking out the clear path of historical progress. With this he arrives at a call for each person to make their own judgments.

This word "history" is very abstract. But all the factors that make history and propel it forward, especially people, are concrete and complicated, a cornucopia of every sort and kind. ... The history of a people, of an era, is a convergence of the histories of millions and millions of individuals. In the course of this convergence, each person must walk their own road. (251)

In a later scene, Sun Yue's narration is also used to mock the mechanistic thinking that continues to dominate party orthodoxy. She decides that history cannot be categorized and periodized according to a simple dialectic. She rejects the seductive oversimplification that whatever happened during the Cultural Revolution must be bad, and whatever happened before or since must be good and speaks directly to the intellectual legacy in her doubts, musing, "I'm not sure if logic can be considered a science, but this much seems simple: seventeen years [of socialism prior to the Cultural Revolution] – the Cultural Revolution – the present. Affirm – deny – affirm. It's a deductive syllogism. If Hegel were alive today, he would have many Chinese disciples" (286). She rejects the premise that transitional justice means closure on the past, for part of history's complexity is its painful continuity. As she says, "To me, history is not in the past. History and the present reality share a single belly that no one can split open. It's swallowing up my future.... I'm so tired of it" (22). Later Sun Yue explains that she was overjoyed to hear the Gang of Four had been smashed, "but the feeling of elation soon passed. When I thought about everything we had been through, the pain was worse than ever. What hurt was not just the results of that chaotic decade, but also its origins. And more than that, both the results and the origins remain realities today!" (163).

In addressing the fate of the Gang of Four so forthrightly, Dai Houying's character argues for the value of doubt. Part of the complexity of history is its stubborn refusal to look the same from all perspectives. The complexity of human history, exacerbated by the limits of human knowledge, together militate against the validity of totalizing ideologies. In a magazine interview in 1988, Dai Houying contrasted herself with Confucius, who offered this account of his self-cultivation: "The Master said: At fifteen, I set my mind upon learning; at thirty, I took my place in society; at forty I became free of doubts; at fifty, I understood Heaven's Mandate; at sixty, my ear was attuned; and at seventy, I could follow my heart's desires without overstepping the bounds of propriety."[33] The Master found self-certainty by aligning himself with the order of the universe. By contrast, Dai Houying came to reject the certainty of ideology and to embrace doubt:

"At forty I was free of doubts." But for me, at forty my doubts had just begun. I had a definite fault: for decades I had given my mind over to other people. It

---

[33] *Analects* 2.4. Translation by Edward Slingerland, transl., *Confucius, the Essential Analects: Selected Passages with Traditional Commentary* (Indianapolis, IN: Hackett, 2006), p. 4.

never occurred to me that I too was a person and that I too had a mind, and a rather intelligent mind at that. I had to take responsibility for myself. From that point on I used my own mind to think, my own eyes to perceive, my own voice to sing – I didn't worship anyone. Looking at my generation from my own perspective, I saw that other people suffered the same way, but the extent of suffering and the ways of expressing it were different. This entire generation of ours had been trapped, and we could not go on that way. I thought I should write out my thoughts – this was the impetus for my literary production.[34]

Dai Houying's emphasis on the importance of individual testimony – on using one's own lived experiences and critical faculties to develop and express a personal perspective – gives primacy to firsthand perceptual knowledge (*ganxing renshi*: based on sensory and emotional "feeling") over abstract rational knowledge (*lixing renshi*).

In the novel, He Jingfu, the embattled author of the manuscript *Marxism and Humanism*, is the character who makes the case for doubt to Sun Yue. Sun Yue (like Dai Houying) has just turned forty, and she is questioning all the so-called wisdom received through books and teachers. In her own narration, Sun Yue admires the hard-earned wisdom of He Jingfu's certainty in the value of doubt. She concludes, "When he [He Jingfu] turned forty, he really did become 'free of doubts'; as for me, my doubts grew greater and greater. But he was right: doubt is not a bad thing" (172).

Another metaphor Dai Houying uses in the novel to undermine ideological certainty is blindness. He Jingfu says, "Sun Yue, ah, Sun Yue. I can see you still don't quite understand. You've muddled blindness with certainty, and you think that doubt and certainty are irreconcilable opposites" (166). Sun Yue recalls that as a child her teachers made the students eat lunch next to a maggot-filled manure pile "to cultivate their proletarian feelings." She forced herself to eat, repeating the mantra, "I haven't seen anything" (166). Sun Yue, awakened from her dream of blind certainty, finds a world of shit and maggots staring her the face. This retrospective revelation is reinforced by its opposite, the experience of He Jingfu who escaped the indoctrination of the Cultural Revolution, ironically, because of his status as an outcast. For years he wandered the countryside as a vagrant, living off his labor and developing his own understanding of the world. He tells the reader that certainty and doubt are not irreconcilable opposites. He explains that "It is only knowledge attained through doubt that is relatively certain" (167).

---

[34] Dai Houying quoted in Xu Hong, "Liuxia yige lishi de zuyi: zhuiji 1998 nian 5 yue caifang Dai Houying" [May 1998 interview with Dai Houying], *Shiji* [Century] (June 1996), p. 22.

Ah: Sounding the Gaps

The title *Humanity, Ah Humanity!* offers a window into the meaning of the novel. Undoubtedly the main topic of Dai Houying's work is "humanity," as the word appears twice in the very brief title. But the rest of the title is important, too. The conspicuous punctuation of the title with an exclamation mark – called an "emotion mark" (*ganqing hao*) in Chinese – tells us that the novel is charged with emotion.[35] The nature and importance of emotional expression in the novel is suggested by the word *ah* (*a*), which first appears in the title and then reappears several times in the narration of the story.

The word *ah* (*a*) in the novel signifies both the emotive expression of subjective truth and the gaps in our knowledge of objective truth. The word *ah* indicates emotion (often as an onomatopoeia of human vocalization), but it is on its own ambiguous in value and content. Being semantically void, *ah* is an example of what the Chinese call an "empty" (*xu*) word. The antonym of empty (*xu*) is *shi* (substantial, actual, real), a character found in terms like *facts* (*shishi*) and *practice* (*shijian*) in the official epistemological slogans "seek truth from facts" and "practice is the sole criterion of truth." The legal process embraced such slogans under the assumption that facts and truth can be established with certainty. The goal of the Special Court's inquiry, including the introduction of evidence and testimony, was to *substantiate* the accusations made in the indictment. From this perspective, an empty word like *ah* would seem to be the last place to seek out truth. But this is precisely the point Dai Houying is making in her novel: truths can also be found in the empty spaces between seeming certainties.

For Dai Houying, digging into past actions is a forensic demonstration of practical realities and objective facts, but facts and truth are not necessarily the same. Whether in reality or in a novel, the reality observed by one person can be called into question by the reality of another. Testimony is inherently subjective. Moreover, political power can be used to trump or exclude or redefine the truth, but this does not mean that might makes right. Dai Houying's critique should not be mistaken for nihilism or moral relativism. Her view is not a denial of material reality or the importance of getting to the truth at the bottom. She is merely pointing out that there is a gap between what is and what ought to be that can make it hard to be sure. She is interested in truth above all else,

---

[35] The mark (!) is also known as an "emotional sigh mark" (*gantanhao*) or an "exclamation mark" (*jingtanhao*); see *Xinhua cidian* [New China dictionary], revised edn. [1988] (Beijing: Shangwu yinshuguan, 1993), Appendix 3, pp. 1264–6.

but she is not convinced that impersonal facts alone will get us there. If there is more to truth than the actual and substantive, then where is the rest to be found?

Dai Houying's answer is this tiny word *ah*, which gives expression to emotion and complexity of human circumstances. *Ah* can express a wide variety of affective states, including surprise, admiration, agreement, or doubt, depending on the context. Dai Houying was very conscious of this ambiguity. In the following, narrated by Sun Yue's ex-husband Zhao Zhenhuan, a single syllable of emotional expression reveals the multiplicity, complexity, and uncertainty of human experience:

> Xu Hengzhong asked me, "How is life now?"
> "I've received my just deserts," I replied simply.
> "Ah!" All three spoke together, but the implications were varied and complex. At that moment I could not make out all the different meanings. (209)

Throughout the text, Dai Houying uses *ah* to signify the fragility of human interconnectedness and relatedness. The semantic void represented by this particle discloses the gulf of darkness and uncertainty that keeps people apart. At the same time, by juxtaposing her narrators' testimony, she proposes to sound the gap, to discern its emotional content and bring people together. Dai Houying states the problem in the epigraph to Part 3 of the novel: "This sort of thing happens every day: Two hearts collide; sometimes there are fireworks, sometimes just an echo" (183). The meaning of particular echoes or fireworks is left for each of us to ponder.

The thematic significance of *ah* is sensitively depicted in the cover art for the novel, drawn by Yang Baizi for the first edition from Huacheng Publishing (Figure 14). The emotional visage of the main character Sun Yue is shown at center over the word *ah* (*a*). Her ex-husband Zhao Zhenhuan is shown at upper left, and the wanderer He Jingfu is shown at lower right, each drawn over the word *person* or *humanity* (*ren*) writ both small and large. The characters are not only individual people, but also representatives of our collective humanity. What connects them together – and holds them (us) apart – is a complex world of emotion. This is the space that Dai Houying wants to explore.

In any given interaction, will there be sparks or just an echo? The novel offers some examples of both. The first example is spoken by Party Secretary Xi Liu, who uses the novel's title phrase to express his unwillingness to accept or to join in the humanist cause:

> It's been criticized so many times, and still people want to talk about humanism. "Think how wonderful it would be if everyone loved each other and everyone was equal, if there were no need for class struggle all the time! I don't want to

Figure 14. Yang Baizi's cover illustration for the first Huacheng Publishing edition of Dai Houying's *Humanity, Ah Humanity!* (November 1980).

struggle against other people, yet everyone else wants to struggle against me."
Humanity, ah, humanity! Human beings are all like this: The only thing they
can't stand more than struggle is *not* to struggle. (283)

For the party secretary, who suffered during the Cultural Revolution and
has witnessed the human capacity for violent struggle, idealistic thinking
is belied by the fallibility of man. The party secretary is one of the less
sympathetic characters in the novel, but when he speaks about humanism, the reader can appreciate the frustration with humanity captured in
the syllable *ah*.

In another, more hopeful example this gap also implies a possibility
for connection. He Jingfu, a more sympathetic narrator, uses *ah* when
groping to reestablish an emotional connection with Sun Yue. Though
they were once close friends, she now addresses him in an unnaturally
distancing manner, which he alternately describes as "business-like"
(37), "bureaucratic" (161), or "cadre-like" (170). He Jingfu addresses
Sun Yue's doubts about his intentions, saying, "Sun Yue, ah, Sun Yue.
I can see you still don't quite understand" (166). Here the *ah* signals the
transformative power of human communication, the potential to connect
two individuals. It is used to express empathy, bridge the gap, move from
confusion and alienation to mutual understanding. Just as the space
between can keep us apart, so too can it bring us together.

A poem treasured by the schoolgirl Hanhan is another example of
how Dai Houying brings out the mix of pathos and ambivalence in *ah* to
signal the complexity of human relationships. Hanhan keeps a poem hidden in the bottom of her book bag. The poem is about her name, which
used to be Huanhuan (Little Ring), a name that borrowed a character
from her father's name. After the divorce, Sun Yue changed the girl's
name to Hanhan (Regret). Little Hanhan is haunted by her tragic name,
the missing paternal character, and the vanished, connective "little ring."
The poem gives voice to this.

> Name ah name,
> You are not just a symbol of people's characters,
> You can also recall certain circumstances
> That produce an echo in people's hearts. (54)

This small poem, Hanhan's plangent apostrophe to her own name
betrays both her self-alienation and her effort to overcome it. The *ah*
echoes the title of the novel as she reaches toward the history of her
absent, abstracted self – an empty space overflowing with meaning and
emotion. As the second line indicates, Hanhan's name is a sign referring
to multiple characters: the graphic character in her father's name, the
affective character of her mother's unresolved regret, and the quality of

her own personal character. In the third line the tension between these multiple referents marks off the circumstances of Hanhan's familial- and self-fragmentation. She has all the evidence but instead of feeling certain, she is immersed in the difficulty of it all.

Testimony recalls "certain circumstances" (*shiqing*) of the past, but also dredges up repressed emotions (*renqing*). The return of the repressed is indicated by the uncanny doubling of the name and its return in altered form: the familiar Huanhuan (which is already a homonym for "return") is transformed into the alien Hanhan, and returns as a disembodied echo of the connection implied by the play on "little ring" and "return." The final line of the poem affirms that the speech act produces an emotional effect in people's hearts. Though her voice is alienated as an echo, sounding out the empty space produces a shared experience. Even if testimony fails to spark off fireworks, even if it merely resonates in emptiness, at least the act of echolocation produces an awareness of space and the possibility of connection.

It is precisely the communicative power of speech that makes it dangerous. Hanhan vows to keep her name contained inside her, so it will not grind down other people as it grinds her down. The single *ah* in the poem's first line represents the alienation, emotionality, multiplicity, and complexity of human relations, as well as the possibility of finding oneself by sounding out the emptiness. The poem is treasured and, by implication, Dai Houying's argument should also be treasured. Emotion is a necessary element in human nature, not something to be contained, pacified, or treated as an alien force. As human emotion is developed and given play, human beings will move closer to actualization. The narrators who speak from emotion may be closer to the truth than those who pose as stalwart and objective.

Ends and Means

China's post–Cultural Revolution humanists cited Marx's early works in philosophy and, based on these, asserted that the teleological end of History is none other than the actualization of human nature in society. Revolutionary means should be appropriate to that ultimate end, which is the full realization of human dignity. In the novel, He Jingfu and his effort to publish give voice to such aspirations. Early in the novel, He Jingfu diagnoses the failure of the Cultural Revolution as follows:

You've read some Marx and Engels. Keep reading and you will see: in the hearts of these two great men is "MAN" [*ren*] written in large strokes. All their theories and all their revolutionary practice was for the realization of this Man, for the elimination of all the conditions that prevent men from becoming Man. Sadly, some self-styled Marxists remember only the means, forgetting or disposing of the ends. It's as if the goal of revolution were to ruin men's characters, to break up their families, to build all sorts of walls around people to keep them apart. (87)

The gap between means and ends has reinforced the gaps between people. The prescription, in He Jingfu's narration, is to reevaluate and reform revolutionary means to be more respectful of human dignity. This line of analysis leads Dai Houying to reject the general strategy of class struggle under socialism and to repudiate the specific tactic of attacking people's personal characters. These criticisms get at the basic impetus behind the Cultural Revolution. On the one hand, it sought to completely raze the remnants of feudal and capitalist culture and, on the other hand, it tried to reconstruct the socialist person from the fundaments of personal and familial identity.

At the time Dai Houying wrote *Humanity, Ah Humanity!* there was little disagreement in China that the continuous class struggle of the Cultural Revolution had gone too far. Within a year of the novel's publication the Chinese Communist Party declared the class struggle completely erroneous and in no way revolutionary. Marxist orthodoxy holds that socialist revolution creates a qualitatively different form of society, liberated from class oppression. Just as this issue was "on trial" in the trial of the Gang of Four, it comes into play in the novel. At one point in the story, He Jingfu states the conventional wisdom that class struggle was necessary to bring about the 1949 revolution, but goes on to say that it became an unnecessary and destructive force. He Jingfu also points out how the instrumentalism of phony class struggle transformed the people into inhuman objects, alienated from the party leadership:

It is necessary, lofty, and great to wage class struggle to eliminate class oppression and exploitation; but it is preposterous and wicked to wage "class struggle" by artificially creating classes, dividing the people, and ruining families. Our predecessors liberated the people; their successors harmed the people. Our predecessors truly treated the people like "human beings"; their successors simply treated the people like tools that speak. (262)

Dai Houying's fiction also persuades readers that turning criticism and struggle into character assassination can only lead to psychological repression and social pathology. In the course of the novel, the reader learns of several people whose diaries and personal letters were publicized and used against them during the Cultural Revolution. Hearing about this, Sun Yue asks, "Who invented this method of class struggle? Baring people's privacy and exposing their most intimate feelings to drive them to the gallows!" (108). As the scope of struggle grew wider and wider, more and more people got caught on the wrong side of arbitrary and constantly shifting lines. The tactics of class struggle turned to the exposure and mockery of people's private thoughts and feelings.

Sun Yue recalls the death of her own humanity (*renge*: personal character) this way. She recounts a Cultural Revolution struggle session in which another character accused Xi Liu of feudal attitudes and implicated Sun Yue as his associate. She traces her experience back to the day she lost faith in her role model Party Secretary Xi Liu, human dignity, the salvation of History, and the possibility of revolution. She laments, "At first I did not fear that placard labeling me 'Xi Liu's concubine'; I had faith that someday the rains would wash the dirty water from my body. But from that day forward I lost my faith. Dirty water has insoluble oils" (15). Sun Yue knows that "dirty water" not only leaves an indelible mark, it also flows in a continuous stream from the past to the present. Sun Yue is stained again with dirty water, this time *after* the Cultural Revolution. Xi Liu resents the former radical Xu Hengzhong and blocks his ability to publish. However, Sun Yue defends Xu: she has reconciled with her tormenter and even helps the widower care for his young son. Xi Liu warns Sun Yue that her relationship with Xu could be misconstrued. When Xi Liu threatens to sully Sun Yue's reputation with unseemly rumors, his ugly smear is more of the same "dirty water" spilled in the Cultural Revolution: "Dirty water, dirty water. Wherever you go there's liable to be dirty water. Especially for a woman, and especially for a woman like me" (17). As she stews over Xi Liu's threat, defiantly sewing new shoes for Xu's young son, she pricks her finger. Through a Freudian slip of the needle, Sun Yue's psychic pain manifests as bodily pain:

A little red pearl of blood beaded up on my fingertip. Every part of the human body is filled with blood and spirit. When we're wounded, we bleed and feel pain. Old wounds heal and new ones open; we keep on flowing blood and feeling pain until we die.

I put my finger in my mouth and sucked on it – mustn't let anyone see. Some people are fixated on blood and are fond of taking other people's blood for conducting "scientific experiments." They study how to turn blood into dirty water and spill it all over the ground. (17)

To the extent that blood and pain are revealed, they become the objects of detached, scientific experiments or sadistic voyeurism. In the name of inhuman science and progress, human blood and spirit become grist for the mill of revolution. Sun Yue's authentic experience of suffering is not spoken publicly, but instead becomes a secret concealed in her closed mouth.[36]

---

[36] Blood has been used in modern Chinese literature to signify authentic bodily experience. See Yomi Braester, *Witness against History: Literature, Film, and Public Discourse in*

And, as The Novelist remarks, stifled emotion leads to hypocrisy and artifice, literally a *"false* emptiness" (*xuwei*). "Forcing people will only make them feel oppressed; they will learn to hide away their true feelings or even to become hypocrites (*xuwei*). If a society accepts hypocrisy as the norm and views natural spontaneity as an evil aberration, it will lead to many silent tragedies" (170). Dai Houying's novel is filled with the silent tragedies of burned diaries, hidden wounds, concealed poetry, and unspoken words.

Another transparent symbol of struggle in the novel is white hair. Throughout the novel, white hair reveals the human toll of class struggle and personal attacks. Though the main characters are just forty years old, many have white hair. As the novel opens, Zhao Zhenhuan, the man who had married Sun Yue in his more optimistic youth, blames his white hair on that lurking and inscrutable monster, History. He says "History is a cunning and capricious creature. It launches sudden strikes against me at night. My hair has gone white" (10–11). He is alienated from the past, yet cannot escape it. His ex-wife Sun Yue also has white hair. Though she is coming to terms with her past, the damage cannot be reversed. When she talks about this Sun Yue she refers to herself in the third person, a sign of her alienation.

Such a lovely day! The storm has long since passed. But when will everything regain its original color? You can't just whitewash and plaster over. The bones must mend. The flesh must be tempered. The blood must be refreshed. Look at Sun Yue – the hair on her temples has gone completely white. (110)

Later, in a confessional letter, Zhao Zhenhuan accepts his white hair as a just punishment, a deserved stigma. He draws on the language of humanism to make his plea, asking "Sun Yue, am I still human? Am I still fit to be father to a child? ... I've taken my punishment; my hair has gone all white" (128). Zhao Zhenhuan's reconciliation with his daughter and with his past on the last page of the book is expressed as a sense of loss and recovery. He says, "I've lost what I ought to lose; I've found what I ought to find" (345).

Thus Dai Houying admits some possibility of justice or even redemption. However, in scenes like this, she is clear that this is not a return to normalcy, at least not in the sense of *status quo ante*. In the wake of dehumanizing disaster, life will never be the same for these characters. Nothing will restore their innocence, youth, or faith. The irreversible passage of time defies the notion of a fully commensurable past. Liu Binyan wanted an end to the perverted exchange that he saw as the root of injustice and inhumanity. For Dai Houying the diagnosis may be stated correctly, but it has little remedial value. Sun Yue refers to this as an inversion (*diandao*) and she says that it cannot simply be reversed. "These past few years have taught me: it's best to keep your most precious feelings stored up inside. What's toppled is not readily turned upright. What's muddied is not readily cleared up" (20).

There is no returning to the past, yet the past will always threaten to make violent incursions into the present. History can neither be paid off nor contained. Under these conditions, justice is not an objective state of affairs, but a subjective acceptance of humanity's shared fate. Holding a trial in order to close the door on the past is fallacious. In the novel, the result of testimony is not a consensus. It is the first step in the opening up of contradictions that raise more questions than they answer.

Questions about individual and collective responsibility, natural and sociological laws, and the extent of human agency – these are the questions at the heart of the contradiction between materialist and voluntarist interpretations of Marxism. The task of the Special Court was to answer a much simpler question, to determine the specific criminal responsibility of certain people for certain historical events. But the larger issue of historical responsibility could not be adjudicated in a court of law. Moreover, for Dai Houying, the question of historical responsibility was neither individual nor collective, but was inextricably entangled with the emotional aspect of human relationships.

Acceptance of personal responsibility was especially important for Dai Houying who, in the postscript to the novel, frankly acknowledges her own enthusiastic participation in the radical politics of the Cultural Revolution. There is the danger that placing a confession like this at the end of the novel will be interpreted as an effort to shift guilt away from the writer and transform her into a victim. Sun Yue, apparently speaking for Dai Houying, does the opposite. She claims ownership of her crimes:

I'm not willing to accept other people's pity and sympathy. And I certainly don't want their charity. I chose every step of the road. Though some choices did not fully realize my feelings and intentions, or sometimes even went against my conscience, in the end they still reflect my understanding and attitude towards life. I'm not willing to erase my own footprints, nor am I willing to let other people help me cover them up. These footprints have caused me suffering and shame, but because of this I treasure them. (135)

The evident sincerity of her confession must have had a powerful effect on its readers. During the struggle sessions of the Cultural Revolution, readers would have witnessed again and again confessions of intrinsically limited reliability: coerced, calculated, or self-serving. Yet the widespread experience of confession remained genuinely painful. As David Wang has explained,

The confessional mode of narrative must have sounded familiar yet strange to mainland [Chinese] readers at the same time, as it has been well practiced by everybody in a broader social context of public self-criticism, even if mostly it was done against personal wishes. History thus conceived implies a (re)collection of incomplete memories, piecemeal evidence, personal prejudices, psychological and ideological motives, all defining and undercutting one another.[37]

Here Sun Yue embraces a sincere form of self-criticism, closer to the ideal than to how it was actually practiced: that is, the ideal of acceptance and reconciliation with one's own culpability and shortcomings. The confession in the postscript, and the confessions by certain characters who earn the respect of the reader, are meant to be sincere and deeply felt.

In this way, Dai Houying's self-criticism and the counterpoint of testimonials she presents in her fiction are a settling of accounts with herself and an invitation to her readers to settle accounts with themselves. Dai Houying seems to say that each individual is ultimately accountable to his or her own conscience: there is no one else who can fully settle accounts for us. This is why, when Sun Yue reports to He Jingfu that the University Party Committee has reversed its 1957 judgment on him, He Jingfu does not thank her. He says, "History was restored to its original shape – what was there to be thankful for? And to feel thankful would be to settle accounts, and with whom could I settle them?" (36). Later, Sun Yue uses similar language to refuse Xu Hengzhong's apology for struggling against her.

Old Xu, what's the point in saying that? We ought not to talk about who is sorry to whom. If I'm supposed to be like you – the sort of person who can bear the burden for that episode of history – then surely I've completely settled that account with you. It's a pity, back then we weren't equipped to bear responsibility for history; rather, History should have borne responsibility for us. As for each individual's lessons, that's another matter. You have your lessons, I have mine. In that regard, no one can cover up for anyone else, no one can stand in for anyone else. (57)

[37] Wang, "Tai Hou-ying," p. 75.

Individuals are not responsible for the grand scope of history, she says, however, our responsibility for ourselves cannot be shirked or foisted onto others.

The problem of individual responsibility for history pervades Dai Houying's novel, and it was also the central issue in the Gang of Four trial. The state could rightly try and convict the political leaders of the Cultural Revolution, but such a courtroom drama could not reconcile the myriad people with their pasts. Dai Houying confessed in a magazine interview that the inclination in her work has been to "sum up history," even if such a complex settling of accounts were not possible.[38] In *Humanity, Ah Humanity!*, Dai Houying assesses the central flaw of the Cultural Revolution as a lack of shared human emotion. The meaning and value of objective facts are determined by empathetic understanding, which fills the gaps between us and provides the moral guide to human actualization through history. This is the ultimate end of revolutionary struggle. According to Dai Houying, testimony has value in itself, beyond its contribution to a totalizing verdict – testimony *is* history.

[38] Xu Hong, "Liuxia yige lishi de zuyi," p. 22.

5   Verdict

After six weeks of grueling testimony and debate, and another four weeks of deliberations, the Special Court at last announced its verdict. The verdict redressed the accusations of injustice raised by the indictment and brought order out of the chaos of testimony. The verdict was a "settling" account, a conclusive narrative resolution that established the final legal truth. As an authoritative interpretation of the past, issued and enforced by the state, the written judgment of the court exemplified the power of the traditional genre of official history (*zhengshi*). Moreover, the power of the official claim to truth was inherent in the trial's claim to justice (*zhengyi*). This connection is evident in the very word for justice, a modern neologism derived by combining the classical terms *zheng* and *yi*.[1]

The classical term *zheng* denotes straightness, correctness, or moral rectitude. The classical term *yi* denotes righteousness, as discussed previously in connection with righteous indignation. Thus the modern term for justice encompasses the moral or ethical values of rectitude and righteousness. However, this same combination of characters also had another use in classical Chinese, as it was appended to the titles of books where it referred to the orthodox or authoritative version of a text and its interpretive commentary. This usage derived from the alternate sense of *yi* as meaning or significance, so that *zhengyi* meant the "correct" (*zheng*) "meaning" (*yi*) of a text.[2] The Special Court's verdict provided just such an example of *zhengyi* – an authoritative interpretation that "did justice" to the past.

---

[1] The modern term is likely derived from classical Chinese by way of the modern Japanese *seigi*. For a discussion of Chinese neologisms of this type, see Lydia Liu, *Translingual Practice: Literature, National Culture, and Translated Modernity – China, 1900–1937* (Stanford, CA: Stanford University Press, 1995).

[2] Some examples of classical texts with titles of this type are *Correct Interpretation of the Records of the Grand Historian* (*Shiji zhengyi*), *Correct Interpretation of the Five Classics* (*Wujing zhengyi*), and *Correct Interpretation of the Imperial Formulae for Musical Temperament and Tuning* (*Yuzhi lülü zhengyi*).

The verdict (like the indictment it responded to) was a performative or operative linguistic act, a speech act that brought into being new social realities. The authority of the legal state validated the judgment's stated findings of fact as truths. Moreover, the text of the verdict contained "sentences" that subjected the defendants to the loss of their freedoms or potentially even their lives.[3] For the language of the verdict to be operative, it had to be performed as an ordained ritual in a proper ceremonial context. At a somber ceremony held in the Tianjin Room of the Great Hall of the People, the judges of the full court affixed their names and seals to the text of the verdict.[4] Two days later, in the symbolic space of the courtroom, the judges pronounced their verdict aloud to the defendants and before the public. This marked the conclusion to the trial. At the signing ceremony, President of the Special Court Jiang Hua had congratulated the assembled judges for "seizing victory" by "seeking truth from facts" and "using law as a weapon."[5] His words were apt, for they pointed to another fundamental conception of justice embodied by the trial: justice as comprehension.

Settling Accounts: Justice as Comprehension

The image of "using law as a weapon" exemplified Chinese socialism's unapologetically instrumental view of law. The instrumental view of law was justified by Lenin's theory of the state as a class dictatorship. In media accounts of the trial, the type of instrument that the law was most often likened to was a weapon. For example, an article about the Gang of Four trial in *Liberation Army Daily* insisted that the people "must be good at using law as a weapon to strike our enemies, to protect the people, to punish criminals, to preserve social order, and to consolidate the people's democratic dictatorship."[6] In another example, this one from *Guangming Daily*, law was described as an indispensable tool for power:

This experience is a painful historical lesson that has told the people, loudly and clearly, this truth: the law of socialist China is a magic weapon [*fabao*] in the people's hands, used to govern the nation, stabilize the state, and ward off harm. "It is something as indispensable as cloth and grain." The people need only

---

[3] Robert M. Cover, "Violence and the Word," *Yale Law Journal* 95.8 (July 1986), pp. 1601–29.

[4] The full court was present, except Judge Fei Xiaotong. For one participant's retrospective account emphasizing ritual aspects of the signing ceremony, see Tumen and Xiao Sike, *Tebie shenpan: Lin Biao, Jiang Qing fangeming jituan shoushen shilu* [Special trial: True account of the trial of the Lin Biao and Jiang Qing counterrevolutionary groups] (Beijing: Zhongyang wenxian chubanshe, 2003), p. 332.

[5] Entry for January 23, *TBFTJS*, p. 427.

[6] "Renmin de shengli" [Victory of the people], *JFJB*, January 26, 1981.

grasp the power in their hands and use the law as a weapon to strike down these counter-revolutionary criminals.[7]

Law in this account was not just any weapon, but the mystical *ne plus ultra* of weaponry: the "magic weapon" (Chinese *fabao*, Sanskrit *dharma-ratna*, literally "dharma-jewel" or "law-treasure") of Buddhist folklore. In the popular imagination, the term *fabao* conjured the image of Monkey wielding his magical staff to strike down the White-Boned Demon and her evil minions, an image previously presented in connection with the trial (Figure 3). In the special cant of Chinese socialism, the term *fabao* usually was reserved for the "magic weapon" of Mao Zedong Thought, as illustrated in the poster in Figure 15. However, the official discourse surrounding the Gang of Four trial revealed that in the era of reform, law too had the power of a magical "law-treasure" weapon. In a political culture that policed every linguistic nuance, this new usage of *fabao* was highly significant, for law now took the place of Mao Zedong Thought as the ultimate weapon of socialism.

To "seize victory" the people would have to grasp the magic weapon and wield it mercilessly against their enemies. One of the most ubiquitous images of socialist power in Mao's China was a raised fist grasping the weapons of revolution, whether a rifle, an industrial tool, a farming implement, or a book of Mao's quotations.[8] It is highly significant that this grasping motif depicts weapons that are both material and intellectual; wielding power entails the ability to craft knowledge and grasp truth. This idea was well established in Mao's China. As Frederick Engels had argued, the dialectical coevolution of the prehensile hand and the comprehending mind through labor differentiates human beings from other creatures.[9] According to Engels, it is this dual "grasp" that builds society and literally makes us human. Law is another powerful tool, like the paleolith or the rocket in depicted in the poster in Figure 16, for the development of human society and the realization of our human potential. A special commentator's piece for the *People's Daily* described law as implemented in the Gang of Four trial as a tool to grasp "truth from facts":

[7] "Huo guo yang min, guo fa bu rong." Similarly, from the official Xinhua News Agency's description of the sentencing of the defendants: "punishment by the people's law ... has struck down on the heads of Jiang Qing and Zhang Chunqiao like a merciless iron fist." See *Xinhua* wire report, January 25, 1981.

[8] See further discussion of grasping at Alexander C. Cook, "The Spiritual Atom Bomb and Its Global Fallout," in Alexander C. Cook, ed., *Mao's Little Red Book: A Global History* (New York: Cambridge University Press, 2014), pp. 1–22.

[9] Frederick Engels, "The Part Played by Labour in the Transition from Ape to Man" (1876), www.marxists.org/archive/marx/works/1876/part-played-labour/.

Figure 15. "Mao Zedong Thought is a magic weapon to victoriously combat all enemies at home and abroad!" (*Mao Zedong sixiang shi zhansheng guoneiwai yiqie dirende fabao!*) (ca. 1967).
Source: Private Collection, International Institute of Social History (Amsterdam).

The proceedings take facts as the basis and law as the standard [literally, plumbline]. Right is right, wrong is wrong. From their crimes, not one bit is subtracted; to what are not their crimes, not one bit is added. We put weight on evidence, not on confessions. All the accusations against [the defendants] are based on verified and original documents and evidence, such as files, letters, diaries, notes, audio recordings, video recordings, and so on. *Truth is in the people's hands.*[10]

By taking into their hands the material facts of evidence and the interpretive apparatus of law, the people could grasp the truth of history. In this way, law is a tool for intellectual comprehension.

[10] "Shehuizhuyi minzhu he fazhi de lichengpai: ping shenpan Lin Biao, Jiang Qing fangeming jituan" [Milestone in socialist democracy and legality: On the trial of the Lin Biao and Jiang Qing counterrevolutionary groups], *RMRB*, December 22, 1980; emphasis added.

Figure 16. Zhou Ruizhuang, "Love labor: Labor creates the human world" (*Ai laodong: Laodong chuangzao renlei shijie*) (1983).
Source: Landsberger Collection, International Institute of Social History (Amsterdam).

Moreover, the socialist ideal of comprehension was comprehensive. Media coverage of the trial depicted law as totalizing in its reach. A headline in the *Worker's Daily* assured readers that "[t]he law's net is vast; legal responsibility is not easily evaded."[11] The phrase "the law's net is vast" (*fa wang huihui*) plays on an aphorism from the ancient Daoist classic, Laozi's *Daodejing* (*Classic of the Way and Virtue*), which says, "Heaven's net is vast; its mesh is coarse yet nothing escapes" (*tian wang huihui, shu er bu shi*).[12] No one can escape justice. Like the universal extent and karmic accuracy of the traditional notion of justice as retribution (*bao*), this

[11] Chen Qingmei and Zhang Zhaoyin, "Fa wang hui, zui ze nan tao: Jielu Wang Hongwen yi shou zhizao 'Za Shang Zi Lian Si' xue'an de zhenxiang" [The law's net is vast, no escape from guilt], *Gongren ribao*, December 6, 1980.

[12] Laozi, *Dao de jing* [Classic of the way and virtue], Chinese with English transl. by James Legge, http://ctext.org/dao-de-jing, section 73, my translation.

modern variant replaced the all-encompassing net of heaven with that of the law. The lines of legal statute are woven into a vast and inescapable net, both capturing and comprehending everything.

The Judgment Is Announced

The full court convened again at No. 1 Justice Road on January 25, 1981 to announce its verdict. The hall, filled with the ten defendants and more than eight hundred spectators, was flooded with television lights. Outside, armed police and sentries cordoned off the building.[13] At precisely 9:00 AM, Jiang Hua called the court to order, announced the roll call, and summoned the accused.[14] The defendants entered one by one, escorted by court officers in smartly pressed blue uniforms with holstered pistols.[15] The president of the court intoned: "The case of the ten prime culprits of the Lin Biao and Jiang Qing Counter-revolutionary Cliques has been heard by the First and Second Tribunals of the Special Court and has undergone the deliberations of the Special Court. Now we shall announce our judgment."[16] He began with a summary of the Special Court's work:

This court held 42 sessions of investigation and debate, during which 49 witnesses and victims appeared in court to testify, and 873 pieces of evidence of all types were examined. The aforementioned criminal offenses of the principal culprits of the Lin Biao and Jiang Qing counter-revolutionary cliques have been amply demonstrated by a great preponderance of material and documentary evidence, expert analysis, witness testimony, and victims' statements. The facts are clear and the evidence is conclusive.[17]

He explained that the verdict was binding and final: this was the court of last resort, and there could be no appeals.[18] It was time to read the verdict, formally called the "Written Judgment of the Special Court

---

[13] Wu Xiuquan, *Wangshi cangsang* [Vicissitudes of bygone days] (Shanghai: Shanghai wenyi chubanshe, 1986), p. 325.

[14] All were present except for Jiang Tengjiao's lawyer Wang Shunhua, who begged off due to illness. Fei Xiaotong had finally returned from overseas, looking weary from his travels (Yu Fucun and Wang Yongchang, *Renmin de shenpan: shenpan Lin Biao, Sirenbang fangeming jituan* [People's trial: Trial of the Lin Biao and Gang of Four counterrevolutionary groups] (Hefei: Anhui renmin chubanshe, 1998), p. 219).

[15] Entry for January 25, *TBFTJS*, p. 428; Yu and Wang, *Renmin de shenpan*, pp. 218–21.

[16] Entry for January 25, *TBFTJS*, p. 429.

[17] "Zhonghua renmin gongheguo zuigao renmin fayuan tebie fating panjueshu" (Te fa #1) [Verdict of the Special Court of the Supreme People's Court], *TBFTJS*, p. 55.

[18] Associate Justice Wu Xiuquan reported in his memoirs, erroneously, that it was he who read aloud the sentences (*Wangshi cangsang*, p. 326). According to official court records, Wu read aloud only the middle section of the verdict detailing individual criminal responsibility of the defendants. Jiang Hua's personal secretary Zhang Wei cleared up the issue in a letter dated August 16, 1988 to the editors of the periodical *Fazhi wenxue xuan kan* [Legal system literary digest]. The letter is reprinted in its entirety in Ye Yonglie,

under the Supreme People's Court of the People's Republic of China"
(Special Court Document No. 1).[19] At fourteen thousand characters
long, the verdict took more than an hour and a half to be read aloud.
An overview of the document reveals its basic structure and content.

The verdict begins by introducing the circumstances of its own creation. With regard to jurisdiction, the verdict explains the establishment
of the Special Court and the Special Procuratorate by the Standing
Committee the National People's Congress (NPC) and lists the parties to
the case: first the prosecutors and then the defendants and their counsel.
The verdict states that it takes as its legal standard the new *Criminal Law*,
with special reference to Article 9 of the code, which concerned prosecution of acts committed after the founding the socialist state in 1949 but
before the current code came into force in 1980. (The code stipulates
that acts may be prosecuted only if they are considered offenses under
the current code and also would be considered offenses "under the laws,
decrees, and policies then in force.") The document carefully delimits
the scope of its findings, as follows:

The duty of this court is to hear the criminal offenses committed by the principal
culprits in the case of the Lin Biao and Jiang Qing counterrevolutionary cliques
and pursue their criminal liability, in strict accordance with the Criminal Law of
the People's Republic of China. This court does not handle other problems of the
defendants that do not fall under the category of criminal offenses.[20]

The verdict claims to be a strictly legal document, even though the verdict's legal interpretation was later integrated into a more comprehensive
account of history.

Now to the substance of the verdict. The next section of the document
first summarizes the basic finding of the court. The summary states that
all ten defendants have been found guilty of serious crimes as members of
a counterrevolutionary conspiracy designed to seize supreme power over
the party and state. Next, the verdict contextualizes this basic finding
within the unusual historical circumstances of the Cultural Revolution,
when normal structures and institutions of social order – including the
legal system – had been severely compromised. This part of the verdict is
worth quoting at length:

During the great Cultural Revolution, the political life of the state became
extremely abnormal and the socialist legal system was seriously undermined.

Jiang Qing zhuan [Biography of Jiang Qing], Sirenbang quan zhuan (Urumqi: Xinjiang
renmin chubanshe, 2000), pp. 889–91.
[19] "Zhonghua renmin gongheguo zuigao renmin fayuan tebie fating panjueshu," *TBFTJS*,
pp. 40–67 [hereafter abbreviated as Verdict].
[20] Ibid., p. 44.

Taking advantage of their positions and power at that time and resorting to every possible means, overt and covert, by pen and by gun, the Lin Biao and Jiang Qing counter-revolutionary cliques framed and persecuted state leaders and leaders of the Chinese Communist Party and the democratic parties in a premeditated way; conspired to overthrow the government and sabotage the army; suppressed and persecuted large numbers of cadres, intellectuals and ordinary people; and endangered the life and property and right of autonomy of the people of various national minorities. The Lin Biao counter-revolutionary clique plotted to stage an armed coup d'état and conspired to assassinate Chairman Mao Zedong. The Jiang Qing counter-revolutionary clique plotted to stage an armed rebellion in Shanghai.[21]

According to the verdict, these criminal actions caused vast damage with very real and potentially counterrevolutionary consequences:

The criminal activities of the Lin Biao and Jiang Qing counter-revolutionary cliques lasted for a whole decade, bringing calamities to all fields of work and all regions of the country, subjecting the system of the people's democratic dictatorship and socialist public order to extraordinarily grave danger, inflicting great damage on the national economy and all other undertakings, and causing enormous disasters to the people of all ethnic nationalities throughout the country.[22]

This basic finding of counterrevolutionary conspiracy is then elaborated in a long section that narrates the conspirators' criminal activities in roughly chronological order.

With the basic finding established and the details laid out, the verdict proceeds to assign personal criminal liability to each defendant. The verdict finds all ten defendants guilty of counterrevolutionary conspiracy under Article 98 of the Criminal Code, but significantly, three levels of criminal liability are distinguished: Jiang Qing assumed the greatest responsibility as "ringleader" of a counterrevolutionary group; most of the others were found to have "organized and led" counterrevolutionary activities; while Chen Boda and Jiang Tengjiao were assigned a somewhat lesser level of responsibility as "active participants" in counterrevolutionary crimes. Nine of the ten defendants, with the exception of Jiang Tengjiao, were found guilty of conspiring to overthrow the state (Article 92) and of falsely persecuting people (Article 138). However, only Wang Hongwen and Jiang Tengjiao were found guilty of killing or injuring people for counterrevolutionary purposes (Article 101). Zhang Chunqiao, Wang Hongwen, and Jiang Tengjiao were found guilty of instigating officials to commit treason or rebellion (Article 93). Jiang Qing, Zhang Chunqiao, Yao Wenyuan, and Chen Boda were

---

[21] Ibid., pp. 43–4.
[22] Ibid., p. 44.

found guilty of inciting the masses for counterrevolutionary purposes (Article 102).

In its final section, the verdict imposes penalties on the defendants. Notably, none of the defendants were sentenced to immediate execution. Jiang Qing and Zhang Chunqiao were sentenced to death with a two-year reprieve. Wang Hongwen was sentenced to life imprisonment. The other defendants were sentenced to fixed terms of imprisonment ranging from fifteen to twenty years. The verdict also deprived the defendants of their political rights for five years following completion of their terms of imprisonment, if applicable. This supplemental penalty, levied against those who committed counterrevolutionary crimes or other serious offenses, formally excluded the offenders from the political community of "the people" by depriving them of:

(1) the right to vote and to stand for election; (2) the rights provided for in Article 45 of the 1978 Constitution [i.e., the freedoms of speech, the press, correspondence, association, assembly, procession, and various forms of public debate]; (3) the right to hold a position in a state organ; and (4) the right to hold a leading position in any enterprise, institution or people's organization.[23]

Although these sentences were by no means light, they do seem lenient relative to the severity of the charges in the indictment, especially when taking into account credit for as much as ten years time served.

The defendants' courtroom reactions to the verdict varied. Zhang Chunqiao nervously wiped sweat from his brow. Yao Wenyuan closed his eyes and lowered his head. Wang Hongwen stared vacantly. Chen Boda looked frightened, his lip shaking. In contrast, the Lin Biao group defendants were visibly relieved.[24]

When the judge came to Jiang Qing's sentence, he slowed his pace for dramatic effect.[25] "Defendant Jiang Qing is sentenced to death," he announced, pausing before saying, "with a two year reprieve." But before he got to the reprieve, Jiang Qing interrupted, shouting out wildly. Vice-President of the Court Wu Xiuquan recalls the scene in his memoir:

Jiang Qing usually put on a composed air, but at this moment she could not contain her emotions.... Since this was the end of the trial and there was no need for the offenders to answer questions, the dock was not outfitted with microphones. Therefore many people could not hear what she was yelling. But as it happened she was facing me directly and I heard her shout, [Cultural Revolution slogans]

[23] *Criminal Code of the People's Republic of China* (1979), Section 7, Articles 50–54; *Constitution of the People's Republic of China* (1978), Article 45.
[24] Yu and Wang, *Renmin de shenpan*, pp. 220–1.
[25] Ye, *Jiang Qing zhuan*, p. 891.

"Rebellion is reasonable!" and "Revolution is not a crime!" and also something like "Down with counter-revolutionary revisionism!"[26]

In order to maintain the solemn and orderly atmosphere of the court-room, the judge ordered Jiang Qing out of the room. Two female guards dragged her away, in handcuffs and still yelling. According to the report in *People's Daily*, "When the people in the audience saw Jiang Qing's hob-bled and shameful exit, they could no longer control the elation in their hearts, and unable at last to obey court procedures, they burst into fer-vid applause."[27] As the remaining defendants were led away, Jiang Hua announced that the Special Court's trial was now over. The gallery once more erupted in cheers. These were the last residues of excess emotion – briefly discharged and wiped away, so the edge could be neatly sealed around this verdict on the Cultural Revolution.

The Deliberations of the Court

Law is meant to remove the authority to exercise violence away from indi-viduals and deliver authority into the hands of such abstract actors as the people or the state. In light of this, it is worth considering the concrete, decidedly nonabstract process by which the legal verdict was rendered by these agents.

The Special Court did not merely rubber-stamp the Special Procuratorate's indictment. All ten defendants were found guilty as expected and although the general outcome was never in doubt, the specifics were worked out in the course of the trial and not scripted ahead of time. Despite heavy, and at times inappropriate, political pres-sure placed on the Special Court, the judges did assert some measure of judicial autonomy. Beginning from a widespread public assumption of guilt, and with procedural inequities and political pressures tilting the field, it is difficult to imagine the Gang of Four emerging innocent from the Special Court trial. Nevertheless, there were significant differences between the indictment and the verdict. According to an official posttrial work report by President of the Court Jiang Hua, the court's delibera-tions resulted in the dismissal of sixteen indictment counts and findings of guilt in an additional seven instances.[28] The deliberation phase reveals

---

26 Wu, *Wangshi cangsang*, p. 326. Looking back, Judge Wu Xiuquan admits that he too lost composure. Though he was within his powers to eject Jiang Qing from the court, he says, he felt he should have done so with less enthusiasm, first explaining that she had violated courtroom regulations.

27 "Renmin de panjue" [Just verdict], *RMRB*, January 26, 1981.

28 Because the verdict assigned criminal liability according to which articles of the criminal code were violated – and not in direct reference to the counts listed in the

some of the issues raised by the trial that remained unsettled prior to the verdict.

The Special Court entered into deliberations shortly after completing its inquiry on December 29, 1980. The purpose of the deliberations phase was to determine the facts of the case in order to assign appropriate criminal liability to each defendant and to compile the findings into a final verdict. Most observers initially expected the verdict to be announced within a week or two, but they seriously underestimated the work that would be required. Eventually, state authorities issued the court a deadline of January 25. (According to Wang Xiuquan, that date was given because Premier Zhao Ziyang was scheduled to travel overseas, and the state did not wish to have the verdict announced while he was out of the country or to have him face questions about the trial before an official verdict had been rendered.[29]) The protracted timeline strongly suggests that the verdict was not scripted ahead of time, but instead resulted from the interpretive work of the judges.

For the first several weeks, the judges met in the small groups that had been assigned to each defendant's case. The small groups made definite findings of fact and assigned criminal responsibility to individual defendants, then submitted these preliminary results for compilation into a first draft of the verdict. According to participant Wu Xiuquan, the presidents and vice-presidents of the court then "held long and repeated discussions on every issue in the judgment, continuously revising the content, evaluating reference materials, and contemplating the wording."[30] This ongoing process of compilation and editing resulted in twenty-six drafts of the verdict.[31] Next the full court met to debate issues, set sentences, and finalize the document. At this stage the full court paid particularly close attention to the language of the document – editing the text line by line and word by word, correcting errors of fact, and assiduously eliminating all references to the defendants' (noncriminal) political "errors."[32] By the time the document reached its thirtieth draft version, the text had been honed down to about two-thirds its original length.[33] These meetings occurred in the Tianjin Hall of the Great Hall of the People over the

indictment – these figures are somewhat difficult to decipher. See "Zuigao renmin fayuan tebie fating guanyu shenpan Lin Biao, Jiang Qing fangeming jituan an zhufan de xiaojie" [Brief summary of the trial of the principal culprits in the Lin Biao and Jiang Qing counterrevolutionary groups by the Special Court under the Supreme People's Court] (February 9, 1981), *TBFTJS*, p. 491.

29 Wu, *Wangshi cangsang*, p. 325.
30 Ibid.
31 Entry for January 20, *TBFTJS*, p. 415.
32 Ibid., p. 416.
33 Wu, *Wangshi cangsang*, p. 325.

course of three days, from January 20 to January 22. Court records indicate that the deliberations "gave full play to democracy, heard a variety of views, and pooled useful ideas from all judges."[34] Substantive issues were put to vote, with the majority view prevailing. The final verdict was approved unanimously by the full court.

From the differences between the verdict and the indictment, it is evident that the judges made an active contribution to the construction of the final narrative. Although the process took place behind closed doors and the court issued no minority or dissenting opinions, the terse official records can be further supplemented by other sources to illuminate a few key points of deliberation.[35] Legal Consultant to the Special Court Qiu Shaoheng has identified three types of issues that were open to deliberation: (1) whether or not the facts were demonstrated conclusively, (2) whether or not demonstrated actions constituted crimes, and (3) whether or not the law was applied appropriately. One example in which the facts had not been demonstrated conclusively was the charge that Jiang Qing conspired with Kang Sheng and Xie Fuzhi to fabricate a list of "61 Traitors" in the leadership. The court found that Kang Sheng gave the list to Jiang Qing at an opera performance and that she passed it along to Chairman Mao, but the court could not establish that Jiang Qing had helped to create the list. The charge was dismissed.[36] An example in which the established facts did not imply criminal liability was the so-called Changsha Report, when the Gang of Four dispatched Wang Hongwen to secretly report to Chairman Mao on the activities of Deng Xiaoping in hopes of preventing his promotion.[37] The court determined that this incident had occurred as alleged in the indictment, but that it did not constitute a crime because the law did not prohibit Politburo members from working together in private or from making private recommendations to the party chairman. Dismissal of this charge was an important omission from the verdict, for the court had opened its inquiry with this charge and spent several sessions establishing the facts. The official press cited dismissal of this charge as proof of the court's strict adherence to the law. An example of deliberation over application of the law is the charge that Yao Wenyuan incited armed rebellion in Shanghai.

---

[34] Entry for January 20, *TBFTJS*, p. 415.

[35] Account of meeting based on entry for January 20, *TBFTJS*, p. 415. All judges were present, except Fan Zhi (assigned to the Wang Hongwen case), who was ill, and Fei Xiaotong (assigned to the Zhang Chunqiao case), who was overseas on assignment for the Chinese Academy of Social Sciences. Deputy Chief Procurator Yu Ping and Procurator Jiang Wen attended as nonvoting delegates.

[36] Ma Lingguo, "Tebie Fating de falü guwen Qiu Shaoheng" [Special Court legal consultant Henry Chiu], *Shiji* [Century] (September 1999), p. 21.

[37] Ibid.

The court found that a preplanned armed rebellion had been staged in response to the smashing of the Gang of Four in October 1976, and Yao Wenyuan admitted in court that he had approved an article in *Red Flag* calling for workers' militias to struggle against "the bourgeoisie in the Party." However, Yao denied that he intended these statements to incite a violent uprising in Shanghai, and the court agreed that no direct connection could be drawn between his words and later events. Therefore, the law against inciting counterrevolutionary violence was not applicable.

Most of the issues raised for deliberation were resolved in the initial meeting of January 20, but the judges met again on January 21 to deal with one vexing problem that remained. This problem was proper application of Article 101, which concerned the killing or injuring of people for counterrevolutionary purposes. Judge Wang Wenzheng has shared her recollections of the debate over whether or not this law was applicable to Jiang Qing.[38] Although Jiang Qing had organized the frame-up of numerous persons, there was no evidence she had directly ordered that anyone be beaten, tortured, or killed. Nor was there any allegation that she had committed such crimes herself. On this basis, judges Wang Wenzheng, Ren Lingyun, and Qu Yucai argued that Jiang Qing should not be found criminally liable for violation of Article 101. According to Judge Wang, they even refused to sign the verdict if it contained such a finding. Wang Wenzheng points to this principled stand as evidence of the judges' integrity. The judges of the full court were unable to reach consensus on this issue and authorized the presidents and vice-presidents of the court to make a ruling.[39] After further discussion, the minority view prevailed: Jiang Qing was not found liable for violating Article 101. There also seems to have been some disagreement over the applicability of Article 101 to Zhang Chunqiao. The indictment implicated him in two violent episodes: the clash of armed worker groups on Kang Ping Road in Shanghai, and the purge of the party apparatus in Ji'nan. Some internal court records show Zhang Chunqiao to have been found in violation of Article 101, but the final version of the verdict finds him not guilty.[40] The reason for this discrepancy has not been explained, but it provides another instance in which the verdict seems to have resulted from active debate and judicial interpretation.

The full court met again on January 22 to determine sentences. The new *Criminal Code* provided specific sentencing guidelines for each of

---

[38] Wang Wenzheng, "Wang Wenzheng faguan huiyi shenpan si ren bang de xiangxi jingguo" [Judge Wang Wenzheng recalls details of his experience of the Gang of Four trial], www .tianshui.com.cn/news/whzx_news/200907140745066442_3.htm.

[39] Entry for January 21, *TBFTJS*, p. 416.

[40] Ibid., p. 420.

its listed crimes. However, judges could consider a wide array of possible mitigating factors and could even calculate successive or concurrent terms for multiple counts.[41] The general principle was quite flexible: "When sentencing a criminal, a punishment shall be imposed based on the facts, nature and circumstances of the crime, the degree of harm done to society and the relevant provisions of this Law."[42] One of the factors that could be weighed was the attitude of each defendant at trial, and these were duly recorded in the verdict:

Defendants Wang Hongwen, Chen Boda, Wu Faxian, Li Zuopeng, Qiu Huizuo, and Jiang Tengjiao confessed to the facts of their criminal activities; Jiang Tengjiao voluntarily surrendered on the second day after Lin Biao fled the country; Wu Faxian, Qiu Huizuo, and Jiang Tengjiao revealed the facts of the criminal activities of Lin Biao, Jiang Qing, and others; Huang Yongsheng confessed to the facts of some of his criminal activities; Yao Wenyuan stated that his criminal activities were errors and did not acknowledge they were crimes; Zhang Chunqiao did not respond to inquiries put to him by the court; Jiang Qing disrupted order in the court.[43]

In the cases of Chen Boda and the five Lin Biao group defendants, the court had little difficulty using its discretion to arrive at a more lenient sentence. The fact that they had cooperated with the investigation and expressed remorse for their crimes was taken into consideration. The court also took into account the advanced age and past meritorious service of these defendants.[44] Therefore, despite the apparent rigidity of sentencing guidelines, it is clear that in practice the judges were able to exercise broad discretion within the wide bounds set by the code.

In the deliberations over sentencing, the most important debate was over which defendants, if any, should receive the death penalty. Because all had been found guilty of serious counterrevolutionary crimes, they were eligible for death sentences under Article 103 of the criminal code. There was enormous public and political pressure in favor of the death penalty, especially for Jiang Qing. Prior to the trial, prominent political leaders, including Deng Xiaoping, Hua Guofeng, and Li Xiannian, had made prejudicial public statements about the guilt of the defendants. Moreover, as the trial wore on, unsolicited advice poured in from every direction: party committees, the State Council, military generals such as Qu Wu and Li Huiwen, various work units, and even regular

---

[41] On mitigating factors, see *Criminal Code of the People's Republic of China* (1979), Chapter II: Crimes, Sections 1–3, Articles 10–26; on multiple counts, see Article 64.
[42] See *Criminal Code of the People's Republic of China* (1979), Article 57.
[43] Verdict in *TBFTJS*, p. 65.
[44] Wu, *Wangshi cangsang*, p. 323.

people.[45] Nearly all of these voices assumed the defendants' guilt and called for the death penalty for Jiang Qing if not for all. For example, Judge Wu Xiuquan reports that he received a letter from a school teacher in Guangdong that read in part, "These people are guilty of monstrous crimes; only by killing them can you appease the people's indignation and uphold justice. If the crimes of planning to kill the former Chairman and of killing the former President are not answered with executions, then our country should just announce the abolition of the death penalty."[46] The Special Court even felt pressure from other parts of the judiciary. Just as the sentencing phase of the Gang of Four trial was about to begin, the Shanghai Municipal People's Court requested permission to seek the death penalty against accomplice Ma Tianshui – surely the Special Court would be expected to deal as harshly with the main culprits.[47] Because the defendants faced the possibility of the death penalty, it was widely assumed to be the inevitable outcome.

In spite of widespread calls for the death penalty, there were compelling reasons to forego the death sentence. Several foreign governments and international organizations had expressed opinions discouraging executions.[48] Chinese supporters of this view argued that carefully measured sentences would bring an end to the deadly cycle of violence that had characterized the Cultural Revolution. Wu Xiuquan recalls in his memoirs:

At that time the whole nation was calling for death. This put pressure on us. When the full court held meetings, everyone reckoned that even death would be too good for people like Jiang Qing and Zhang Chunqiao, and that failing to execute them would not ease the people's anger. So to start with we were prepared to rule in favor of the death penalty, but after mulling it over it felt not quite right. For one thing, we had to consider the international and domestic influence of such a ruling, and for another we had to imagine the opinion of posterity. We could not be governed by feelings of righteous indignation.[49]

At first, most of the judges favored the death penalty for Jiang Qing and Zhang Chunqiao, but others were uneasy with the idea. The judges debated back and forth.[50]

---

[45] Tumen and Xiao, *Tebie shenpan*, pp. 315–18; Yu and Wang, *Renmin de shenpan*, pp. 210–13.
[46] Quoted in Tumen and Xiao, *Tebie shenpan*, p. 318.
[47] Ibid., p. 321; Yu and Wang, *Renmin de shenpan*, p. 213. In the end, Ma Tianshui was found mentally incompetent to stand trial. As far as I know, none of the accomplices tried in lower courts were sentenced to death.
[48] Wu, *Wangshi cangsang*, pp. 326–7; Yu and Wang, *Renmin de shenpan*, p. 217.
[49] Wu, *Wangshi cangsang*, p. 323.
[50] Yu and Wang, *Renmin de shenpan*, p. 217. Wu Xiuquan's recollections of sentencing are suspect because he was hospitalized due to illness during part of the deliberations.

When protracted discussion failed to produce consensus, the court appealed to Deng Xiaoping for advice. The rules governing this decision are worth reviewing. According to the *Organic Law of the People's Courts* (1979), China's courts "shall exercise judicial power independently, subject only to the law."[51] Despite this apparently unqualified declaration of independence from political influence, the people's courts at all levels were (and are) subject to supervision by adjudication committees appointed by the people's congresses at equivalent levels.[52] Although the NPC neglected to name a formal adjudication committee when it established the Special Court, an ad hoc adjudication committee was formed, headed by Chairman of the NPC Legal Affairs Committee Peng Zhen.[53] This ad hoc adjudication committee dealt with the death penalty question in an enlarged meeting attended by Deng Xiaoping, Hu Yaobang, Hua Guofeng, and others.[54] Deng Xiaoping, who had been following the case closely, proposed the final decision: Jiang Qing and Zhang Chunqiao should be sentenced to death with a two-year reprieve.

Despite political pressure, President of the Court Jiang Hua reminded the judges of their duty to uphold the rule of law. "Though the Special Court is special," he said, "even the special and extraordinary must not deviate from the principle of handling matters according to law."[55] In his summation to the meeting, prior to putting the proposed sentences to a vote, he again emphasized the legal authority and judicial autonomy

---

Though Wu was chief judge of the Second Tribunal, Judge Liu Jiguang was appointed to summarize their findings at the sentencing meeting. See entry for January 22, *TBFTJS*, p. 422.

[51] *Organic Law of the People's Courts of the People's Republic of China* (1979), http://www .china.org.cn/english/government/207253.htm, Article 4. This article was revised in 1983 to be even more specific: "The people's courts shall exercise judicial power independently, in accordance with the provisions of law, and shall not be subject to interference by any administrative organ, public organization or individual."

[52] See Margaret Woo, "Adjudication Supervision and Judicial Independence in the PRC," *American Journal of Comparative Law* 39 (1991), pp. 95–119.

[53] The committee's members included Secretary of the Politburo Standing Committee Peng Chong, President of the Special Court Jiang Hua, Chief of the Special Procuratorate Huang Huoqing, Minister of Public Security Zhao Cangbi, Chief Judge of the Second Tribunal Wu Xiuquan, and Deputy Secretary of the Central Commission for Discipline Inspection Wang Heshou. Reported by Special Court judge Ren Lingyun, who coordinated the work of the court; see Li and Wang, *Shiji duihua*, p. 93.

[54] The meeting also included Secretary of the Central Commission for Discipline Inspection Huang Kecheng, Vice-Chairman of the NPC Legal Affairs Committee Liu Fuzhi, and several members of the Politburo's elite Standing Committee. See Ren Lingyun's account in Li and Wang, *Shiji duihua*, p. 95. For more on the relationship between the Politburo and the Special Court, see Tumen and Xiao, *Tebie shenpan*, p. 326–7; Wu, *Wangshi cangsang*, p. 323; Yu and Wang, *Renmin de shenpan*, pp. 214–16. Deng Xiaoping is said to have viewed video recordings and transcripts of the trial almost daily.

[55] Entry for January 22, *TBFTJS*, pp. 423–4.

of the Special Court. His speech is worth quoting at length, because it expresses a view contrary to the concern shared by Dai Houying in Chapter 4. Jiang Hua held that law, conscientiously applied by people, can be capacious enough to accommodate the complexities of human circumstances (*renqing*):

In weighing sentences we must take account of all views, even those of the defendants.... We have heard from witnesses, defense counsel, and prosecutors. We must consider views from all sides. This, too, is about our handling matters according to law. Today we have contemplated the times, places, and conditions of the crimes, and in particular the special attributes of these crimes and their historical conditions. We are handling the task of sentencing in accordance with the findings of our verdict and in accordance with the criminal code. Therefore, we are acting according to the law – and let us pay no mind to what [those outside the court] might say.[56]

Following Jiang Hua's speech, the judges put the sentences to a vote.[57] The sentences passed unanimously except for Wang Hongwen's life sentence, which was passed by majority vote.[58] Though the court reached nearly unanimous agreement, several issues had been brought forward for debate from multiple perspectives. However, Jiang Hua stressed that the complexity of human circumstances did not imply some flaccid, subjective relativism. Law provided a rational process to cut through complexity and arrive at objective truth: "The Special Court's sentencing of these ten main culprits is on the basis of facts and law, and is definitely not a case of substituting emotions for law."[59] Legal justice had been meted out by human actors following a rational, deliberative process.

Accomplice Trials and Lustration

The case before the Special Court dealt with the crimes of the main culprits of the Lin Biao and Jiang Qing counterrevolutionary groups. However, the wide-ranging criminal conspiracy elaborated by the Special Court trial necessarily involved a large number of participants. A comprehensive "settling of accounts" would require prosecution of the counterrevolutionary groups' many accomplices. Furthermore, the party would have to address the noncriminal political "errors" made by

---

[56] Ibid., p. 424.
[57] Judge Fei Xiaotong, still absent, left a letter deferring to the judgment of the majority. See entry for January 23, *TBFTJS*, p. 425.
[58] On the issues related to Wang Hongwen's sentence, see Tumen and Xiao, *Tebie shenpan*, p. 331; Wu, *Wangshi cangsang*, p. 323.
[59] Entry for January 23, *TBFTJS*, p. 426.

countless activists and opportunists in pursuit of the erroneous political line of the Cultural Revolution.

Besides the ten main defendants in the Lin Biao and Jiang Qing counterrevolutionary groups, scores of accomplices were directly implicated in the case. Many of these accomplices were prosecuted in lower courts in trials closely patterned on the Gang of Four trial. A few of these accomplice trials were concluded prior to the Special Court trial, but most occurred in the two years after the trial, between January 1981 and March 1983. The new *Organic Law of the People's Courts* (1979) provided that cases involving counterrevolutionary crimes (as with other cases carrying a possible penalty of death or life imprisonment) should be tried in the first instance before an Intermediate People's Court or (in cases of unusual complexity or importance) a High People's Court. The majority of accomplice trials were conducted in Intermediate People's Courts, and verdicts were eligible for appeal to higher courts. At least one defendant did appeal his conviction to the Supreme People's Court, without success.[60] Military defendants were tried before courts martial of the People's Liberation Army (PLA). The accomplice trials were meant to hold to account additional Cultural Revolution radicals for their counterrevolutionary crimes. Significantly, though, authorities took pains to limit the number and scope of legal cases that would issue from the Special Court's trial.

Planning for the accomplice trials was coordinated through a series of national conferences held between August 1979 and November 1981. The conferences produced guidelines for prosecution meant to ensure that punishment would be meted out cautiously. Prosecutors were directed to differentiate contradictions among the people from contradictions between the people and their enemies; look at the big picture rather than small details; narrow the scope of investigation rather than broaden it; seek truth from facts in a detached and level-headed way; assess comrades holistically and from a historical perspective; avoid legal prosecution where disciplinary remedies would be more appropriate; prefer no punishment to punishment, and light punishment to harsh punishment; be strict in criticizing ideological deviation but lenient in seeking sanctions; and emphasize education and persuasion rather than coercion. The general principle was "to fight the disease in order to save the patient."[61] In this medical metaphor the disease was radicalism and

---

[60] "Zhonghua renmin gongheguo zuigao renmin fayuan xingshi caidingshu" [Sentencing Ruling by the Supreme People's Court of the PRC] (April 26, 1982), in *LSSP*, vol. 2, pp. 346–7.

[61] "Zhonggong zhongyang guanyu pi zhuan di wu ci quanguo 'Liang An' shenli gongzuo zuotan hui jiyao de tongzhi" [Notification of the CCP CC Forwarding *Summary of the*

the patient the people – the individuals under investigation and also the body politic. Chinese society was still in the vulnerable early stages of recovery from the Cultural Revolution. Prosecutors were urged to operate only where necessary and to do so with surgical precision, so as to avoid inflicting additional wounds.

The total number of defendants was quite small. An official document from 1988 gives an exact number of cases directly issuing from the case of the Lin Biao and Jiang Qing counterrevolutionary groups, but the figure has been redacted from the published version and remains unknown to us.[62] Nevertheless, an estimate is possible. The example of Yunnan Province gives a general indication of just how narrow was the scope of prosecution. According to a previously classified document summarizing the investigation in Yunnan, officials there investigated 7,569 persons. Of these, 335 were found to have committed violations serious enough to warrant expulsion from the party, but only 24 faced prosecution for crimes committed during the Cultural Revolution. Just six were publically tried as direct accomplices to the counterrevolutionary conspiracy.[63] Investigations of similar scale were conducted in other regions. References in media sources and declassified documents account for more than seventy specific cases heard in the courts of fourteen provinces (Anhui, Fujian, Guizhou, Heilongjiang, Henan, Hubei, Hunan, Jiangsu, Jiangxi, Jilin, Liaoning, Sichuan, Yunnan, and Zhejiang), two provincial-equivalent municipalities (Beijing and Shanghai), and by the

---

Fifth National Work Conference on "Two Case" Trials] (January 31, 1982), Zhongfa #9 [Central Directive No. 9 (1982)] in *Chinese Cultural Revolution Database (Zhongguo wenhua da geming wenku)*, Song Yongyi, ed., 3rd edn. (University Service Centre for Chinese Studies, Chinese University of Hong Kong, 2010), http://ccrd.usc.cuhk.edu .hk/ [hereafter abbreviated *CCRD*]. Guidelines for trials of military accomplices were established separately, but with a similar tone. Military cases were to be reviewed according to regulations set by the CCP Central Military Commission on January 20, 1978 and supplemented by the Commission for Military Discipline in May 1980. "Zong zhengzhi bu, zhongyang junwei jilü jiancha weiyuanhui guanyu yinfa 'Liang An' jielun shenpi quanxian de tongzhi" [Notification of PLA General Political Office and Discipline Inspection Commission of the CCP Central Military Commission at Conclusion of "Two Cases" Issuance of Clarification of Authority for Examination and Approval] (March 30, 1982), Junji lian zi #1 [PLA Discipline Commission Joint Document No. 1 (1982)], in *CCRD*.

[62] "Zhonggong zhongyang pizhuan zhongyang 'Liang An' shenli lingdao xiaozu *Guanyu 'Liang An' shenli gongzuo de zongjie baogao* de tongzhi" [Notification of the CCP CC Forwarding the CC "Two Case" Leading Small Group's *Summary Report on the "Two Case" Trial Work*] (February 12, 1988), Zhongfa #2 [Central Directive No. 2 (1988)], in *CCRD*. The original Small Group report is dated September 25, 1987; the redaction appears at the end of section 2.

[63] Yunnan Provincial Party History Office, "Yunnan 'Wenhua da geming' yundong dashi jishi" [Record of major events in Yunnan's "Cultural Revolution" movement] (May 18, 2005), in *CCRD*.

courts martial of the PLA.[64] This preliminary tally is almost certainly incomplete. It is likely that every (or nearly every) provincial-level jurisdiction conducted accomplice trials, but figures are not available for the provinces of Gansu, Guangdong, Hebei, Qinghai, Shaanxi, Shandong, and Shanxi; the provincial-level municipality of Tianjin; or the provincial-level autonomous regions of Guangxi, Inner Mongolia, Tibet, and Xinjiang. The picture is even sketchier when considering the trials of military defendants. Military trials are rarely publicized in China and few details relating to these cases have been forthcoming.[65] Of the sixty or more military officers purged in the immediate aftermath of the Lin Biao incident in September 1971, the legal fates of only a handful are known to us.[66] Based on this admittedly incomplete information, a reasonable estimate is that perhaps one hundred to two hundred accomplices faced criminal prosecution in civilian or military courts.

In January 1983, as the accomplice trials were well underway, the Supreme People's Court reviewed the Special Court's suspended death sentences against Jiang Qing and Zhang Chunqiao. The court elected to commute their sentences to life in prison, having found that the two had not resisted correctional reform through labor during the two-year reprieve.[67] (As mentioned previously, commutation was the normal outcome of such

---

[64] The best source is *LSSP*, vol. 2, a compilation of materials relating to trials of fifty-five defendants. This compilation overlaps incompletely with the partial list of trial locations and defendants in Zhong fa #2 [1988], above, in which sometimes a single defendant is named for a location where it is otherwise known that multiple defendants were tried. E.g., only Xia Bangyin is named for Hubei Province, but was just one of four defendants tried simultaneously there. See Liang Xia, "Wuhan shi zhongji renmin fayuan dui Xia Bangyin, Zhu Hongjia, Hu Houmin, and Zhang Liguo fangeming an jinxing gongkai shenpan de qingkuang" [Wuhan city intermediate people's court public trial of the Xia, Zhu, Hu, and Zhang counterrevolutionary case], classified for internal-use only by *Hubei Daily* editorial staff (August 24, 1982), in *CCRD*; See also, Amnesty International, *China's Ultra-Left on Trial: Unfair Legal Procedure and Political Imprisonment in the Anti-Gang of Four Purge, 1976–1987*, pp. 25–30 and Appendix 2, pp. 58–60.

[65] Captain David C. Rodearmel, JAGC, "Military Law in Communist China: Development, Structure, and Function," thesis presented to Judge Advocate General School, United States Army (1987) in *Military Law Review* 119 (1988).

[66] For a partial list of purged military officers, see Jèurgen Domes, *China after the Cultural Revolution: Politics between Two Party Congresses* (Berkeley: University of California Press, 1977), pp. 140–1. For materials relating to the trials of military defendants Wang Weiguo, Gu Tongchuan, and Hu Ping, see *LSSP*, vol. 2, pp. 312–46. On the sentencing of additional military defendants, see "Lin Biao jituan Li Weixin deng shiyi ren bei kongjun fayuan panxing" [Li Weixin and eleven other members of the Lin Biao group sentenced by Court Martial of the PLA Air Force], *Wenhuibao* [Literary Gazette], July 6, 1981. A few likely defendants can be ruled out: e.g., Wang Fei, formerly Deputy Chief of Staff of the Air Force Command, whose written deposition was entered into evidence before the Special Court, was diagnosed with mental illness and declared incompetent in 1974.

[67] Commutation was allowed in accordance with Article 46 of the criminal code; full text of the Supreme People's Court ruling was published in *RMRB*, January 26, 1983.

cases.) A directive preparing party cadres for the decision took pains to emphasize that the commutation of sentences should not be misconstrued as a sign that the offensive against the Gang of Four was over:

All jurisdictions must continue to pay close attention to [*zhua jin*: lit. "firmly grasp"] the trials of other culprits in the Lin Biao and Jiang Qing Counterrevolutionary Groups, using law to render verdicts expeditiously, and absolutely must not be influenced in any way by the reduction in sentences for Jiang Qing and Zhang Chunqiao. We must guard against remnants of the Lin Biao and Jiang Qing Counterrevolutionary Groups and other hostile forces who seize opportunities to sow chaos and destruction; we must use law to resolutely crack down on every substantiated case of counterrevolutionary activity.[68]

Despite the tough talk of using law to suppress the remnants of the counterrevolutionary forces, the official legal response to the Cultural Revolution was already nearing its conclusion.

The Special Court had established a legal and procedural model for the lower court trials. Beyond the limited number of accomplice trials, though, the Gang of Four trial set no lasting legal precedent. Almost as soon as the new era of socialist legality was trumpeted, the new procedural guarantees were compromised for the sake of a nationwide anticrime campaign.[69] Once again the state demonstrated that socialist criminal law would be nothing more than a tool for social control. More important than the legal precedent, the Gang of Four trial established a rhetorical script that was strictly adhered to in local media coverage of lower court cases. The public accounts of accomplice trials rehearsed *verbatim* the very same tropes first presented in stories about the Gang of Four trial.[70]

Even the limited promise of delivering legal accountability for Cultural Revolution crimes was not really delivered. The vast majority of crimes committed during the Cultural Revolution period – including very serious violent crimes like rape and murder – were never prosecuted.[71] After the spectacle of the Gang of Four trial, the focus of legal reform shifted from criminal law to civil law – the better to support the developing market economy.

---

[68] "Zhongyang bangong ting guanyu dui Lin Biao, Jiang Qing fangeming jituan zhufan Jiang Qing, Zhang Chunqiao jiang yifa yuyi jianxing de tongzhi" [CCP Central Committee General Office on Notification of Legal Commutation of Sentences for Main Culprits of the Lin Biao and Jiang Qing Counterrevolutionary Groups Jiang Qing and Zhang Chunqiao] (January 3, 1983), Zhong ban fa #3 [General Office Directive No. 3 (1983)], in *CCRD*.

[69] Harold M. Tanner, *Strike Hard! Anti-Crime Campaigns and Chinese Criminal Justice, 1979–1985* (Ithaca, NY: Cornell University East Asia Program, 1999).

[70] Examples are easily adduced from the materials gathered in *LSSP*, vol. 2.

[71] Sue Trevaskes, "People's Justice and Injustice: Courts and the Redressing of Cultural Revolution Cases," *China Information* 16 (October 2002), pp. 1–26.

As for the party, it preferred whenever possible to handle its problems in-house through the extralegal process of party discipline. In the study of transitional justice, this type of political purge is called lustration. Lustration refers specifically to "the disqualification and (where in office) the removal of certain categories of office-holders under the prior regime from certain public or private offices under the new regime."[72] The trial of the most notorious leaders of the Cultural Revolution had decapitated the radical faction within the party.[73] Regarding the vast body of radicals who still held lower-level positions of power, the party elected to remove only those personnel who had particularly checkered pasts and now refused to conform to the new orthodoxy of reform. This cautious approach to purging the party after the Cultural Revolution reflected a long-standing generational problem. The revolutionaries who founded the party in 1921 and founded the state in 1949 had been born around the turn of the twentieth century. A new generation was needed to carry on their legacy. Just as Mao had hoped to find worthy "revolutionary successors" to wage his Cultural Revolution, the post-Mao leaders were keen to promote younger cadres with moderate political views to implement the program of reform.[74] During the decade of the Cultural Revolution, membership in the Chinese Communist Party (CCP) had doubled from seventeen million to thirty-five million, and grew to forty million by 1980. Reformists were concerned about the quality and political leanings of these recruits, and about the advanced age of the senior leadership.[75] To ensure the health and integrity of its Leninist organization, in November 1983 the CCP initiated a comprehensive party rectification (*zheng dang*) campaign.

The rectification had multiple goals: to unify party ideology, strengthen organizational discipline, correct "unhealthy tendencies" in work style, and cleanse the party of unqualified, incompetent, corrupt, opportunistic, and politically radical cadres.[76] Unlike the violent purges of the

---

[72] Herman Schwartz, "Lustration in Eastern Europe" in Neil J. Kritz, ed., *Transitional Justice: How Emerging Democracies Reckon with Former Regimes* (Washington, DC: United States Institute of Peace Press, 1995), vol. 1, p. 461.

[73] There are rumors of a purge in the late 1970s of as many as one million people, but I am unable to independently verify this figure. See Amnesty International, *China's Ultra-Left on Trial*, pp. 3–7.

[74] See, e.g., Chen Yun, "Cheng qian shang wan di tiba zhong-qing nian ganbu" [On the promotion of thousands or tens of thousands of middle-aged and younger cadres] (July 2, 1981), http://cpc.people.com.cn/GB/69112/83035/83317/83597/5738417.html.

[75] See, e.g., Deng Xiaoping, "Adhere to the Party Line and Improve Methods of Work," http://dengxiaopingworks.wordpress.com/2013/02/25/adhere-to-the-party-line-and-improve-methods-of-work/.

[76] On the goals, see FBIS CHI October 12, 1983. For an overview of results, see "Bo Yibo report winds up party rectification" (May 31, 1987), *Daily Report China*, FBIS-CHI-87–105 (June 2, 1987), pp. K3–K18; and Bruce J. Dickson, "Conflict and Non-compliance

Cultural Revolution period, the rectification was supposed to adhere to and reinforce "normal" procedures for auditing the party rolls.[77] In the course of rectification, all forty million party members were required to resubmit their applications for registration. The rectification was conducted first at the national and provincial levels, then extended down to prefectural and county levels, and finally implemented at the local level. At each level, rectification involved group study of party policies and standards, evaluation of party members against the standards, correction of deviations, and reregistration of properly qualified party members. This exhaustive audit lasted three and a half years, ending in mid-1987.

Among the forty million registrations vetted, roughly three million were considered problematic and subjected to closer scrutiny. The investigation resulted in more than four hundred thousand party members, or slightly more than 1 percent of the total membership, suffering sanctions of one kind or another.[78] Nationwide, thirty to forty thousand people were expelled from the party for "serious problems" of incompetence, corruption, or ideological infirmity. Another forty to fifty thousand were expelled specifically for committing serious "Leftist" errors. Between five and ten thousand were branded as the "three kinds of people": opportunists who had made their careers by following the radical line of Lin Biao and Jiang Qing, ideologues who still harbored serious factional tendencies, and hooligans who had participated in beating, smashing, and looting during the Cultural Revolution. A high-level party document described the problem with this last category:

The "three kinds of people" are still to be found in leadership positions and must be cleaned out from all levels. Their cases are to be dealt with according to facts, based on principles and policies laid down by the center, making concrete analyses using specific methods, and handled by the normal authorities for cadre management in the relevant departments of organization, personnel, and discipline inspection. [Cases are to be] resolved one by one.[79]

in Chinese Politics: Party Rectification, 1983–1987," *Pacific Affairs* 63.2 (Summer 1990), pp. 170–90.

[77] For more on the history of this issue, see Frederick Teiwes, *Politics and Purges in China: Rectification and the Decline of Party Norms, 1950–1965* (Armonk, NY: M. E. Sharpe, 1979).

[78] Figures based on "Bo Yibo report winds up party rectification." The report did not include results from Guangxi, where party rectification was complicated by an unstable border with Vietnam, unresolved political issues from the Cultural Revolution, poor economic conditions, and a series of natural disasters. See "Chuli 'Wen ge' yiliu wenti, qingli 'san zhong ren' wenjian huibian" [Compilation of documents on handling residual problems from the Cultural Revolution and purging the three kinds of people] (Nanning: Guangxi Zhuangzu zizhiqu dangwei zheng dang bangongshi, 1986), vol. 5, p. 326. For figures from Guangxi, some redacted, see "Chuli 'Wen ge' yiliu wenti," vol. 5, p. 337; and vol. 4, pp. 47 and 62.

[79] "Zhonggong zhongyang guanyu pi zhuan di wu ci quanguo 'Liang An' shenli gongzuo zuotan hui jiyao de tongzhi."

The disclosure of enemies in leadership positions at all levels may have echoed the ominous warnings that launched the Cultural Revolution, but the main substance of the directive was that the purge must be conducted in a sober and orderly fashion. Some unknown number of the "three kinds of people" were referred to legal authorities for criminal prosecution, but this was not the principal outcome. The purpose of rectification was to remove political radicals from positions of authority at every level of the party, state, and military.

In the decade following the Cultural Revolution, four hundred to eight hundred thousand people were stripped of their titles and removed from office.[80] However, at the end of the day, many of the bureaucrats staffing the new regime were the same as in the old. China was not exceptional in this regard. Historical examples include de-Nazification in Germany after World War II, the removal of fascist parties from Southern Europe in the late 1970s and from Latin America in the 1980s, and the ban on communist parties in Eastern Europe in the 1990s. Due to the institutional inertia of modern bureaucracy – and especially the need to staff offices with the people possessing education, experience, and expertise – lustration has rarely been thorough, even under the most tenacious programs of de-Nazification and decommunization. Lustration in China was further hampered by the persistence of communist party rule. The CCP did not banish itself from power, but instead removed a faction of party members associated with the prior regime. This reality prevented a truly clean break with the political culture of the past.

The persistence of communist party rule also contributed to a lack of transparency in settling accounts with the past. Just as the official archives relating to the Gang of Four trial have remained sealed, as a general rule the post-Mao regime has declined to open the archives of the Cultural Revolution era. The archival situation in China remains a serious impediment to the discovery of historical truth. Also closed are the personnel dossiers and other documents that would have exposed the ubiquitous system of secret police and informants used against Chinese citizens during the Mao years.[81] While in some cases victims of unlawful persecution were allowed to review heavily redacted copies of their own personnel files, neither the extent of domestic surveillance nor the identities of informants have been fully revealed. As a result, regular Chinese people have not had a chance to confront the everyday

---

[80] "Bo Yibo report winds up party rectification," p. K6.
[81] Michael Schoenhals, *Spying for the People: Mao's Secret Agents, 1949–1967* (New York: Cambridge University Press, 2013). Professor Schoenhals recently has extended his research on this topic into the Cultural Revolution era.

police state system that was (and continues to be) arrayed against them. Impunity extended all the way to the top of the state security apparatus. The deceased Kang Sheng and Xie Fuzhi were identified as principal culprits in the Lin Biao and Jiang Qing groups but did not face trial for their crimes committed during the height of the Cultural Revolution. More troubling is the fact that the living Hua Guofeng, who succeeded Xie Fuzhi as minister of public security in the latter years of the Cultural Revolution, was shielded from criminal prosecution – probably in order to secure his political support for the trial. The ongoing secrecy surrounding archives, dossiers, and documents means that despite the rhetoric of comprehensive justice, much of the historical truth has been withheld from the hands of the people.

Mao and the Laws of History

The post-Mao regime carefully crafted its own version of historical truth. In late June 1981, six months after the Special Court verdict, the Central Committee of the CCP adopted the much anticipated "Resolution on Certain Questions in the History of the Party since the Founding of the State."[82] The state's legal verdict and the party's historical resolution were devised together as complementary parts of a coherent interpretation of the past. The public trial of Cultural Revolution leaders would become a showcase for the new socialist legal system, enabling the state to deliver legal retribution, create closure, and establish a factual record of past crimes. Likewise, the official reevaluation of history would provide an opportunity for the party to acknowledge its mistakes, control damage to its reputation, and put forward a vision for moving forward. In the wake of mass violence over which they had presided, the state and party crafted these two narratives to reestablish their legitimacy to govern.

These two official interpretations of the Cultural Revolution were separate but related attempts to settle accounts, in the sense of establishing a definitive account of the violent and contested past. The two official accounts were complementary, issuing a binding and authoritative interpretation of the past in separate but related registers: the law and the laws of history. The verdict provides an account of the Cultural Revolution in terms of crimes at the level of law. Meanwhile, the resolution analyzes the Cultural Revolution at the level of objective historical laws as a series of "errors" in revolutionary thought and practice.

---

[82] "Guanyu jianguo yilai dang de ruogan lishi wenti de jueyi" [Resolution on certain questions in the history of the party since the founding of the state], *RMRB*, July 1, 1981 [hereafter abbreviated as Resolution].

Taken together, the verdict and the resolution attempted to characterize the Cultural Revolution in such a way as to demonstrate that Chinese socialist law and historiography are capable of interpreting and drawing lessons from the violent past and are just as worthy of leading the way to the future.

To succeed, the party's resolution on history would have to achieve a number of difficult goals. First, it would have to protect the historical legacy of the CCP without shirking responsibility for its failures. The good of the party's historical accomplishments would have to outweigh the bad of the disastrous recent decade. Second, the party would have to analyze and explain the failures of the Cultural Revolution in socialist terms, in a theoretically coherent and defensible way. The interpretation would have to demonstrate that socialist ideology could provide solutions to its own problems. Third, the historical model would have to isolate and contain the failures of the Cultural Revolution era, putting brackets around the period as an aberration or rupture that has now ended. At the same time, it would have to provide continuity around that rupture, connecting the past glories of the CCP to the present. Finally, it would have to explain why Chinese socialism was the best option for moving forward into the future.

The basis for this double judgment was a further distinction between crimes and errors. These were not the ordinary errors of political judgment committed by followers of a radical line, but a special kind of error committed by those in leadership. The theoretical basis for this distinction was presented in an authoritative Special Commentator article published in *People's Daily* on December 22, 1980. The article, "Milestone in Socialist Democracy and Legality," reminded readers that the Special Court would only address the crimes of the Cultural Revolution and would not consider noncriminal errors.[83] The article then went on to discuss particularly grave errors with disastrous consequences, which nevertheless were also to be considered as fundamentally different in nature from crimes. A crime, it said, is "an action harmful to society that is subject to punishment under the law," while an error is "a discrepancy between the subjective and the objective, an action that does not conform to objective laws."[84] These parallel definitions refer to parallel normative standards: the statutory laws (*falü*) that govern a particular society, and the objective laws (*guilü*) that govern social and historical

---

[83] "Shehuizhuyi minzhu he fazhi de lichengpai: ping shenpan Lin Biao, Jiang Qing fangeming jituan" [Milestone in socialist democracy and legality: On the trial of the Lin Biao and Jiang Qing counterrevolutionary groups], *RMRB*, December 22, 1980.

[84] Ibid.

development in general.[85] Violations of the former are crimes, while violations of the latter are errors. The nature of this distinction would figure in several important projects: in the exculpation of Chairman Mao from legal responsibility, in the official condemnation of the Cultural Revolution as an erroneous disaster, and in the authorization of law as a valid tool for analysis under socialism.

It is the system of Mao Zedong Thought that defines errors as violations of *guilü*, or the objective "laws of history." In reviving the Maoist maxim, "seek truth from facts" (*shishi qiushi*), the post–Cultural Revolution reformers reaffirmed Mao Zedong Thought as a correct and scientific system, to be distinguished from its flawed and all-too-human progenitor. Basically, "seek truth from facts" describes the inductive process of social science, by which one studies specific examples in order to divine general principles. In Mao's own explanation of "seek truth from facts," he defines truths as expressions of *guilü*: "'truth' means the internal relations of objective things, namely their regularities (*guilüxing*) [i.e., their *guilü*-ness, or the extent to which their internal relations constitute *guilü*]."[86] By this definition, truths are those constant or regular principles ("laws") that govern how society works: in Marxism, the law of class struggle; in liberal economics, the law of supply and demand; in Maoism, the law of the unity of opposites; and so on. Maoism is concerned in particular with discovering certain kind of laws, namely, the laws of historical development. Mao's central project was the "Sinification of Marxism" – the application of abstract Marxist theories to concrete Chinese realities. Mao recognized that the complexity and contingency of history make it impossible to replicate and "mechanically apply" the laws induced from European history to other places and times.[87] Because the objective laws of history (*guilü*) are universal only to the degree that they are abstract and devoid of specific content, the truth of abstract theories constantly must be tested in practical application. This is the meaning of the second important epistemological slogan of the post-Mao period: "practice is the sole criterion for testing truth." Because it relies on practice to test inductive reasoning, Mao Zedong Thought is neither predictive nor infallible. Inevitably,

---

[85] According to advisers to the Special Court Wu Jianfan and Ouyang Tao, errors are "mistakes in ideology"; see Wu Jianfan and Ouyang Tao, "Lun shenpan Lin Biao, Jiang Qing fangeming jituan de jige falü wenti" [Discussion of a few legal questions in the trial of Lin Biao and Jiang Qing counterrevolution groups], *Faxue yanjiu* [Research in jurisprudence] (June 1980), p. 2.

[86] Quoted in and translated by Nick Knight in "The Form of Mao's 'Sinification of Marxism,'" *Australian Journal of Chinese Affairs* 9 (January 1983), p. 19.

[87] Mao Zedong's phrase, quoted in ibid., p. 20.

errors will arise from imperfect knowledge or the misapprehension of true facts and conditions, leading to the subjective misinterpretation of objective laws. If crime and punishment was the central concern of the verdict, the Maoist understanding of error assumed paramount importance for the drafters of the resolution.

The verdict and resolution sought to mark with perfect clarity the relationship and distinction between crimes (violations of statutory laws) and errors (violations of objective laws). The Chinese character *lü*, common to the terms "statutory laws" (*falü*) and "objective laws" (*guilü*), links the two concepts. At the most basic etymological level, *lü* denotes a restraint; in classical usage, *lü* refers to the formal codification of abstract normative principles: most commonly legal codes, but also codified systems of pitch and tone in music, and rules of tone and rhyme in regulated verse. Correlating statutory law with the objective laws of history implicitly places both within a broader spectrum of normative orders or restraints: the self-discipline or autonomy of the individual (*zilü*), the group discipline of the party or other social unit (*jilü*), the legal discipline of society as a whole (*falü*), the objective laws of history (*guilü*), and, finally, the immutable laws of nature (*dinglü*). This correlative model, which has ample precedents in the long history of Chinese thought, lends socialist legal thought a moral authority similar to that of natural law.[88] Mao Zedong Thought provides that revelation of the higher order is accessible to human beings through practical experience and applied reason. The conceptual and etymological connection between law and restraint is not unique to the Chinese tradition. For example, St. Thomas Aquinas notes in the introduction to his "Treatise on Law" (1269–70): "Law is a rule or measure for action by which one is led to action or restrained from acting. The word law (*lex*) is derived from *ligare*, to bind, because it binds one to act."[89] It is the binding necessity of law that is normative or repressive.

Just as the creation of a legal indictment against the Gang of Four elevated the violence of the Cultural Revolution from an issue of party

---

[88] According to Benjamin Schwartz, correlative cosmology was well established in Chinese thought by the third century BCE and reached its height in the Huang-Lao syncretism of the Han dynasty, "leaving its lasting mark on the entire subsequent development of the 'philosophy of nature' in China." Schwartz notes that while correlative thinking is "considered by some to be a primordial and quintessential expression of the Chinese mind," he agrees with A. C. Graham that correlative cosmology as an expression of general proto-scientific thinking along the lines of Levi-Strauss's primitive "science of the concrete." See Benjamin I. Schwartz, *The World of Thought in Ancient China* (Cambridge, MA: Belknap Press of Harvard University Press, 1985), pp. 350–2.

[89] Compare St. Thomas Aquinas, *Summa of Theology*, I-II, Qu. 90, 1, Qu. 91, 3 and Qu. 93, 3.

discipline (*jilü*) to a matter of law (*falü*), so too did the party's resolution elevate the discussion of transgressions to yet another level, from law (*falü*) to the laws of history (*guilü*). The conflation of human laws and scientific laws is a powerful ideological concept, which Northrup Frye has rightly called "a violent and foolish pun."[90]

The Gang of Four trial and the historical resolution were planned simultaneously. Deng Xiaoping and his reformist protégé Hu Yaobang were put in charge of the project, while party veteran Hu Qiaomu and leading theoretican Deng Liqun were tasked with drafting the document. At the outset, Hu Qiaomu identified two major difficulties: on the one hand, to identify the errors of the Cultural Revolution and to explain why they occurred; and on the other hand, to define the (correct) essence of the party's guiding ideology and its relationship to Mao Zedong Thought. In March 1980, in the same meeting at which the Secretariat approved plans to conduct the Gang of Four trial, party leaders also discussed the resolution. Deng Xiaoping suggested to Hu Qiaomu three basic principles to uphold in drafting the document: First, the resolution must acknowledge the historical importance of Mao Zedong Thought and reaffirm its value as an ideology to be adhered to and developed. Second, the document must "seek truth from facts" to analyze the events of the past thirty years, including a fair evaluation of correct and erroneous policies as well as the merits and demerits of responsible cadres. Third, the resolution must provide a basic but comprehensive summary of events, painted in broad strokes rather than close detail, in order to help people understand the past and "unite as one and look toward the future." Deng Xiaoping also noted that the party leadership must accept some measure of collective responsibility for past errors, which were certainly not all the errors of a single person.

The complete text was publicized on July 6, 1981.[91] The new resolution was consciously patterned after the earlier "Resolution on Certain Historical

---

[90] Northrop Frye, *Myth and Metaphor: Selected Essays, 1974–1988*, Robert D. Denham, ed. (Charlottesville: University Press of Virginia, 1990), p. 265.

[91] The trial and the resolution were devised to be the final business of the Eleventh Central Committee. The first stable draft was dated November 22, 1980, coinciding precisely with the start of Gang of Four trial, with revisions to be postponed until conclusion of the trial. A revised draft was put before an enlarged session of the Politburo in late May 1980 and formally approved by the plenary session in late June of that year. For a recent account of the drafting process, see Huang Li, "Guanyu jianguo yilai dang de ruogan lishi wenti de jueyi" qicao taiqian muhou [Behind the scenes of the drafting of the "Resolution on Certain Questions in the History of Our Party since the Founding of the People's Republic of China"] from Zhongguo Gongchandang xinwen wang [CCP News Network] (April 2, 2009), http://dangshi.people.com.cn/GB/85040/9070755 .html, (accessed March 10, 2014).

Questions" passed by the Seventh Plenum of the Sixth CCP Central Committee in April 1945.[92] This original 1945 resolution, also drafted by Hu Qiaomu, was the first document of institutionalized party history and solidified the new orthodoxy of Maoist historiography. Decades later, the 1981 resolution "shows that the [Central Committee] still conceived of itself as being the only source of authoritative interpretations of Party history."[93]

The periodization found in the resolution marks the major ruptures and continuities of party history. The era of state socialism is divided into three periods: "basic completion of the socialist transformation" (1949–56), "beginning to build socialism in all spheres" (1956–66), "the ten years of the 'Cultural Revolution'" (1966–76), and the present "great turning point in history" (1976–81). The resolution formally dates the beginning of the Cultural Revolution to May 1966 and its end to October 1976 (§ 19), coinciding exactly with the temporal scope of the counterrevolutionary conspiracy described in the legal verdict. Both documents bridge ten years of history into a single, coherent period. The resolution reinforces the historical periodization implicit in the verdict, its only innovation being to supplant the term "decade of catastrophe" with the more neutral phrase "decade of internal chaos."[94] This basic periodization still dominates the study of China's political history, both in China and the West.

The resolution completed the rhetorical work of positioning the chaotic Cultural Revolution as a period of rupture between the progressive early years of the People's Republic and the historical present of the post-Mao Reform Era. The resolution judges that rupture to be entirely erroneous in orientation. The resolution does not hold back in describing the magnitude of the disaster, calling the Cultural Revolution "a

---

[92] See Tony Saich, "Writing or Rewriting History? The Construction of the Maoist Resolution on History," in Tony Saich and Hans van de Ven, eds., *New Perspectives on the Chinese Communist Revolution* (Armonk, NY: M. E. Sharpe, 1995), pp. 299–338.

[93] Susanne Weigelin-Schwiedrzik, "Party Historiography," in Jonathan Unger, ed., *Using the Past to Serve the Present: Historiography and Politics in Contemporary China* (Armonk, NY, and London: M. E. Sharpe), p. 171.

[94] Based on frequency of usage in *RMRB*. The phrase *shinian haojie* (decade of catastrophe) first appeared June 8, 1979; usage peaked from July 1980 through June 1981 (more than twenty-five usages per month). However, the phrase *shinian neiluan* (decade of internal chaos) appeared with equal frequency in July 1981 and thereafter with much greater frequency. The phrase *shinian neiluan* (decade of internal chaos) became common only after mid-June 1981: There are only five examples prior to June 15, 1981, the earliest on October 28, 1980, compared to 137 examples from the latter half of 1981. "Decade of internal chaos" remained a common phrase throughout 1982–3, before declining in 1984. Note that the term *catastrophe* (*haojie*) does not appear at all in the *Resolution* as adopted, while the term *internal chaos* (*neiluan*) does appear in the section on the Cultural Revolution period (see resolution, § 20).

grave Left-deviation error comprehensive in nature and protracted in scope" (§ 22). Utterly unlike the truly progressive revolution of 1949, the Cultural Revolution was interpreted as a chaotic rupture in the history of socialism characterized by violations of both positive (statutory) and natural (objective) law. Such an abnormal and regressive "Left-deviation error" demanded explanation in terms of the socialist laws of history. Accordingly, the resolution's explanation of the Cultural Revolution rested on the concept of "error":

Owing to our Party's meager experience in leading the cause of socialism and to subjectivist errors in the Party leadership's analysis of the situation and its understanding of Chinese conditions, prior to the Cultural Revolution there were mistakes of enlarging the scope of class struggle and of rash, premature development in economic construction. Afterwards, there occurred the comprehensive, protracted, and grave error of the Cultural Revolution. (§ 8)

The party leadership's lack of practical experience, limited knowledge of objective facts, and mistaken analysis of the overall situation resulted in unintended violations of the objective laws governing historical development. Such violations could not but result in disaster. However, these errors were fundamentally different in nature from crimes, which were those violations of law described in the verdict.

The resolution characterized as the four erroneous theses that formed the general political theory of the Cultural Revolution. The four erroneous theses were: (1) The Cultural Revolution was a struggle against the revisionist line or the capitalist road. This had no grounding in fact, and many of the policies negated had been correct. (2) The confusion of right and wrong led to the confusion of friends and enemies. The facts show that many of the people attacked and persecuted had been wrongly labeled. (3) The Cultural Revolution was supposed to rely on the masses for support. In fact, the movement was divorced from party organizations and the masses and even had been resisted or rejected by people at all levels. (4) The Cultural Revolution was said to be a revolution. Here the refutation is very strong: "Practice has shown that in fact the Cultural Revolution did not – and indeed *could not possibly have* – constituted a revolution or social progress *in any sense*" (§ 20). The errors made were contrary to fact, the objective laws of history, and the great tradition of Mao Zedong Thought.

Nor does the resolution stint in its criticism of Chairman Mao.[95] By contrast, the resolution also stresses Mao's lasting and overwhelmingly

---

[95] Party leaders Ye Jianying, Deng Xiaoping, and Huang Kechang all provided critical evaluations of Mao Zedong that predated the Resolution; see Brantly Womack, "Where Mao Went Wrong: Epistemology and Ideology in Mao's Leftist Politics," *Australian Journal of Chinese Affairs* 16 (July 1986), p. 25n2.

positive contributions to the cause of Chinese socialism, even acknowledging his good intentions in launching the Cultural Revolution. The resolution urged a balanced view of history, equally condemning those who supported or attacked Mao without qualification: "These two attitudes fail to draw a distinction between Mao Zedong Thought, a scientific theory formed and tested over a long period of time, and the errors made by Comrade Mao Zedong in his later years. Yet this distinction is absolutely necessary" (§ 31). This is to say that in evaluating history, the distinction must be drawn between the person and his thought, between the subjective and the objective; people's actions must be measured separately against the law and the objective laws of history.[96] The resolution affirms that the enduring historical philosophy of Mao Zedong Thought can and must be salvaged and applied to the challenges ahead. Only through the guiding principles of Marxism-Leninism and Mao Zedong Thought – seeking truth from facts, and testing it through revolutionary practice – can the nation achieve unity, stability, and modernization as it moves forward.

From the ambition of the party's historical resolution, and from its direct and complementary relationship to the earlier legal verdict, it is clear that the Gang of Four trial aimed to achieve much more than a public shaming of Cultural Revolution leaders. The trial attempted to define the scope and function of law in socialist society, demonstrate its proper exercise by state power, and render a judgment on the past rooted in the ostensibly lawlike and scientific regularities of human history. The "magic weapon" of Mao Zedong Thought – wrested from the radicals, redeemed by law, and once again grasped by the people – appeared to have regained its luster.

---

[96] Haiyan Lee, "Mao's Two Bodies: On the Curious (Political) Art of Impersonating the Great Helmsman," in Jie Li and Enhua Zhang, eds., *Red Legacies in China: Cultural Afterlives of the Communist Revolution* (Cambridge, MA: Harvard East Asia Center, 2016); applying the metaphor developed by Ernst Hartwig Kantorowicz, *The King's Two Bodies: A Study in Mediaeval Political Theology* (Princeton, NJ: Princeton University Press, 1957).

6   Vanity

Literary Verdict

Yang Jiang's *Six Records of a Cadre School* (*Gan xiao liu ji*) (1981) was the first memoir of the Cultural Revolution to be written by an established author and widely distributed in socialist China.[1] It is also widely recognized as a work of considerable literary merit.[2] The memoir recounts episodes from the author's time in a May Seventh Cadre School, a labor camp for urban intellectuals "sent down" to the remote countryside for reeducation. The cadre schools were named for a letter dated May 7, 1966, in which Chairman Mao suggested to Lin Biao that cadre members in the People's Liberation Army should go to the countryside to broaden their practical experience, learn from the peasant masses, and develop greater class consciousness (see Figure 17). Mao later urged expansion of this "rustification" program beyond the army because all able-bodied cadres could benefit from this "excellent opportunity to renew their studies."[3] At the height of the Cultural Revolution, some seventeen million urban youth were sent "up the mountains and down to the countryside," soon to be followed by about three million adult intellectuals.

Despite the idealistic origins of the cadre schools, in reality many were hastily improvised internment camps to which "petty bourgeois" social elements like Yang Jiang could be banished from the overcrowded cities.

---

[1] In this chapter parenthetical references to page numbers refer to the following edition: Yang Jiang, *Gan xiao liu ji* [Six records of a cadre school], 2nd edn. [1981] (Hong Kong: Guangjiaojing chubanshe, 1988). Translations are my own, except as indicated, but in consultation with the translation by Howard Goldblatt, transl., *Six Chapters from My Life Downunder* (Hong Kong: Chinese University of Hong Kong; Seattle: University of Washington Press, 1984).

[2] E.g., in 1989 the Chinese Writers Association commended this book first among twenty-four "Outstanding Works of Prose" written since 1979; reported by Xinhua Overseas News Service (Beijing), March 15, 1989.

[3] Mao Zedong quoted in "Liuhe 'wu-qi' ganxiao wei jiguan geming hua tigongle xin de jingyan" [Liu River 'May Seventh' cadre school offers new experience to revolutionize organizations], *RMRB*, October 5, 1968.

Figure 17. "Advance courageously along the glorious road of Chairman Mao's *May Seventh Directive*" (*Yanzhe Mao zhuxi Wu-Qi Zhishi de guanghui dadao fenyong qianjin*) (no date).
Source: Landsberger Collection, International Institute of Social History (Amsterdam).

Yang Jiang's life, including her experience in the cadre school, was in some ways representative of an older generation of Chinese intellectuals who came of age in the prerevolutionary era. Yang Jikang (Yang Jiang is her pen name) was born in 1911 to an elite, cosmopolitan family in Jiangsu Province.[4] Her family prized scholarship for both boys and girls, and she enjoyed a world-class education.[5] A student of Romance languages

[4] For biographical information on Yang Jiang, see Kong Qingmao, *Yang Jiang ping zhaun* [Critical biography of Yang Jiang] (Beijing: Huaxia chubanshe, 1998); Luo Yinsheng, *Yang Jiang zhuan* [Biography of Yang Jiang] (Beijing: Wenhua yishu chubanse, 2004); Wu Xuezhao, *Ting Yang Jiang tan wang shi* [Listening to Yang Jiang talk about the past] (Beijing: Sanlian shudian, 2008). Yang Jiang has also written a number of autobiographical works, as surveyed in Christopher Rea, "Yang Jiang's Conspicuous Inconspicuousness: A Centenary Writer in China's 'Prosperous Age,'" *China Heritage Quarterly* 26 (June 2011), www.chinaheritagequarterly.org/features .php?searchterm=026_yangjiang.inc&issue=026; and Jesse L. Field, "Writing Lives in China: The Case of Yang Jiang," PhD diss. (University of Minnesota, 2012).

[5] Yang Jiang's father was a noted jurist with degrees from Waseda University in Japan and the University of Pennsylvania; her aunt earned a master's degree in education from Columbia University, later becoming China's first female university president.

and literature, she graduated from Soochow University and undertook graduate studies at the renowned Tsinghua University in Beijing. There she met her future husband, Qian Zhongshu, and the two of them continued their studies at the University of Oxford and the University of Paris before returning to a war-torn China in 1938. Living in the international haven of Shanghai, Yang Jiang became a respected translator, literary critic, and playwright. Her husband, already a noted essayist and a leading scholar of classical Chinese poetry, wrote a commercially successful comedy of manners, *Fortress Besieged* (*Wei cheng*) (1947), considered one of the great Chinese novels of the twentieth century. Yang Jiang and her husband belonged to an established cohort of educated Chinese who chose to remain in or return to their homeland to build the New China. Her mature worldview was not a product of the revolution or of state socialism, but she invested in the success of New China and shared in its losses.

Yang Jiang was assigned to a cadre school in a remote section of Henan Province in July 1970. Her husband had already been sent to an adjoining camp in November 1969. Both were released in March 1972, though the last of the cadre schools remained open until 1979. Yang Jiang finished writing her memoir in August 1980, shortly before formation of the Special Court. The book was published first in Hong Kong in May 1981 by the current-events monthly *Wide Angle* (*Guangjiaojing*) and subsequently published on the mainland in July 1981 by the Joint Publishing Bookstore (*Sanlian shudian*), a commercial affiliate of the People's Publishing House (*Renmin chubanshe*).[6] Yang Jiang went through back channels to publish her memoir in Hong Kong because she was worried the work would be too controversial. To her surprise, the memoir caught the attention and approval of Minister of Propaganda Hu Qiaomu, the principal author of the party's official "Resolution on Certain Questions in the History of the Party since the Founding of the People's Republic of China." Hu Qiaomu offered the following endorsement, which appeared (without attribution) in an advertisement for the book on the back cover of the literary journal *Dushu*: "Written with true feeling, true meaning, true scenery; sorrowful but not wounded, wronged but not angry; a sketch of that 'historically unprecedented' decade drawn by someone there against her will."[7] As she states in the

---

[6] Kong, *Yang Jiang ping zhaun*, pp. 295–6; Li Guoqing, "Ganxiao liuji zai Xianggang shouban" [Initial Hong Kong publication of Six Records of a Cadre School], http://news.takungpao.com/paper/q/2014/0313/2347571.html. Li Guoqing was editor-in-chief of *Wide Angle* magazine at the time and personally arranged for publication of Yang Jiang's memoir.

[7] Back cover of *Dushu*, August 1981.

last line of the memoir, "Eight years have passed since I returned to Beijing, yet these little incidents are as clear to me as the present day. That stage of my life was a hard-won experience, and so I have written these six records" (68). The memoir recounts personal hardships, but it does not dwell on grisly details nor does it directly touch upon the most sensitive political issues of the Cultural Revolution. Instead Yang's work is suffused with a regretful ambivalence about socialism as a failed ideology of salvation and redemption. Publication of the book in mainland China constituted a tacit but powerful admission by the socialist state of the injustices inflicted on Chinese intellectuals.

Yang Jiang's timing was uncanny. The memoir was placed before mainland Chinese readers simultaneously with, and added a personal dimension to, the party's official resolution on history. The spirit of the memoir also coincided with that of the official judgments, in the important sense that Yang Jiang desired to record and reflect upon the recent past, and to draw lessons for the future. Yang Jiang's quiet but disquieting approach stirred a powerful response from her readers, as attested by the influential literary critic Min Ze: "Once I picked up the manuscript I could not put it down, and once I read it I could not put it out of my mind.... For a long time my emotions would not be settled."[8]

Yet despite the apparent sympathy between her memoir and the official judgments, Yang Jiang's writing challenged the official project of reconciliation in subtle ways. First, as in the other literary works studied here, Yang Jiang's memoir addresses the crisis of Chinese socialism through the theme of socialist humanity rather than socialist legality. Compared to the sweeping verdicts of the party resolution and the court of law, her personal accounts seek meaning on a much smaller scale. In rejecting the delusion of justice as comprehension, Yang Jiang provides a sort of literary "antiverdict," a provocative rumination on the vanity of grand plans and the falsity of neat conclusions. Yang Jiang's memoir describes the outer limits of human community at the fringes of survival, and reveals the inhumanity of wasted talent (rencai, human resources). In the end, Yang reluctantly concedes the vanity of human efforts to affect great change in the face of grand historical forces. Reflecting on the ultimate pointlessness of her experiences in the cadre school, she turns inward and is ashamed at her own inability to be reformed through labor. While lamenting the suffering brought by the failed radical vision of socialism, her memoir also subtly suggests that the ostensibly scientific approach to socialism is a vain

---

[8] Min Ze, "*Ganxiao liuji* du hou" [After reading Six Chapters of Cadre School], *Dushu* (September 1981), p. 9.

utopian dream. Exhausted by revolution, she implies that grand narratives – and the grand projects that issue from them – could only result in further dehumanization, disappointment, and disaster. Instead, she says, it is agency on the smaller scale of human experience that might yet hold us together. The legal verdict and the historical resolution linked justice to the authoritative and comprehensive interpretation of official history (*zhengshi*). The opening "Record of Parting" in Yang Jiang's memoir marks her account as an unofficial or "outside history" (*waishi*). She has departed Beijing, the world of official politics, for the hastily-improvised world of the cadre school.

Multiple, Small, Fragmented, Incomplete

The form of Yang Jiang's memoir reinforces its critique of the grand claims of authoritative verdicts. Unlike the comprehensive judgments of the court's legal verdict and the party's historical resolution, Yang Jiang's memoir is fragmentary: small and broken, multiple yet incomplete, with the disjointed pieces gathered into six chapters, each devoted to the distinctive theme announced by its title: (1) "Sent Down: A Record of Parting"; (2) "Drilling a Well: A Record of Labor"; (3) "Tending the Plot: A Record of Leisure"; (4) "Little Qu: A Record of Sentiment"; (5) "Risky Adventure: A Record of Fortune"; and (6) "False Rumor: A Record of Vanity." Apart from the first chapter recounting the couples' departure for cadre school and the final chapter describing their return home, the narrative follows no fixed chronology and insists on recounting the same events multiple times through different thematic lenses. The fragmentary form, under the guise of so much order, is a vehicle for implicitly questioning and revising the official lessons of the Cultural Revolution.

We have already seen how the Special Court's legal verdict and the party's historical resolution provided two interlocking conclusions to the Cultural Revolution. The need for two such verdicts – one legal and one historical – already suggested that a single narrative interpretation was not sufficient. But at least these two official judgments were articulations of a single, coherent ideological vision, complementary statements in the corresponding registers of criminal law and the laws of history. Yang Jiang's memoir is never really integrated into a coherent narrative whole. Unlike the interlocking verdicts of the legal trial and official history, Yang Jiang's six chapters present multiple overlapping and disconnected accounts, whose pieces do not fit together neatly at the edges. The sense of multiplicity is further heightened by the memoir's close relationship with two other texts.

First, Yang Jiang's *Six Records of a Cadre School* is patterned on a beloved classic of Chinese literature, Shen Fu's *Six Records of a Floating Life (Fu sheng liu ji)* (completed ca. 1809; published 1877).[9] Despite the gap of nearly two hundred years, these two memoirs bear much in common: similar book titles, chapter titles, and chapter structure; similar autobiographical content; and similar themes and tone. In the estimation of Jonathan Spence, "Yang Jiang has recaptured Shen [Fu]'s moods with uncanny skill: in her work one finds a similar gentle melancholy concerning the individual's helplessness in the face of a tyrannical society, along with a similar celebration of the tiny victories that are made possible by aesthetic sensitivity or by the strength of personal love."[10] Before returning to the content and tone of her work, a few words should be said about its form. The multiplicity in Yang Jiang's memoir functions very differently from the multiplicity in Dai Houying's novel. Dai Houying's use of multiple narrators in *Humanity, Ah Humanity!* was a modernist experiment intended to defamiliarize the stable subject position; her purpose was to represent the alienation felt by the Chinese people and to demonstrate the irreducible truth of their multiple perspectives. Yang Jiang's multiple essays, by contrast, recall a traditional literary form (the casual *sanwen* essay) in order to situate the reader on familiar ground. Yang Jiang utilized the parallel structure of Shen Fu's classic as an intertextual support to reinforce themes subtly developed inside the text. In Chinese culture this was a tried and true strategy for self-preservation in a situation in which the author could only go so far and say so much: Yang Jiang used a text outside the text to partially shelter herself against tempestuous political conditions.

However short and seemingly simple, *Six Records of a Cadre School* is a remarkably rich and complex work. This can be seen in its relationship to a second text – actually an addendum to the text proper – the brief foreword to the memoir written by the author's husband Qian Zhongshu.[11] While Shen Fu's classic memoir supports the text from the outside, Qian Zhongshu's foreword destabilizes it from the inside. Yang Jiang's memoir is simultaneously in dialogue with both of these texts,

---

[9] Shen Fu probably completed *Six Records of a Floating Life* in the first decade of the nineteenth century, though we know little of the memoir or its author than what is found in the text. The earliest known edition was published in 1877. Lin Yutang's bilingual edition is available as Shen Fu, *Fu sheng liu ji* [Six records of a floating life], Lin Yutang, transl. (Hong Kong: Sanmin tushu gongsi, 1956); a more recent English translation is Shen Fu, *Six Records of a Floating Life*, Leonard Pratt and Chiang Su-hui, transl. (New York: Penguin Classics, 1983), and includes a chronology of Shen Fu's life reconstructed from the text; see pp. 16–17.

[10] Jonathan Spence, preface to Goldblatt, transl., *Six Chapters*, p. vii.

[11] Qian, "Foreword," pp. 1–2.

sometimes producing unexpected effects. For example, Shen Fu's classic memoir was prized for its rare depiction of romantic love within the traditional institution of arranged marriage; likewise, Yang Jiang's loving marriage to Qian Zhongshu (referred to throughout by his pet name, Mo Cun) is a constant theme throughout her work. But her husband was also a scathing satirist. In a scant two pages of biting, enigmatic humor, his foreword manages to shake the foundations of his wife's memoir, criticizing its structure, style, and themes. He frankly informs us, for example, that the classic memoir she has taken as a model is a book he "never did like very much."[12] The prominent placement of Qian Zhongshu's essay at the front of his wife's book, to be read prior to the memoir, frames the reader's journey with ambivalence and contradiction. The interplay of Yang Jiang's text with Shen Fu's *Six Records of a Floating Life* and with Qian Zhongshu's foreword is integral to its function – to quietly undercut the very idea that any text, and certainly not grand proclamations like legal verdicts and party resolutions, can provide comprehension and closure at the human level.

Perhaps the most striking feature of Yang Jiang's episodic memoir is its small narrative scope. As literary scholar Theodore Huters puts it, "Yang Jiang's account restricts itself to what can only be called a tenderly ironic account of personal feelings."[13] The irony is that the larger political context of the Cultural Revolution, known to the reader, is only dimly visible in the background of these characters' lives. Instead, Yang Jiang foregrounds everyday action of seemingly trivial consequence: planting vegetables, sitting through study sessions, feeding a dog. Her husband Qian Zhongshu reminds us in the foreword that such incidents are but brief interludes within a larger movement of political upheaval: "'A Record of Labor,' 'A Record of Leisure,' a record of this, a record of that – all these are no more than small adornments to this great backdrop, minor episodes in a grand story."[14] Yang Jiang's focus is so narrow that even the most serious and personal family crises are passed over with great dispatch. For example, the suicide of her son-in-law is mentioned in passing as a brief disruption amidst the elaborate arrangements for packing and moving to the cadre school. For a personal memoir, these omissions are striking; it is plain to see that a great deal is repressed by the narrative. Because the story is so fragmented and incomplete, it demands of the reader a more alert and imaginative interpretative effort.

---

[12] Ibid., p. 2.
[13] Theodore Huters, "Speaking of Many Things: Food, Kings, and the National Tradition in Ah Cheng's 'The Chess King,'" *Modern China* 14.4 (October 1988), p. 392.
[14] Qian, "Foreword," p. 1.

In its small narrative scope, Yang Jiang's post-Mao memoir resembles Shen Fu's earlier *Six Records*. Like Yang Jiang, Shen Fu confines his account to the minor joys and sorrows in the life of a married couple. He elaborately details the minutiae of arranging flowers and entertaining guests; meanwhile, the reader is well into the third chapter learning that he has a daughter, and the eventual death of his beloved wife is mentioned only briefly. Also missing from Shen Fu's memoir is the broader context, the mounting structural crisis of a government that could offer no suitable employment for his literary skills – much less for his talented wife. This is no small matter, either, for the systemic failure of the Qing to employ its literati contributed to the eventual collapse of China's dynastic system. Shen Fu perhaps did not perceive the empire on the precipice because he lived at the tail end of the Qing's "prosperous age" (*sheng shi*) and a hundred years before the fall of the dynasty, but his memoir testifies to an experience of dislocation and anomie.

Why does Yang Jiang maintain such a narrow scope? She was no ingénue. Why write a tale of "gentle melancholy" and "tiny victories" in the face of great violence and losses? Writing in 1980, with the benefit of hindsight, Yang Jiang clearly understood the larger context of her internment. "Now, the affair is over and the situation has changed; the water has subsided and the rocks have emerged," writes Qian Zhongshu in the foreword.[15] Apparently Yang Jiang has made a *deliberate* decision to focus on small, concrete narratives at the exclusion of abstract, grand ones. Unlike the grand pretensions of the legal verdict and the historical resolution, for Yang Jiang it is arguably the small narratives that are more significant.

The authenticity of her subjective, personal experiences forms the basis for her authority as a reliable recorder of events. As a later biography of Yang Jiang puts it, "[S]he has written down her personal experiences and true feelings extremely prosaically and naturally, without the artifice of symbolism, fabrication, or imagery."[16] This description closely matches Shen Fu's opening to *Six Records of a Floating Life*: "My only regret is that I was not properly schooled as a child; I know only simple language, and so my aim is merely to record the real facts and true sentiments."[17] The directness of Yang Jiang's experience and the simplicity of her writing make for a highly credible account. Nevertheless, her rhetorical method is sophisticated and often tends toward irony and

---

[15] Ibid., p. 2.
[16] Kong Qingmao, *Qian Zhongshu yu Yang Jiang* [Qian Zhongshu and Yang Jiang] (Haikou: Hainan guoji xinwen chuban zhongxin, 1997), pp. 280–1.
[17] Shen, *Fu sheng liu ji*, p. 3 [translation modified].

allegory.[18] A good example of her allegorical layering of the literal and the figurative is the way she writes simply of knowledge gathered locally and personally, without the aid of distant landmarks or abstract latitudes and longitudes; she is, after all, a prisoner. She describes herself (both literally and figuratively) as walking in the dark, but close to the ground: "Besides, I enjoyed walking in the dark. If I had used a flashlight, then I could only see the small area around me without knowing where I was. But by walking in darkness I could get to know the area quite clearly" (33). Her knowledge arises from directly engaging blind necessity: necessity as arising from literal imprisonment and as a theoretical preoccupation of socialism. Alone on that literal and figurative dark road, covering the same ground in multiple journeys and focused on the smallest possible view, she at last feels "free and easy" (33), with a clear understanding of her place in the world, her own resources, and thus her freedom.

Oddly enough, as Yang Jiang zooms in on minor facets of her life in the cadre school, the increasing detail only increases the reader's sense that her story is incomplete. The seed of this thought is planted by Qian Zhongshu's foreword, which suggests that a chapter of the book is missing: "After Yang Jiang finished writing *Six Records of a Cadre School*, she gave me the manuscript to look over. I felt she had left out a chapter, which we might as well call 'Political Campaigns: A Record of Shame.'"[19] Indeed the missing piece is not just any chapter, but seemingly the most important one. For him, the incessant political campaigns of struggle and criticism were the defining feature of life in cadre school – the "grand story" that has not been told. Thus the foreword begins by presenting Yang Jiang's intimate account as incomplete in a painfully troubling way, for it lacks the very element that her most intimate friend and partner considers to be the most significant part.

But then Qian Zhongshu cuts back again, and ends the foreword by mocking our desire for completeness. "[Shen Fu's] *Six Records of a Floating Life* ... in fact has only four extant chapters," Qian Zhongshu reminds us, "while *Six Records of a Cadre School* should in theory have seven."[20] Qian's observation calls to mind scholar Lin Yutang's wish that two more chapters might someday be added to the four known chapters of Shen Fu's classic: "I have the fond hope that some complete copy of

---

[18] An early review of Yang Jiang's memoir, having missed or chosen to ignore the overall irony of the work, draws the same legalistic lesson as that promulgated by the party: "Lin Biao and the 'Gang of Four' took advantage of the cadre schools to destroy human resources and decimate the cadre" (Min Ze, *Ganxiao liuji* du hou," p. 10).

[19] Qian, "Foreword," p. 1.

[20] Ibid., p. 2.

the book is still lying somewhere in the private collections or second-hand shops of Soochow [Suzhou], and if we are lucky, it is not altogether impossible that we may discover it still."[21] Lin Yutang's fond hope was fulfilled almost immediately: later that same year a Shanghai publisher discovered Shen Fu's missing chapters in Suzhou and published a "complete" edition. The discovered chapters were forgeries.[22] In his foreword, Qian wickedly echoes and expands upon Lin Yutang's wistful sentiment for humorous effect:

These days, when collectors, antiquarians, and scholars combine their skills and work together, the discovery of unpublished manuscripts, as yet unwritten by authors great and small, has become a flourishing new enterprise in the field of literary studies. So who can say that the day will not come when the missing chapters of these two books will surface to fill the gaps, thereby lessening somewhat the number of defects in the world of man.[23]

The falsification of chapters "as yet unwritten" might meet the interests of commercial profit, but it would be naïve to believe that completion of the text on those terms could somehow mend the human condition. With his whimsical remarks, Qian Zhongshu draws out a central lesson of Yang Jiang's tale: the desire for totality is delusion, no more than a plea for comforting falsehood.

Human Resources: A Record of Waste

If there is one theme that unites the six disparate records, it is the inhuman waste of talent. Talent (*rencai*: literally, "human resources") is in Chinese an innate *human* characteristic that must be as properly developed or cultivated as any other natural resource. Through intertextual reference to Shen Fu's *Six Records of a Floating Life*, Yang Jiang draws together traditional and contemporary discourses on the importance of human resources to society. It is an enduring preoccupation of Chinese thought that the proper role of the state is to identify, cultivate, and employ talented and worthy people. An enlightened ruler is one who makes economical and appropriate use of his subjects; a good subject is one who applies his talents in service of the commonweal. The ideal of the state in search of talent pervades the statecraft tradition, but is perhaps most evident in the characteristic institution of the Chinese imperial bureaucracy: the civil service examination, a system devoted to the meritocratic goal of producing and identifying "elegant talents" (*xiucai*).

---

[21] Lin Yutang, preface to *Fu sheng liu ji*, p. xiv.
[22] See Shen, *Fu sheng liu ji*, pp. 13–14 and 145–6.
[23] Translation of final sentence of the passage following Goldblatt, *Six Chapters*, p. 3.

Conversely, the reliable sign of misgovernment and social disorder is the state's failure to employ society's most valuable resource, its people. The theme of talents in search of a state – be they knights-errant, reclusive poets, or wandering sages – pervades multiple fiction and nonfiction genres in traditional Chinese literature. Shen Fu's unemployed scholar story belongs to this tradition, as does Yang Jiang's.[24] Like Shen Fu, Yang Jiang sees herself and her husband and their fellow cadre school students as unappreciated talents thrown to waste.

Chinese socialism inherited this tradition and translated it into the modern language of Marxism-Leninism and Mao Zedong Thought. The Marxian concept of productive justice is at its core a theory of human resources – an ethical prescription for the free employment of human creativity.[25] Leninism likewise is a theory of organizational management in service of revolution.[26] Mao, too, attached fundamental importance to the management of human resources: "In the final analysis, leadership involves two main responsibilities: to work out ideas, and to use cadres well."[27] It would not be far-fetched to say that Mao's last revolution, the Cultural Revolution, was at its heart a huge and ill-fated exercise in human resource management. As Deng Xiaoping lamented in connection with the party's resolution on history, "We say that the Cultural Revolution wasted the talents of a whole generation of our people. In fact, it didn't stop with just one generation. It opened the floodgates to anarchism and ultra-individualism, and seriously debased standards of social conduct."[28] The human resources problem was a major concern of the post-Mao transition.

It was impossible to reconcile the socialist state's supposedly emancipatory approach to human resources with actual life in the cadre schools. Cadre school labor was compulsory and alienating, and therefore dehumanizing. Yang Jiang describes the first agricultural task of the school as if it were the systematic dismantling of the physical body and its spiritual capacity. The students are forced to break ground in a dry, fallow

---

[24] Shen Fu offers no sociological explanation for his failures, but he has no doubt its causes are external: "Why is it that there are sorrows and hardships in this life? Usually they are due to one's own fault, but this was not the case with me." Shen Fu, *Fu sheng liu ji*, p. 123.

[25] Robert C. Tucker, *The Marxian Revolutionary Idea* (New York: W. W. Norton and Company, 1969), pp. 33–53.

[26] Vladimir Ilyich Lenin, *What Is to Be Done?* (1902), www.marxists.org/archive/lenin/works/1901/witbd/.

[27] Mao Zedong, "The Role of the CCP in the National War" (October 1938), in *Quotations from Chairman Mao Tsetung* (Peking: Foreign Languages Press, 1972), pp. 282–3.

[28] Deng Xiaoping, "Talk with some leading comrades of the Central Committee" (March 19, 1980) in "Remarks on Successive Drafts of the *Resolution on Certain Questions in the History of Our Party since the Founding of the People's Republic of China*" (March 1980–June 1981), http://english.peopledaily.com.cn/dengxp/vol2/text/b1420.html.

field strewn with clods of dirt "bigger than human heads and harder than bone" (17) that must be smashed into a fine meal. It is a telling and frightful description of reeducation – the difficult labor of cultivating a new society by grinding (metaphorical) skulls to bits. Throughout Yang Jiang's memoir, the reader glimpses intellectuals performing menial and pointless tasks. From the moment of her husband's initial departure to the cadre school, the experience exemplifies the demoralizing condition that Chinese idiom calls "great resources put to petty use" (*da cai xiao yong*). In an early scene, Yang Jiang witnesses the undignified cadre school matriculation of a noted senior scholar who happened to be the foremost expert on Shen Fu's *Six Records of a Floating Life*.[29]

Those ready to be "sent down" fell into formation. The red flag was unfurled, with the esteemed Yu Pingbo and his schoolmistress wife leading the way. These scholars in their seventies were lined up like children and marched off to cadre school. I couldn't bear to see it, so I turned and left early. Along the way I noticed that many people had lost their enthusiasm and were wandering back to work. On everyone's face was a blank expression. (9)

Once at the cadre school, the nation's most renowned intellectuals passed their days building ramshackle dorms and growing inedible food. Qian Zhongshu, a hopeless failure at his initial work assignment of water boiler, is demoted to watchman to befit his meager practical skills. He later finds an outlet for his literary accomplishments deciphering miswritten postal addresses.

Here, as in Shen Fu's memoir, the waste of the spouse's talent is vividly portrayed as even greater than that of the author. Shen Fu's career is frustrated, but his wife's situation is much worse, with no prospect whatsoever that her talents will be recognized. Shen Fu knows her only hope for fulfillment is to be reincarnated as a man. (In one scene he even invites her to masquerade as a man so she can attend a poetry reading.) Shen Fu cites the saying, "Lack of talent in a woman is a virtue," for unusable talent can only lead to waste and disappointment (73). Yang Jiang's memoir switches the spousal roles, with the writer wife lamenting her unrecognized husband. In both works, lamenting the waste of the spouse's talent succeeds in underscoring the pathos while avoiding self-pity. Consider Yang Jiang's dry report on the sequelae to her own crowning achievement: a makeshift outhouse at the vegetable plot for the collection of fertilizer. After the curtain is stolen by locals, one of her more important "duties" was to act as a human screen for people squatting over the potty. Unfortunately, most of the collected feces were

---

[29] See, e.g., Shen Fu, *Fu sheng liu ji zhu* [Annotated edition of Six Record of a Floating Life], annotated by Yu Pingbo (Beijing: Beijing shi fan xue yuan chu ban she, 1992).

stolen, as well, because locals knew that "the cadre school waste was the best around" (24).

The notion of the "best" waste points up Yang Jiang's ironically elitist characterization of the rustification program, namely the notion that intellectuals are innately more talented than their rural brethren and therefore more entitled to labor in relative comfort. The supposedly natural division between physical and mental labor was well established in traditional Confucian thought, which viewed agriculture as the economic basis of the state, but upheld governance as the purview of intellectuals. The *locus classicus* for this position is *Mencius* 3A:4:

Great men have their proper business, and little men have theirs.... Thus it is said, "Some labor with their minds, and some labor with their strength. Those who labor with their minds govern others; those who labor with their strength are governed by others. Those who are governed by others feed them; those who govern others are fed by them." This is a universal principle.[30]

Shen Fu expressed this idea allegorically in his *Six Records of a Floating Life*: "A crane can dance but cannot plow; an ox can plow but cannot dance. That is just the nature of things. To teach one to be the other – isn't that a wasted effort?"[31] The Cultural Revolution was supposed to eradicate such elitist ideas.[32]

Given the advanced age of many cadre school inmates, it was singularly futile and unproductive to have subjected them to the hardships of peasant life. Was this cruel practice not a damning metaphor for the entire socialist project, which had laid waste to its loyal, talented, experienced, and young?[33] For to make matters worse, the wasted humanity of the Cultural Revolution was at the same time grotesquely caricatured by its systematic cultivation of *in*humanity, a theme now familiar to us from media coverage of the Gang of Four trial and from the other literary

---

[30] *Mencius*, Chinese with English translation by James Legge, http://ctext.org/mengzi, 3A:4 [translation modified].

[31] Shen, *Six Records of a Floating Life*, p. 47 [translation modified].

[32] In fact, Mao's pointed rejection of the label "genius" (*tiancai*, literally "natural or heavenly talent") was the pretense for the purge of defendant Chen Boda in 1970 and perhaps set in motion the fall of Lin Biao in 1971.

[33] There is not space here to explore the many similarities of setting, theme, outlook, and content between Yang Jiang's *laogai* memoir and Fyodor Dostoevsky's gulag masterpiece *Memoirs from the House of the Dead*. However, it is worth noting Dostoevsky's comment on the waste of talent: "And how much youth had gone to waste within those walls, what great powers had perished uselessly there! For the whole truth must be told: these indeed were no ordinary men. Perhaps indeed they were the most highly gifted and the strongest of all our people. But these powerful forces were condemned to perish uselessly, unnaturally, wrongfully, irrevocably. And whose is the blame?" Fyodor Dostoevsky, *Memoirs from the House of the Dead*, Jesse Coulson, transl. (Oxford: Oxford University Press), p. 360.

works studied here. From the radicals' rapid promotion of "mediocre talent" (*yongcai*) Wang Hongwen, to the social inversion of man and monster in Liu Binyan's reportage, this trope was repeated everywhere. One additional example will bring us to the topic of the next section, a discussion of Yang Jiang's dog. An article published in *People's Daily* described how the Gang of Four raised man-eating beasts: "Jackals and wolves have their uses, and so there are some who will groom jackals and wolves."[34] This play on the word jackal (*chai*) – a cognate and near homonym of talent (*cai*), but written with the inhuman radical for beasts – drives home the point that where virtuous leaders are supposed to cultivate talent, the Gang of Four instead raised packs of predators.

Yang Jiang's Dog

The boundary between the human and the non-human is a persistent theme in the writings of Yang Jiang and her husband Qian Zhongshu. The earlier writings of Qian Zhongshu in particular profess a belief in the exceptional qualities of human beings, who are distinguished from base creatures by their attachment to transcendent values. Here is an example from an essay published in 1941:

The difference between civilized humans and savage beasts is that humans possess a point of view that transcends their own subjectivity. For this reason, humans are able to divorce questions of right and wrong, authenticity and falsity from their own personal gain and loss, and separate questions of good and evil, beauty and ugliness from their individual likes and dislikes. Man is not, in fact, inextricably bound to daily life…. Though he cherishes life, he also understands the value of sacrificing oneself for one's country or religion. Being born of humankind, he will inevitably do stupid things and make mistakes, eat forbidden fruit and love unworthy things. Yet his mind will stay balanced and he will not confound right and wrong or blur good and bad in order to protect himself.[35]

Human beings have the potential for attachment to values that transcend their own immediate survival or material gain. To rely solely on instrumental reason, then, would rob us of our innate humanity and reduce us to conniving animals. Despite our human imperfections, our attachment to values enables us to avoid an error that cold calculation cannot; namely, to avoid the error (and here Qian Zhongshu uses the same formulation found in Guo Moruo's poem and Liu Binyan's reportage) of

---

[34] Cong Linzhong, "Huan yang chai lang de ren" [Grooming jackels and wolves], *RMRB*, December 5, 1980.

[35] Qian Zhongshu, "Explaining Literary Blindness" [1941], in Christopher G. Rea, ed., *Humans, Beasts, and Ghosts: Stories and Essays* (New York: Columbia University Press, 2011), p. 69; translation modified.

"confounding right and wrong." Qian Zhongshu wrote this essay during wartime, having witnessed both heroic sacrifices and brutal violations of human dignity. He responded by affirming the intrinsic goodness of human nature. Yang Jiang responded to the Cultural Revolution with less confidence in the boundary between man and beast. In *Six Records of a Cadre School*, her relationship with a stray dog exposes the limits of human community on the fringes of survival.

Yang Jiang devotes an entire chapter to her canine friend, far more space than is given to any person besides her husband – including the author's daughter, son-in-law, or her other cadre school companions. Though Yang Jiang's *Six Records* (like Shen Fu's before it) is commonly considered a husband-and-wife love story, the dog is an important third character. The reader observes from the outset that this little dog has many human qualities, and even a human name: Little Qu is a pun on the name of the cadre school poet who first found her. (The poet's surname was Ou, which the illiterate locals misread as Qu. Yang Jiang changed this to another Chinese character pronounced *qu*, meaning swift.) It was fortunate that no one outside the vegetable plot deciphered the human origins of Little Qu's name, Yang Jiang explains, because it was ideologically suspect to have a "running dog," much less to treat it as a human being (36). In the dehumanizing conditions of the cadre school, however, this sympathetic creature proves more humane than many of the author's fellow humans.

The titular theme of Little Qu's chapter is sentiment or emotion (*qing*), the same quality that Dai Houying's *Humanity, Ah Humanity!* identified as the essence of human relations. In a fablelike vignette reminiscent of a struggle session, a pack of local boys and their ferocious dogs hunt down a rabbit. Yang Jiang cannot bear the hooting and barking as the rabbit makes a final, vain attempt to escape. Little Qu fears these local dogs (who have no names), just as Yang Jiang fears her fellow humans. The dog follows her about with wagging tail, and when she is transferred from the outlying vegetable plot to the Central Compound, the loyal dog finds its way to join her. Sadly, at the Central Compound Yang Jiang cannot openly repay the dog's affection: "Many people in the company loved dogs; but some others felt that dogs were just playthings for ladies of the capitalist class. So I always treated Little Qu lightly, never daring to spoil her" (39). Later, the whole company is relocated to an even more distant camp and Yang Jiang is forced to leave Little Qu behind. A colleague returning from a visit to the old compound reports the heartbreaking scene: "That little dog of yours refuses to eat, running about here and there, just running and barking everywhere, as if looking for something" (44).

In another scene, the canteen serves up dog meat as a holiday treat. Little Qu's namesake, the fellow cadre school inmate surnamed Ou, reports that when the dog was offered a table scrap she refused to eat:

According to poet Ou, Little Qu cradled the meat in her mouth, dug a hole, and buried it in the ground. I don't trust the words of poets, but when I asked again she insisted she had personally seen Little Qu bury the dog meat. However, I still believe the story may have been poetic license. (43)

That the story may be an anthropomorphized interpretation of the canine instinct to bury a valued treat does not detract from the human significance of the event. To both the inmates and to the reader it seems as if the dog meat has received a more decent burial than the school's human suicides, who are unceremoniously dumped in shallow, unmarked graves by the river. Unlike the many people who scramble over each other to ruin the lives of others, Little Qu will not resort to cannibalism to survive. She prefers to live on feces than to betray her innate caninity (read: humanity).

Little Qu's chapter ends with Yang Jiang and her husband wondering about the dog's fate. Qian Zhongshu muses, "'Perhaps she's already been eaten by somebody and become a pile of manure.'" But Yang Jiang is more hopeful: "Maybe she's been eaten; but then again, maybe she's become a mother, eating manure to survive, having one puppy after another" (44). Eating shit is the most dignified option among several debasing strategies: to eat others, eat just enough shit to survive, or be eaten by others and become shit. Which of these choices represents freedom? In discussions of transitional justice, these roles are more commonly known as perpetrator, collaborator, and victim. Qian Zhongshu discusses these roles when in the foreword he calls for recovery of a seventh, "missing" chapter: "Political Campaigns: A Record of Shame."

Political Campaigns: A Record of Shame

Qian Zhongshu does not count his wife and himself among the most sympathetic victims of the Cultural Revolution – that is, among those who could rightly author "A Record of Injustice" or "A Record of Indignation." *Six Records of a Cadre School* is pointedly not a typical tale of victimhood in the mold of Scar Literature. Neither is Yang Jiang's story a litany of accusations as found in the indictment, nor a testimony of righteous indignation. She produces a more conflicted and ambivalent account. "This sort of 'laughter with tears,'" says one recent reviewer, "has greater literary vitality and artistic merit than those indignant, accusatory denunciations."[36] The essential missing chapter is "A Record of Shame" because, as Qian Zhongshu insists, he and his wife belong instead to that vast majority of people who were "passive participants" caught between the perpetrators and the victims. Some of these passive collaborators were "unwitting insects," unable to make out false or erroneous charges, he says, while still others saw the injustice unfolding, but were too cowardly to protest. (He confesses himself to be a member of this latter group.) Their "not very active" participation in the political campaigns of the Cultural Revolution deserves its own chapter as a cause for shame.[37]

And what about the shame of the active perpetrators, of "those who persisted in serving as flag-wavers, drum-beaters, and hatchet-men; those who pushed to settle trumped-up cases though they knew the accounts were hopelessly muddled?" "Logically, these are the people most suited to write a Record of Shame," says Qian Zhongshu, but most likely they have forgotten the past and feel no shame.[38] Here he unleashes his caustic wit on the post-Mao reforms, intimating that the modernizers' mantra of "uniting as one and looking towards the future" is a self-serving project of forgetting shame. Qian Zhongshu, parodically aping the modernizers, dismisses shame as a weakness that can only retard the drive for modernization:

Shame also causes fear and doubt, which can lead to critical hesitation in the desperate struggle for survival; for those who harbor shame, a moment of retreat could leave them stragglers their entire lives. Therefore, shame is an emotion that ought to be eliminated, not fostered; nor is it listed among the "seven emotions" handed down from antiquity. With the increasing stress of life in today's modern society, this psychological state is not only useless, but quite harmful – best not to feel it at all, if you wish to keep a sound body and peace of mind.[39]

As he sees it, the state's shameless modernizing agenda has little use for honest introspection, for a sense of shame is one of the "sprouts" of our basic humaneness.[40] But because shame has no instrumental purpose, it places values in the way of instrumentality and therefore is detrimental to modernization.

Following this logic, it is easy to see why the post-Mao state chose to focus narrowly on individual legal guilt, rather than addressing the much broader problem of shame. Shame and guilt are both affective

---

[36] Kong, *Qian Zhongshu yu Yang Jiang*, p. 285.
[37] Qian, "Foreword," pp. 1–2.
[38] Ibid., p. 2.
[39] Ibid.
[40] *Mencius*, 2A:6.

responses to the realization that one has done something wrong. But guilt is based on a negative evaluation of a wrongful *action*, while shame is based on a negative evaluation of the *self*.[41] Because guilt directs attention outward, to the harmful consequences of the action on its victim, it is more closely associated with empathy; shame is directed inward, focusing on the inadequacies and faults of the perpetrator. Shame may even lead the perpetrator to feel *ressentiment* toward the victim for exposing these weaknesses.[42] The other problem is that the protracted period of mass violence made it difficult to draw neat distinctions between perpetrator and victim. It must be noted that the Chinese state has not hesitated to cultivate a collective sense of "national humiliation" or shame (*guo chi*) when victimhood could be used to inspire anti-Western or anti-Japanese nationalism. But the victimhood and shame of the Cultural Revolution was as self-inflicted as it was pervasive, a fact that precluded too much rallying around the flag. Instead the party relied on the extravagantly theatrical Gang of Four trial, with its sharp focus on individual guilty actors, to neutralize the shameful past.

Vanity and Efficacy in History

Yang Jiang's introspective memoir does not say much about political campaigns, but it does record her shame. It is not shame of the sort Qian Zhongshu has mentioned, but rather a troubling and ambivalent shame at her failure to be reformed by the cadre school. Yang Jiang admits to shame at the "unequal division of labor" (19) in the labor camp and to her poor class consciousness. Several times she contrasts the extreme physical exertion endured by others with her light duties tending a vegetable plot (32):

Everyone in our company was a hard worker and a hearty eater – isn't this a case of "from each according his ability, to each according to his need"? Of course eating was just part of the story since we were compensated at different levels of the pay scale. I ate little food and did little work; my duties were very light but my pay was extremely high. You could say I was "taking advantage of the superiority of socialism" at considerable expense to the nation. I felt ashamed about it, but

---

[41] Helen B. Lewis, *Shame and Guilt in Neurosis* (New York: International University Press, 1971).

[42] Recent social science research suggests that in transitional justice contexts, collective shame may promote efforts to repair the self-worth or public image of the *perpetrator* group at the expense of reparations for the *victim* group. See Rupert Brown and Sabina Cehajic, "Dealing with the Past and Facing the Future: Mediators of the Effects of Collective Guilt and Shame in Bosnia and Herzegovina," *European Journal of Social Psychology* 38.4 (2008), pp. 682–3.

nobody took much notice of my remorse. So I just went about my business, dutifully planting vegetables at the cadre school. (24)

Moreover, there are moments when she feels that hard labor might really change her. For example, when helping the company dig a well, with her bare feet squishing about in the mud, she begins to feel an intimacy with the soil. The movement of her feet in the mud becomes an amusing metaphor for personal transformation. "I silently laughed at myself: you could say I was changing my standpoint or gaining a foothold" (18). She describes in that moment a sense of solidarity with her fellow workers at the cadre school, a sentiment she likens to "collective identity" (*jiti gan*) or "social connectedness" (*hequn gan*). Unfortunately, the solidarity that ought to grow from common experience did not materialize; quite the contrary.

In Yang Jiang's experience, cadre school labor did not foster socialist class consciousness, but merely strengthened bonds among the intellectuals. On the one hand, the cadre school inmates grew closer as they closed ranks against their supervisors: "The difference between 'us' and 'them' was not the same as class difference, but working alongside the group in collective labor was very educational: I began to develop a slight grasp of 'class sympathy'" (21). On the other hand, this sympathy among the intellectual workers never extends to their supposed models and teachers, the middle to lower peasants. Likewise, the put-upon locals view the outsiders with suspicion, as an unwelcome nuisance: "We were not a part of their 'us'; we were 'poorly dressed, well fed people with wristwatches' – i.e., 'them'" (21). There remains a total lack of collective identity between the intellectuals and peasants: This complete failure to bridge solidarity and understanding across class lines must count among the major ideological failures of the Cultural Revolution. Here Yang Jiang's small narratives mount a major rebuttal of socialism's grand projects.

The stated theme of her chapter on the vegetable plot is "Leisure," even though her time there was hardly fun and she seems to have worked as hard as her physical constitution would allow. Yang Jiang's personal failure at reform mirrors the overall failure of the Cultural Revolution to meld individual subjects into the socialist collective. When news arrives that she has been selected for early release among the old, feeble, sick, and disabled, her heart jumps. Despite her regret at leaving the others behind, she cannot suppress her selfish joy. It is a moment of shameful self-realization: "After more than ten years of reform, and another two years at the cadre school, I could not say I had attained the progress for which we all strived. This selfish heart of mine had not changed a bit. I was the same old me" (67). Just as labor has no lasting effect on her character, it also has no lasting effect on the land. When the cadre school picks up to move to another location, Yang Jiang surveys the scene: no trace of the camp is left; their toil and suffering has amounted to nothing (33). Yang Jiang begins her cadre school experience ashamed that others labor harder than she does; she ends up ashamed at the failure of her personal transformation.

The end of the memoir brings us back around to the beginning, with Yang Jiang returning to Beijing and discovering herself to be "the same old me." Despite the passage of biographical and historical time, there has been no progress. Her work at the cadre school has been toilsome and fruitless; she has failed in her personal struggle to conquer selfishness for the sake of collective identity; and the political movement of the Cultural Revolution has failed to remake the material world through human will. The reader cannot help but be struck by the pointlessness of it all. And yet in the memoir's very last line, the author claims some value for her time at the cadre school: "It has been eight years since I returned to Beijing," she writes, "yet these little incidents are as clear to me as the present moment. Since that period of my life was a hard-won experience, I have written these six records" (68). Yang Jiang's justification for the existence of her memoir is that it records a hard-won experience. What, then, was won? What is the lesson to draw from her experience? The lesson of *Six Records of a Cadre School* is the vanity of making and remaking human beings through mass political mobilization.

Human beings are simply too hard to change. The premise of reeducation is that labor is an effective way to reform (or re-form) people, but Yang Jiang points out time and again that human beings are not so easily molded by the crude methods of the cadre school. In the opening scene, as her colleagues prepare for departure to the cadre school by packing their goods into wood and metal crates, Yang Jiang laments there is no comparable protection for their selves. There is no suitable preparation for the journey, she says, save "tempering" – learning to endure abuse. Still she takes solace in the observation that "nothing endures abuse as readily as flesh and blood" (7). Shortly afterward, the students are enduring another round of predeparture tempering, this time pointlessly transporting books on carrying poles so heavy they rip through the fabric of their shirts. At the sight of their bare shoulders, she remarks, "Again I was amazed that what suffers wear and tear the best is human flesh and blood" (10). The durability of their physical bodies is, of course, a figure for the immutability of human nature. Through all the abuse, the old intellectuals barely change at all. In frustration their tormenters are prompted to complain: "tempering people is harder than tempering steel" (10). Later at the cadre school, the students arrive at a similar conclusion: "Changing one's nature is like teaching a dog to give up eating shit" (37), a point driven home by the rare moments when it seems that Yang Jiang might be changing. Once, for example, she identifies with the collective spirit while drilling the well. But a closer reading reveals that her apparent transformation is merely resignation to Necessity. Note well her characterization: "After months and months at the cadre school, *with no other prospects in sight*, a feeling of 'us' gradually took hold" (20; italics added). Her situation of internment is the very definition of Necessity – confined against her will in a situation she cannot change, with no other prospects in sight.

Toward the end of her imprisonment, a false rumor of her husband's impending release reveals her unreformed, selfish character. In this crucial scene, she realizes she cannot maintain the collective feeling of "us" without her husband by her side. She recalls that in the days before the Communist liberation of 1949, they felt a sense of nationalism or patriotism. Back then, Qian Zhongshu says, he frequently quoted a line of classical verse from a poem by Liu Yong: "With no regret, though my sash hangs loose about the waist / it is for her that I pine and wither away" (65). Yang Jiang explains that the one she and her husband pined for was China:

We could not give up the motherland. We could not abandon "her" – for she was also "we" or "us". Although we had never met the one billion other people who were "we" or "us", we formed a single body. We suffered together, and lived and breathed as one, each inseparable parts of a single self. (65)

For the sake of the nation, they could feel "no regret." An editorial for *People's Daily* seized upon this line from the memoir and cited its patriotic message: "Young friends, think of Qian Zhongshu and Yang Jiang! Have their lives not been more sorrowful than yours? ... So how is it that they survived the apocalypse [*jiebo*; Sanskrit *kalpa*] without resentment, 'with no regret though their sashes hang loose about the waist'? In their hearts is a 'her' above all others – the motherland."[43] Yang Jiang had always agreed with this sentiment, but in the misery of the cadre school she was not so sure. Her husband reaffirms their decision to remain in China after the revolution, yet still she wavers: "Since liberation I had been forged in the fires of reform, but I feared that now I was even worse than before" (65).

[My husband] normally reached decisions very quickly, almost without thinking; and afterwards, he would not change his mind. As for me, I couldn't help thinking a thing through forwards and back. Yet our decisions were always the

---

[43] Xin Hong, "Women zhi shi shebude zuguo" [We can't give up our motherland], *RMRB*, December 5, 1981.

same. These were the choices we had made, and what's more they were not blind choices. From that point on, I resolved to hold my ground and put a rest to vain hopes. (65)

Yang Jiang ultimately accepts their current position because, she says, it was not "blind choices" that brought them there.

This is a curious statement: certainly they had not *chosen* to end up prisoners in the cadre school? Her meaning can be illuminated by Engels's well-known statement on freedom and Necessity. According to Engels, the illusion of many possible choices is actually a sign of blindness, while recognition of the one correct and inevitable choice shows insight into Necessity:

Therefore the *freer* a man's judgment is in relation to a definite question, the greater is the *necessity* with which the content of this judgment will be determined; while the uncertainty, founded on ignorance, which seems to make an arbitrary choice among many different and conflicting possible decisions, shows precisely by this that it is not free, that it is controlled by the very object it should itself control.[44]

Yang Jiang and Qian Zhongshu chose to remain in China, to suffer without regrets, because they could not do otherwise. They were unwilling and unable to abandon the collective with which they genuinely identified. The inevitability of this choice is proven when – even now, after all their suffering, and despite her wavering judgment – they both arrive again at the same conclusion. Vanity is false hope, a belief in illusory freedom. True freedom comes from insight into the necessity of what is not possible and the recognition of what is possible.

Thus Yang Jiang describes her wavering judgment, her passing illusion of choice, as a vain (*wang*) hope. This word *wang* appears in the chapter title and again throughout the chapter; in various contexts it means absurd, ridiculous, rushed, ill-considered, or vain. Yang Jiang's view of human history is encapsulated in the idea of *wang*, or vanity: the realization that grand plans are foolish and deluded, and will result in disappointment or disaster. Yang Jiang seems to agree with Engels's view of freedom, but rather than celebrating the emancipatory promise of harnessing Necessity, she emphasizes the modest and cautionary view that prevails in the conclusion to Engels's essay: "how young the whole of human history still is, and how ridiculous it would be to attempt to ascribe any absolute validity to our present views."[45] We are walking in

[44] Friedrich Engels, "Part I: Philosophy, XI. Morality and Law, Freedom and Necessity," *Anti-Dühring: Herr Eugin Dühring's Revolution in Science* (1877), www.marxists.org/archive/marx/works/1877/anti-duhring/.
[45] Ibid.

the dark, to borrow a seminal image from Yang Jiang's memoir. It would be ridiculous to turn on our flashlight and, on the basis of that tiny light, pretend to see and comprehend the entire landscape around us. And how much more ridiculous and vain it would be on this basis to embark on a sudden and sweeping plan to remake that world. "Theory becomes aimless if it is not connected with revolutionary practice, just as practice gropes in the dark if its path is not illuminated by revolutionary theory," wrote Stalin.[46] The sharpest political implication of the nation's groping advance is that revolutionary theory has failed to illuminate a path.

For Yang Jiang, human freedom consists of understanding Necessity, and seeking insight into its inner workings. But this does not mean thinking on the grand scale: rashly claiming to know the laws of history, irresponsibly exploiting nature, or imperiously imposing our will over other human beings. Instead, human freedom is a recognition of our position, floating in a maelstrom of barely visible yet overwhelming forces. Indeed, this is the central image of Shen Fu's *Six Records of a Floating Life*, the title of which is derived from the classical poetry of Li Bo: "This floating life is like a dream, how rare our chances for happiness." The line alludes to Buddhism's fatalistic vision of an ephemeral, transient, and unreal world, where human lives are tossed about and carried along like leaves floating on a rushing stream. In the nightmare world of the cadre school, happiness was rare indeed. But Yang Jiang's vision is not so much fatalistic as it is modest. Recognition of the great forces arrayed against her brings Yang Jiang a sense of freedom and perhaps even some measure of happiness.

Freedom from the Laws of History

Yang Jiang neatly sums up the futility of their situation at the cadre school: "To tell the truth, though he [Qian Zhongshu] tried to console me, we both understood that 'freedom is insight into Necessity'; if you clearly know that the cell door is bolted fast, then pushing and pounding against it is futile" (62). The delicate irony of this statement can be appreciated once it is imbedded back into context, in this quotation from Engels:

Hegel was the first to state correctly the relationship between freedom and necessity. To him, freedom is the insight into necessity. "Necessity is *blind* only *in so far as it is not understood*." Freedom does not consist in any dreamt-of independence

---

[46] Joseph Stalin, *Foundations of Leninism* (Honolulu: University Press of the Pacific, 2001), p. 28.

from natural laws, but in the knowledge of these laws, and in the possibility this gives of systematically making them work towards definite ends.[47]

Here Engels argues that true freedom arises from our insight into the laws of the material world. This insight allows us to master the objective conditions of our existence and thereby to transform the forces that work against us into forces that work for us. This is what Lenin calls, in his later analysis of the passage, "the transformation of blind, unknown necessity, 'necessity-in-itself,' into the known 'necessity-for-us.'"[48] For Lenin, the relationship between history and will is clear: "the necessity of nature is primary and human will and mind secondary. The latter must necessarily and inevitably adapt themselves to the former."[49] And yet, this unbending historical materialism still creates space for human agency. The laws of the objective, external world may be immutable, but our knowledge and insight into them allow the possibility for meaningful action by consciously harnessing them to our own ends. Instead of pounding locked doors, so to speak, it is better to direct one's energies toward a more effective route of escape. This emancipatory claim lays the philosophical foundation for post-Mao socialism's emphasis on modernization through objective and scientific knowledge.[50] The reader may guess Yang Jiang's uneasiness with the post-Mao reaffirmation of historical materialism, however; for in the preceding quotation, in place of the usual Chinese translation for Necessity (*biran*), she substitutes the term *guilü* (the laws of history). For her, the so-called laws of history are not a guide to modernization and progress, but an obstacle to freedom. Insight into the existence and workings of the bolted door offers no solace – only an awareness of futility.

At times this awareness surfaces as a fatalistic resignation, as when Yang imagines herself in a painting she had seen, of an old man walking down a giant mountain and into his grave. (In the preface to her 2007 memoir, she writes in a similar vein, "Birth, aging, sickness, death: these are the *guilü* of life – no one can avoid them."[51]) More often, though,

---

[47] Engels, *Anti-Dühring*.

[48] Vladimir Ilyich Lenin, "Chapter 3: The Theory of Knowledge of Dialectical Materialism of Empirio-Criticism, Part 6: Freedom and Necessity," in *Materialism and Empirio-Criticism: Critical Comments on a Reactionary Philosophy in Collected Works*, 45 vols. (Moscow: Progress Publishers, 1972), vol. 14, p. 189.

[49] Ibid., p. 188.

[50] The original passage in Engels's *Anti-Dühring* (1877) and Lenin's commentary on it in *Materialism and Empirio-Criticism* (1909) greatly influenced Mao's understanding of historical materialism as expressed in his philosophical writings of the late 1930s. These writings were identified in the post-Mao era as the correct and essential core of Mao Zedong Thought; see Frederic Wakeman Jr., *History and Will: Philosophical Perspectives of Mao Tse-tung's Thought* (Berkeley: University of California Press, 1973), pp. 223 and 229.

[51] Yang Jiang, *Zou dao rensheng bian shang: Zi wen zi da* [Arriving at the margins of life: Answering my own questions] (Taibei: Shibao wenhua chuban, 2007), p. 3.

she emphasizes possibilities for agency albeit on a smaller, human scale. Though human will may be for Lenin secondary to the necessities of history and nature, it remains for Yang Jiang the issue of primary importance. Though she is not idly waiting for religious salvation (hoping for the bared door to miraculously open), the spirit of her interpretation resembles the serenity prayer attributed to theologian Reinhold Niebuhr: "Give us courage to change what must be altered, serenity to accept what cannot be helped, and the insight to know the one from the other."[52]

Yang Jiang quietly challenged the authority of the official verdict on the Cultural Revolution by adding six small records of her own. She records how she turned away from the locked cell door and, like Shen Fu before her, toward the small joys and sorrows of an embodied human life. In focusing on local knowledge, personal relationships, and everyday activities, she comes closer to realizing her humanity than any grand socialist project could ever hope. Her political disillusionment represents the experience of a generation, says the reviewer for *Dushu*, who points out that the Cultural Revolution sullied the great name of socialism:

Cadre school was a term that once had a good connotation in our revolutionary history, and was something that served a positive purpose. But the "cadre schools" of the decade of chaos had a different character, in just the same way that Marxism-Leninism, socialism, and so on, suddenly became the trademarks of repugnant thugs pushing odious counterrevolutionary scams.[53]

This reviewer's remarks aligned Yang Jiang's position with that of the party-state. But Yang Jiang's personal and unassuming memoir, precisely *because* it lacked the coercive efficacy of the legal verdict or the party resolution, was all the more powerful in its impact upon the imagination of Chinese readers. Yang Jiang's memoir, like Liu Binyan's reportage and Dai Houying's novel, dramatizes that it is inhumanity – not illegality – that lies at the root of societal dysfunction; and this is the ultimate injustice of the Cultural Revolution. *Six Records of a Cadre School* was just the beginning of an outpouring of personal memoirs on the hardships and injustices of that period. (There are dozens available in English translation alone.) The very proliferation of other, unsettling accounts about the Cultural Revolution and its aftermath proves how naïve was the notion that the Special Court could pronounce a final verdict on the past, or that any one narrative gesture alone could dispel lingering anxieties and social contradictions. Already by 1984 the central

---

[52] There are several versions of this saying; here as quoted in "Serenity Prayer Skeptic Now Credits Niebuhr," *New York Times*, November 28, 2009.

[53] Min, "*Ganxiao liuji* du hou," p. 10.

authorities were so fed up with the torrent of "recollections, memoirs, reportage, etc." and other unofficial histories of the Cultural Revolution that for a time they recommended no more be approved for publication, save perhaps a few "seriously and conscientiously written recollections with a definite value;" and these they further stipulated "must be factually accurate, must not violate the spirit of the 'Resolution on Certain Questions in the History of the Party,' must not freely cite historical materials not yet declassified, and must not touch upon the moral character of leading party and state officials."[54] Clearly the official comprehensive verdicts were not comprehensive enough, and the party and state found themselves fighting a losing battle to contain the range of testimony.

[54] "Document 63. CCP Central Propaganda Department and State Press and Publications Administration, Regulations Governing the Publication of Books about the 'Great Cultural Revolution'" (December 10, 1984) in Michael Schoenhals, ed., *China's Cultural Revolution, 1966–1969: Not a Dinner Party. An Eastgate Reader* (Armonk, NY: M. E. Sharpe, 1996), pp. 310–12 [translation modified].

Conclusion

Transitional justice following the Cultural Revolution was complex and multifaceted. The Gang of Four trial played an important part, not least for its social symbolism. But official efforts to settle accounts with the past were by no means limited to a "show" trial. After the trial, the regime tried to tie up loose ends using party discipline, law, and even the laws of history. Although the results were necessarily incomplete and not every loose end could be tied up satisfactorily, transitional justice did achieve some measure of success. Old wounds were sutured sufficiently for Chinese society to move forward into a new era of political stability and economic growth. Above all, the reversal of verdicts on the Cultural Revolution preserved the socialist party-state system from self-inflicted disaster and fortified it enough to outlast the collapse of communism in Eastern Europe and the Soviet Union. Moreover, the post-Mao regime has not just survived, it has thrived.

The legitimacy of the post-Mao regime has rested on the promise of modernization. The Gang of Four trial took up a debate that had animated Chinese political thought since the late nineteenth century: Should modernization be motivated by instrumental rationality and material development or by humanistic values and spiritual renewal? The official discourse on justice that surrounded the trial proposed an apparently paradoxical resolution to this dilemma: that socialist values could find expression in instrumental rationality.[1] The end of the Cultural Revolution marked an end to continuous revolution in the political and economic spheres, and especially to the idea that the motive force of revolution was subjective consciousness. Chinese socialism took up the task of transforming the material conditions of an agrarian economy, of developing and harnessing the continuous revolution of the advanced

---

[1] Xue-liang Ding, "The Disparity between Idealistic and Instrumental Chinese Reformers," *Asian Survey* 28.11 (November 1988), pp. 1117–39; and Feng Chen, "An Unfinished Battle in China: The Leftist Criticism of the Reform and the Third Thought Emancipation," *China Quarterly* (June 1999), pp. 447–67.

productive forces historically associated with industrial capitalism. Deng Xiaoping pointed out that even after decades of socialist revolution, China still faced the problem of poverty:

During the "Cultural Revolution" the Gang of Four raised the absurd slogan, "Better to be poor under socialism and communism than to be rich under capitalism." ... To build socialism it is necessary to develop the productive forces. Poverty is not socialism. To uphold socialism, a socialism that is to be superior to capitalism, it is imperative first and foremost to eliminate poverty.[2]

For those who measure success macroeconomically, the past three decades of sustained economic growth have vindicated the program of reform and proved the efficacy of the instrumental approach to modernization. Though the reforms were introduced in an incremental and uneven fashion, cumulatively they have produced changes amounting to an economic revolution. In just a few decades, China has transformed itself from a largely agrarian country to a highly urbanized, industrialized, and globally oriented export economy. From 1980 to 2010, China enjoyed a nearly 10 percent average annual increase in nominal gross domestic product (GDP), becoming by the end of that period the world's second-largest economy, largest exporter, and largest creditor. There is no question that the program of market reform and structural transformation has brought tremendous economic growth. The post-Mao leadership, more than any other Chinese regime of the previous two centuries, has delivered on the promise of modernization – at least insofar as modernization means the attainment of wealth and power for the Chinese nation and the betterment of the material standard of living for its people.

At the heart of this successful economic growth has been an experimental approach to development. The embrace of instrumentalism as a core value of Chinese socialism was best expressed by Deng Xiaoping's pragmatic approach to "*mao* theory": "It doesn't matter whether a cat [*mao*] is white or black; if it catches mice, then it's a good cat."[3] It doesn't matter if the means are socialist or capitalist, if the end result is economic modernization. Consistent commitment to trial and error accounts for China's supposedly inconsistent approach to reform, including its cycles

---

[2] Deng Xiaoping, "To Uphold Socialism We Must Eliminate Poverty" (April 26, 1987), https://dengxiaopingworks.wordpress.com/2013/03/18/to-uphold-socialism-we-must-eliminate-poverty/.

[3] Deng is supposed to have first uttered this Sichuanese proverb at a Communist Youth League conference in July 1962, where he was arguing against the rural commune system and in favor of the household responsibility system. In some versions of the proverb, the choice is between a black cat and a yellow cat.

of political repression and relaxation.[4] Because the adjustments and reversals integral to this experimental process will likely continue, the observer should be cautious about finding too much significance in specific policies and reforms. These are all provisional means to a purposive end.

China's post-Mao leadership needed to discover a new route to the future communist utopia in unique historical conditions; a route unforeseen by classical Marxism, indicated only generally by Leninism, and charted incorrectly by Mao. To navigate this perilous journey through unknown waters, its leadership would need to understand and exploit the underlying patterns and flows that guide historical development. Deng Xiaoping described development as "crossing the river by feeling for stones." The metaphor of "feeling for stones" expresses faith in the existence of objectively existing structures (the laws of history) lying just below the surface, waiting to be discovered. Such discovery arises from practice: getting your feet wet and feeling about for the hard facts upon which to stand as you make your way. But anyone who has crossed a stream in this manner will tell that when you reach the other bank you may not end up in the spot that you intended. The metaphor is strongly deterministic but weakly teleological: you will go wherever the stones lead you. As Chinese society moves step by step farther from the lived experience of socialist revolution, this unresolved contradiction raises some provocative questions about the overall direction of China's modernization. Once the Chinese master capitalism in the name of socialism, will they still be interested in communism? What if the other shore is not the communist utopia?

Moreover, the journey is fraught with hidden dangers: conceptually, Mao's treacherous shoals and Deng's stepping-stones are, after all, much the same thing. To what extent can China's experiments in the laws of historical development be fully controlled by and contained within the socialist model? The real world is not a laboratory, hermetically sealed and sterilized. The opening of Special Economic Zones (SEZs) is an illustrative example. When the Chinese Communist Party (CCP) implemented market-oriented laws in selected coastal cities beginning in the late 1970s, the strategy was to harness the productive power of capitalism and foreign investment while containing capitalism's ill effects to the trade ports. The SEZs have been no more successful at containing capitalism than the treaty ports of the nineteenth century were at containing imperialism. Like Dr. Frankenstein's monster, the economic

---

[4] Sebastian Heilmann and Elizabeth J. Perry, eds., *Mao's Invisible Hand: The Political Foundations of Adaptive Governance in China.* Harvard Contemporary China Series 17 (Cambridge, MA: Harvard University Press, 2011).

experiment has taken on a life of its own, unleashing the energies of global capitalism that constantly threaten to envelop and destroy the scientists who unleashed them.

China's successful economic revolution has been attended by profound social changes. These include positive changes like the emergence of a middle class, increased entrepreneurial opportunities, access to global culture, and overall improved standards of living. However, China is still very much a developing country. Although it boasts the world's second-largest economy by GDP, the *per capita* figure ranks around ninetieth, comparable to nations like Thailand, Cuba, the Dominican Republic, and Angola. China also has one of the world's highest Gini coefficients, indicating severe income inequality. Not surprisingly, such rapid and uneven economic growth in the post-Mao period has produced some undesirable consequences. The deleterious side effects of reform include inequalities between coastal and inland regions, urban and rural communities, men and women, and between majority Han Chinese and minority ethnic groups; disappearance of the social safety net, exacerbating the effects of unequal access to social resources like housing, education, and medical care; displacement and destruction of existing communities to make way for development, often forcibly or without adequate compensation; environmental degradation, marked by rapacious exploitation of scarce natural resources and dangerous pollution of soil, water, and air; and sharp increases in violent crime and property crime, including widespread official corruption and gross corporate malfeasance. The social fabric, torn by revolution, has been mended only hastily by economic reform, only to be subjected to new and no less profound stresses from many forces and directions.

Equally as obvious as the economic and social transformation of post-Mao China, though somewhat more difficult to quantify, is the profound change in Chinese culture. This cultural change is produced by, exacerbated by, and, in turn, contributes to the more visible social and economic changes. Arthur Kleinman and others have pointed to "a pivotal transformation in the moral context and in the personhood of the Chinese today ... that has been obscured by the enormous economic, political, and security interests that still dominate our understanding of modern China."[5] Signs of this subjective transformation were already evident in the earliest social scientific data collected in the post-Mao period.[6] Faced with a greater variety of economic opportunities,

---

[5] Arthur Kleinman, "Introduction: Remaking the Moral Person in a New China," in Arthur Kleinman et al., eds., *Deep China: The Moral Life of the Person* (Berkeley: University of California Press, 2011), p. 31.

[6] Stanley Rosen, "Value Change among Post-Mao Youth: The Evidence from Survey Data," in Perry Link, Richard Madsen, and Paul G. Piocwicz, eds., *Unofficial China: Popular Culture and Thought in the People's Republic* (Boulder, CO: Westview Press, 1989), pp. 193–216.

weaker imposition of social control, the declining prestige of official (state, party, military) institutions relative to private enterprise, and a reduced emphasis on politics in everyday life, more and more Chinese, especially young people, have turned away from the collectivist values of socialism and toward the pursuit of personal satisfaction. Most remarkable is the strength of hedonistic consumerism, which stands in complete contrast both to the self-sacrificing communitarian ideals preached during the Mao era and to the humanistic values championed in the works of literature examined here.[7] Perhaps in resignation to such transformations, the party-state has tried recently to rally collective identity around nationalism and patriotism, but these sentiments are, of course, not specifically socialist.

The cultural transformation has been felt most acutely at the level of the individual. This transformation in subjectivity has been marked by the individualization of morality, the loosening of ties to the traditional family and the modern state, increased dislocation and mobility, the emergence of new types of elective sociality, the rise of conspicuous consumption, the acknowledgment of sexuality and desire, and the embrace of personal enterprise.[8] The pervasive disconnectedness from larger norms and institutions, and deep change in the basic character of personhood in post-Mao China amounts to a shift of macrohistorical significance, "one of the great historical pivots in Chinese society."[9] The Gang of Four trial, and the conversations it raised about socialist legality and humanity, helped to define this moment of historical pivot.

In historical perspective, the major significance of the trial was its failure to make a compelling case for the justice – and not just the economic efficacy and political expedience – of Chinese socialism. From this failure to model and nurture a more just society has emerged the Faustian bargain that saved Chinese socialism as a ruling ideology but cost it its revolutionary soul. Concern for socialist humanity was rooted

---

[7] Judith Farquhar, *Appetites: Food and Sex in Post-Socialist China* (Durham, NC: Duke University Press, 2002); Jiwei Ci, *Dialectic of the Chinese Revolution: From Utopianism to Hedonism* (Stanford, CA: Stanford University Press, 2004). An online survey conducted in September 2013 in twenty countries by the French market research firm Ipsos found that Chinese respondents were most likely to respond affirmatively to the statements "I measure my success by the things I own" (71 percent) and "I feel a lot of pressure to be successful and make money" (68 percent); Ipsos, "The Global Trends Survey: A Public Opinion Report," www.ipsos-na.com/download/pr.aspx?id=13284 (accessed January 25, 2014). Chinese reaction to the poll was covered by Bree Feng, "Chinese Respondents Top Materialism Poll," http://sinosphere.blogs.nytimes.com/2013/12/20/chinese-respondents-top-materialism-poll/?_php=true&_type=blogs&_r=0 (accessed January 25, 2014).

[8] Arthur Kleinman, Yunxiang Yan, Jing Jun, Sing Lee, Everett Zhang, Pan Tianshu, Wu Fe, and Guo Jinhua, *Deep China: The Moral Life of the Person* (Berkeley: University of California Press, 2011).

[9] Kleinman, "Introduction," p. 30.

in the conviction that China's socialist society, if it were to be truly just and good, must be governed according to principles rooted in humanistic values. This meant that socialist legality was welcome, but only so far as it could promote the end goal of socialism, namely the realization of human dignity.

The conversation documented here, between socialist legality and socialist humanity, was short-lived. The humanist position was considered briefly, gaining traction in leading academic journals and even for a time in the official media, but then just as quickly dismissed. Even so, the conversation occasioned by the trial helped to define the post-Mao era. In those few years, from about 1979 to 1983, it was possible for Chinese people to speak, without cynicism or irony, of the possibility of a reformed socialism based on genuine, transcendent values. The conversation about socialist humanity was soon choked off, but it showed that the party-state no longer had a monopoly on the definition of justice. When that conversation was finally muted, the moral imperative of socialism was reduced to obedience to authority in the name of law and order (see Figure 18). What remained was an official ideology bereft of positive values that people could believe in.

Talk of humanistic values has not disappeared completely. In the official ideology of the post-Mao successor regimes, the scientistic discourse on material development has been dominant, but the submerged discourse on the human side of socialism still surfaces now and again. In the 1980s, the Deng Xiaoping regime called for the development of material civilization and "socialist spiritual civilization," though, of course, more attention was paid to the former than the latter. In the 1990s, Deng Xiaoping's successor Jiang Zemin, "proceeding from the perspective of the laws of historical development, ... comprehensively and incisively elaborated the scientific meaning of the important thought of the Three Represents."[10] The lofty scientific pretensions are obvious, but Jiang Zemin also initiated a campaign to complement the rule of law with the rule of virtue (dezhi), arguing that law promotes material and political civilization while virtue promotes spiritual civilization. Jiang Zemin's successor Hu Jintao articulated the Scientific Development Concept, which

[10] International Department, Central Committee of the CPC, "On the Three Represents" (July 1, 2001), www.idcpc.org.cn/english/policy/3represents.htm. This formulation stated that the CCP has historically represented and must continue to represent "the development trend of China's advanced productive forces, the orientation of China's advanced culture, and the fundamental interests of the overwhelming majority of the Chinese people." See Joseph Fewsmith, "Studying the Three Represents," *China Leadership Monitor* 8 (Fall 2003), p. 2.

个个遵守秩序 人人注意社会公德

Figure 18. Wu Min, "Everyone observe order, everybody attend to social morality" (*Gege zunshou zhixu, renren zhuyi shehui gongde*) (1983). *Source:* Landsberger Collection, International Institute of Social History (Amsterdam).

supposedly embraced the "laws of history" concerning the development of human societies in general and socialist societies in particular.[11] The Scientific Development Concept proposed an all-around approach to growth that would be more diverse, equitable, ecologically responsible, and sustainable. Borrowing a phrase from the classic statecraft text *The Great Learning*, Hu Jintao said that good government must "take people as the root" (*yi ren wei ben*) and recognize "comprehensive human development" as the ultimate end goal of socialism. Hu Jintao's successor Xi Jinping advanced the doctrine of Four Comprehensives: comprehensively build a moderately prosperous society, deepen reform, govern the country according to the law, and apply strictness in governing the party.

---

[11] Wang Xiuzhi, "'San ge daibiao' yu 'san da guilü'" [The "Three Represents" and "three great laws of history"], *RMRB*, November 11, 2003.

In addition to pairing law with party discipline, Xi Jinping also asserted that laws should "accord with objective laws (*guilü*) and with the will of the people."[12] As even this cursory account indicates, the core dilemma laid bare at the time of the Gang of Four trial has not been resolved.[13]

The courtroom spectacle of the Gang of Four getting their just deserts must have been a satisfying moment for their many victims. In the long run, though, the trial could not deliver on its more ambitious goals: to punish the many crimes of the Cultural Revolution era, achieve closure on the trauma of the violent past, and construct an authoritative interpretation of history. Some of these shortcomings owed to the specific political and historical circumstances surrounding the trial. Other failures, arguably the most important ones, point to inherent limitations in the mode of narrative production employed by transitional justice trials in general. Like other postconflict trials, the Gang of Four trial responded to a disillusioning nightmare. A main purpose of transitional justice is to reformulate the narrative of the shared community, to overcome the debilitating wounds of a scarred past by retelling its relationship to the present and future. However, the crisis of Chinese socialism was evidently not only a crisis of legal justice, but also a crisis of narratives marked by profound skepticism over the power and function of totalizing narratives. In the apparently modernist literary works that accompanied the Gang of Four trial are buried roots of Chinese literary postmodernism, a cultural phenomenon that would not be felt as a reflexive aesthetic choice until the experimental avant-garde movement starting in the mid-1980s. Yet Chinese culture of the late 1970s and early 1980s already was imbued with a deep sense of post-ness – that is, of a present defined by a rejection of the past. In the wake of the Cultural Revolution, meaning was not found in the certainty of a new normative order (*nomos*) of socialist justice, but instead gave way to an alienating sense of normlessness (*anomie*). Thus the Chinese post–Cultural Revolution reckoning belongs to the global experience of postmodernity. The disasters wrought by mass violence and modern political ideologies inevitably shake their victims' faith in grand plans to reorganize the human community. To those who wish for legal trials – and the grand narratives they create – to adjudicate history, this realization should be unsettling.

[12] "Zhonggong zhongyang guanyu quanmian tuijin yifa zhiguo ruogan zhongda wenti de jueding" [CCP Central Committee resolution on certain important issues in the comprehensive promotion of the rule of law] (October 23, 2014) in Xinhua wire report, October 28, 2014, http://news.xinhuanet.com/politics/2014-10/28/c_1113015330.htm.

[13] For a more complete account of ideological debates during the Deng Xiaoping era, see Yan Sun, *The Chinese Reassessment of Socialism, 1976–1992* (Princeton, NJ: Princeton University Press, 1995).

Bibliography

Althusser, Louis, "Ideology and Ideological State Apparatuses (Notes towards an Investigation)," in *Lenin and Philosophy and Other Essays*, Ben Brewster, transl. (New York: Monthly Review, 1971).

Althusser, Louis, and Étienne Balibar, *Reading Capital*, Ben Brewster, transl. (New York: Pantheon Books, 1979).

Amnesty International, *China's Ultra-Left on Trial: Unfair Legal Procedure and Political Imprisonment in the Anti-Gang of Four Purge, 1976–1987* (unpublished manuscript, 1987?).

Anagnost, Ann, *National Past-Times: Narrative, Representation, and Power in Modern China* (Durham, NC, and London: Duke University Press, 1997).

Anderson, Marston, *The Limits of Realism: Chinese Fiction in the Revolutionary Period* (Berkeley: University of California Press, 1990).

Apter, David E., and Tony Saich, *Revolutionary Discourse in Mao's Republic* (Cambridge, MA: Harvard University Press, 1994).

ARIC Press, "China Lays Down the Law," *Newsweek* (September 7, 1981), p. 47.

Aristotle, *The Rhetoric and Poetics of Aristotle*, W. Rhys Roberts and Ingram Bywater, transl. Modern Library College edn. (New York: Random House; dist. by McGraw-Hill, 1984).

Arthur, Paige, "How 'Transitions' Reshaped Human Rights: A Conceptual History of Transitional Justice," *Human Rights Quarterly* 31.2 (2009), pp. 321–67.

Austin, J. L., *How to Do Things with Words* (London: Oxford University Press, 1962).

Baeher, Peter, "The 'Iron Cage' and the 'Shell as Hard as Steel': Parsons, Weber, and the Stahlhartes Gehäuse Metaphor in the Protestant Ethic and the Spirit of Capitalism," *History and Theory* 40.2 (May 2001), pp. 153–69.

Bai mao nü [The White-Haired Girl], film version completed March 1950 by Dongbei dianying zhipianchang; adapted by Shui Hua, Wang Bin, and Yang Runshen from the original opera script collectively produced by the Yan'an Lu Xun yishu gongzuotuan and written by He Jingzhi and Ding Yi, in *Zhongguo dianying juben xuanji* (Beijing: Zhongguo dianying chubanshe, 1962), vol. 1, pp. 95–148.

Balibar, Etienne, "The Nation Form: History and Ideology," in *Race, Nation, Class: Ambiguous Identities*, Etienne Balibar and Immanuel Wallerstein, eds. (New York: Verso, 1991).

Balibar, Etienne, and Pierre Macherey, "Interview," *Diacritics* 12.1 (Spring 1982), pp. 46–52.

Balint, Jennifer L., "Accountability for International Crimes and Serious Violations of Human Rights," *Law and Contemporary Problems* 59.4 (Autumn 1996), pp. 231–47.

Bao Zhongwen, *Dangdai Zhongguo wenyi lilun shi* [History literary and art theory of contemporary China] (Nanjing: Jiangsu jiaoyu chubanshe, 1998).

Barmé, Geremie, *In the Red: On Contemporary Chinese Culture* (New York: Columbia University Press, 1999).

   "For Truly Great Men, Look to This Age Alone: Was Mao a New Emperor?," in Timothy Cheek, ed. *A Critical Introduction to Mao* (New York: Cambridge University Press, 2010), pp. 243–72.

   "New China Newspeak," *China Heritage Quarterly* 29 (March 2012), www.chinaheritagequarterly.org/glossary.php?searchterm=029_xinhua .inc&issue=029.

Barthes, Roland, *Mythologies*, Annette Lavers, transl. (New York: Noonday Press, 1972).

Bartov, Omer, Atina Grossman, and Mary Nolan, eds., *Crimes of War: Guilt and Denial in the Twentieth Century* (New York: The New Press, 2002).

Baum, Richard, *Burying Mao: Chinese Politics in the Age of Deng Xiaoping* (Princeton, NJ: Princeton University Press, 1994).

Berman, Marshall, *All That Is Solid Melts into Air: The Experience of Modernity* (New York: Simon and Schuster, 1982).

Bernstein, Michael André, *Foregone Conclusions: Against Apocalyptic History* (Berkeley: University of California Press, 1994).

Best Chinese Idioms (Chinese-English), comp. by Situ Tan, Zhao Shuhan, and Tang Bowen, transl., 9th edn. (Hong Kong: Hai Feng Publishing, 1994).

Bhabha, Homi, "Introduction: Narrating the Nation," in *Narrating the Nation* (New York: Routledge, 1990), pp. 1–7.

Binder, Guyora, and Robert Weisberg, *Literary Criticisms of Law* (Princeton, NJ: Princeton University Press, 2000).

Bingham, Tom, *The Rule of Law*, reprint edn. (London: Penguin UK, 2011).

Blecher, Marc, *China against the Tides: Restructuring through Revolution, Radicalism, and Reform*, 3rd. ed. (London: Bloomsbury Academic, 2009).

"Bo Yibo report winds up party rectification" (May 31, 1987), *Daily Report China*, FBIS-CHI-87-105 (June 2, 1987), pp. K3–K18.

"Bochi Jiang Qing wuchi guibian" [Refuting Jiang Qing's shameless sophistry], Xinhua wire report reprinted in *Zhonggong shenpan "Lin Jiang jituan" an*, vol. 1, pp. 160–8; *LSSP*, vol. 1, pp. 70–8.

Bonavia, David, *Verdict in Peking: The Trial of the Gang of Four* (London: Burnett Books, 1984).

Borneman, John, *Settling Accounts: Violence, Justice, and Accountability in Postsocialist Europe* (Princeton, NJ: Princeton University Press, 1997).

Braester, Yomi, *Witness against History: Literature, Film, and Public Discourse in Twentieth-Century China* (Stanford, CA: Stanford University Press, 2003).

Brecher, John, and Melinda Liu, "Mao's Widow Hangs Tough," *Newsweek* (November 17, 1980), p. 63.

Brooks, Peter, "Storytelling without Fear? Confession in Law and Literature," in Peter Brooks and Paul Gewirtz, eds., *Law's Stories: Narrative and Rhetoric in the Law* (New Haven, CT: Yale University Press, 1996), pp. 114–34.

Brooks, Peter, and Paul Gewirtz, *Law's Stories: Narrative and Rhetoric in the Law* (New Haven, CT: Yale University Press, 1996).

Brown, Jeremy, and Paul G. Pickowicz, *Dilemmas of Victory: The Early Years of the People's Republic of China* (Cambridge, MA: Harvard University Press, 2010).

Brown, Rupert, and Sabina Cehajic, "Dealing with the Past and Facing the Future: Mediators of the Effects of Collective Guilt and Shame in Bosnia and Herzegovina," *European Journal of Social Psychology* 38.4 (2008), pp. 669–84.

Brugger, Bill, and David Kelly, *Chinese Marxism in the Post-Mao Era* (Stanford, CA: Stanford University Press, 1990).

Burke, Peter, *Eyewitnessing: The Uses of Images as Historical Evidence* (Ithaca, NY: Cornell University Press, 2001).

Cai, Chang, *Trials of Sovereignty: Chinese Nationalist Trials of Japanese War Criminals, 1946–1949*, undergraduate honors thesis (University of California, Berkeley, 2010).

Cao, Deborah, *Chinese Law: A Language Perspective (Shuo fa)* (Burlington, VT: Ashgate, 2004).

Carr, E. H., *What Is History? The George Macaulay Trevelyan Lectures Delivered in the University of Cambridge, January–March 1961*, R. W. Davies, ed., 2nd edn. (London: Macmillan, 1982).

Cathcart, Adam, and Patricia Nash, "War Criminals and the Road to Sino-Japanese Normalization: Zhou Enlai and the Shenyang Trials, 1954–1956," *Twentieth Century China* 34.2 (April 2009), pp. 89–111.

CCP Central Committee, "Nongcun shehuizhuyi jiaoyu yundong zhong muqian de yixie wenti" [Some current problems in the rural socialist education movement] (January 14, 1965), news.xinhuanet.com/ziliao/2005-02/02/content_2539348.htm.

Chao Feng, ed., *"Wenhua da geming" cidian* [Dictionary of the "Great Cultural Revolution"] (Hong Kong: Xiang-Long chubanshe, 1993).

Chase, Cynthia, *Decomposing Figures: Rhetorical Readings in the Romantic Tradition* (Baltimore, MD: The Johns Hopkins University Press, 1986).

Chen, Albert H. Y., "Toward a Legal Enlightenment: Discussions in Contemporary China on the Rule of Law," *UCLA Pacific Basin Law Journal* 17.125 (Fall 1999/Spring 2000), pp. 125–65.

Chen Boda, "Hengsao yiqie niugui sheshen" [Sweep away all ox-ghosts and snake-spirits], *RMRB* (June 1, 1966).

Chen, Li, *Chinese Law in Imperial Eyes: Sovereignty, Justice, and Transcultural Politics* (New York: Columbia University Press, 2015).

Chen, T. H., "Law and Poetry in Ancient China," *Asian Culture Quarterly* 16.4 (Winter 1988), pp. 39–54.

Chen, Xiaomei, *Acting the Right Part: Political Theater and Popular Drama in Contemporary China* (Honolulu: University of Hawai'i Press, 2002).

Chen, Yu-Shih, "Efforts and Achievements: A Profile of the 1986 Jinshan Conference on Contemporary Chinese Literature," *Modern Chinese Literature* 2.1 (Fall 1986), pp. 235–44.

Chen Duxiu, *Chen Duxiu wenzhang xuanbian* [Selected essays of Chen Duxiu] (Beijing: Sanlian shudian, 1984).

Chen Jingliang, "Lun Liang Shuming de fa wen hua guan. Zhongnan caijing zhengzhi daxue, faxue yuan tushuguan," http://fxylib.znufe.edu.cn/new/ShowArticle.asp?ArticleID=4974.

Chen Qingmei and Zhang Zhaoyin, "Fa wang hui, zui ze nan tao: Jielu Wang Hongwen yi shou zhizao 'Za Shang Zi Lian Si' xue'an de zhenxiang" [The law's net is vast, no escape from guilt], *Gongren ribao*, December 6, 1980.

Chen Shijin, *Jiangjun juanjin xuanwo: "Sirenbang" Shanghai yudang fumie ji* [The general drawn into the whirlpool: The destruction of the remnants of the "Gang of Four" in Shanghai], *Jishi wenxue congshu*, vol. 8 (Jiangsu wenyi chubanshe, 1987).

Chen Xianyi, and Chen Ruiyue, eds., *Wangshi: 1978 xie zhen* [Bygone days: true stories of 1978] (Nanchang: Baihuazhou wenyi chubanshe, 1998).

Chen Yun, "Cheng qian shang wan di tiba zhong-qing nian ganbu" [On the promotion of thousands or tens of thousands of middle-aged and younger cadres] (July 2, 1981), cpc.people.com.cn/GB/69112/83035/83317/83597/5738417.html.

Cheng Zhensheng, "'Sirenbang' shi zheyang beizhuade" [This is how the Gang of Four was apprehended], *Wode beijilu*, http://xingguolian.com/mymemo/article/210.htm.

Chi Hsin [pseudonym], *The Case of the Gang of Four*. China News Analysis 1231 (Hong Kong: Cosmos Books, 1977).

Chiang, Yung-chen, *Social Engineering and the Social Sciences in China, 1919–1949* (New York: Cambridge University Press, 2001).

"China Reports Plot by Four to Seize Power 'Shattered' by Hua; Mao's Widow Named in Group," *New York Times*, October 22, 1976.

Chinese Cultural Revolution Database (Zhongguo wenhua da geming wenku), Song Yongyi, ed., 3rd edn. (University Service Centre for Chinese Studies, Chinese University of Hong Kong, 2010), http://ccrd.usc.cuhk.edu.hk/.

Chiu, Hungdah, "Certain Legal Aspects of the Recent Peking Trials of the 'Gang of Four' and Others," in James C. Hsiung, ed., *Symposium: The Trial of the "Gang of Four" and Its Implication in China*. Occasional Papers/Reprints Series in Contemporary Asian Studies 40 (Baltimore: University of Maryland School of Law, 1981), pp. 27–39.

"The Development of Chinese International Law Terms and the Problem of Their Translation," *The Journal of Asian Studies* 27.3 (May 1968), pp. 485–501.

Chong, Woei Lien, ed., *China's Great Proletarian Cultural Revolution: Master Narratives and Post-Mao Counternarratives* (New York: Rowman and Littlefield, 2000).

Chou Yunzhou, "Xiang 'Sirenbang' yudang duoquan: Su Zhenhua jieguan Shanghai" [Seizing power from the Gang of Four: Su Zhenhua assumes control of Shanghai], *Bainian chao* (May 2002), pp. 4–11.

Christenson, Ron, *Political Trials: Gordian Knots in the Law* (Piscataway, NJ: Transaction Publishers, 1986)

Christenson, Ronald, "A Political Theory of Criminal Trials," *Journal of Criminal Law and Criminology* 74.2 (1983), pp. 547–77.

"Chuli 'Wen ge' yiliu wenti, qingli 'san zhong ren' wenjian huibian" [Compilation of documents on handling residual problems from the Cultural Revolution and purging the three kinds of people], 5 vols. (Nanning: Guangxi Zhuangzu zizhiqu dangwei zheng dang bangongshi, 1986).

"Chumu jingxin faren shenxing: da tanwu fan Wang Shouxin weishenme you name da de shentong?" [Shocking and thought-provoking: How did the corrupt Wang Shouxin attain such supernatural powers?], *RMRB*, August 16, 1979.

Ci, Jiwei, *Dialectic of the Chinese Revolution: From Utopianism to Hedonism* (Stanford, CA: Stanford University Press, 2004).

"Circular and Materials of the CCP Central Committee on Organizing the Distribution and Discussion of *The Struggle to Smash the Lin-Chen Anti-Party Clique's Counterrevolutionary Coup* (Materials, Part 1)" (December 11, 1971), Zhongfa #77 [Central Directive No. 77 (1971)].

Clark, Phil, and Nicola Palmer, "Challenging Transitional Justice," in Nicola Palmer, Phil Clark, and Danielle Granville, eds. *Critical Perspectives on Transitional Justice* (Cambridge: Intersentia, 2012), pp. 1–16.

Clark, Phil, Nicola Palmer, and Danielle Granville, eds., *Critical Perspectives on Transitional Justice*. Series on Transitional Justice 8 (Cambridge: Intersentia, 2012).

Cohen, Paul, *History in Three Keys: The Boxers as Event, Experience, and Myth* (New York: Columbia University Press, 1997).

Cong Linzhong, "Huan yang chai lang de ren" [Grooming jackels and wolves], *RMRB*, December 5, 1980.

Cook, Alexander C., "Settling Accounts: Law as History in the Trial of the Gang of Four," in Andrew Lewis and Michael Lobban, eds., *Law and History*, Current Legal Issues 6 (Oxford: Oxford University Press, 2003), pp. 413–32.

"The Spiritual Atom Bomb and Its Global Fallout," in Alexander C. Cook, ed., *Mao's Little Red Book: A Global History* (New York: Cambridge University Press, 2014), pp. 1–22.

Cover, Robert M., "*Nomos* and Narrative: Foreword to the Supreme Court 1982 Term," *Harvard Law Review* 97.1 (November 1983), pp. 4–68.

"Violence and the Word," *Yale Law Journal* 95.8 (July 1986), pp. 1601–29.

Criminal Law of the People's Republic of China (Beijing: Foreign Languages Press, 1984).

Criminal Procedure Law of the People's Republic of China (Beijing: Foreign Languages Press, 1984).

Crocker, David A., "Reckoning with Past Wrongs: A Normative Framework," *Ethics and International Affairs* 13 (April 1999), pp. 43–64.

Crockett, George W., Jr., "Criminal Justice in China," in Maud Russell, ed., *Some Observations on Law in China* (New York: Far East Reporter, 1976), pp. 3–17.

Culler, Jonathan, "Apostrophe," *diacritics* 7.4 (Winter 1977), pp. 59–69.

"Da tanwu fan Wang Shouxin fufa" [Corruption criminal Wang Shouxin executed], *RMRB*, February 29, 1980.

Dai Houying, *Ren a, ren!* [Humanity, Ah humanity!] [1980] (Hong Kong: Xiangjiang chuban youxian gongsi, 1996).

Dalby, Michael, "Revenge and the Law in Traditional China," *The American Journal of Legal History* 25.4 (October 1981), pp. 267–307.

Day, Alexander, *The Peasant in Post-Socialist China: History, Politics, and Capitalism* (New York: Cambridge University Press, 2013).

de Bary, Wm. Theodore, and Richard Lufrano, eds., *Sources of Chinese Tradition*. 2 vols., 2nd edn. (New York: Columbia University Press, 1999).

Deng Liqun, "Answers to Questions Concerning the 'Resolution on Certain Questions in the History of the Party since the Founding of the PRC,'" *Chinese Law and Government* 19.6 (Fall 1986), pp. 12–54.

Deng Xiaoping, *Deng Xiaoping Wenxuan (1975–1982)* [Selected works of Deng Xiaoping] (Beijing: Renmin chubanshe, 1983).

"Jiefang sixiang, shishi qiushi, tuanjie yizhi xiang qian kan" [Emancipate the mind, seek truth from facts, and unite as one in looking to the future] (December 13, 1978), *Deng Xiaoping wenxuan* [Selected works of Deng Xiaoping] (Beijing: Renmin chubanshe, 1994), vol. 2, pp. 140–53.

"Adhere to the Party Line and Improve Methods of Work" (February 29, 1980), http://dengxiaopingworks.wordpress.com/2013/02/25/adhere-to-the-party-line-and-improve-methods-of-work/.

"Talk with some leading comrades of the Central Committee" (March 19, 1980) in "Remarks on Successive Drafts of the *Resolution on Certain Questions in the History of our Party since the Founding of the People's Republic of China*" (March 1980–June 1981), english.peopledaily.com.cn/dengxp/vol2/text/b1420.html.

Speeches and Writings, 2nd expanded edn. (Oxford: Pergamon Press, 1987).

"To Uphold Socialism We Must Eliminate Poverty" (April 26, 1987), https://dengxiaopingworks.wordpress.com/2013/03/18/to-uphold-socialism-we-must-eliminate-poverty/.

Denton, Kirk A., *Modern Chinese Literary Thought: Writings on Literature, 1893–1945* (Stanford, CA: Stanford University Press, 1996).

"Dianshiji qian kan minxin" [In front of the television set, watching the people's heart], *RMRB*, November 23, 1980.

Dickson, Bruce J., "Conflict and Non-compliance in Chinese Politics: Party Rectification, 1983–1987," *Pacific Affairs* 63.2 (Summer 1990), pp. 170–90.

Dictionary of Chinese-Japanese Words in the Japanese Language (London: John Harington Gubbins, 1889).

Dimock, Wai Chee, *Residues of Justice: Literature, Law, Philosophy* (Berkeley: University of California Press, 1996).

Ding Qi, "Fensui 'Sirenbang' jishi" [True account of smashing the Gang of Four], in Zhou Ming, ed., *Lishi zai zheli chensi* [Where history ruminates], 6 vols. (Beijing: Beiyue wenyi chubanshe, 1989), vol. 5, pp. 414–52.

Ding Xueliang, "Xin Makesizhuyi dui Zhongguo delu de yingxiang" [Influence of Neo-Marxism on the Chinese mainland], in Chen Guide, ed., *Zhongguo dalu dangdai wenhua bianqian (1978–1989)* [Changes in mainland Chinese contemporary culture] (Taipei: Guiguan, 1991), pp. 115–44.

Ding, Xue-liang, "The Disparity between Idealistic and Instrumental Chinese Reformers," *Asian Survey* 28.11 (November 1988), pp. 1117–39.

Dirlik, Arif, and Xudong Zhang, eds. *Postmodernism and China* (Durham, NC: Duke University Press, 2000).

Dittmer, Lowell, "Introduction," in Woei Lien Chong, ed., *China's Great Proletarian Cultural Revolution: Master Narratives and Post-Mao Counternarratives* (New York: Rowman and Littlefield, 2000), pp. ix–xix.

"Rethinking China's Cultural Revolution amid Reform," in Woei Lien Chong, ed., *China's Great Proletarian Cultural Revolution: Master Narratives and Post-Mao Counternarratives* (New York: Rowman and Littlefield, 2000), pp. 3–26.

"The Structural Evolution of Criticism and Self-Criticism," *China Quarterly* 53 (March 1973), pp. 708–29.

Dittmer, Lowell, and Chen Ruoxi, *Ethics and Rhetoric of the Cultural Revolution*. Studies in Chinese Terminology 19 (Berkeley: Center for Chinese Studies, Institute of East Asian Studies, University of California, 1981).

"Di wu jie quanguo renmin daibiao hui changwu weiyuanhui guanyu chengli zuigao renmin jianchayuan tebie jianchating he zuigao renmin fayuan tebie fating jiancha, shenpan Lin Biao, Jiang Qing fangeming jituan an zhufan de jueding" (September 29, 1980) [Resolution of the Standing Committee of the Fifth National People's Congress Regarding Establishment of the Special Procuratorate of the Supreme People's Procuratorate and the Special Court of the Supreme People's Court to Investigate and Try the Main Culprits of the Lin Biao and Jiang Qing Counterrevolutionary Groups], in *TBFTJS*, pp. 1–2.

Doležalová, Anna, "Liu Binyan's Comeback to the Contemporary Chinese Literary Scene," *Asian and African Studies* (Bratislava) 20 (1984), pp. 81–100.

Dolin, Kieran, *Fiction and the Law: Legal Discourse in Victorian and Modernist Literature* (Cambridge: Cambridge University Press, 1999).

Domes, Jeurgen, *China after the Cultural Revolution: Politics between Two Party Congresses* (Berkeley: University of California Press, 1977).

Donahoe, Eileen, "The Promise of Law for the Post-Mao Leadership in China," *Stanford Law Review* 41.1 (November 1988), pp. 171–85.

Dong Yushun and Ding Longjia, eds., *Chen yuan zhao xue: Pingfan yuan, jia, cuo an* [Righting old wrongs: reversing unjust, false, and wrong cases] (Hefei: Anhui renmin chubanshe, 2003).

Dostoevsky, Fyodor, *Memoirs from the House of the Dead*, Jesse Coulson, transl. (Oxford: Oxford University Press).

Douglas, Lawrence, *The Memory of Judgment: Making Law and History in the Trials of the Holocaust* (New Haven, CT: Yale University Press, 2001).

"The Didactic Trial: Filtering History and Memory in the Courtroom," *European Review* 14.4 (2006), pp. 513–22.

Dowling, William C., *Jameson, Althusser, Marx: An Introduction to The Political Unconscious* (Ithaca, NY: Cornell University Press, 1984).

Doyle, Sir Arthur Conan, "Silver Blaze" (1892) in *New Annotated Sherlock Holmes*, Leslie S. Klinger, ed. (New York and London: W. W. Norton, 2005), vol. 1, pp. 378–421.

Du Jiankun, "Wo wei Dai Houying bianji" [I was Dai houying's editor], in Wu Zhongjie and Gao Yun, eds., *Dai Houying ah Dai Houying* [Dai Houying, ah, Dai Houying] (Haikou: Hainan guoji xinwen chuban zhongxin, 1997), pp. 195–202.

Duke, Michael, *Blooming and Contending: Chinese Literature in the Post-Mao Era* (Bloomington: Indiana University Press, 1985).

Dutton, Michael, *Streetlife China* (Cambridge: Cambridge University Press, 1999), pp. 238–71.

Eagleton, Terry, "Estrangement and Irony," *Salmagundi* 73 (2005), pp. 25–32.

Ellul, Jacques, *Propaganda: The Formation of Men's Attitudes* (New York: Alfred A. Knopf, 1965).

Elster, Jon, *Closing the Books* (New York: Cambridge University Press, 2004).

The Encyclopedia of Genocide and Crimes against Humanity, 3 vols. (New York: Macmillan Reference, 2004).

Engels, Freidrich, "The Part Played by Labour in the Transition from Ape to Man" (1876), www.marxists.org/archive/marx/works/1876/part-played-labour/.

"Part I: Philosophy, XI. Morality and Law, Freedom and Necessity," in *Anti-Dühring: Herr Eugin Dühring's Revolution in Science* (1877), www.marxists .org/archive/marx/works/1877/anti-duhring/.

Esherick, Joseph W., Paul G. Pickowicz, and Andrew G. Walder, eds., *The Chinese Cultural Revolution as History* (Stanford, CA: Stanford University Press, 2006).

Fang Zhouzi, "Fan kexue mangren he Yao Wenyuan" [Yao Wenyuan and the anti-science ignoramuses] (April 11, 2003), www.taosl.net/dir1/fzz030.htm.

Farquhar, Judith, *Appetites: Food and Sex in Post-Socialist China* (Durham, NC: Duke University Press, 2002).

Farquhar, Mary, and Chris Berry, "Speaking Bitterness: History, Media, and Nation in Twentieth Century China," *Historiography East and West* 2.1 (2004), pp. 116–43.

Fazhi yu renzhi wenti taolun ji [Collected theses on the rule of law and the rule of man]. China Forum on the Rule of Law, reprint edn. [1981] (Beijing: Shehui kexue wenxian chubanshe, 2003).

Fei Xiaotong, "Yi ge shenpanyuan de ganshou" [Impressions of a judge], *RMRB*, January 30, 1981.

"Reflections of a Judge," in *A Great Trial in Chinese History* (Beijing: New World Press; dist. by New York: Pergamon Press, 1981), pp. 1–11.

From the Soil: The Foundations of Chinese Society, a Translation of Fei Xiaotong's Xiangtu Zhongguo, Gary G. Hamilton and Wang Zheng, transl. (Berkeley: University of California Press, 1992).

Feng, Bree, "Chinese Respondents Top Materialism Poll," sinosphere.blogs.nytimes.com/2013/12/20/chinese-respondents-top-materialism-poll/?_php=true&_type=blogs&_r=0.

Feng Chen, "An Unfinished Battle in China: The Leftist Criticism of the Reform and the Third Thought Emancipation," *China Quarterly* (June 1999), pp. 447–67.

Ferguson, Robert A., "Untold Stories in the Law," in Peter Brooks and Paul Gewirtz, eds., *Law's Stories: Narrative and Rhetoric in the Law* (New Haven, CT: Yale University Press, 1996), pp. 84–98.

Fewsmith, Joseph, "Studying the Three Represents," *China Leadership Monitor* 8 (Fall 2003), pp. 1–11.

Field, Jesse L., "Writing Lives in China: The Case of Yang Jiang," PhD diss. (University of Minnesota, 2012).

Fingarette, Herbert, "Human Community as Holy Ritual: An Interpretation of Confucius' *Analects*," *Harvard Theological Review* 59.1 (January 1966), pp. 53–67.

Fisch, Andrea, *The Invention of the Eyewitness: Witnessing and Testimony in Early Modern France*. North Carolina Studies in the Romance Languages and Literatures 279 (Chapel Hill: University of North Carolina Press, 2004).

Forster, Keith, "China's Coup of 1976," *Modern China* 18.3 (July 1992), pp. 263–303.

Friedman, Geraldine, "The Spectral Legacy of Althusser: The Symptom and Its Return," *Depositions: Althusser, Balibar, Macherey, and the Labor of Reading.* Yale French Studies 88 (1995), pp. 165–82.

Fromm, Erich, *Marx's Concept of Man* [1961] (New York: Continuum, 1992).

Frye, Northrop, *Anatomy of Criticism: Four Essays* (Princeton, NJ: Princeton University Press, 1957).

   Myth and Metaphor: Selected Essays, 1974–1988, Robert D. Denham, ed. (Charlottesville: University Press of Virginia, 1990).

Fung, Edmund S. K., "The Human Rights Issue in China, 1929–1931," *Modern Asian Studies* 32.2 (May 1998), pp. 431–57.

Furet, François, *The Passing of an Illusion: The Idea of Communism in the Twentieth Century*, Deborah Furet, transl. (Chicago: University of Chicago Press, 1999).

Gaensbauer, Monika, "The Cultural Revolution in Feng Jicai's Fiction," in Woei Lien Chong, ed., *China's Great Proletarian Cultural Revolution: Master Narratives and Post-Mao Counternarratives* (New York: Rowman and Littlefield, 2000), pp. 319–44.

"'Gaichao huandai' zhi meng de pomei" ['Change of dynasty' dream destroyed], *RMRB*, November 28, 1980.

Gao, Mobo, *The Battle for China's Past: Mao and the Cultural Revolution* (Ann Arbor, MI: Pluto Press, 2008).

Gao Ji, "Mori fengkuang" [Madness of the final days], in Zhou Ming, ed., *Lishi zai zheli chensi* [History ruminates], 6 vols. (Beijing: Beiyue wenyi chuban-she, 1989), vol. 2, pp. 317–25.

Gelatt, Timothy A., *Criminal Justice with Chinese Characteristics: China's Criminal Process and Violations of Human Rights* (New York: Lawyers Committee for Human Rights, 1993).

Gilkerson, Christopher P., "Poverty Law Narratives: The Critical Practice and Theory of Receiving and Translating Stories," *Hastings Law Journal* 43 (April 1992), pp. 861–945.

Ginzburg, Carlo, "Clues: Roots of an Evidential Paradigm," in *Clues, Myths, and the Historical Method*, John and Anne C. Tadeshi, transl., reprint ed. (Baltimore: The Johns Hopkins University Press, 2013), pp. 96–125.

Gold, Thomas B., "'Just in Time!': China Battles Spiritual Pollution on the Eve of 1984," *Asian Survey* 24.9 (September 1984), pp. 947–74.

Goldblatt, Howard, ed., *Chinese Literature for the 1980s: The Fourth Congress of Writers and Artists* (Armonk, NY: M. E. Sharpe, 1982).

   transl., *Six Chapters from My Life Downunder* (Hong Kong: Chinese University of Hong Kong; Seattle: University of Washington Press, 1984).

Gouldner, Alvin W., *The Two Marxisms: Contradictions and Anomalies in the Development of Theory* (Oxford: Oxford University Press, 1982).

Gramsci, Antonio, *Selections from the Prison Notebooks [1929–1935]* (New York: International Publishers, 1971).

A Great Trial in Chinese History (Beijing: New World Press; dist. by New York: Pergamon Press, 1981).

Gregor, A. James, and Maria Hsia Chang, "Anti-Confucianism: Mao's Last Campaign," *Asian Survey* 19.11 (November 1979), pp. 1073–92.

Gu Baozi, "1976 nian qiutianli de shujian: Du Xiuxian tan 'Sirenbang' zai zheng de zuihou jingtou" [Autumn 1976: Du Xiuxian discusses the "Gang of Four's" final hours in power], in Yi Qiming, ed., *Zhiqingzhe shuo: Lishi guanjian renwu liugei houshi de zhenxiang [Insiders' accounts: Key historical figures leave facts to posterity]*, serial edn. (Beijing: Zhongguo qingnian chubanshe, 1998), vol. 4, pp. 254–76.

"Guanyu jianguo yilai dang de ruogan lishi wenti de jueyi" [Resolution on certain questions in the history of the party since the founding of the state], *RMRB*, July 1, 1981.

Gulik, Robert van, transl. *Celebrated Cases of Judge Dee; Dee Goong An: An Authentic Eighteenth–century Chinese Detective Novel* (New York: Dover Publications, 1976).

Guo Moruo, "Kan Sun Wukong san ci da Bai Gu Jing" in *Mao zhuxi shici xuexi xiaozu, Mao zhuxi shici qianshi* [Classical Poetry of Chairman Mao] (Guangdong Yueju xuexiao, 1988), p. 231.

Habermas, Jürgen, "Technology and Science as 'Ideology,'" in *Toward a Rational Society: Student Protest, Science, and Politics* (Boston, MA: Beacon Press, 1971), pp. 81–122.

Hacking, Ian, *Rewriting the Soul: Multiple Personality and the Sciences of Memory* (Princeton, NJ: Princeton University Press, 1998).

Hanawalt, Barbara A., and Susan Noakes, "Trial Transcript, Romance, Propaganda: Joan of Arc and the French Body Politic," *Modern Language Quarterly* 57.4 (December 1996), pp. 605–31.

Hansen, Chad, "Fa (Standards: Laws) and Meaning Changes in Chinese Philosophy," *Philosophy East and West* 44.3 (July 1994), pp. 435–88.

Hanyu da cidian [Chinese dictionary] (Shanghai: Hanyu da cidian chubanshe, 2000).

Harris, Lillian Craig, "Images and Reality: Human Rights and the Trial of the 'Gang of Four,'" in James C. Hsiung, ed., *Symposium: The Trial of the "Gang of Four" and Its Implication in China*. Occasional Papers/Reprints Series in Contemporary Asian Studies 40 (Baltimore: University of Maryland, 1981), pp. 40–56.

Hatamen, Horace, ed. and transl., *Pékin: Un procès peut en cacher un autre: Les minutes du procès de Jiang Qing, la veuve de Mao*. Bibliotèque Asiatique 69 (Paris: Christian Bourgois, 1982).

Hegel, Robert, *True Crimes in Eighteenth-Century China: Twenty Case Histories* (Seattle: University of Washington Press, 2009).

Heidegger, Martin, "The Question Concerning Technology," in *Basic Writings*, Harper Perennial Modern Classics, revised and expanded edn. (New York: HaperCollins, 2008), pp. 307–41.

Heilmann, Sebastian, and Elizabeth J. Perry, eds., *Mao's Invisible Hand: The Political Foundations of Adaptive Governance in China*. Harvard Contemporary China Series 17 (Cambridge, MA: Harvard University Press, 2011).

"Heilongjiang Sheng pohuo yiqi yanzhong tanwu jituan anjian" [Heilongjiang Province uncovers serious corruption group case], *RMRB*, April 23, 1979.

Heinrich, Larissa N., *The Afterlife of Images: Translating the Pathological Body between China and the West* (Durham, NC: Duke University Press, 2008).

Hellbeck, Jochen, "With Hegel to Salvation: Bukharin's Other Trial," *Representations* 107 (Summer 2009), pp. 56–90.

"Henan sheng Zhengzhou shi zhongji renmin fayuan xingshi panjue shu" [Verdict of the Henan Province Zhengzhou City Intermediate People's Court, Criminal Division Document No. 50] (December 4, 1979), *LSSP*, vol. 2, pp. 387–9.

Hershatter, Gail, *Dangerous Pleasures: Prostitution and Modernity in Twentieth-century Shanghai* (Berkeley: University of California Press, 1999).

Hesse, Carla, and Robert Post, eds., *Human Rights in Political Transitions: Gettysburg to Bosnia* (New York: Zone Books, 1999).

He Yuhuai, *Cycles of Repression and Relaxation: Politico-Literary Events in China, 1976–1989*. Chinathemen, Serie Europäisches Projekt zur Modernisierung in China 6 (Bochum: N. Brockmeyer, 1992).

He Zai, ed., *Yuan jia cuo an shi zheyang pingfande* [This is how unjust, false, and wrong cases were reversed] (Beijing: Zhonggong zhongyang dangxiao chubanshe, 1999).

Hobsbawm, Eric, *The Age of Extremes: A History of the World, 1914–1991* (New York: Pantheon Books, 1994).

Ho Ching-chih, and Ting Yi, *The White-Haired Girl: An Opera in Five Acts,* Yang Hsien-yi and Gladys Yang, transl. (Beijing: Foreign Languages Press, 1954).

Holley, David, "Chinese Journalist Punished in Crackdown to Teach at UCLA," *Los Angeles Times*, March 18, 1988.

Hong, Junhao, *The Internationalization of Television in China: The Evolution of Ideology, Society, and Media since the Reform* (Westport, CT: Praeger, 1998).

Horkheimer, Max, *The Critique of Instrumental Reason* (London: Verso, 2013).

Hsia, C. T., "Obsession with China: The Moral Burden of Modern Chinese Literature," in *A History of Modern Chinese Fiction*, 3rd. edn. (Bloomsbury: University of Indiana Press, 1999), pp. 533–54.

Hsiung, James C., "Introduction," in James C. Hsiung, ed., *Symposium: The Trial of the "Gang of Four" and Its Implication in China*. Occasional Papers/ Reprints Series in Contemporary Asian Studies 40 (Baltimore: University of Maryland, 1981), pp. 1–4.

    ed., *Symposium: The Trial of the "Gang of Four" and Its Implication in China*. Occasional Papers/Reprints Series in Contemporary Asian Studies 40 (Baltimore: University of Maryland, 1981).

Hsu, Vivian Ling, ed., *A Reader in Post-Cultural Revolution Chinese Literature* (Hong Kong: Chinese University Press; New Haven, CT: Yale University Far Eastern Publications, 1990).

Hua Junwu, "Manhua: Bai hua zhi yi hua" [Cartoons: One flower among one hundred], *RMRB*, June 4, 1978.

Hua, Shiping, *Scientism and Humanism: Two Cultures in Post-Mao China (1978–1989)* (Albany: State University of New York Press, 1995).

Huang, Philip, "'Public Sphere'/'Civil Sphere' in China? The Third Realm between State and Society," *Modern China* 19.2 (1993), pp. 216–40.

    "Theory and the Study of Modern Chinese History: Four Traps and a Question," *Modern China* 24.2 (1998), pp. 183–208.

Hu Fuming, "'Shijian shi jianyan zhenli de weiyi biaozhun' yi wen chansheng jingguo" [My experience producing the slogan "Practice is the sole criterion of truth"], in Lü Lin, Wei Hua, and Wang Gang, eds., *Hongse jiyi: Zhongguo Gongchandang lishi koushu shilu* [Red memories: An oral history of the communist party of China] (Ji'nan: Ji'nan chubanshe, 2002), vol. 2, pp. 3–15.

Hu Sisheng, "Kaiting zhi ri" [Opening day of court], *RMRB*, November 21, 1980.

Hu Qiaomu, "On the Question of Humanism and Alienation," *Hongqi* [Red flag] (February 1984), pp. 2–28.

Huang Li, "Guanyu jianguo yilai dang de ruogan lishi wenti de jueyi" qicao taiqian muhou [Behind the scenes of the drafting of the "Resolution on Certain Questions in the History of Our Party since the Founding of the People's Republic of China"] from Zhongguo Gongchandang xinwen wang [CCP News Network] (April 2, 2009), dangshi.people.com.cn/GB/85040/9070755.html.

"Huo guo yang min, guo fa bu rong" [Calamity for the nation, prohibited by law], *GMRB*, September 30, 1980.

Huters, Theodore, "Speaking of Many Things: Food, Kings, and the National Tradition in Ah Cheng's 'The Chess King,'" *Modern China* 14.4 (October 1988), pp. 388–418.

International Department, Central Committee of the CPC, "On the Three Represents" (July 1, 2001), www.idcpc.org.cn/english/policy/3represents.htm.

Ip, Hong-Yok, "Liang Shuming and the Idea of Democracy in Modern China," *Modern China* 17.4 (October 1991), pp. 469–508.

Ipsos, "The Global Trends Survey: A Public Opinion Report," www.ipsos-na.com/download/pr.aspx?id=13284.

Jameson, Fredric, *The Political Unconscious: Narrative as a Socially Symbolic Act* (Ithaca, NY: Cornell University Press, 1981).

Postmodernism or, the Cultural Logic of Late Capitalism (Durham, NC: Duke University Press, 1991).

Jenco, Leigh K., "'Rule by Man' and 'Rule by Law' in Early Republican China: Contributions to a Theoretical Debate," *Journal of Asian Studies* 69.1 (February 2010), pp. 181–203.

Ji Fengyuan, *Linguistic Engineering: Language and Politics in Mao's China* (Honolulu: University of Hawai'i Press, 2004).

Ji Xichen, Lin Gang, and Lü Nan, "Changsha wugao qianhou," [Circumstances surrounding the Changsha report], in Zhou Ming, ed., *Lishi zai zheli chensi*, [Where history ruminates] 6 vols. (Beijing: Beiyue wenyi chubanshe, 1989), vol. 2, pp. 196–203.

Jian, Guo, Yongyi Song, and Yuan Zhou, *Historical Dictionary of the Chinese Cultural Revolution* (Lanham, MD: Scarecrow Press, 2006).

Jiang Fan, "Yuyu dengqing wanli ai" [Ten thousand miles of dust cleared from the Palace of Heaven], in Zeng Jinshun, ed., *Lishi de shenpan: jiepi "Sirenbang" manhua xuan* [History's trial: selected cartoons criticizing the Gang of Four] (Shanghai: Shanghai renmin meishu chubanshe, 1979).

Jiang Hua, *Jiang Hua sifa wenji* [Selected legal writings of Jiang Hua] (Beijing: Renmin fayuan chubanshe, 1989).

Jiang Hua, and Zuo Mingxing, "Yige ceng kanya Jiang Qing de nübing huiyi Jiang Qing yuzhong rizi" [A female guard recalls Jiang Qing's time in custody], *Wode beijilu* (mymemo.cn99.com), excerpt from *Nanfang zhoumo* [Southern Weekly] (May 10, 1995), xingguolian.com/mymemo/article/211.htm.

"Jiang Qing, Zhang Chunqiao, Wu Faxian de yusheng" [The final days of Jiang Qing, Zhang Chunqiao, and Wu Faxian] *Sichuan zaixian* online (April 15, 2003).

Jiang Wen, "Dui beigaoren Jiang Qing suo fan zuixing de fayan" [Statement on defendant Jiang Qing's criminal conduct] (December 24, 1980), *LSSP*, vol. 1, pp. 67–70.

Jiang Yihua and Roderick MacFarquhar, "Two Perspectives on Mao," in Timothy Cheek, ed. *A Critical Introduction to Mao* (Cambridge: Cambridge University Press, 2010), pp. 332–51.

"Jieshou Lin, Jiang fangeming jituan wu ming beigao de weituo shi ming lüshi jiang chuting bianhu" [Accepting the commission to represent five of the accused in the Lin and Jiang counterrevolutionary groups: Ten lawyers to appear in court for the defense], *RMRB*, November 20, 1980.

Jin Chunming, *"Wenhua da geming" shi gao* [Draft history of the Great Cultural Revolution] (Chengdu: Sichuan renmin chubanshe, 1995).

——— ed., *Sirenbang fuchenji* [Vicissitudes of the Gang of Four] (Chenyang: Liaoning renmin chubanshe, 1997).

Jin Chunming, Huang Yuchong, and Chang Huimin, eds., *"Wenge" shiqi guaishi guaiyu* [Strange events and terminology of the Cultural Revolution period] (Beijing: Qiushi chubanshe, 1989).

Jin Fang in Su Gui, *Mao Zedong shi ci dadian [Compendium of Mao Zedong's poetry]* (Nanning: Guangxi renmin chubanshe, 1993), pp. 227–35.

"Jiji ganyu shenghuo, tuidong shehui qianjin: tujian Liu Binyan de texie 'Renyao zhi jian'" [Actively delve into life, promote social advancement: recommending Liu Binyan's special report "Between Man and Monster"], *RMRB*, October 9, 1979.

"Jingtun guojia ju kuan de 'Binzhou meiba' shoudao guofa zhicai; da tanwu fan Wang Shouxin bei panchu sixing yu gai an youguan de qita zuifan Ma Zhanqing deng fenbie panchu tuxing" [Bin County Coal Tyrant who devoured state funds is subjected to legal sanction; Major embezzler Wang Shouxin sentenced to death; Ma Zhanqing and other defendants in the case sentenced to imprisonment], *RMRB*, October 25, 1979.

"Jiuchu tanwu fan, qiye huo xinsheng: bei Wang Shouxin panju shi nian zhi jiu de Bin xian ranliao gongsi jingguo yi nian de zhengdun, meitan gouxiao gongzuo zhua de jin, gongzuo zuofeng da bianyang" [Embezzlers excised, enterprise given new life: Bin County fuel company occupied for a decade by Wang Shouxin undergoes a year of retrenchment, work of buying and selling coal is grasped firmly and work style changes greatly], *RMRB*, November 26, 1979.

"Jiuyi renmin de shenpan" [Nine hundred thousand people's trial], *RMRB*, November 21, 1980.

Johnson, Barbara, "Anthropomorphism in Lyric and Law," in Tom Cohen et al., eds., *Material Events: Paul de Man and the Afterlife of Theory* (Minneapolis: University of Minnesota, 2001), pp. 201–25.

Kantorowicz, Ernst Hartwig, *The King's Two Bodies: A Study in Mediaeval Political Theology* (Princeton, NJ: Princeton University Press, 1957).

Kao, Karl S. Y., "Bao and Baoying: Narrative Causality and External Motivations in Chinese Fiction," *Chinese Literature: Essays, Articles, Reviews* 11 (December 1989), pp. 115–37.

Kau, Michael Y. M., and John K. Leung, *Writings of Mao Zedong, 1949–1976*, vol. 2: January 1956–December 1957 (Armonk, NY: M. E. Sharpe, 1992).

Kavanaugh, James H., Thomas E. Lewis, and Terry Eagleton, "Interview: Terry Eagleton," *diacritics* 12.1 (Spring 1982), pp. 52–64.

Keith, Ronald C., "Chinese Politics and the New Theory of 'Rule of Law,'" *China Quarterly* 125 (March 1991), pp. 109–18.

Kelly, David A., "The Emergence of Humanism: Wang Ruoshui and the Critique of Socialist Alienation," in Merle Goldman et al., eds., *China's Intellectuals and the State: In Search of a New Relationship* (Cambridge, MA: Harvard University Council on East Asian Studies, 1987), pp. 159–82.

King, Richard, "'Wounds' and 'Exposure': Chinese Literature after the Gang of Four," *Pacific Affairs* 54 (January 1981), pp. 82–100.

Kinkley, Jeffrey C., *Chinese Justice, the Fiction: Law and Literature in Modern China* (Stanford, CA: Stanford University Press, 2000).

      ed., *After Mao: Chinese Literature and Society, 1978–1981* (Cambridge, MA: Harvard University Council on East Asian Studies, 1985).

Kirchheimer, Otto, *Political Justice: The Use of Legal Procedure for Political Ends* (Princeton, NJ: Princeton University Press, 1961).

Kleinman, Arthur, "Introduction: Remaking the Moral Person in a New China," in Arthur Kleinman et al., *Deep China: The Moral Life of the Person* (Berkeley: University of California Press, 2011), pp. 1–35.

Kleinman, Arthur, Yunxiang Yan, Jing Jun, Sing Lee, Everett Zhang, Pan Tianshu, Wu Fe, and Guo Jinhua, *Deep China: The Moral Life of the Person* (Berkeley: University of California Press, 2011).

Kneale, Douglas J., "Romantic Aversions: Apostrophe Reconsidered," *ELH* 58.1 (Spring 1991), pp. 141–65.

Knight, Nick, "The Form of Mao's 'Sinification of Marxism,'" *Australian Journal of Chinese Affairs* 9 (January 1983), pp. 17–33.

      Marxist Philosophy in China: From Qu Qiubai to Mao Zedong, 1923–1945 (Dordrecht, The Netherlands: Springer, 2005).

      Rethinking Mao: Explorations in Mao Zedong's Thought (New York: Lexington Books, 2007), pp. 249–69.

Knight, Sabina, *The Heart of Time: Moral Agency in Twentieth-Century Chinese Fiction*. Harvard East Asian Monographs 276 (Cambridge, MA: Harvard University Press, 2006).

Koelb, Janice Hewlett, *The Poetics of Description: Imagined Places in European Literature* (New York: Palgrave Macmillan, 2006).

Kolakowski, Leszek, *Main Currents of Marxism*, P. S. Falla, transl., 3 vols. (New York: Oxford University Press, 1981).

Kong Qingmao, *Qian Zhongshu yu Yang Jiang* [Qian Zhongshu and Yang Jiang] (Haikou: Hainan guoji xinwen chuban zhongxin, 1997).

      Yang Jiang ping zhaun [Critical biography of Yang Jiang] (Beijing: Huaxia chubanshe, 1998).

Konstan, David, *The Emotions of the Ancient Greeks: Studies in Aristotle and Classical Literature*. Robson Classical Lectures (Toronto: University of Toronto, 2007).

Köppel-Yang, Martina, *Semiotic Warfare: A Semiotic Analysis, The Chinese Avant-Garde, 1979–1989* (Hong Kong: Timezone 8, 2003).

Koselleck, Reinhart, "'Neuzeit': Remarks on the Semantics of the Modern Concepts of Movement," in *Futures Past: On the Semantics of Historical Time* (Cambridge, MA: MIT Press, 1985).

Kritz, Neil J., ed., *Transitional Justice: How Emerging Democracies Reckon with Former Regimes*, 3 vols. (Washington, DC: United States Institute of Peace Press, 1995).

Kuo, Joseph C., *Huayu Guangbo Special Series: The Trial of the Lin Biao and Jiang Qing Cliques*. International Studies East Asian Language Texts 13. (Lawrence: University of Kansas Press, 1986).

Kushner, Barak, *Men to Devils, Devils to Men: Japanese War Crimes and Chinese Justice* (Cambridge, MA: Harvard University Press, 2015).

Kwok, D. W. Y., *Scientism in Chinese Thought, 1900–1950* (New Haven, CT: Yale University Press, 1965).

Kwong, Julia, "The 1986 Student Demonstrations in China: A Democratic Movement?," *Asian Survey* 28.9 (September 1988), pp. 970–85.

Lamb, Malcolm, *Directory of Officials and Organizations in China, 1968–1983*. Contemporary China Papers of the Australian National University Contemporary China Centre (Armonk, NY: M. E. Sharpe, 1984).

Laozi, *Dao de jing* [Classic of the way and virtue], Chinese with English transl. by James Legge, ctext.org/dao-de-jing.

Larson, Wendy, "Realism, Modernism, and the Anti-'Spiritual Pollution' Campaign in China," *Modern China* 15.1 (January 1989), pp. 37–71.

Laughlin, Charles A., *Chinese Reportage: The Aesthetics of Historical Experience* (Durham, NC: Duke University Press, 2002).

Law, Kam-yee, ed., *The Chinese Cultural Revolution Reconsidered: Beyond Purge and Holocaust* (New York: Palgrave Macmillan, 2003).

Law Annual Report of China 1982/3 (Hong Kong: Kingsway International, 1982).

Lean, Eugenia, *Public Passions: The Trial of Shi Jianqiao and the Rise of Popular Sympathy in Republican China* (Berkeley: University of California Press, Los Angeles, 2007).

Lee, Haiyan, "Mao's Two Bodies: On the Curious (Political) Art of Impersonating the Great Helmsman," in Jie Li and Enhua Zhang, eds., *Red Legacies in China: Cultural Afterlives of the Communist Revolution* (Cambridge, MA: Harvard East Asia Center, 2016).

Leese, Daniel, *Mao Cult: Rhetoric and Ritual in China's Cultural Revolution* (New York: Cambridge University Press, 2013).

"Revising Verdicts in Post-Mao China: The Case of Beijing's Fengtai District," in Jeremy Brown and Matthew Johnson, eds., *Maoism at the Grassroots: Everyday Life in China's Era of High Socialism* (Cambridge, MA: Harvard University Press, 2015), pp. 102–28.

Leng, Shao-chuan, with Hungdah Chiu, *Criminal Justice in Post-Mao China: Analysis and Documents* (Albany: State University of New York Press, 1985).

Lenin, Vladimir Ilyich, "Chapter 3: The Theory of Knowledge of Dialectical Materialism of Empirio-Criticism, Part 6: Freedom and Necessity," in *Materialism and Empirio-Criticism: Critical Comments on a Reactionary Philosophy in Collected Works*, 45 vols. (Moscow: Progress Publishers, 1972), vol. 14, pp. 187–93.

"The State and Revolution," in Henry M. Christman, ed., *Essential Works of Lenin: "What Is to Be Done?" and Other Writings* (New York: Dover, 1987), pp. 271–364.

What Is to Be Done? (1902), www.marxists.org/archive/lenin/works/1901/witbd/.

Lewis, Helen B., *Shame and Guilt in Neurosis* (New York: International University Press, 1971).

Lewis, Mark Edward, *Sanctioned Violence in Early China* (Albany: State University of New York Press, 1990).

Li Gengchen, "Rebutting Jiang Qing's Theory of Legal Illegality" [*Chi Jiang Qing de fanfa hefa lun*], *JFRB*, December 28, 1980.

Li, Huaiyin, "Challenging the Revolutionary Orthodoxy: 'New Enlightenment' Historiography in the 1980s," in *Reinventing Modern China: Imagination and Authenticity in Chinese Historical Writing* (Honolulu: University of Hawai'i Press, 2013), pp. 170–203.

Li, Wei, "Research Note: The Security Service for Chinese Central Leaders," *China Quarterly* 143 (September 1995), pp. 814–27.

Liang Xiao zuizheng cailiao [Material on the crimes of the Liang Xiao group] (Beijing: Liang Xiao Special Case Group, unpublished, 1978).

Liang Zhiping, "Explicating 'Law': A Comparative Perspective of Chinese and Western Legal Culture," *Journal of Chinese Law* 3.1 (1989), pp. 55–91.

Li Guoqing, "Ganxiao liuji zai Xianggang shouban" [On the initial publication of Six Records of a Cadre School in Hong Kong], news.takungpao.com/paper/q/2014/0313/2347571.html.

Li Haiwen, and Wang Yanling, eds., *Shiji duihua: yi Xin Zhongguo fazhi zunjiren Peng Zhen* [A century of conversations: remembering Peng Zhen, the key figure in New China's legal system] (Beijing: Qunzhong chubanshe, 2002).

Li Jie, "Confessions and Denunciations of the Cultural Revolution: The Practice of Everyday Graphomania," unpublished paper.

Li Kuaicai, ed., *"Wenge" midang*, [Secret files of the Cultural Revolution] 6 vols., (Hong Kong: Xianggang Zhonghua wenhua chubanshe, 2003).

Li Yonghai, "Ah, lishi – wuqing de faguan" [Ah, History – merciless judge], *Renmin gong'an* [People's Public Security] 269 (January 1981), p. 33.

Liang Xia, "Wuhan shi zhongji renmin fayuan dui Xia Bangyin, Zhu Hongjia, Hu Houmin, and Zhang Liguo fangeming an jinxing gongkai shenpan de qingkuang" [Wuhan city intermediate people's court public trial of the Xia, Zhu, Hu, and Zhang counterrevolutionary case], classified for internal-use only by *Hubei Daily* editorial staff (August 24, 1982), in *CCRD*.

Lin Biao, "Foreword to the Second Edition of Quotations of Chairman Mao Tse-tung" (December 16, 1966), www.marxists.org/reference/archive/lin-biao/1966/12/16.htm.

"Report to the Ninth National Congress of the Communist Party of China" (April 1, 1969), www.marxists.org/reference/archive/lin-biao/1969/04/01.htm.

Selected Works of Lin Piao. China Problems Research Center (Hong Kong: Chih Luen Press, 1970).

"Lin Biao jituan Li Weixin deng shiyi ren bei kongjun fayuan panxing" [Li Weixin and eleven other members of the Lin Biao group sentenced by Court Martial of the PLA Air Force], *Wenhuibao* [Literary Gazette], July 6, 1981.

Lin Yutang, "Preface" [1935] in Shen Fu, *Fu sheng liu ji* [Six records of a floating life], Lin Yutang, transl. (Hong Kong: Sanmin tushu gongsi, 1956), pp. 1–5.

Link, Perry, ed., *People or Monsters? And Other Stories and Reportage from China after Mao* (Bloomington: Indiana University Press, 1983).

——— ed., *Stubborn Weeds: Popular and Controversial Chinese Literature after the Cultural Revolution* (Bloomington: Indiana University Press, 1983).

——— "Fiction and the Reading Public in Guangzhou and Other Chinese Cities, 1979–1980," in Jeffrey C. Kinkley, ed., *After Mao: Chinese Literature and Society, 1978–1981* (Cambridge, MA: Harvard University Council on East Asian Studies, 1985), pp. 221–74.

——— *The Uses of Literature: Life in the Socialist Chinese Literary System* (Princeton, NJ: Princeton University Press, 2000).

——— *Evening Chats in Beijing: Probing China's Predicament* (New York: Norton, 1992).

Lipman, Jonathan N., and Stevan Harrell, eds. *Violence in China: Essays in Culture and Counterculture* (Albany: State University of New York Press, 1990).

Lishi de shenpan: Shenpan Lin Biao, Jiang Qing fangeming jituan an jishi [Historic trial: Records of the trial of the Jiang Qing and Lin Biao counterrevolutionary groups], 2 vols., reprint edn. [orig. 1981 and 1985] (Beijing: Qunzhong chubanshe, 2000).

"Lishi wuqing, renmin liliang bu ke shengli" [History is merciless and the people's strength is invincible], *RMRB*, January 28, 1981.

Liu Binyan, "Wenxue yao yi zheng, yi jing, yi wen" [Literature should discuss politics, economics, and culture], *Shanghai wenxue* [Shanghai literature] 16 (January 1979), p. 76.

——— "Guanyu 'xie yin an mian' he 'gan yu shenghuo'" [On 'writing about the dark side' and 'intervening into life'], *Shanghai wenxue* [Shanghai literature] 18 (March 1979), pp. 49–57.

——— "Ren shi mudi, ren shi zhongxin [Human beings are the aim, human beings are the center], *Wenxue pinglun (Literary review)* 6 (1979), pp. 10–15.

——— "Ren yao zhi jian" [Between man and monster], *Renmin wenxue* [People's literature] 240 (September 1979), pp. 83–102.

——— "Qingting renmin de shengyin" [Listen carefully to the voice of the people], *RMRB*, November 26, 1979.

——— "Shidai de zhaohuan" [Call of the times], *Wenyi bao* [Literature and art news] 359–60 (November–December 1979), pp. 36–46 [speech given at Third Congress of the Chinese Writers Association].

——— "Guanyu 'Ren yao zhi jian' da duzhe wen" [Answers to readers' questions about *Between Man and Monster*], *Renmin wenxue* [*People's Literature*], January 1980, pp. 99–101.

——— "People or Monsters?," James V. Feinerman with Perry Link, transl., in *People or Monsters? And Other Stories and Reportage from China after Mao*, Perry Link, ed. (Bloomington: Indiana University Press, 1983), pp. 11–68.

——— *A Higher Kind of Loyalty: A Memoir by China's Foremost Journalist [Liu Binyan zi zhuan]*, Zhu Hong, transl. (New York: Pantheon Books, 1990).

Liu Fuzhi, "Woguo shehuizhuyi fazhide zhuyao dianji ren: Peng Zhen" [Peng Zhen, a founder of our nation's socialist legal system] *Renmin wang* [People's web] (September 29, 2002), www.people.com.cn/GB/shizheng/252/9114/9116/20020929/834024.html.

Liu Guohang, "Yu Jiang Qing da san nian jiaodao 'nü baogong': Liu Liying chenzhuo yingdui feibang" [Three years of dealings with Jiang Qing: female "Judge Bao" Liu Liying handled slanders with calm] (December 11, 2002), http://news.tom.com/Archive/1002/2002/12/11-38889.html.

Liu Hainian, interview by author at Institute of Law, Chinese Academy of Social Sciences (Beijing: September, 30, 2003).

Liu, Lydia, *Translingual Practice: Literature, National Culture, and Translated Modernity – China, 1900–1937* (Stanford, CA: Stanford University Press, 1995).

Liu Zhuanzeng, ed., *Liu zai dangqi shang de jiyi* [Memories left on the Party banner] (Beijing: Zhongyang wenyi chubanshe, 2001).

"Liuhe 'wu-qi' ganxiao wei jiguan geming hua tigongle xin de jingyan" [Liu River 'May Seventh' cadre school offers new experience to revolutionize organizations], *RMRB*, October 5, 1968.

Llamas, Regina, "Retribution, Revenge, and the Ungrateful Scholar in Early Chinese Southern Drama," *Asia Major* 2 (2007), pp. 75–101.

Lo, Carlos W. H., "Deng Xiaoping's Ideas on Law: China on the Threshold of a Legal Order," *Asian Survey* 32.7 (July 1992), pp. 649–65.

Lotman, J. M., "Point of View in a Text," *New Literary History* 6 (Winter 1975), pp. 339–50.

Lu, Jingyu, "The Structure and Function of Chinese Television, 1979–1989," in Chin-chuan Lee, ed.. *Voices of China: The Interplay of Politics and Journalism* (New York: The Guilford Press, 1990), pp. 69–87.

Lubman, Stanley, *Bird in a Cage: Legal Reform in China after Mao* (Stanford, CA: Stanford University Press, 1999).

Lu Hong, *Zhonggong zhengzhi wutai shang de "Fu Jiang": Wu Xiuquan chuanqi* ["Lucky General" on the government stage: the legend of Wu Xiuquan] (Beijing: Zhongguo qingnian chubanshe, 2000).

Lukács, Georg, *The Historical Novel* [1937] (Boston: Beacon Press, 1962).

Lu Lin, Wang Gang, and Jin Baochen, eds., *Hongse jiyi: Zhongguo Gongchandang lishi koushu shilu* [Red memories: An oral history of the communist party of China], vol. 2, 1978–2001 (Ji'nan: Ji'nan chubanshe, 2002).

Luo Yinsheng, *Yang Jiang zhuan* [Biography of Yang Jiang] (Beijing: Wenhua yishu chubanse, 2004).

Lu Xun, *Lu Hsün: Selected Stories*, Yang Hsien-yi and Gladys Yang, transl. (New York: Norton, 1977).

Macauley, Melissa, *Social Power and Legal Culture: Litigation Masters in Late Imperial China* (Stanford, CA: Stanford University Press, 1998).

MacFarquhar, Roderick, *The Origins of the Cultural Revolution*, 3 vols. (New York: Columbia University Press for the Royal Institute of International Affairs, the East Asian Institute of Columbia University, and the Research Institute on Communist Affairs of Columbia University, 1974–83).

MacFarquhar, Roderick, and Michael Schoenhals, *Mao's Last Revolution* (Cambridge, MA: Belknap Press of Harvard University Press, 2008).

Madsen, Richard, "The Politics of Revenge in Rural China during the Cultural Revolution," in Jonathan N. Lipman and Stevan Harrell, eds., *Violence in China: Essays in Culture and Counterculture* (Albany: State University of New York Press, 1990), pp. 175–200.

Ma Lingguo, "Tebie Fating de falü guwen Qiu Shaoheng" [Special Court legal consultant Henry Chiu], *Shiji* [Century] (September 1999), pp. 18–21.

Mao Dun, "Guanyu 'baogao wenxue'" [On Reportage], *Zhong liu* [Chinese tide], November 1937.

Mao Zedong, "Oppose Book Worship" (1930), www.marxists.org/reference/archive/mao/selected-works/volume-6/mswv6_11.htm.

"On Contradiction" (1937), www.marxists.org/reference/archive/mao/selected-works/volume-1/mswv1_17.htm.

"The Chinese People Have Stood Up!" (Opening address at the First Plenary Session of the Chinese People's Political Consultative Conference, September 21, 1949), www.marxists.org/reference/archive/mao/selected-works/volume-5/mswv5_01.htm.

"On the People's Democratic Dictatorship" (1949), www.marxists.org/reference/archive/mao/selected-works/volume-4/mswv4_65.htm.

"Where Do Correct Ideas Come From?" (1963), www.marxists.org/reference/archive/mao/selected-works/volume-9/mswv9_01.htm.

Mao Tsetung Poems (Beijing: Foreign Languages Press, 1976).

"He Guo Moruo tongzhi," in *Mao zhuxi shici xuexi xiaozu, Mao zhuxi shici qianshi* [Classical Poetry of Chairman Mao] (Guangdong: Huanan shiyuan Zhongwen xi, Guangdong Yueju xuexiao, 1988), p. 231.

Quotations from Chairman Mao Tsetung (Peking: Foreign Languages Press, 1972).

Marcuse, Herbert, *One Dimensional Man* (Boston, MA: Beacon Press, 1991).

Marrus, Michael R., *The Nuremberg War Crimes Trial, 1945–46: A Documentary History* (Boston: Bedford Books, 1997).

Marx, Karl, "Speech at the Anniversary of the People's Paper" (April 14, 1856), www.marxists.org/archive/marx/works/1856/04/14.htm.

Mazower, Mark, *Dark Continent: Europe's Twentieth Century* (New York: Vintage Books, 2000).

McCabe, Edward J., "Structural Elements of Contemporary Criminal Justice in the People's Republic of China," in Ronald J. Troyer, John P. Clark, and Dean G. Rojek, eds., *Social Control in the People's Republic of China* (New York: Praeger, 1989), pp. 115–29.

Mei, Ju-ao, "China and the Rule of Law," *Pacific Affairs* 5.10 (October 1932), pp. 863–72.

Meierhenrich, Jens, and Devin O. Pendas, "Political Trials in Theory and History," in Jends Meierhenrich and Devin O, Pendas, eds., *Political Trials in Theory and History* (New York: Cambridge University Press, forthcoming), np.

Meijer, Marinus J., *Murder and Adultery in Late Imperial China: A Study of Law and Morality*. Sinica Leidensia 25 (New York: E. J. Brill, 1991).

Meijer, Marinus Johan, *Introduction of Modern Criminal Law in China. Studies in Chinese Government and Law*, ed. Joseph En-pao Wang, reprint edn. (Arlington, VA: University Publications of America, 1976).

Meisner, Maurice, *The Deng Xiaoping Era: An Inquiry into the Fate of Chinese Socialism, 1978–1994* (New York: Hill and Wang, 1996).

Mao's China and After: A History of the People's Republic (New York: Free Press, 1986).

"Marx, Mao and Deng on the Division of Labor in History," in Arif Dirlik and Maurice Meisner, eds., *Marxism and the Chinese Experience: Issues in Contemporary Chinese Socialism* (Armonk, NY: M. E. Sharpe, 1989), pp. 79–116.

Michel, Jean-Baptiste, Yuan Kui Shen, Aviva Presser Aiden, Adrian Veres, Matthew K. Gray, William Brockman, The Google Books Team, Joseph P. Pickett, Dale Hoiberg, Dan Clancy, Peter Norvig, Jon Orwant, Steven Pinker, Martin A. Nowak, and Erez Lieberman Aiden, "Quantitative Analysis of Culture Using Millions of Digitized Books," in *Science* (published online December 16, 2010).

Miller, H. Lyman, "The Cultural Revolution in the Dock: The Trials in Political Perspective," in James C. Hsiung, ed., *Symposium: The Trial of the "Gang of Four" and Its Implication in China.* Occasional Papers/Reprints Series in Contemporary Asian Studies 40 (Baltimore: University of Maryland, 1981), pp. 5–26.

Miller, William Ian, *An Eye for an Eye* (New York: Cambridge University Press, 2007).

Minow, Martha, *Between Vengeance and Forgiveness: Facing History after Genocide and Mass Violence* (Boston: Beacon Press, 1998).

"Stories in Law," in Peter Brooks and Paul Gewirtz, eds., *Law's Stories: Narrative and Rhetoric in the Law* (New Haven, CT: Yale University Press, 1996), pp. 24–36.

Min Ze, "*Ganxiao liuji* du hou" [After reading Six Chapters of Cadre School], *Dushu* (September 1981), pp. 9–13.

Misra, Kalpana, *From Post-Maoism to Post-Marxism: The Erosion of Official Ideology in Deng's China* (New York: Routledge, 1998).

Moran, Thomas Elton, "True Stories: Contemporary Chinese Reportage and Its Ideology and Aesthetics," PhD diss. (Cornell University, 1998).

Mühlhahn, Klaus, *Criminal Justice in China: A History* (Cambridge, MA: Harvard University Press, 2009).

Munro, Donald J., *The Concept of Man in Contemporary China* (Ann Arbor: Center for Chinese Studies, University of Michigan, 1977).

The Concept of Man in Early China. Michigan Classics in Chinese Studies (Ann Arbor: Center for Chinese Studies, University of Michigan, 2001).

Mu Qing, Guo Chaoren, and Lu Fuwei, *Lishi de shenpan* [Historic trial], in Zhou Ming, ed., *Lishi zai zheli chensi* [Where history ruminates], 6 vols. (Beijing: Beiyue wenyi chubanshe, 1989), vol. 2, pp. 326–41.

New Princeton Encyclopedia of Poetry and Poetics, Alex Preminger and T. V. F. Brogan, eds. (Princeton, NJ: Princeton University Press, 1993).

Newton, Scott, "Post-war to New World Order and Post-socialist Transition: 1989 as Pseudo-Event," in Fleur Johns, Richard Joyce, and Sundhya Pahuja, eds., *Events: The Force of International Law* (London: Routledge, 2011), pp. 106–16.

Nino, Carlos Santiago, *Radical Evil on Trial* (New Haven, CT: Yale, 1996).

Nussbaum, Martha C., *The Fragility of Goodness: Luck and Ethics in Greek Tragedy and Philosophy* (New York: Cambridge University Press, 1986).

Hiding from Humanity: Disgust, Shame, and the Law (Princeton, NJ: Princeton University Press, 2004).

Onate, Andres D., "Hua Kuo-feng and the Arrest of the 'Gang of Four,'" *China Quarterly* 75 (September 1978), pp. 540–65.

Orentlicher, Diane F., "Settling Accounts: The Duty to Prosecute Human Rights Violations of a Prior Regime," *Yale Law Journal* 100.8 (June 1991), pp. 2537–2615.

Organic Law of the People's Courts of the People's Republic of China (1979), http://www.china.org.cn/english/government/207253.htm.

Orwell, George, *Collected Essays, Letters and Journalism of George Orwell, Volume IV: In Front of Your Nose, 1945–1950*, Sonia Orwell and Ian Angus, eds. (New York: Harcourt, Brace and World, 1968).

Oxford Classical Dictionary, 3rd edn. (Oxford: Oxford University Press, 1996).

Oxford English Dictionary, online edition, www.oed.com/.

Palmer, Nicola, Phil Clark, and Danielle Granville, eds., *Critical Perspectives on Transitional Justice*. Series on Transitional Justice 8 (Cambridge, Antwerp, and Portland, OR: Intersentia, 2012).

Paperno, Irina, *Stories of the Soviet Experience: Memoirs, Diaries, Dreams* (Ithaca, NY: Cornell University Press, 2009).

Peerenboom, Randall P., *China's Long March toward Rule of Law* (New York: Cambridge University Press, 2002).

Lawyers in China: Obstacles to Independence and the Defense of Rights (New York and Washington, DC: Lawyers Committee for Human Rights, 1998).

Pinto, António Costa, "Settling Accounts with the Past in a Troubled Transition to Democracy: The Portuguese Case," in Alexandra Barahona De Brito, Carmen Gonzalez Enriquez, and Paloma Aguilar, eds., *The Politics of Memory and Democratization* (Oxford: Oxford University Press, 2001).

Pochu Lin Biao, "Sirenbang" de xiandai mixin [Do away with Lin Biao and the Gang of Four's modern superstition] (Beijing: Renmin chubanshe, 1978) [front matter pagination changed to Roman numerals].

Poovey, Mary, *A History of the Modern Fact: Problems of Knowledge in the Sciences of Wealth and Society* (Chicago: University of Chicago Press, 1998).

Pruyn, Carolyn S., *Humanism in Modern Chinese Literature: The Case of Dai Houying*. Chinathemen 35 (Berlin: Bochum, 1988).

Qian Gang, "Watchwords: The Life of the Party," The China Media Project, cmp.hku.hk/2012/09/10/26667/.

Qian Zhongshu, "Explaining Literary Blindness" [1941], in Christopher G. Rea, ed., *Humans, Beasts, and Ghosts: Stories and Essays* (New York: Columbia University Press, 2011), pp. 66–9.

"Qishi niandai zuida nü tanwu fan zhixing sixing quancheng" [Full story of the execution of the greatest female embezzler of the 1970s], legal.gmw.cn/2013-04/30/content_7482682.htm.

"Quanguo renda changweihui guanyu chengli tebie fating gei zuigao renmin fayuan de tong zhi" [Notification by the Standing Committee of the National People's Congress Given to the Supreme People's Court Regarding Establishment of the Special Court] (Standing Committee of the National People's Congress Document No. 27) (September 29, 1980), *TBFTJS*, p. 433.

Rankin, Mary B., "Some Observations on a Chinese Public Sphere," *Modern China* 19.2 (1993), pp. 158–82.

Rea, Christopher, "Yang Jiang's Conspicuous Inconspicuousness: A Centenary Writer in China's 'Prosperous Age,'" *China Heritage Quarterly* 26 (June 2011), www.chinaheritagequarterly.org/features.php?searchterm=026_yangjiang .inc&issue=026.

Reed, Bradly W., *Talons and Teeth: County Clerks and Runners in the Qing Dynasty* (Stanford, CA: Stanford University Press, 2000).

"Regulations for Punishment of Counterrevolutionaries" (1951), chinacopyrightandmedia.wordpress.com/1951/02/20/regulations-on-the-punishment-of-counterrevolutionaries-of-the-peoples-republic-of-china/.

"Renmin de shenpan, lishi de shenpan" [The people's trial, history's trial], *Gongmin ribao* [Workers' Daily], November 21, 1980.

"Relie huanhu Hua Guofeng tongzhi wei women dang de lingxiu, fennu shengtao 'si ren bang' fandang jituan taotian zuaxing" [Comrade Hua Guofeng enthusiastically cheered by our party leaders, 'Gang of Four' angrily denounced for heinous antiparty crimes], *RMRB*, October 26, 1976.

"Renmin de shengli" [Victory of the people], *JFJB*, January 26, 1981.

Ricoeur, Paul, "Between Lived Time and Universal Time: Historical Time," in *Time and Narrative* (Chicago: University of Chicago Press, 1988), pp. 116–26.

Richter, Thomas, *Strafrecht in Reaktion auf Systemunrecht: Vergleichende Einblicke in Transitionsprozesse 9: China* [Criminal law in reaction to state crime: Insights into transition processes 9: China] (Berlin: Duncker and Humblot, 2006).

Roberts, Moss, *Dao de jing: The Book of the Way/Laozi* (Berkeley: University of California Press, 1990).

Rodearmel, Captain David C., JAGC, "Military Law in Communist China: Development, Structure, and Function," thesis presented to Judge Advocate General School, United States Army (1987) in *Military Law Review* 119 (1988).

Rooney, Ellen, "Better Read Than Dead: Althusser and the Fetish of Ideology," in *Depositions: Althusser, Balibar, Macherey, and the Labor of Reading.* Yale French Studies 88 (1995), pp. 183–200.

Rosen, Stanley, "Value Change among Post-Mao Youth: The Evidence from Survey Data," in Perry Link, Richard Madsen, and Paul G. Piocwicz, eds., *Unofficial China: Popular Culture and Thought in the People's Republic* (Boulder, CO: Westview Press, 1989), pp. 193–216.

Rosenberg, Tina, "Confronting the Painful Past," afterword to Martin Meredith, *Coming to Terms: South Africa's Search for Truth* (New York: Public Affairs, 1999).

Ross, Claudia, and Lester Ross, "Language and Law: Sources of Systemic Vagueness and Ambiguous Authority in Chinese Statutory Language," in Karen G. Turner, James V. Feinerman, and R. Kent Guy, eds., *The Limits of the Rule of Law in China* (Seattle and London: University of Washington Press, 2000), pp. 221–70.

Rowe, William T., *Hankow: Commerce and Society in a Chinese City, 1796–1889* (Stanford, CA: Stanford University Press, 1984).

Ruskola, Teemu, *Legal Orientalism: China, the United States, and Modern Law* (Cambridge, MA: Harvard University Press, 2013).

Saich, Tony, "Writing or Rewriting History? The Construction of the Maoist Resolution on History," in Tony Saich and Hans van de Ven, eds., *New Perspectives on the Chinese Communist Revolution* (Armonk, NY: M. E. Sharpe, 1995), pp. 299–338.

Sarat, Austin, and Thomas R. Kearns, eds., *Law's Violence* (Ann Arbor: University of Michigan Press, 1992).

Satin, Allan D., *A Doonesbury Index: An Index to the Daily Syndicated Newspaper Strip "Doonesbury" by Gary Trudeau, 1970–1983* (Metuchen, NJ and London: The Scarecrow Press, 1985).

Schoenhals, Michael, "Unofficial and Official Histories of the Cultural Revolution – A Review Article," *Journal of Asian Studies* 48.3 (August 1989), pp. 563–72.

Doing Things with Words in Chinese Politics: Five Studies (Berkeley: University of California, Berkeley, Center for Chinese Studies, 1992).

"The Central Case Examination Group, 1966–1979," *China Quarterly* 145 (March 1996), pp. 87–111.

ed., *China's Cultural Revolution, 1966–1969: Not a Dinner Party*. An East Gate Reader (Armonk, NY: M. E. Sharpe, 1996).

Spying for the People: Mao's Secret Agents, 1949–1967 (New York: Cambridge University Press, 2013).

Schurmann, Franz, *Ideology and Organization in Communist China* (Berkeley: University of California Press, 1968).

Schwartz, Benjamin I., *The World of Thought in Ancient China* (Cambridge, MA: Belknap Press of Harvard University Press, 1985).

Schwartz, Herman, "Lustration in Eastern Europe," in Neil J. Kritz, ed., *Transitional Justice: How Emerging Democracies Reckon with Former Regimes* (Washington, DC: United States Institute of Peace Press, 1995), vol. 1, pp. 461–83.

Searle, John L., *Speech Acts: An Essay in the Philosophy of Language* (Cambridge: Cambridge University Press, 1989).

Sewell Jr., William H., "Historical Events as Transformations of Structures: Inventing Revolution at the Bastille," *Theory and Society* 25.6 (December 1996), pp. 841–81.

Seymour, James D., and Richard Anderson, *Old Ghosts, New Ghosts: Prisons and Labor Reform Camps in China, Socialism and Social Movements* (New York: Routledge, 1999).

Shang Yiren, "Fang Han Xuezhang lüshi" [Interview with lawyer Han Xuezhang], *Minzhu yu fazhi* [Democracy and legal system] (May 1981), pp. 13–14.

Shao Hua, and You Hu, *Lin Biao de zheyi sheng* [This life of Lin Biao], 2nd edn. (Wuhan: Hubei renmin chubanshe, 2003).

"Shehuizhuyi minzhu he fazhi de lichengpai: ping shenpan Lin Biao, Jiang Qing fangeming jituan" [Milestone in socialist democracy and legality: On the trial of the Lin Biao and Jiang Qing counterrevolutionary groups], *RMRB*, December 22, 1980.

Shen Baoxiang, "Zhenli biaozhun wenti da taolun jishi" [Discussion on the standard of truth issue], in Lu Lin, Wang Gang, and Jin Baochen, eds., *Hongse jiyi: Zhongguo Gongchandang lishi koushu shilu* [Red memories: An oral history of the communist party of China], vol. 2, 1978–2001 (Ji'nan: Ji'nan chubanshe, 2002), pp. 16–34.

Shen Fu, *Fu sheng liu ji* [Six records of a floating life], Lin Yutang, transl. (Hong Kong: Sanmin tushu gongsi, 1956).

Fu sheng liu ji zhu [Annotated edition of Six Record of a Floating Life], annotated by Yu Pingbo (Beijing: Beijing shi fan xue yuan chu ban she, 1992).

Six Records of a Floating Life, Leonard Pratt and Chiang Su-hui, transl. (New York: Penguin Classics, 1983).

Shi Hongdao, "Lishi de shenpan, renmin de shengli" [History's trial, people's victory], *Beijing ribao* [Beijing Daily], November 21, 1980.

Shklar, Judith, *Legalism: Law, Morals, and Political Trials* (Cambridge, MA: Harvard University Press, 1986).

Singh, Chatrapati, *Law from Anarchy to Utopia: An Exposition of the Logical, Epistemological and Ontological Foundations of the Idea of Law, by an Inquiry into the Nature of Legal Propositions and the Basis of Legal Authority* (Oxford: Oxford University Press, 1986).

"Sirenbang" fangeming zuixing cailiao bianlu: 10/1976–4/1977 [Compilation of materials on the Gang of Four's counterrevolutionary crimes] 2 vols., (Beijing: Chinese Academy of Social Sciences, Institute of Philosophy, Library Materials Room, 1977).

Slingerland, Edward, transl., *Confucius, the Essential Analects: Selected Passages with Traditional Commentary* (Indianapolis, IN: Hackett, 2006).

Smith, Anthony, "Introduction," in *Television: An International History*, 2nd edn. (Oxford: Oxford University Press, 1998), pp. 1–6.

Smith, Kathleen E., *Remembering Stalin's Victims: Popular Memory and the End of the USSR* (Ithaca, NY: Cornell University Press, 1996).

Special commentator for *Zhongguo qingnian* [China youth], "Pochu mixin, zhangwo kexue" [Expel superstition, grasp science], in *Pochu Lin Biao, "Sirenbang" de xiandai mixin* [Do away with Lin Biao and the Gang of Four's modern superstition] (Beijing: Renmin chubanshe, 1978), pp. 1–8.

"Special Court Commences Court Debate on the Facts of Yao Wenyuan's Crimes," Xinhua News Agency wire report, December 19, 1980.

Spence, Jonathan, preface to Yang Jiang, *Six Chapters from My Life Downunder*, Howard Goldblatt, transl. (Hong Kong: Chinese University of Hong Kong; Seattle: University of Washington Press, 1984).

Stalin, Joseph, *Foundations of Leninism* (Honolulu: University Press of the Pacific, 2001).

Strassberg, Richard E., ed. and transl., *A Chinese Bestiary: Strange Creatures from the Guideways through Mountains and Seas* [A translation of the *Shan hai jing*] (Berkeley: University of California Press, 2002).

Su Gui, *Mao Zedong shi ci dadian* [Compendium of Mao Zedong's poetry] (Nanning: Guangxi renmin chubanshe, 1993).

Sullivan, Lawrence R., "The Controversy over 'Feudal Despotism': Politics and Historiography in China, 1978–1982," in Jonathan Unger, ed., *Using the Past to Serve the Present: Historiography and Politics in Contemporary China*. Contemporary China Papers, Australian National University, An East Gate Book (Armonk, NY and London: M. E. Sharpe), pp. 174–204.

Sun, Yan, *The Chinese Reassessment of Socialism, 1976–1992* (Princeton, NJ: Princeton University Press, 1995).

Sun Haogang and Qian Gang, "Kaiting di yi tian" [First day of trial], *JFJB*, November 21, 1980.

Sun Haogang, and Li Gengzhen, "Pohui kuang – Jiang Qing" [Mad persecutor – Jiang Qing], in Zhou Ming, ed., *Lishi zai zheli chensi* [Where history ruminates], 6 vols. (Beijing: Beiyue wenyi chubanshe, 1989), vol. 2, pp. 216–22.

Tang Xiaobing, "'Poetic Revolution,' Colonization, and Form at the Beginning of Modern Chinese Literature," in Rebecca E. Karl and Peter Zarrow, eds., *Rethinking the 1898 Reform: Political and Cultural Change in Late Qing China* (Cambridge, MA: Harvard East Asia Center, 2002), pp. 245–68.

Tanner, Harold M., *Strike Hard! Anti-Crime Campaigns and Chinese Criminal Justice, 1979–1985* (Ithaca, NY: Cornell University East Asia Program, 1999).

Teiwes, Frederick C., *Politics and Purges in China: Rectification and the Decline of Party Norms, 1950–1965* (Armonk, NY: M. E. Sharpe, 1979).

"Mao and His Followers," in Timothy Cheek, ed., *Critical Introduction to Mao* (Cambridge: Cambridge University Press, 2010), pp. 129–68.

Teiwes, Frederick, and Warren Sun, *The End of the Maoist Era: Chinese Politics during the Twilight of the Cultural Revolution, 1972–1976* (New York: Routledge, 2007).

ter Haar, Barend J., "China's Inner Demons: The Political Impact of the Demonological Paradigm," in Woei Lien Chong, ed., *China's Great Proletarian Cultural Revolution: Master Narratives and Post-Mao Counter-Narratives* (Oxford: Rowman and Littlefield, 2002), pp. 27–68.

Terrill, Ross, *Madame Mao: The White-Boned Demon*, revised and expanded edn. (Stanford, CA: Stanford University Press, 1999).

Thomas, Aquinas, St., "The Summa of Theology," in *St. Thomas Aquinas on Politics and Ethics*, Paul E. Sigmund, transl. and ed. (New York: W. W. Norton, 1988).

Thompson, E. P., *The Poverty of Theory and Other Essays* (New York: Monthly Review, 1978).

Thurston, Anne F., "Urban Violence during the Cultural Revolution: Who Is to Blame?," in Jonathan N. Lipman and Stevan Harrell, eds., *Violence in China: Essays in Culture and Counterculture* (Albany: State University of New York Press, 1990), pp. 149–74.

Todorov, Tzvetan, "In Search of Lost Crime," *The New Republic* (January 29, 2001).

Trevaskes, Sue, "People's Justice and Injustice: Courts and the Redressing of Cultural Revolution Cases," *China Information* 16 (October 2002), pp. 1–26.

Troyer, Ronald J., John P. Clark, and Dean G. Rojek, eds., *Social Control in the People's Republic of China* (New York: Praeger, 1989).

Trudeau, G. B., *In Search of Reagan's Brain* (New York: Holt, Rinehart and Winston, 1981).

Tsou, Tang, "Back from the Brink of Revolutionary-'Feudal' Totalitarianism," in *The Cultural Revolution and Post-Mao Reforms: A Historical Perspective* (Chicago: University of Chicago Press, 1986), pp. 144–88.

Tucker, Robert C., *The Marxian Revolutionary Idea* (New York: W. W. Norton and Company, 1969).

ed., *The Marx-Engels Reader*, 2nd edn. (New York: Norton, 1978).

Tumen and Kong Di, *Gongheguo zuida yuan'an* [The republic's biggest unjust case] (Beijing: Falü chubanshe, 1993).

Tumen and Xiao Sike, *Tebie shenpan: Lin Biao, Jiang Qing fangeming jituan shoushen shilu* [Special trial: True account of the trial of the Lin Biao and Jiang Qing counterrevolutionary groups] (Beijing: Zhongyang wenxian chubanshe, 2003).

Zhenjing shijie di 77 tian: Lin Biao, Jiang Qing fangeming jituan shoushen jishi [Seventy-seven days that shook the world: The trial of the Lin Biao, Jiang Qing counterrevolution groups] (Beijing: Zhonggong zhongyang dang xiao chubanshe, 1994).

Turk, Austin T., "Political Deviance and Popular Justice in China: Lessons for the West," in Ronald J. Troyer, John P. Clark, and Dean G. Rojek, eds., *Social Control in the People's Republic of China* (New York: Praeger, 1989), pp. 34–42.

Turner, Karen G., James V. Feinerman, and R. Kent Guy, *The Limits of the Rule of Law in China* (Seattle and London: University of Washington Press, 2000).

Uhalley Jr., Stephen, and Jin Qiu, "The Lin Biao Incident: More Than Twenty Years Later," *Pacific Affairs* 66.3 (Autumn 1993), pp. 386–98.

Vanderbilt University Television Archive (Nashville, TN).

Virag, Curie, "'That Which Encompasses the Myriad Cares': Subjectivity, Knowledge, and the Ethics of Emotion in Tang and Song China," PhD diss. (Harvard University, 2004).

Wagner, Rudolf G., "Liu Binyan and the *Texie*," *Modern Chinese Literature* 2.1 (Spring 1986): pp. 63–98.

"Monkey King Subdues the White-Bone Demon: A Study in PRC Mythology," in *The Contemporary Chinese Historical Drama: Four Studies* (Berkeley: University of California Press, 1990), pp. 139–235.

Inside a Service Trade: Studies in Contemporary Chinese Prose. Harvard-Yenching Institute Monograph Series 34 (Cambridge, MA: Harvard University Council on East Asian Studies, 1992).

Wakeman Jr., Frederic, "The Civil Society and Public Sphere Debate," *Modern China* 19.2 (1993), pp. 108–38.

History and Will: Philosophical Perspectives of Mao Tse-tung's Thought (Berkeley: University of California Press, 1973).

Walder, Andrew, "Rebellion and Repression in China, 1966–1971," *Social Science History* 38.3–4 (2014): 513–39.

Waldron, Arthur, "Chinese Analyses of Soviet Failure: Humanitarian Socialism," *China Brief* 10.11 (May 27, 2010), www.jamestown.org/programs/chinabrief/archivescb/cb2009/.

Walker, David M., *Marx, Methodology and Science: Marx's Science of Politics* (Burlington, VT: Ashgate, 2001).

Wang, Ban, "Conclusion: In the Beginning is the Word," in Alexander Cook, ed., *Mao's Little Red Book: A Global History* (New York: Cambridge University Press, 2014), pp. 266–77.

The Sublime Figure of History: Aesthetics and Politics in Twentieth-Century China (Stanford, CA: Stanford University Press, 1997).

Wang, David D. W., "Tai Hou-ying, Feng Chi-ts'ai, and Ah Ch'eng: Three Approaches to the Historical Novel," *Asian Culture Quarterly* 16.2 (Summer 1988), pp. 71–88.

Wang, David Der-wei, *The Monster That Is History: History, Violence, and Fictional Writing in Twentieth-Century China* (Berkeley: University of California Press, 2004).

Wang Haiguang, Zhe ji chen sha Wendu'erhan [Crash in the sands of Öndörkhaan] (Beijing: Jiuzhou chubanshe, 2012).

"Wang Hongwen, Zhang Chunqiao, Jiang Qing, Yao Wenyuan fangeming jituan zuizheng (cailiao zhi yi, er, san)" [Evidence against the Wang Hongwen, Zhang Chunqiao, Jiang Qing, Yao Wenyuan counterrevolutionary group (materials parts 1, 2, 3)] (October 18, 1976; March 3, 1977; September 23, 1977), Zhongfa [Central Directive] No. 16 [1976], No. 10 [1977], and No. 37 [1977].

Wang Man, "Women cengjing yiqi zhandou" [We fought a battle together], in Wu Zhongjie and Gao Yun, eds., *Dai Houying ah Dai Houying* [Dai Houying, ah, Dai Houying] (Haikou: Hainan guoji xinwen chuban zhongxin, 1997), pp. 208–12.

Wang Meng, "Yi wei xiansheng yu tade da fangxiang" [One gentleman and his path], in *Wang Meng zizhuan* [Autobiography of Wang Meng] (Guangzhou: Huacheng chubanshe, 2007), vol. 2, pp. 131–40.

"Wang Shouxin tanwu an gongkai shenpan gao jieshu" [Public trial of Wang Shouxin corruption case concluded], *Heilongjiang ribao* [Heilongjiang Daily], October 21, 1979.

Wang Wenfeng, *Dou Mo: Mian dui mian shencha Jiang Qing fangeming jituan qin liji* [Battling demons: Personal memoirs of investigating the Jiang Qing counterrevolutionary group face-to-face] (Beijing: Zhongguo shehui kexue chubanshe, 2000).

"Geli shencha shijian de 'Sirenbang' zhuyao chengyuan" [A main member from the time of the separate investigations of the Gang of Four] (May 31, 2002), *Sixiang zhengzhi gongzuo wang* [Ideological and political work web], www.chinatelecom.com.cn/sxgz/20020531/00000155.html.

Wang Wenzheng, "Wang Wenzheng faguan huiyi shenpan si ren bang de xiangxi jingguo" [Judge Wang Wenzheng recalls details of his experience of the Gang of Four trial], www.tianshui.com.cn/news/whzx_news/200907140745066442_3.htm.

Wang Xingzhi, "Wo du *Ren a, ren!*" [My reading of *Man Ah, Man!*], *Dushu* (November 1981), pp. 37–42.

Wang Xiuzhi, "'San ge daibiao' yu 'san da guilü,'" *RMRB*, November 11, 2003.

Wang Yiyan, "Dai Houying," in Lily Xiao, Hong Lee, and A. D. Stefanowska, eds., *Zhongguo funü zhuanji cidian* [Biographical Dictionary of Chinese Women] (Armonk, NY: M. E. Sharpe, 2003), vol. 2, pp. 120–3.

Wang-Zhang-Jiang-Yao Zhuan An Zu [Wang-Zhang-Jiang-Yao Special Case Group], Zhongfa [1976] #16, [1977] #10, [1977] #37, "Wang Hongwen, Zhang Chunqiao, Jiang Qing, Yao Wenyuan fangeming jituan zuizheng (cailiao zhi yi, er, san)" [Evidence against the Wang Hongwen, Zhang Chunqiao, Jiang Qing, Yao Wenyuan counterrevolutionary group (materials parts 1, 2, 3)] (October 18, 1976; March 3, 1977; September 23, 1977).

"Washington Whispers," *US News and World Report* (December 15, 1980), p. 14.

Weber, Max, "Economic and Social History" [1922], in W. G. Runciman, ed.; E. Matthews, transl., *Selections in Translation* (New York: Cambridge University Press, 1978), pp. 287–354.

Weigelin-Schweidrzik, Susanne, "Party Historiography," in Jonathan Unger, ed., *Using the Past to Serve the Present: Historiography and Politics in Contemporary China* (Armonk, NY: M. E. Sharpe, 1993), pp. 151–73.

"In Search of a Master Narrative for 20th-Century Chinese History," in Julia Strauss, ed., *The History of the People's Republic of China* (Cambridge: Cambridge University Press, 2007), pp. 216–37.

"Coping with the Cultural Revolution: Competing Interpretations," in Agnes Schick-Chen and Astrid Lipinsky, eds., *Justice Restored? Between Rehabilitation and Reconciliation in China and Taiwan* (Frankfurt and New York: Peter Lang GmbH, Internationaler Verlag der Wissenschaften, 2012).

Weisberg, Robert, "Proclaiming Trials as Narratives," in Peter Brooks and Paul Gewirtz, eds., *Law's Stories: Narrative and Rhetoric in the Law* (New Haven, CT: Yale University Press, 1996), pp. 61–83.

Weschler, Lawrence, *A Miracle, A Universe: Settling Accounts with Torturers* (Chicago: University of Chicago Press, 1990).

Westad, Odd Arne, "The Great Transformation: China in the Long 1970s," in Niall Ferguson, Charles S. Maier, Erez Manela, and Daniel J. Sargent, eds., *The Shock of the Global: The 1970s in Perspective* (Cambridge, MA: Belknap Press of Harvard University Press, 2010).

White, Hayden, *Metahistory: The Historical Imagination in Nineteenth-Century Europe* (Baltimore: Johns Hopkins University Press, 1973).

White, James Boyd, *Heracles' Bow: Essays on the Rhetoric and Poetics of Law* (Madison: University of Wisconsin Press, 1985).

White III, Lynn T., and Kam-yee Law, "Explanations for China's Revolution at Its Peak," in Kam-yee Law, ed., *The Chinese Cultural Revolution Reconsidered: Beyond Purge and Holocaust* (New York: Palgrave Macmillan, 2003), pp. 1–24.

Winks, Robin W., *The Historian as Detective: Essays on Evidence* (New York: Harper and Row, 1969).

Womack, Brantly, "Where Mao Went Wrong: Epistemology and Ideology in Mao's Leftist Politics," *Australian Journal of Chinese Affairs* 16 (July 1986), pp. 23–40.

Woo, Margaret, "Adjudication Supervision and Judicial Independence in the PRC," *American Journal of Comparative Law* 39 (1991), pp. 95–119.

Wood, Elizabeth A., *Performing Justice: Agitation Trials in Early Soviet Russia* (Ithaca, NY: Cornell University Press, 2005).

Wood, Frances, transl., *Stones of the Wall* [Ren ah, ren! By Dai Houying] (London: Michael Joseph, 1985).

Wu Kailiu, "Renmin de shenpan, lishi de shenpan" [The people's trial, history's trial], *GMRB*, November 21, 1980.

Wu, Tien-wei, *Lin Biao and the Gang of Four: Contra-Confucianism in Historical and Intellectual Perspective* (Carbondale: Southern Illinois University Press, 1983).

Wu De, *Wu De kou shu: Shi nian fengyu ji shi* [Wu De's oral account: Recording the ups and downs of a decade] (Beijing: Dangdai zhongguo chubanshe, 2004).

Wu Jianfan, Interview by author at Institute of Law, Chinese Academy of Social Sciences, Beijing (September 30, 2003).

"Wode yanjiu zhi lu (3)" [The course of my research (Part 3)], Chinese Academy of Social Sciences Institute of Law web site (2003), iolaw.org.cn/shownews.asp?id=2705.

Wu Jianfan, and Ouyang Tao, "Lun shenpan Lin Biao, Jiang Qing fangeming jituan de jige falü wenti" [Discussion of a few legal questions in the trial of Lin Biao and Jiang Qing counterrevolution groups], *Faxue yanjiu* [Research in jurisprudence] (June 1980), pp. 1–5.

Wu Jianhua, "Jiang 'Sirenbang' yajie Qin Cheng shilu" [Account of escorting the Gang of Four to Qincheng prison], *Shiji* [Century] (March 2002), pp. 4–7.

Wu Jicheng, and Wang Fan, *Hongse jingwei: Zhongyang Jingweiju yuan fuju zhang Wu Jicheng huiyilu* [Red sentry: Memoir of Wu Jicheng, former deputy chief of the Central Security Bureau] (Beijing: Dangdai zhongguo chubanshe, 2003).

Wu Xiuquan, "Canyu shenpan Lin Biao, Jiang Qing fangeming jituan zhuzui" [Attending the trial of the main criminals of the Lin Biao and Jiang Qing counterrevolutionary groups], Text of speech given at Chinese Academy of Social Sciences, Chinese Communist Party History Meeting (June 2001), www.cass.net.cn/zhuanti/y_party/yd/yd_i/yd_i_012.htm.

Wangshi cangsang [Vicissitudes of bygone days] (Shanghai: Shanghai wenyi chubanshe, 1986).

Wu Xuezhao, *Ting Yang Jiang tan wang shi* [Listening to Yang Jiang talk about the past] (Beijing: Sanlian shudian, 2008).

Wu Zhongjie, and Gao Yun, eds., *Dai Houying ah Dai Houying* [Dai Houying, ah, Dai Houying] (Haikou: Hainan guoji xinwen chuban zhongxin, 1997).

Xiao Sike, *Chaoji shenpan: Tumen jiangjun canyu shenli Lin Biao fangeming jituan qin liji* [Super trial: A personal account of the trial of the Lin Biao counter-revolutionary group], 2 vols. (Jinan: Jinan chubanshe, 1992).

"Zai gongkai shenpan beihou: Lin Biao, Jiang Qing fangeming jituan you mimi dao gongkai shenpan shimo" [Behind the public trial: From secret to public trial of the Lin Biao and Jiang Qing counterrevolutionary groups], in Yi Qiming, ed., *Zhiqingzhe shuo: lishi guanjian renwu liugei houshi de zhenxiang* (Beijing: Zhongguo qingnian chubanshe, 2000), vol. 2, pp. 419–36.

Xin Hong, "Women zhi shi shebude zuguo" [We can't give up our motherland], *RMRB*, December 5, 1981.

Xing Yixun, *Quan yu fa* [Power versus law], in *Juben* [Drama] (October 1979), pp. 31–91; cf. English translation by Gladys Yang, in *Chinese Literature* (June 1980), pp. 92–7.

Xinhua cidian [New China dictionary], revised edn. [1988] (Beijing: Shangwu yinshuguan, 1993).

Xu Hong, "Liuxia yige lishi de zuyi: zhuiji 1998 nian 5 yue caifang Dai Houying" [A May 1998 interview with Dai Houying], *Shiji* [Century] (June 1996), pp. 21–3.

Xu Xinhua, "Nühuang meng de zhongjie" [The end of an empress' dream], in *Mingren mingshi lu* (Taiyuan: Shanxi renmin chubanshe, 1992), pp. 189–91.

"*Xue hao wenjian zhuazhu gang*" [Study the documents well and grasp the key link], joint editorial of *RMRB, HQ*, and *JFRB*, February 7, 1977.

Yan Jiaqi, "Zongjiao, lixing, shijian: fang sange shidai guanyu zhenli wenti de sange 'fating' (Zhexue huanxiang xiaoshuo)" [Religion, rationality, practice: Paying a visit to three "courts" of truth in three different ages (An imaginary philosophical story)], in *Pochu Lin Biao, "Sirenbang" de xiandai mixin* [Do away with Lin Biao and the Gang of Four's modern superstition] (Beijing: Renmin chubanshe, 1978), pp. 42–66; revised, originally published in *Guangming ribao*, September 14, 1978.

Yan Jiaqi and Gao Gao, *Zhongguo "wenge" shinian shi* [Ten year history of the Chinese Cultural Revolution], 2 vols. (Hong Kong: Xianggang dagong baoshe, 1986).

Yang, Lien-sheng, "The Concept of Pao as a Basis for Social Relations in China," in John K. Fairbank, ed., *Chinese Thought and Institutions* (Chicago: University of Chicago Press, 1957), pp. 291–309.

Yang Jiang, *Ganxiao liuji* [Six Records of a Cadre School], 2nd edn. [1981] (Hong Kong: Guangjiaojing chubanshe, 1988).

    Lost in the Crowd, Geremie Barmé, transl. (Melbourne: McPhee Gribble, 1989).

    "Shishi – gushi – zhenshi" [Facts, stories, truths], *Wenxue pinglun* [Literary criticism] (May 15, 1980), pp. 15–21.

    Six Chapters from My Life Downunder, Howard Goldblatt, transl. (Hong Kong: Chinese University of Hong Kong; Seattle: University of Washington Press, 1984).

    Zou dao rensheng bianshang: Zi wen zi da [Arriving at the margins of life: Answering my own questions] (Taibei: Shibao wenhua chuban, 2007).

"Yansu dangji guofa; hen hen daji tanwu fan: duzhe fenfen laixin, dui Wang Shouxin de fanzui xingwei biaoshi jida fenkai, yizhi yaoqiu yifa yancheng" [Stern discipline and law; severe crackdown on corruption: Flood of reader letters express utmost indignation at the crimes of Wang Shouxin and unanimously demand serious legal punishment], *RMRB*, May 17, 1979.

Yao Lun, "Wo canyu shenxun 'Sirenbang' de yidian huiyi" [Some recollections of participating in the interrogation of the "Gang of Four"], *Bainian chao* (April 2002), pp. 17–18.

Ye Yonglie, "Chen Boda chu yu yihou" [Chen Boda after leaving prison], in *Mingren beihuan lü* [Record of the joys and sorrows of famous people] (Hefei: Anhui wenyi chubanshe, 1992), pp. 289–301.

    Jiang Qing zhuan [Biography of Jiang Qing], Sirenbang quan zhuan (Urumqi: Xinjiang renmin chubanshe, 2000).

    Mingren fengyun lu [How famous people weathered the storm] (Nanjing: Jiangsu wenyi chubanshe, 2002).

    Zhang Chunqiao zhuan [Biography of Zhang Chunqiao] (Beijing: Zuojia chubanshe, 1993).

    Zhuixun lishi zhenxiang: wode xiezuo shengya [Seeking the true face of history: My writing career], 2 vols. (Shanghai: Shanghai wenyi chubanshe, 2001).

Yin Changlong, *1985: Yanshen yu zhuanzhe* [1985: Extension and transition], Bainian Zhongguo wenxue zongxi (Jinan: Shandong jiaoyu chubanshe, 1998).

Yin Jiamin, ed., *Zhiqingzhe shuo: lishi guanjian renwu liugei houshi de zhenxiang* [Insiders speak: Truth left to posterity by historical personages], comp. edn. (Beijing: Zhongguo qingnian chubanshe, 2000).

Yin Yungong, "Lun chenggong fensui 'sirenbang' de guanjian qunti" [On the key group that successfully overthrew the Gang of Four], paper presented at the International Senior Forum on the Contemporary History of China: Contemporary China and the World, Beijing (September 2004).

Ying Zhu, *Two Billion Eyes: The Story of China Central Television* (New York: The New Press, 2014).

Youd, Daniel M., "Beyond Bao: Moral Ambiguity and the Law in Late Imperial Chinese Narrative Literature," in Robert E. Hegel and Katherine Carlitz, eds., *Writing and Law in Late Imperial China: Crime, Conflict, and Judgment* (Seattle: University of Washington Press, 2007), pp. 215–33.

Yuan Shuo, "'Sirenbang' fumie ji" [Record of exterminating the Gang of Four], in Zhang Hua and Su Caiqing, eds., *Huishou "Wenge": Zhongguo shinian "Wenge" fenxi yu fanxiang* [Looking back on the Cultural Revolution: Analysis and reflection on China's ten year Cultural Revolution], 2 vols. (Beijing: Zhonggong dangshi chubanshe, 2000), vol. 2, pp. 1253–70.

Yue, Gang, *The Mouth That Begs: Hunger, Cannibalism, and the Politics of Eating in Modern China* (Durham, NC: Duke University Press, 1999).

Yu Fucun and Wang Yongchang, *Renmin de shenpan: shenpan Lin Biao, Sirenbang fangeming jituan* [People's trial: Trial of the Lin Biao and Gang of Four counterrevolutionary groups] (Hefei: Anhui renmin chubanshe, 1998).

Yu Shutong and He Bingsong, "Lin Biao, Jiang Qing fangeming jituan de tedian ji qi zhufan de xingshi zeren" [Characteristics of the Lin Biao and Jiang Qin counterrevolution cliques and the criminal liability of the Principal culprits], in Zhang Hua and Su Caiqing, eds., *Huishou "Wenge": Zhongguo shinian "Wenge" fenxi yu fanxiang* [Looking back on the Cultural Revolution: Analysis and reflection on China's ten year Cultural Revolution], 2 vols. (Beijing: Zhonggong dangshi chubanshe, 2000), vol. 1, pp. 559–67.

Yu Youhai, "Jiang Qing he Lin Biao de goujie" [The collusion of Jiang Qing and Lin Biao], in Zhou Ming, ed., *Lishi zai zheli chensi* [Where history ruminates], 6 vols. (Beijing: Beiyue wenyi chubanshe, 1989), vol. 2, pp. 223–7.

Yu Zongqi, *Zhongguo wenxue yu zhongguo falü* [Chinese literature and Chinese law] (Beijing: Zhongguo zhengfa daxue chubanshe, 2002).

Yunnan Provincial Party History Office, "Yunnan 'Wenhua da geming' yundong dashi jishi" [Record of major events in Yunnan's "Cultural Revolution" movement] (May 18, 2005), in *CCRD*.

"Zai beigao zhushang" [In the defendants' seats], *RMRB*, November 21, 1980.

Zanasi, Margherita, "Globalizing Hanjian: The Suzhou Trials and the Post-World War II Discourse on Collaboration," *American Historical Review* 113.3 (June 2008), pp. 731–51.

Zarrow, Peter, "He Zhen and Anarcho-Feminism in China," *The Journal of Asian Studies* 47.4 (November 1988), pp. 796–813.

Zeng Jinshun, *Lishi de shenpan: jiepi "Sirenbang" manhua xuan* [History's trial: Selected cartoons criticizing the Gang of Four] (Shanghai: Shanghai renmin meishu chubanshe, 1979).

Zhang, Chunhou, and C. Edwin Vaughan, *Mao Zedong as Poet and Revolutionary Leader: Social and Historical Perspectives* (Lanham, MD: Lexington Books, 2002).

Zhang Hua and Su Caiqing, eds., *Huishou "Wenge": Zhongguo shinian "Wenge" fenxi yu fanxiang* [Recovering the "Cultural Revolution": Analysis and reflection on China's ten-year "Cultural Revolution"], 2 vols. (Beijing: Zhonggong dangshi chubanshe, 2000).

Zhang Sizhi, "Meiyou ren zuo Jiang Qing de bianhushi: fang liang an shenpan bianhuzu zuzhang Zhang Sizhi" [No one was Jiang Qing's defender: Interview with head of the defense team for the two cases trial Zhang Sizhi], in Wang Fan, Xiao Sike, Gu Baozi, and Wang Yufei, eds., *Zhiqingzhe shuo* [Insiders' accounts] (Beijing: Zhongguo qing nian chu ban she, 2000), vol. 1, pp. 115–32.

"Wo ceng bei zhiding zuo Jiang Qing de bianhu lüshi" [I was once assigned to be Jiang Qing's defense lawyer], in Wang Fan, ed., *Muji lishi: guanyu dangdai Zhongguo dashi weiren de koushu shilu* [Witness history: An oral record of the major events and figures in contemporary China] (Changsha: Hunan wenyi chubanshe, 1998), pp. 339–64.

Zhang Xinqing, ed., *Tebie Fating jishi* [True stories of the Special Court], Fazhi yu Xinwen jingxuan congshu, Lishi Changhe juan (Beijing: Guofang daxue chubanshe, 1998).

Zhang Yaoci, "Wo fuze yige xingdong xiaozu zhua Jiang Qing" in Zhang Yaoci, "Wo fuze yige xingdong xiaozu zhua Jiang Qing" [I led a tactical unit to capture Jiang Qing] in Lü Lin, Wei Hua, and Wang Gang, eds., *Hongse jiyi: Zhongguo Gongchandang lishi koushu shilu* [Red memories: An oral history of the communist party of China] (Ji'nan: Ji'nan chubanshe, 2002), vol. 1, pp. 645–51.

Zhang Yinjing, "Narrative, Ideology, Subjectivity: Defining a Subversive Discourse in Chinese Reportage," in Liu Kang and Tang Xiaobing, eds., *Politics, Ideology, and Literary Discourse in Modern China* (Durham, NC: Duke University Press, 1993), pp. 211–42.

Zhang Youyu, *Zhang Youyu wenxuan* [Selected works of Zhang Youyu], 2 vols. (Beijing: Falü chubanshe, 1997).

Zhang Youyu et al., *Faxue lilun lunwenji* [Collected theses on jurisprudence]. China Forum on the Rule of Law, reprint edn. [1984] (Beijing: Shehui kexue wenxian chubanshe, 2003).

Zhang Youyu and Wang Shuwen, eds., *Zhongguo faxue sishi nian* [Forty years of PRC legal studies, 1949–1989] (Shanghai: Shanghai renmin chubanshe, 1989).

Zhang Zhanwu, ed., *Zhengzhi fazhan yu dangdai Zhongguo* [Political development and contemporary China] (Changchun: Jilin wenshi chubanshe, 1990).

Zhao Bin, "Greater China," in Anthony Smith with Richard Paterson, eds., *Television: An International History*, 2nd edn. (Oxford: Oxford University Press, 1998), pp. 247–53.

Zhao Xin, "Tebie shenpan: yifa zhiguo de lichengpai – fang zhongyang junwei fazhiju yuan juzhang Tu Men jiangjun," in *China Judge* [journal online], www.jc.gov.cn/personal/ysxs/fzhm/fzhm80.htm, reprinted from *Jiancha ribao* (August 30, 1999).

"Zhejiang sheng Kangzhou shi yifa kangbu Zhang Yongsheng, panchu Weng Senhe wuqi tuxing" [Zhejiang Province's Kangzhou City arrests Zhang Yongsheng and sentences Weng Senhe to life imprisonment according to law], *Zhejiang ribao* [Zhejiang Daily] (August 14, 1978), *LSSP*, vol. 2, pp. 442–6.

"Zhejiang sheng Kangzhou shi zhongji renmin fayuan xingshi panjue shu" [Verdict of the Zhejiang Province Kangzhou City Intermediate People's Court, Criminal Division Document No. 27] (August 13, 1978), *LSSP*, vol. 2, pp. 453–5.

"Zhengyi de shenpan, renmin de xinyuan" [Justice's trial, the people's aspiration], *JFJB*, November 21, 1980.

Zhonggong shenpan "Lin Jiang jituan" an [Communist China's trial of the Lin and Jiang groups], 2 vols., Zhonggong yuanshi ziliao xuanji zhuanti lei 1 (Taibei: Zhonggong yanjiu zazhi shehui, 1981).

"Zhonggong zhongyang guanyu pi zhuan di wu ci quanguo 'Liang An' shenli gongzuo zuotan hui jiyao de tongzhi" [Notification of the CCP Central Committee Forwarding of the *Summary of the Fifth National Work Conference on "Two Case" Trials*] (January 31, 1982), Zhongfa #9 [Central Directive No. 9 (1982)] in *CCRD*.

"Zhonggong zhongyang guanyu quanmian tuijin yifa zhiguo ruogan zhongda wenti de jueding" [CCP Central Committee resolution on certain important issues in the comprehensive promotion of the rule of law] (October 23, 2014) in Xinhua wire report, October 28, 2014, news.xinhuanet.com/politics/2014-10/28/c_1113015330.htm.

"Zhonggong zhongyang pizhuan zhongyang 'Liang An' shenli lingdao xiaozu *Guanyu 'Liang An' shenli gongzuo de zongjie baogao* de tongzhi" [Notification of the CCP Central Committee Forwarding the Central Committee's "Two Case" Leading Small Group's *Summary Report on the "Two Case" Trial Work*] (February 12, 1988), Zhongfa #2 [Central Directive No. 2 (1988)], in *CCRD*.

"Zhongguo gongchandang di shiyi jie zhongyang weiyuanhui di san ci quanti huiyi gongbao" [Communiqué of the Third Plenum of the Eleventh Central Committee of the Chinese Communist Party] (December 22, 1978), cpc. people.com.cn/GB/64162/64168/64563/65371/4441902.html.

"Zhonghua renmin gongheguo zuigao renmin fayuan tebie fating guize" [Regulations of the Special Court of the Supreme People's Court of the People's Republic of China] (Passed by the first meeting of the Special Court of the Supreme People's Court, November 6, 1980), *TBFTJS*, pp. 453–4.

"Zhonghua renmin gongheguo zuigao renmin fayuan tebie fating panjueshu" [Written Verdict of the Special Court under the Supreme People's Court of the People's Republic of China] (January 23, 1981), Te Fa zi #1 [Special Court Document No. 1], *TBFTJS*, pp. 40–67; cf. English translation in *A Great Trial in Chinese History*, pp. 199–234.

Zhonghua renmin gongheguo zuigao renmin fayuan tebie fating shenpan Lin Biao, Jiang Qing fangeming jituan an zhufan jishi [Records of the Special Court of the Supreme People's Court of the PRC trial of the main culprits in the Lin Biao and Jiang Qing counterrevolutionary groups], Zuigao renmin fayuan yanjiushi, ed. (Beijing: Falü chubanshe, 1982) [labeled neibu faxing: internal distribution only].

"Zhonghua renmin gongheguo zuigao renmin fayuan xingshi caidingshu" [Sentencing Ruling by the Supreme People's Court of the PRC] (April 26, 1982), in *LSSP*, vol. 2, pp. 346–7.

"Zhonghua renmin gongheguo zuigao renmin jianchayuan tebie jianchating qisushu" (November 2, 1980) [Indictment by the Special Procuratorate of the Supreme People's Procuratorate of the PRC, Special Procuratorate Document No. 1], *TBFTJS*, pp. 3–39; cf. English translation in *A Great Trial in Chinese History*, pp. 149–98.

"Zhongyang bangong ting guanyu dui Lin Biao, Jiang Qing fangeming jituan zhufan Jiang Qing, Zhang Chunqiao jiang yifa yuyi jianxing de tongzhi" [CCP Central Committee General Office on Notification of Legal Commutation of Sentences for Main Culprits of the Lin Biao and Jiang Qing Counterrevolutionary Groups Jiang Qing and Zhang Chunqiao] (January 3, 1983), Zhong ban fa #3 [General Office Directive No. 3 (1983)], in *CCRD*.

Zhou Ming, ed., *Lishi zai zheli chensi* [Where history ruminates], 6 vols. (Beijing: Beiyue wenyi chubanshe, 1989).

"Zong zhengzhi bu, zhongyang junwei jilü jiancha weiyuanhui guanyu yinfa 'Liang An' jielun shenpi quanxian de tongzhi" [Notification of PLA General Political Office and Discipline Inspection Commission of the CCP Central Military Commission at Conclusion of "Two Cases" Issuance of Clarification of Authority for Examination and Approval] (March 30, 1982), Junji lian zi #1 [PLA Discipline Commission Joint Document No. 1 (1982)], in *CCRD*.

"Zuigao renmin fayuan tebie fating guanyu shenpan Lin Biao, Jiang Qing fangeming jituan an zhufan de xiaojie" [Brief summary of the trial of the main culprits in the Lin Biao and Jiang Qing counterrevolutionary groups by the Special Court under the Supreme People's Court] (February 9, 1981), *Zhonghua renmin gongheguo zuigao renmin fayuan tebie fating shenpan Lin Biao, Jiang Qing fangeming jituan an zhufan jishi* [Records of the Special Court of the Supreme People's Court of the PRC trial of the main culprits in the Lin Biao and Jiang Qing counterrevolutionary groups] (Beijing: Falü chubanshe, 1982), pp. 480–92.

"Zuigao renmin fayuan tebie fating guanyu shenpan renyuan fengong de yijian" [Suggestions of the Special Court of the Supreme People's Court Regarding Division of Work among Judges (Passed by the First Meeting of the Special Court of the Supreme People's Court, dated 6 November 1980)], *TBFTJS*, pp. 455–6.

"Zuigao renmin fayuan tebie fating he Beijing shi falü guwenchu guanyu wei beigaoren zhipai bianhu lüshi de laiwang xinhan" [Correspondence between the Special Court of the Supreme People's Court and the Beijing Legal Consultancy regarding assignment of defense lawyers to the defendants], *TBFTJS*, pp. 459–62.

"Zuigao renmin fayuan tebie fating kaiting shenpan Lin Biao, Jiang Qing fangeming jituan an zhufan gaikuang biao" [Overview chart of sessions of the Special Court of the Supreme People's Court of the PRC's trial of the main culprits in the Lin Biao and Jiang Qing counterrevolutionary groups], *TBFTJS*, pp. 439–51.

"Zuigao renmin fayuan tebie fating kaiting shenwen shi ming beigao ren chushi zhengju zongji biao" [Statistical chart of the presentation of evidence in sessions of the Special Court of the Supreme People's Court of the PRC's trial of the main culprits in the Lin Biao and Jiang Qing counterrevolutionary groups], *TBFTJS*, p. 452.

"Zuigao renmin fayuan tebie fating sifa jingcha gongzuo shouze" [Rules and regulations for judicial police work of the Special Court of the Supreme People's Court] (Court Oversight Group, October [*sic*] 13, 1980), *TBFTJS*, pp. 457–58.

"Zuigao renmin jianchayuan tebie jianchating jueding dui Lin Biao, Jiang Qing fangeming jituan an shi ming zhufan tiqi gongsu zhi zuigao renmin fayuan han" [Letter to the Supreme People's Court from the Special Procuratorate of the Supreme People's Procuratorate Resolving to Seek Public Prosecution of the Ten Main Culprits of the Lin Biao and Jiang Qing Counterrevolutionary Cases] (Supreme People's Procuratorate Criminal Case Letter #59 (80), dated November 5, 1980), *TBFTJS*, pp. 436–7.

Index

accomplice trials, 185–89
Aeschylus, 133
agency, 6, 205, 224, 225
  Marxism and, 166
Ah, History – Merciless Judge
  (poem), 133–35
alien class element, 46
alienation, 26, 129
  political, 49
  socialist alienation, 152
  work of Dai Houying and, 139, 140,
  151, 161, 162, 165, 206
Aristotle, 132
audience expectations, 75

Balibar, Etienne, 104
Barmé, Geremie, 29
Baum, Richard, 6
Between Man and Monster (Liu Binyan),
  32, 78, 79, 148, *See also* Liu Binyan
  call for continued struggle in, 100
  criticism of, 102
  as discursive space, 97
  as literary indictment, 80–83, 90, 99–100
  as literature, 92
  as social space for intervention, 96–98
  Wang Meng on, 88
  Wang Shouxin in, 93–96
Bin County, 93, *See also Between Man and
  Monster*
Bin County Coal Tyrant. *See* Wang Shouxin
Bird in a Cage (Lubman), 6
blindness, 157
Bonavia, David, 7
Book of Rites, 76
bourgeois humanism, 146
Buddhism, 223
bureaucratic rationalization, 27

cadre schools, 201, 225, *See also Six
  Records of a Cadre School* (Yang Jiang)
  human resources and, 211

labor at, 211
  Yang Jiang's, 203, 211, 223
Central Archives (Bejing), 4
Central Security Bureau (CSB), 41
Chen Boda, 1, 17, 19, 88
  defense counsel and, 113
China's Long March toward Rule of Law
  (Peerenboom), 6
China Youth Daily (*Zhongguo qingnian
  bao*), 85
Chinese Academy of Social Sciences
  (CASS), 85
Chinese Academy of Social Sciences
  Institute of Law, 50, 52
Chinese Communist Party (CCP), 1
  founding of PRC by, 15
  party rectification (*zheng dang*)
  campaign, 190
Chinese literature of post-Mao
  transition, 76, 77
Chiu, Hungdah, 5
circumstances (*shiqing*), 162
class struggle, 15, 16, 163, 165
clear sky, symbolism of, 152
close reading, 9, 28
coal enterprise, 79
commensurate repayment, justice as, 39,
  74, 75, *See also* requital (*bao*)
Committee on the Trial of the "Two
  Cases," 53
comprehension
  justice as, 170–74
confession, 115–18
  during Cultural Revolution, 167
  narrative function of in Chinese
  law, 117
  in work of Dai Houying, 166, 167
Confucius, 76, 93, 156, 213
  righteousness and, 131
containment, strategies of, 129
contestation, 118–21
corruption, 80, 83, 89, 93

271

Studies of the Weatherhead East Asian Institute,
Columbia University

Selected Titles

Oral and Literary Continuities in Modern Tibetan Literature: The Inescapable Nation, by Lama Jabb. Lexington Books, 2015

Neither Donkey Nor Horse: Medicine in the Struggle over China's Modernity, by Sean Hsiang-lin Lei. University of Chicago Press, 2014

When the Future Disappears: The Modernist Imagination in Late Colonial Korea, by Janet Poole. Columbia University Press, 2014

Bad Water: Nature, Pollution, & Politics in Japan, 1870–1950, by Robert Stolz. Duke University Press, 2014

Rise of a Japanese Chinatown: Yokohama, 1894–1972, by Eric C. Han. Harvard University Asia Center, 2014

Beyond the Metropolis: Second Cities and Modern Life in Interwar Japan, by Louise Young. University of California Press, 2013

From Cultures of War to Cultures of Peace: War and Peace Museums in Japan, China, and South Korea, by Takashi Yoshida. MerwinAsia, 2013

Imperial Eclipse: Japan's Strategic Thinking about Continental Asia before August 1945, by Yukiko Koshiro. Cornell University Press, 2013

The Nature of the Beasts: Empire and Exhibition at the Tokyo Imperial Zoo, by Ian J. Miller. University of California Press, 2013

Public Properties: Museums in Imperial Japan, by Noriko Aso. Duke University Press, 2013

Reconstructing Bodies: Biomedicine, Health, and Nation-Building in South Korea since 1945, by John P. DiMoia. Stanford University Press, 2013

Taming Tibet: Landscape Transformation and the Gift of Chinese Development, by Emily T. Yeh. Cornell University Press, 2013

Tyranny of the Weak: North Korea and the World, 1950–1992, by Charles K. Armstrong. Cornell University Press, 2013

The Art of Censorship in Postwar Japan, by Kirsten Cather. University of Hawai'i Press, 2012

Asia for the Asians: China in the Lives of Five Meiji Japanese, by Paula Harrell. MerwinAsia, 2012

Lin Shu, Inc.: Translation and the Making of Modern Chinese Culture, by Michael Gibbs Hill. Oxford University Press, 2012

Occupying Power: Sex Workers and Servicemen in Postwar Japan, by Sarah Kovner. Stanford University Press, 2012

Redacted: The Archives of Censorship in Postwar Japan, by Jonathan E. Abel. University of California Press, 2012

Empire of Dogs: Canines, Japan, and the Making of the Modern Imperial World, by Aaron Herald Skabelund. Cornell University Press, 2011

Planning for Empire: Reform Bureaucrats and the Japanese Wartime State, by Janis Mimura. Cornell University Press, 2011

Realms of Literacy: Early Japan and the History of Writing, by David Lurie. Harvard University Asia Center, 2011

Russo-Japanese Relations, 1905–17: From Enemies to Allies, by Peter Berton. Routledge, 2011

Behind the Gate: Inventing Students in Beijing, by Fabio Lanza. Columbia University Press, 2010

Imperial Japan at Its Zenith: The Wartime Celebration of the Empire's 2,600th Anniversary, by Kenneth J. Ruoff. Cornell University Press, 2010